THOMAS POTTS OF CANTERBURY

THOMAS POTTS OF CANTERBURY

Colonist and conservationist

PAUL STAR

OTAGO UNIVERSITY PRESS
Te Whare Tā o Te Wānanga o Ōtākou

Published by Otago University Press
Te Whare Tā o Te Wānanga o Ōtākou
533 Castle Street
Dunedin, New Zealand
university.press@otago.ac.nz
www.otago.ac.nz/press

First published 2020

ISBN 978-1-98-859242-8

A catalogue record for this book is available from the National Library of New Zealand.

Editor: Imogen Coxhead
Index: Imogen Coxhead
Author photograph: Adrienne Mulqueen

Cover illustrations: A relaxed Thomas Henry Potts in his fifties with a stuffed specimen of the great spotted kiwi, *Apteryx haastii.* Hocken Collections, Uare Taoka o Hākena, University of Otago: Box-025-002, S19-203a; *Celmisia angustifolia*, collected in the Ashburton Mountains by T.H. Potts. Museum of New Zealand Te Papa Tongarewa: SP046568

Printed in China through Asia Pacific Offset

FSC www.fsc.org
MIX
Paper from responsible sources
FSC® C136333

Contents

Preface

In about 1858 naturalist Thomas Henry Potts (1824–1888) protested against the destruction of stands of tōtara on the Port Hills near Christchurch. A decade later, as a member of Parliament, he made forest conservation a national issue. Through his journalism he raised the idea of protecting native birds on island reserves, and he argued that New Zealand should have national 'domains' or parks. As a pioneering colonist, acclimatist and runholder, however, Potts' own actions, as first described in his early diary, threatened the very environments he sought to maintain. His life's narrative is engaging and his writings have their charm, and both also inform us on the problems we still face in balancing development and conservation. This book is about, and partly by, Potts, and through him about New Zealand and the course and consequences of its European settlement.

Very few colonists anywhere wrote or spoke in sufficient detail for us to chart their personal 'acclimatisation' to a new environment. It is partly the rarity of such detail that justifies examination of the anxieties this involved. Knowing about these few people becomes more relevant as others adopt the attitudes and understandings that they were the first to voice. Over a century after the colonists have passed away, respect and protection for indigenous biota has become an intrinsic component of the national identity of New Zealand and other ex-colonies.

At present Herbert Guthrie-Smith of Tūtira, a settler and station owner from the late nineteenth century, is virtually alone among New Zealanders in receiving recognition for his environmental records and ruminations. A generation earlier, however, Potts also noted changes to Aotearoa New Zealand's environment, and expressed more trenchant concern about them. *Thomas Potts of Canterbury* is designed to give the man and his writing the prominence they deserve.

In Part One I describe and interpret Potts' life, beginning with his early years in England (1824–53) as a prelude to the account of his later years in Canterbury, New Zealand, from 1854 until his death in 1888. His fascination with the changes going on around him – particularly in animal and plant life, and in landscapes – is what makes Potts special. What I have written reflects this, for I refer not only to Potts' life, but also to New Zealand's natural environment and what he made of it. My account explores the subjects that interested Potts and how he came to be possessed by them. At the same time, I leave room enough to display Thomas Potts 'the man'.

Part Two presents a selection of passages from his diary (1855–58), kept while living near Rockwood in inland Canterbury, close to present-day Windwhistle and some 80 kilometres west of Christchurch. At the time, this placed him close to the edge of European settlement. The poem by Potts that opens this part of the book was written in his diary in 1856 and provides the title for my selection. Here, 'Seeking a stranger-land' can refer not only to Potts' search for an understanding of his new home, but also to our search for an understanding of Potts and his environment. Potts' use of the term 'stranger-land' may have stemmed from his reading of Tennyson's popular poem, 'In Memoriam' (1850), which includes the line 'We live within the stranger's land', and itself references the biblical text 'I have been a stranger in a strange land.'[1]

I know of only one other occurrence of the term in the nineteenth century – in a letter written in 1854 by Isabella Gascoyne, a reluctant emigrant whose family is the subject of the memoir *Strangerland* by English writer Helena Drysdale.[2] Coincidentally, Gascoyne came to New Zealand on the same voyage as Potts: in a retrospective article about that voyage he referred to her as 'Mrs. G.':

> There was an excellent female barometer amongst the passengers, whose spirits rose and fell in exact sympathy with the weather … her custom was to make herself as disagreeable and unamiable as possible to the other lady passengers, that is during fair weather, but let the sea get up, the ship creak and strain and tumble about a bit, Mrs. G. became an angel for kindliness and good nature, only breaking off to pray aloud for mercy on her soul outside her cabin; very often at the cuddy doorway … When the sea moderated, her fretful temper made her as intolerable as ever; a civil remark or a smile from her warned her fair neighbours bad weather was coming, and to look out for squalls.[3]

Potts was a superb observer, both of the natural environment and – as here – of human quirks, and nothing reveals Potts' own character more than his own writing.

I have chosen from the longer entries in his diary, since these provide the clearest windows into Potts' world. Potts began writing his station diary in 1854, but only the volumes from April 1855 to April 1858 have survived, and then only as a later typescript.[4] A parallel Rockwood Station journal (1855–57), mostly written by Potts' father-in-law Henry Phillips, still exists, as does a later Rockwood journal (1863–69) kept by Henry's son George. There is also a journal (1866–71) from another of Henry's sons, Tom, which is centred on The Point, the station next to Rockwood.[5] None of these volumes has been published, but Thomas Potts' diary is the one that cries out to be in print. Time and again he breaks free from the straitjacket of listed weather changes, stock movements, gardening and farming activity, visiting and visitors that are the sum total of many such records.

Potts' journal is perhaps most valuable for its many references to a natural environment during a time of great change. It also provides a rare and vivid description not only of what pioneering life on an early Canterbury station entailed, but also of what it was like. Almost immediately, he makes himself ('pottering about in a purposeless manner') and his wife Emma ('risen this morning from the wrong side of the bed') real to the reader as fellow humans.[6] Other references to Mrs Potts in this journal provide almost the only testimony we have to her good spirits and industrious nature.[7]

Part Three, 'Still Out in the Open', is a selection from among the essays Potts wrote in the final few years of his life (1882–88), mostly from Governors Bay in Lyttelton Harbour. These essays provide a counterpoint to the content of his journal, written three decades earlier when he was a young man in a very young settlement. By the 1880s he was, in his own eyes, an old man reflecting on the 'old times' of the 1850s and the changes that had taken place – to the environment, and to the inhabitants of Canterbury, both Māori and Pākehā.

One twentieth-century reader, while acknowledging that Potts' articles 'displayed his ability as an observer of nature', found his style 'much too flowery for modern tastes'.[8] Although Potts, like many of his era, at times wrote distinctly purple prose, the rewards to be found in his insights far outweigh the effort of adjusting to their expression.

This book does not include Thomas Potts' series of important articles entitled 'On the Birds of New Zealand', which appeared in the *Transactions of the New Zealand Institute* from 1870 to 1874, and which are now available online.[9] Nor does it include the valuable articles first published in the *New Zealand Country Journal* and mostly on natural history themes, that he himself collected in *Out in the Open*

(1882).[10] Many libraries have a copy of this book, often in the reprinted version, so its contents are still accessible if not purchasable. Some of these articles are quoted from and discussed in Part One.

*

In recent years several biographies of key figures in the early history of Canterbury and histories of sheep stations in the area have appeared.[11] Until now, however, there has been no published biography of Potts, and no detailed study of Rockwood or the other stations with which he was associated. Although he was clearly a member of Canterbury's elite, Potts receives only a passing mention in Stevan Eldred-Grigg's *A Southern Gentry*, and he does not figure at all in Jim McAloon's later book on the wealthy in early Canterbury and Otago.[12] The centenary of Potts' death was noted in the *University of Canterbury Chronicle* in 1988, but nowhere else.[13] Although few people are aware of their earliest New Zealand nurseryman, some of the ideas that he planted have continued to grow. There is every reason to remember Potts in the twenty-first century on the grounds of his continuing relevance.

Ohinetahi (or as he spelt it, 'Ohinitahi') is the home Potts established in Governors Bay near Christchurch; it is now open to the public and is much visited. Mt Potts and the surrounding area – once part of his Canterbury high-country station – have become a conservation park, famous lately as the habitat of hobbits. But more than the heritage of the properties he developed or his contribution as an early Canterbury pioneer, the continuing significance of Potts stems from his writings.

Once republished as *Out in the Open*, the essays Potts wrote between 1878 and 1882 received a wide national audience. The book included his 1878 article on national domains, and others that stressed the unique aspects of many native birds and plants. When *Out in the Open* was reprinted in 1976 the publishers described 'the story it has to tell' as 'totally relevant 94 years later'.[14] The collection helped New Zealanders to see the country's natural history as a distinctive component of their national identity, particularly from the 1890s.[15]

Around 1904, when zoologist Frederick Hutton and naturalist James Drummond were preparing their influential book on *The Animals of New Zealand* (which was largely about birds), Emma Potts put her late husband's published papers at their disposal. Hutton and Drummond selected a photograph of him as their frontispiece and quoted extensively from his notes, securing for Thomas Potts his place in the historiography of New Zealand ornithology. They wrote that Potts 'knew our fauna before its destruction had been fairly begun, and he devoted tremendous energy to the study of the habits of our native birds. As a result of his labour of love, New Zealand possesses unique records in its literature on natural history.'[16] These were likely the sentences recrafted 62 years later in A.H. McLintock's *Encyclopaedia of New Zealand* (1966), where it was noted: '[Potts'] acute observations of nature gave to New Zealand literature unique records of birds and flora even then retreating before the progress of European occupation.'[17]

In 1953 Robert Falla of the Dominion Museum wrote that the explorer Charles Douglas 'gives a fuller and more reliable account of the habits of New Zealand birds than any other writer of the period 1850–1900', but then added 'except perhaps T.H. Potts.'[18] The value of Potts' remarks on birds, especially those regarding native quail, laughing owl and other species now extinct, has always been recognised, although his identification of several 'new' species has never been accepted. The quality of Potts' prose, as distinct from the value of his observations, has been less widely acknowledged, despite Leo Acland rating him and Lady Barker as 'two of the best descriptive writers we ever had.'[19] In recent anthologies, Potts' work appeared in Philip Temple's collection of New Zealand natural history essays, but not in Elisabeth Easther's selection of pieces by 'New Zealand writers on birds.'[20]

My choice of articles for this book is based on their maturity, candour and emphasis on environmental themes, but also on their unfamiliarity. Potts produced more than 30 articles after 1882, but until now almost none have been reprinted. They include some of the best pieces he ever wrote, which deserve a wide readership but are largely unknown. His contemporaneous 'recollections' of 'old times' in the *Canterbury Times*, while useful in constructing a narrative of his life, are mostly inferior in quality and have less environmental content.

*

The selections from Potts' early diary and the selected essays are both instructive and enjoyable. I have tried to make my part of the book a similarly good read. Taken as a whole, *Thomas Potts of Canterbury* is also offered as a contribution to the field of environmental history. The overall picture, both in these pages and more generally in this discipline, is of 'the face of nature' changing in the course of humans 'making a new land.'[21]

Environmental history is the study of the relationship between humans and the environment over time. In *Thomas Potts of Canterbury*, the relationships studied were changing rapidly and the humans recorded are mostly European settlers in New Zealand. The environment most discussed is the remaining natural environment of New Zealand. This consisted of indigenous plants and animals, interacting to form different ecosystems – coastal, wetland, dryland, forest, lowland, highland, alpine – in different locations. The time under consideration is the second half of the nineeenth century, when this environment was increasingly affected by the intrusion not only of human settlers like Potts, but also by exotic flora and fauna introduced with or by these settlers.

There are problems in discussing the European impact on this natural environment with only limited reference to the Māori impact that preceded and continued alongside it. There are also problems in writing as though humans and the environment are different entities, when they are really both part of the same overarching 'nature' or 'organism' – or as some would say, of 'God's plan'. Furthermore, differentiating flora and fauna as either indigenous or exotic downplays the reality, now found throughout New Zealand, of their elaborate co-existence. Potts struggled with such matters and so do we.

New Zealand data on human–environment interactions received early attention from geographers, most notably by visiting scholars or imported academics, such as Canadian Andrew Hill Clark and English-born Kenneth Cumberland.[22] Since the 1990s, however, New Zealand-born historians and geographers have been doing their own homework, as displayed in the 2002 collection *Environmental Histories of New Zealand*.[23] Valuable studies include Robert Peden's *Making Sheep Country* (2011), Peter Holland's *Home in the 'Howling Wilderness'* (2013) and Jonathan West's environmental history of the Otago Peninsula, *The Face of Nature* (2017), all of which utilise South Island material.[24] *Thomas Potts of Canterbury* differs from these by focusing on the life, practice and writing of a particular individual. I trust it will sit well in their company.

Acknowledgements

I am grateful, first, to Bryony Macmillan, great-granddaughter of Thomas and Emma Potts, for giving me complete access to the diaries of Thomas Potts and other material by him. So much treasure! I also want to thank Bryony's cousin Ben Richards (a descendant of Henry and Mary Anne Phillips) and his wife Cheryl for their welcome at Rockwood Station, which they own. Many years ago Sir Miles Warren generously drove out from Christchurch to guide me around Ohinetahi in Governors Bay. More recently, Sir Miles' neighbour Paul Ensor took me on a wonderful walk through Potts' pinetum and nearby farmland that had also been part of the Potts estate. Jane Robertson was with us; both in person and through the example of her published history of Governors Bay, she inspired me to bring together my research in the form it now takes.

My thanks also to New Zealand's environmental historians and historical geographers for their research and company over many years, especially James Beattie, Tom Brooking, Ross Galbreath, the late Peter Holland, Eric Pawson, Robert Peden, Alex Wearing, Jonathan West and Vaughan Wood. While Tom is the academic colleague I have worked with most closely, James is the one who persistently urged me to write a book about Potts, and I am now glad of that. Among other historians, I am grateful to John Stenhouse for his early encouragement, and to Geoff Rice for his help in the final stages.

My thanks to Otago University Press for taking on this project, in particular to editor Imogen Coxhead, designer Fiona Moffat, publisher Rachel Scott, and former editorial board member Sigurd Wilbanks. Canterbury History Foundation provided a much-appreciated grant towards the purchase of images and reproduction rights. I have received generous help from more librarians, archivists and museum staff than I can mention, but I do particularly recall the excitement when, at Canterbury Museum, Paul Scofield found me the very specimens that Potts, a century and a half ago, examined and described as *Apteryx haastii*.

Finally, my son Jeremy Star deserves special thanks for having drawn the maps in this book; my wife Adrienne Mulqueen and daughter Anna have been equally important in their support throughout. We've had a great journey.

Part One

Thomas Potts and the New Zealand Environment

The Early Years, to 1853

Take a look at the cover photograph of Thomas Henry Potts in his fifties. To the modern eye, the contrast between the closely cut and combed hair on the top of his head and the unruly bushiness of his facial hair is striking, but many early settlers were similarly 'shaggy-bearded'.[1] His jacket, trousers and waistcoast are of good quality, and a watch-chain is visible. A short and rather stocky man, the tightness of his waistcoat suggests he has put on weight. Though he remained physically active throughout his life, it is unlikely he could still shinny up a tree and crack a stock whip as he had in his thirties.[2] After years in the colonies he still presented as a respectable English gentleman, well dressed, well furnished and well fed.

But the most notable feature of the photograph is a stuffed and mounted kiwi, around which Potts has placed his arm possessively – or protectively. The bird is an example of the great spotted kiwi, *Apteryx haastii*, which he himself had named and differentiated as a separate species in 1871.[3] Its inclusion acknowledges his principal interest: natural history.

In December 1871 Potts spent 16 days in a remote part of the South Island's West Coast with prospector William Docherty, primarily to observe this uncommon kiwi. It rained unremittingly for 11 of those days, however, and they saw none. Sharing a tent in such circumstances is a sure way of getting to know someone. Docherty later declared that Potts was 'a good plain unassuming man, a thorough gentleman'.[4]

Back in Christchurch a few months later Potts fired off a letter to the British journal *Nature*, urging readers to 'help us save our birds'. By 'our birds' he meant the remarkable and increasingly rare birds found only in New Zealand: kiwi, kākāpō, takahē, kōkako and others. His use of the determiner 'our' suggests how much

Potts identified with New Zealand by the 1870s. He himself was becoming a New Zealander – what would later be called a 'Kiwi'.[5]

*

Thomas Potts was 30 when he reached New Zealand in 1854. Many accounts of colonial lives spend only a few lines on the early years before they cut to the chase, to the time when the settler is in the colony and becoming a part of its history. In Potts' case in particular this will not do.

While still in England Potts accumulated the financial capital that determined much of what he would presently achieve in New Zealand. He also acquired the cultural capital of wide reading in the arts and natural sciences, later realised in his New Zealand writings, and the social capital and confidence of a well-bred and well-connected Englishman.

Potts arrived in New Zealand with a long-established interest in English natural history. A second flora and fauna then became equally familiar to him, and in the course of European settlement he witnessed the interaction of the two. Largely in consequence of his appreciation of them both, his understanding of environmental change became unusually acute.

Though Potts' ancestry was primarily English, his inheritance can be traced back to the Branders, anglicised Swedes who were involved in the eighteenth-century ore trade with London.[6] William Brander lived behind the Tower of London and its armoury in the Minories, a centre for England's gunmaking industry. He worked as a gunmaker from 1752–89, at times under contract to the East India Company. William's son Martin Brander was apprenticed into his father's business in 1774, became a master gunmaker in 1792, and had ordnance contracts to make guns for the government between 1793 and 1809.[7] Martin had no sons; his wife's nephew, Thomas Potts senior, became his younger partner. In 1802 the firm of Brander & Potts made flintlock cavalry pistols and fowling guns for hunting game birds. One of the latter went to George Caley, the plant collector in New South Wales for naturalist Joseph Banks.[8]

Brander & Potts was raided during the Spa Field riots in 1816, when anti-monarchists carried out an abortive attack on the Tower of London.[9] In 1828 one of the firm's employees was convicted for stealing a handcart and transported to Tasmania for a seven-year term.[10] Thomas's only son, Thomas Henry Potts, was four by this time, and growing up against a background of poverty and violence, revolt and retribution. But his forebears had capital and were resourceful in every sense of the word. They were supportive of and supported by the law; and so, in due course, was he.

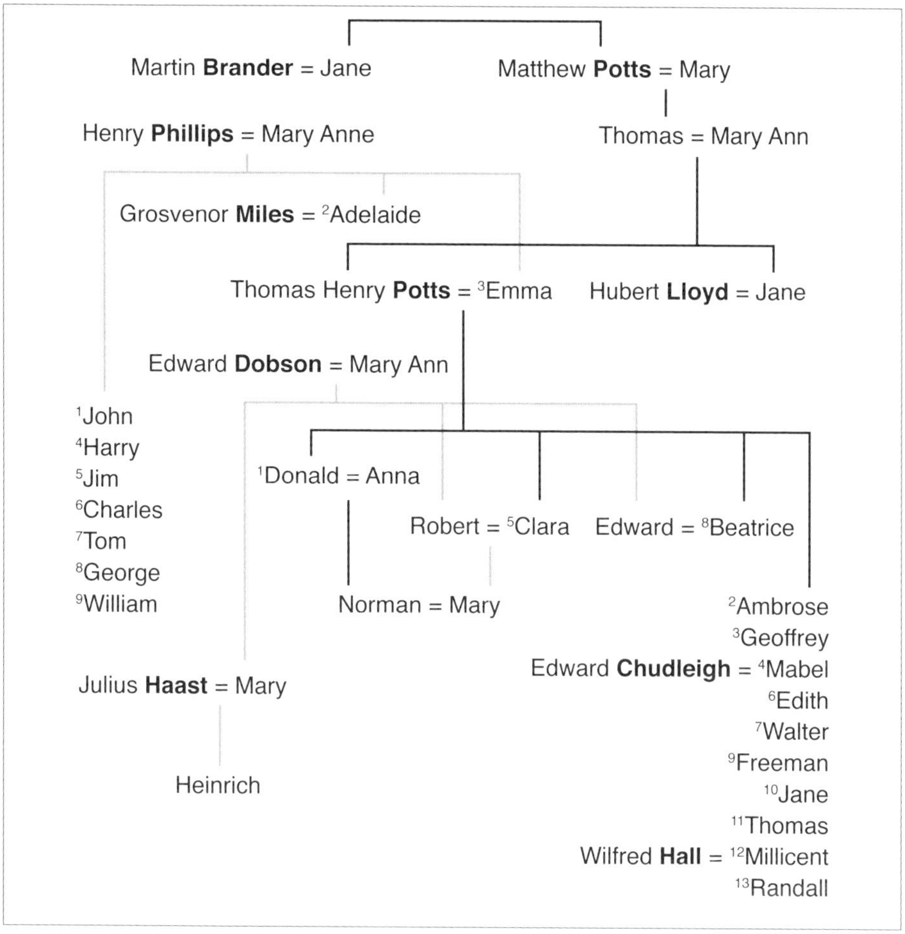

Surnames are in bold. Numerals indicate order of birth. This diagram prioritises clarity over completeness. It shows only the relationships between people featured in the text, and in so doing omits other ancestors, siblings, spouses and descendants. Graphic by Jeremy Star.

Thomas Henry Potts was born in London on 23 November 1824.[11] His family soon moved to the country, for he was baptised into the Church of England at Brandon in Suffolk in 1826. Although Brandon was not linked to London by rail until 1845, Thomas senior would still have been able to divide his time between family in Suffolk and work in London. The family also acquired a new town base in Upper Clapton, and from the time he was apprenticed, probably when 14, Thomas junior would have spent most of his time in London.

Thomas Potts senior was 46 when his son was born, 49 when he became sole owner of the firm, and 64 when he died in 1842.[12] His wife Mary Ann then ran the business, retaining her interest in it until her own death in 1852 aged 54. With Thomas senior's death, the marital links between the Brander and Potts families meant that both fortunes associated with the firm passed to his son.

Thomas Henry Potts mainly spent his earliest years in a rural English setting. His later writings refer to 'hen and chicken' daisies, owls and sycamore leaves, to killing and eating blackbirds, and to rooks nesting in the vicarage elms and in the avenue leading to the squire's hall. Though he never went to university, Thomas had considerable schooling – perhaps with a private tutor. He read widely and at some point acquired Latin and French.[13]

Thomas had not completed his apprenticeship when his father died, and in 1842 he was 'turned over' to another long-established and respected firm of gunmakers in the Minories, Barnett & Sons, where he worked until 1846.[14] In that year, aged 21, he became a freeman, 'took livery' (that is, gained full membership) in the Gunmakers' Company, and returned to his own family's firm. In 1848 at the age of 23, Thomas took over control of the business from his mother and changed its name to T.H. Potts, and by 1849 the firm was operating not only from the Minories in London but also from Birmingham's Gun Quarter.[15] When Thomas Hunt became his partner in 1853 the firm was renamed Potts & Hunt.[16] Hunt is a hard name to find in any archive, but there was a gunmaker called Hunt in Birmingham in 1849, and Potts' association with Thomas Hunt may well have stemmed from or strengthened the firm's Birmingham links.

Potts & Hunt continued until 1874 and achieved considerable renown. Its main product, the P British Pattern 1853 Enfield rifle-musket or B-53, was developed while Potts was still an active partner. Although this gun originated with the Royal Small Arms Company at Enfield in London, many were manufactured under contract by Barnett & Sons and by Potts & Hunt. It became the most important weapon of its day, employed by the British Army in Crimea in 1855, in the so-called Indian Mutiny of 1857, and in the New Zealand Wars of 1858.[17] Enfield rifles also played a significant role in the American Civil War: over 900,000 were imported into America for use in every major engagement from 1862 to 1865.

As a keen supporter of king or queen and country, Potts would have had no reservations about the use of Enfields in defence of the British Empire. We do not know how he viewed later American deals, when Potts & Hunt 'happily sold arms to both the Union and the Confederacy', nor how long he retained a financial interest in the firm that bore his name.[18] If he had any qualms, however, his brief return to England in 1862 would have been a good time to sever any remaining links.

With the escalation in scale of military conflicts, mass machine-production of guns with interchangeable parts became both possible and necessary, and the role of independent skilled gunmakers like Potts & Hunt was increasingly marginalised.[19] Members of the trade reacted by forming a competitive private group called Birmingham Small Arms (BSA) in 1861. According to memoirist David Macmillan, Potts & Hunt was 'one, if not the principal' component of the new company.[20] The military arms trade proved a precarious business in the 1870s, however, and the company secured its future by moving into the manufacture of 'safety bicycles' – alternatives to the penny-farthing – in the 1880s. Had Potts stayed in England he might have ended his days making BSA bikes.

He did not stay. Perhaps the move to mass production encouraged Potts to conclude his time as a British manufacturer as much as other factors attracted him to a very different occupation: that of the New Zealand runholder. Many people felt concern about the way England was heading. Charles Dickens' 'Hard Times' and Elizabeth Gaskell's 'North and South' were published in *Household Words* (edited by Dickens) in 1854–55, shortly after Potts left England.[21] Between them they highlighted growing divisions within English society, contrasting a genteel rural lifestyle still possible in the south of England with the thrusting, numbing, industrialised existence common in the north. Dickens was Potts' favourite writer, so he certainly read these novels; and in the early 1850s he had witnessed the industrial landscape of Birmingham and experienced a rural southern existence on his estate some 24 kilometres south of London.

Potts' retreat to what we might now call his 'lifestyle block', Kingswood Lodge near Croydon, was the kind of move a thousand other wealthy Londoners had already made. The railway had reached the town in 1839, and with the medical profession stressing the purity of the local water supply and the health benefits of the Surrey Hills, many among the better-off left London for this early 'commuter' area.[22] Croydon Parish was home to about 12,500 people in 1831 and around twice this number by the mid-fifties, and Potts was part of the drift. His relocation paralleled that of his future father-in-law, Henry Phillips, who moved into rural Warwickshire.

Henry Phillips belonged to a well-established Midlands dynasty. Several generations of the family had brewed beer, much as the Potts family made guns, though the Phillips' involvement with ale was far more extensive in its ramifications.[23] Henry took on the Phillips' Coventry brewery in 1836; by the time he sold it in 1847, he and his family had moved to the village of Bourton-on-Dunsmore, 11 kilometres south-east of Coventry.

Thomas Potts' only sibling, Jane Brander Potts, married Hubert Lloyd, company secretary of the Warwick & Leamington Bank, in Upper Clapton in 1848. The couple lived in Royal Leamington Spa, a resort nine kilometres south-west of Bourton. Their home, Milverton Lawn, featured a marble staircase and a double-height ballroom, which Hubert hoped might tempt Queen Victoria to visit. She never did.[24] Jane died there in 1860: she was in her thirties and most of her eight children had already passed away.

*

When Thomas Potts married Henry Phillips' daughter Emma in Bourton on 2 April 1850, he was already based at Kingswood Lodge. His estate lay within an extension of Croydon Parish, several kilometres beyond the burgeoning town and midway between the small villages of Sanderstead and Warlingham. To get to London, Potts rode four kilometres to the tiny railway station at Purley to link up with the branch line from Brighton to London. Kingswood Lodge had once belonged to Lieutenant-General Francis Grose, who was governor of New South Wales in the 1790s.[25] When advertised for sale in 1810 the lodge had 'four bedrooms, dining room, drawing room, breakfast parlour, kitchen, dairy, garrets and cellars, also a farmyard with barns, stabling, sheds for thirty bullocks and a thrashing machine'. Potts also owned about 40 hectares of the surrounding woodland and fields. Duties as beadle of the Manor of Croydon came with the estate.[26]

From the windows of his home Potts could see sparrowhawks gliding and kestrels hovering over the adjacent Surrey farmlands. King's Wood was also close by. Described as an oak coppice in 1844, it soon after became a game covert for hunting, with conifers planted as markers for huntsmen. A century and a half later it was still a protected area, a 'public open space' of 60 hectares of woodland surrounded by houses. It remained notable for its oaks, silver birches, maples and hazelnut trees. Beneath this canopy grew bramble and bluebell, wood sorrel and wood anemone, and a rich profusion of male fern and broad buckler. Potts would have hunted, observed birds and collected ferns in these woods.

Less than a kilometre from this reserve is another. Selsdon Wood has been owned by the National Trust since 1936 and is known locally as 'the bird sanctuary'.[27] In the 1980s you could still find ring ouzels, goldcrests, hawfinches, woodcocks and woodpeckers there. In Potts' day it formed part of the Selsdon Park estate and was reserved for game shooting and hunting.[28] Lying as it did within the country of the

Old Surrey and Burstow Foxhounds, with which both Thomas and Emma rode, it was a fine area for a naturalist and hunter.[29]

Potts' interest in nature found full expression in his egg-collecting expeditions around Britain. He later recalled 'long walks around the lakes and over the fells of bonnie Cumberland and Westmoreland [sic], before their romantic charm was broken into by intrusive railway lines and puffing steamboats'. His blanket 'contained choice and highly prized specimens of the eggs of buzzards and ravens, collected mainly through the help of solitary shepherds amongst the untameable wilderness of Alston Moor'.[30] By his mid-twenties he had assembled one of the best collections of birds' eggs in the country. He was especially proud to own three eggs of the great auk, a flightless bird occupying the same niche in the northern oceans as penguins did in the south. As with the New Zealand moa, the great auk was considered either extinct or on the verge of extinction.[31] Potts disposed of two of these precious eggs by auction in May 1853 shortly before his departure for New Zealand; the third he retained for the rest of his life as a prized and valuable possession.[32]

Following Queen Victoria's acquisition of a number of Brahma chickens for her extensive poultry flock in 1843, Asiatic poultry breeds became particularly sought after in mid-century Britain.[33] Potts had a notable collection of Cochin fowl, and one of his Lemon Shanghai hens was sufficiently well regarded to be portrayed in Wingfield and Johnson's *Poultry Book* of 1853.[34] As with his great auk eggs, Potts' poultry went under the hammer (figuratively speaking) once it was certain the family would be moving to New Zealand. At a sale in London in 1853 one of the hens sold for the princely sum of £36 15s.[35]

Thomas and Emma led a privileged life in the early 1850s. Family letters, now lost, mentioned 'long carriage tours in England and abroad'. Macmillan noted that 'portraits in oil ... of Thomas Henry and Emma on their marriage depict gifts from Prince Louis Napoleon and an Indian prince, thus, perhaps, showing their appreciation of an armament maker'.[36] Today these large paintings are found on display at Canterbury Museum in Christchurch.

At the time of Emma's marriage to Thomas her parents were preparing to emigrate to New Zealand; her eldest brother John was already in Moreton Bay, Brisbane.[37] Her six other brothers (aged between four and 18 years) sailed for Canterbury with her father and mother in 1850.[38] Thomas's mother lived long enough to hear of the birth in 1851 of Thomas and Emma's first son, Donald, but died five months before their second son Ambrose was born in 1852. The only one of Emma's siblings left in England to see these babies was her sister Adelaide, who in 1850 had married

Grosvenor Miles in the parish church at Croydon. Miles appears in the 1851 census as a farmer with 65 hectares and living at Bourton.

In 1853, a fortnight after the birth of Thomas and Emma's third son Geoffrey, Grosvenor and Adelaide left for Canterbury on the *John Taylor*.[39] Had Thomas and Emma not then followed the Phillips and Miles families to New Zealand, Emma would have lost the company of all her immediate relations. Thomas did not face such a separation: his parents were both dead, and any responsibility he had for his only sister Jane was limited following her marriage in 1848.

Unlike Potts' gunmaking, Henry Phillips' brewery business was not in decline, as evidenced by the ongoing prosperity of his brothers and cousins and their descendants. But Phillips, himself the fourth of five brothers, could not expect to find good positions in England for all of his sons. In mid-nineteenth-century England many people, particularly younger sons, considered emigration to the colonies; Phillips' sons-in-law not only followed in his footsteps but probably followed a similar train of thought when deciding to emigrate to Canterbury.

Phillips would have known of the earlier settlement schemes initiated or fostered by Edward Gibbon Wakefield, and both men were Anglicans of Quaker descent. Wakefieldian emigration to South Australia commenced in 1836, continued with the New Zealand Company's settlements in the early 1840s in Wellington and elsewhere, and culminated in the Otago and Canterbury Association settlements of 1848 and 1850.[40] Thomas Arnold, the famous headmaster of Rugby School (five kilometres north-east of Bourton), invested in the New Zealand Association in 1839. By 1848 his middle son Tom was in Wellington, claiming the family's 80 hectares and writing enthusiastic letters home.[41]

The Canterbury Association was launched in England in March 1848 and, as Potts later expressed it, 'unsettled people's minds with the prospect of enabling them to found another England at the antipodes'.[42] The proposal called for a specifically English settlement closely connected to the Anglican Church, to which Phillips, Potts and Miles all belonged.

Had he not fallen in love with Emma Phillips, Thomas may well have emigrated to one of Britain's colonies anyway. In part, their attraction for him would have lain in the undiscovered elements of their natural histories. From the time of Banks on the *Endeavour* in the 1770s to Darwin's journey on the *Beagle* in the 1830s, every long voyage with a naturalist on board produced flora and fauna hitherto unknown to science. Potts would also have had some knowledge at least of New Zealand's remarkable forests even before his father-in-law left England: a meeting of potential

Canterbury colonists (including Phillips) in London in May 1850 had discussed 'some interesting specimens of the New Zealand shrubs' received by William Hooker of Kew Gardens.[43]

New Zealand exercised a peculiar fascination for those interested in birds. While it could boast of nothing so colourful as the hummingbirds of South America or the budgerigars of the Australian colonies, it had birds that were 'odd'. Exhibits in the New Zealand Court at the Great Exhibition of 1851 included bones of an extinct bird, the flightless moa; and a live kiwi, smaller but similarly flightless, had just been received at London Zoo and was sketched for the *Illustrated London News*.[44] Kiwi had been described by George Robert Gray of the British Museum in 1845 in the first published list of New Zealand birds, and in 1848 the paleontologist Richard Owen had described the takahē from bones sent to him by Walter Mantell, a settler in Wellington with scientific interests. Late in 1850 the London *Times* announced the arrival of a skin of this giant rail, proof that it was not extinct; and in 1851, details emerged of a flightless New Zealand parrot, the kākāpō. Discoveries such as these suggested the possibility of further species to be found by visiting scientists and settling colonists.[45]

From Croydon, Potts went up to London early in 1851 to view the Great Exhibition in the Crystal Palace. During the six months it was open this exhibition attracted about four million viewers, equivalent to 17 per cent of Britain's population. The exhibition celebrated free trade and the expansion of the British Empire through peace and industry rather than war, and envisioned Pax Britannica as a tree spreading its branches around the world and bearing fruit in plenty. The Royal Society of Arts, which organised the exhibition under Prince Albert's presidency, also oversaw the planting of some 15 million oaks and 20 million firs and larches.[46] Activity of this kind would have appealed to Potts. He visited the exhibition as an 'inventor and manufacturer' to check out the three items of his own that were on display: two double-barrelled guns with improved breeches (the part behind the barrel) and 'an instrument for drawing the breeches'.[47] The extensive New Zealand display also gained his attention. News had just come through of the successful landing of the first Canterbury Association colonists at Lyttelton in December 1850 – among them Henry Phillips and his family.

By 1853 Thomas and Emma's emigration to New Zealand was clearly a matter of when, not if. Thomas purchased in advance a section in the new city of Christchurch at the corner of what would become Tuam and Antigua streets,[48] and as their plans came closer to realisation he visited William Hooker at Kew Gardens; William's son Joseph Dalton Hooker had travelled to New Zealand in 1851 and published his *Flora Novae-Zelandiae* in 1853. Potts sought the Hookers' advice on which plants might usefully be sent to New Zealand, and before leaving England shipped out azaleas, rhododendrons, unspecified ferns and other plants, all expensively and carefully sealed in Wardian cases, an early type of terrarium.[49] Many of the plants mentioned were Asian in origin, not European, and were already popular additions to nineteenth-century English gardens. Clearly the new society that Potts envisioned for New Zealand was not just some rural 'world we have lost', but a world of expanding horticultural horizons.[50]

At the end of that year Thomas, Emma and their three sons sailed from Plymouth on the *Balnaguith*, leaving the bleak Devon winter for the promise of a New Zealand summer. The voyage was something of an ordeal: there was a gale off Cape Grinez, seasickness in the Bay of Biscay, and a squall after Madeira in which the main and mizzen topmasts and the jib-boom were carried away. Thirty-three years later Potts recalled, 'fresh provisions were scarce; poultry, pigs and sheep had all been consumed; there only remained tinned fish and meats, of which the detested soup-and-bully was the more plentiful'. He described the captain as 'a sort of pocket Hercules', a diminutive drunk and an autocrat who 'refused to call at the Cape for water and fresh provisions'.[51] The ship was almost wrecked off the Otago coast, but about four months after leaving England they finally reached Lyttelton Harbour on 24 April 1854. The arrival of any ship was still a major event in those early days, but that of the *Ackbar* a few days earlier had been more dramatic, when John Cracroft Wilson disembarked from Calcutta with a retinue of Indian coolies, plus rhododendrons, bamboos, and a number of antelopes, hare and deer.[52]

The Potts family stepped from the *Balnaguith* into a whaleboat and were rowed ashore in Port Lyttelton by a Māori crew. Potts wrote that at first 'the steep mountains, covered with brown tussocks, that bordered the harbour, surprised and disappointed everyone, after the green fields of the Old Country'. Once he had negotiated the Bridle Path behind Lyttelton his mood lightened, however: 'The summit attained, with a very short walk an excellent view of the great plain was obtained, the universal brown tussock chequered here and there with … woods of magnificent trees.'[53] He strode into Christchurch in search of Grosvenor and Adelaide Miles.

A few days later Emma, Thomas and their three boys set out for Rockwood, further inland, to start their station life with the Phillips family. Thomas was 29, Emma just 26.

Changes at Rockwood, 1854–58

European settlers came to Aotearoa New Zealand with all the usual hopes, seeking love, fulfilment or capital gain. Settlers with vision were keen to replicate the best features of British society while avoiding its flaws, and this desire lay behind Wakefield's ideal of a structured and graded society with a strong rural base, in which a landed élite could flourish while displaying a dutiful regard for the rest of the population. In Wakefield's plan, those who at first could not afford land would in time be able to earn enough from their labour to buy reasonably priced 'waste land' from the Crown. Their development of such land (which, by the bye, was only ever deemed 'wasted' by the settler, certainly not by indigenous Māori) would empower the new landowners to join the middle-ranking yeoman class of small mixed farmers. 'Such advancement towards wealth,' Potts mused, 'could only be esteemed as miraculous amongst the same class in the Old Country.'[1]

The prospect of a new start appealed to everyone who came to the Wakefield settlements in Wellington, Otago, Canterbury and elsewhere from the 1840s to 1860s. Their aspirations were founded on their own experiences. But although some, like Potts, had travelled in Europe, none had encountered a natural environment like that of New Zealand. The new settlers struggled to understand the cultural beliefs of the Māori, the tangata whenua, who viewed land in terms of communal responsibility rather than individual ownership, and forests and wetlands as seasonal destinations for hunting and gathering – mahinga kai – rather than as potential farmland for grazing sheep and cattle.

The 'naturalness' of New Zealand's environment has always been romanticised. Tom Arnold, viewing the landscape in the decade before Potts' arrival, considered the country 'a Paradise'.[2] At the same time – revealing ambiguities in both terminology

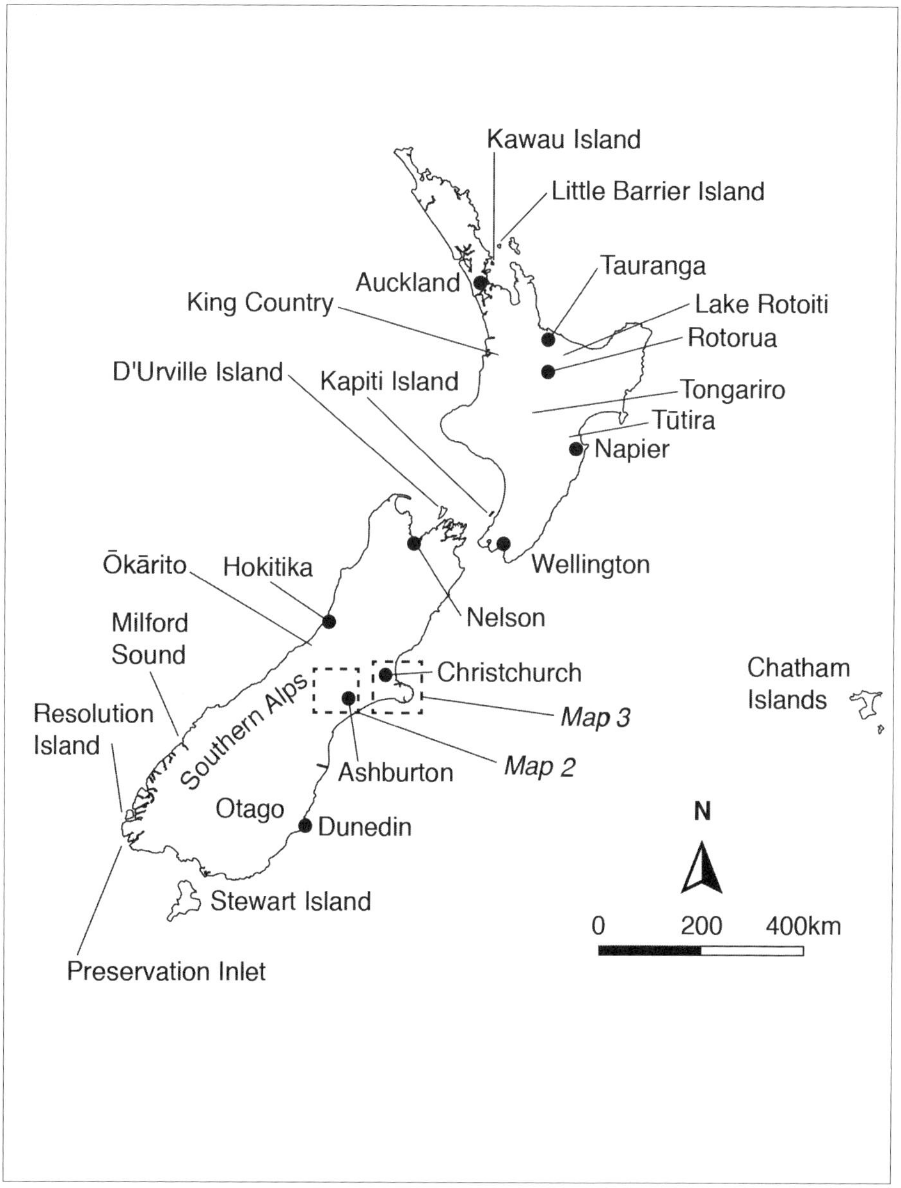

Map 1. *Jeremy Star*

and colonisation – one well-established settler in a remote part of the North Island boasted that he had 'converted the place from a wilderness to a paradise'.[3] From his home in Canterbury in 1854 Henry Sewell voiced a common belief: 'Nature is most perfect, and therefore most to be admired, when she is most cultivated.'[4]

But New Zealand's environment underwent considerable anthropogenic change well before the arrival of Europeans. Compared to other lands, initial human impact began late in Aotearoa. Polynesians and their Māori descendants occupied the land from about the thirteenth century. The extensive plains and lowlands in the region that became Canterbury were forested before their arrival, and substantial fires during the Polynesian period had changed most of these areas into tussockland before Europeans and their sheep ever gazed – and grazed – upon them. It is estimated that about half of New Zealand was still in native forest in 1840 when Pākehā (European) settlement began in earnest.[5]

American historian Alfred Crosby has described New Zealand's transformation after 1840 as the creation of a 'Neo-Europe' by British 'ecological imperialists'.[6] It was one part only of an increasingly rapid and thorough human exploitation of the environment during the nineteenth century, felt as much in Britain as in its colonies. Botanist Eric Godley once compared William Pember Reeves' wistful poem of 1898 about 'the passing of the forest' in New Zealand with lines written in 1865 by Tom Arnold's brother Matthew, who recalled his youth in rural England, where the disappearance of well-loved plants was already apparent:

> Down each bank hath gone the ploughboy's team,
> And only in the hidden brookside gleam
> Primroses, orphans of the flowery prime.[7]

Potts had also witnessed environmental change in England: it was part of what encouraged free agents like himself and Henry Phillips to move to pastures new. He would now see further transformation, this time with a cast of old and new actors playing on a different stage. From the beginning of his residence in New Zealand, Potts was acutely aware of the dilemmas involved in emulating an English way of life in such a place.

There was, and was always meant to be, more to settlement than just new work in a new place. The stated aim of the parent body of the association, the New Zealand Company, was 'not confined to mere emigration': the company planned 'to transplant English society with its various gradations in due proportions, carry out our laws, customs, associations, habits, manners, feelings – everything of England, in short, but the soil'.[8] According to one early historian who knew some of the Canterbury 'pilgrims':

> they dreamed of a new settlement to be peopled by sons and daughters of the Church of England, a chosen band, to pioneer the cause of religion and education in the vast unoccupied territories of the Southern Seas … they set out in high hope to subdue the wilderness and to realise their dream.[9]

*

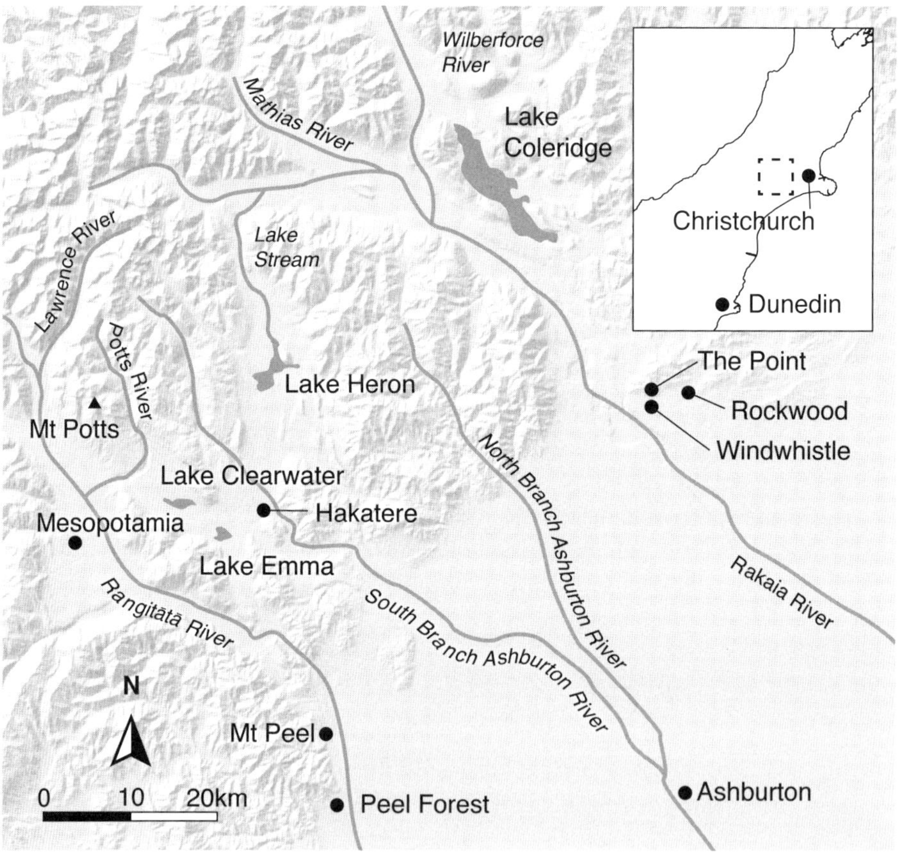

Map 2. *Jeremy Star. Contains data sourced from the LINZ Data Service licensed for reuse under CC BY 4.0.*

When Thomas and Emma Potts and their children reached Canterbury, Henry Phillips and his family had already been there for over three years. In July 1852 Phillips took up 5000 acres (2020ha) east of the Rakaia River, close to present-day Windwhistle, and established Rockwood Station.[10] Grosvenor Miles reached Canterbury with his family in 1853 but opted to remain in Christchurch. He co-founded the mercantile partnership of Gould & Miles in July 1854, just a few weeks after Potts and his family arrived. Thomas did not want to become a city merchant like Miles: he wanted to be a runholder like Phillips, but in order to do so he needed to gain experience, stock and land. With this in mind he and Emma and the children joined her parents at Rockwood. There they shared the Phillips' pioneering lifestyle, and Thomas quickly developed a reputation as an expert cattleman.

We have little information about the beef cattle and sheep brought to Rockwood by the Phillips family and set loose to graze in the surrounding native beech forest and tussock. Henry Phillips' interests were 'his family, his friends, his garden and tree-planting … he had no inclination towards nor interest in sheep farming, but devoted his energies to getting the orchard started and also the asparagus bed.'[11]

Potts described Rockwood as 'nestling well up in a valley at the foot of a sombre beechwood that covered rocky mountain slopes in the very heart of picturesque and romantic landscapes'.[12] Prefiguring Potts' own concerns, Phillips also valued native trees even while cutting many down. Close to Rockwood there still stood 'a few specimens of kahikatea, or white pine … These were very strictly preserved … But some of these pines had been withdrawn from the governor's [Phillips'] *tapu*, sawn up, and used for the inside portion of the house.'[13]

At the end of each day Phillips said grace before tea. Potts noted:

> a glance at the table shows how much families were indebted to their own exertions for provisions in those days when sheep were very scarce and dear; a savoury pie or stew of birds, a goodly joint of cold salted wild pork, excellent vegetables, and a capital salad, were the principal dishes; but no tea was perhaps quite satisfactory, from which a tin of sardines was absent.[14]

Before long Rockwood would offer much more than canned sardines. In a later essay Potts referred to the development of not only an orchard but also a fish pond.[15]

As a staunch Anglican, Henry Phillips made sure that life at Rockwood always maintained a religious tone. On Sunday evenings he read out the evening service and 'a sermon from one of the more orthodox divines'. On other days, according to Potts, they amused themselves with pastimes: 'After the journal or diary was written up, the governor and mistress, themselves excellent players, always made up a rubber at whist.' They played quoits on the lawns, and on wet days there was much 'heavy novel reading'.[16]

Thomas and Emma's fourth child and first daughter, Mabel, was born at Rockwood in July 1854. By the end of that year the family had a separate residence, Valehead, on the hillside above the Phillips' house. The two families maintained almost daily interaction, and the Potts family often walked back up to their cottage in the evening after sharing dinner with the Phillips family. Phillips and Potts jointly took up land on Rakaia Terrace in June 1855, and though they owned cattle separately their stock frequently grazed and browsed together.

Henry Phillips and two of his sons kept diaries, and although these were never expansive and mostly record climate, season and farming activity, nevertheless they provide a valuable outline of events in and around Rockwood after 1858 when Thomas and Emma had moved on.[17] The principal source of information about Potts' activities from 1854 to 1858, when he and Emma lived in the Rockwood area, is his own vividly descriptive diary.[18]

*

One year into their new life, in 1855, Thomas recorded that he and Emma were finding it tough: he wished to 'never experience another twelvemonth of such discomfort'.[19] The weather was often appalling, with frequent nor'westers, snow and fierce storms.[20] Christmas had been a poignant occasion when to wish anyone a 'merry Christmas' seemed 'too ridiculous'.[21] Occasionally one or other of them gained some relief by visiting Christchurch for a few days, but this involved a long journey on horseback or in a dray, and whoever stayed behind faced a near impossible workload.[22] When Emma was absent the situation seemed particularly bleak to Thomas as the house soon became 'rather dirty and our living anything but luxurious'.[23] 'Who wouldn't be an emigrant?' he mused.[24]

If the weather was a constraining factor, so too were his young offspring, who Potts once described as 'three of the noisiest and most tiresome little boys that ever disturbed any father's meditations'.[25] At the time his sons were aged four, three and just under two, their little sister Mabel was not yet one and Emma was four months pregnant. On the bright side, Emma's parents and most of her seven brothers were usually just down the track at Rockwood, and one or more of them was always available to help with childcare or farmwork. Henry Richards (who had some medical training) also lived nearby with his wife and children, and Potts sometimes employed him to do farmwork and to attend to any health problems.[26] Richards was present at the birth of Thomas and Emma's fifth child, Clara, at Valehead in October 1855. Two years later, in anticipation of the birth of their sixth child, Potts would transport his heavily pregnant wife to Rockwood on a sledge.[27]

Raising cattle in the high country in the 1850s meant releasing them into unfenced country where they could wander in search of palatable vegetation. In those early days fencing was erected simply to keep horses and cattle out of the garden and to create a holding paddock and yard where livestock, once mustered, could be drafted or branded. Finding the stock in order to check their offspring or drive them onto the right run when they had strayed elsewhere was an ongoing task. Potts loved traversing the country where he felt 'the world was all before him', but the frequent searches for his cattle could be frustrating.[28]

Potts frequently dwelt on the new circumstances faced by English farm stock and by the people who had brought them to New Zealand: like indigenous species, both displayed 'changes in habits' and the need for adaptation.[29] He compared the conditions at Valehead with the English farming scene where, he quoted, 'The lowing herd winds slowly o'er the lea.'[30] The words were from Thomas Gray's 1751 'Elegy Written in a Country Churchyard', a classic portrayal of the kind of English scene that Potts had enjoyed in the Surrey countryside. It was what he wished to recreate in New Zealand in 1855 – but it was not working. He and Emma had experienced a dramatic change: from a genteel English life in which others did the farmwork and housework for them, to an existence in which even keeping a roof over one's head could be a challenge. The weather was not English weather, there was no milking shed, his money had not come through from England, and he no longer had a skilled worker to do the milking for him. With no fences to contain them the skittish cows simply ran away – and there was not yet much of a garden, either. The problem was one of human adaptation with all parties having much to learn. However strong the urge to transplant English society to this part of Canterbury in 1857, in reality they lived in an isolated rural community in which the demand for amenable or 'good' hired labour far outstripped its availability. Nor did the colony yet have the physical and social barriers that had separated and differentiated the classes in England.

Potts and his brothers-in-law shared the majority of the farmwork with some assistance from hired helpers. William Seal was present throughout their Rockwood years, and initially there was a man called Nurse whose wife worked with Emma around the house. The Nurses were rarely deemed satisfactory. When they left in November 1855 Emma and her youngest child accompanied them to Christchurch to find replacements.[31] Potts found some of their successors even less tolerable, most notably a couple called Jack and Maria whom he felt 'ought to have the prize for dirt'.[32]

Potts took great delight in his children as they grew older but became increasingly frustrated by his wife's relatives.[33] He complained of young Harry Phillips' 'miserable twaddling' and of the stinginess of Emma's mother, Mary Anne.[34] This disharmony was a factor in Thomas and Emma's decision in September 1856 to remove their family five kilometres from Valehead to a rough dwelling on the other side of Rockwood, close to the Rakaia River and the run of their friends the Studholme brothers.[35] Henry and Mary Anne Phillips were opposed to the relocation, particularly because Potts encouraged Harry to stay with him and Emma; he had also encouraged another son, Jim, to seek a run of his own. Mary Anne and Henry were keen to keep their sons at Rockwood, and may also have resented Potts' increased influence once the full extent of his wealth became evident. Potts mused, 'Supposing I get £50,000, let Jim have £10,000 of it.'[36] Most of his money was still in England, but letters from his erstwhile business partner Hunt indicated it would soon flow through to New Zealand.

Moving to their new abode meant that much of the work done on the house and gardens at Valehead was wasted, but for Thomas and Emma this was a necessary step towards the fulfilment of their dreams.The rudimentary building they now inhabited became 'Potts' Castle'. It was further from Rockwood, but closer to where Potts ran his cattle. In later years the run reverted to John Hall and became part of Terrace Station.

*

A few of the comments in Potts' diary make him sound as disagreeable as the people he complains about, which might shed light on Heinrich von Haast's description of him as 'an alert, vivacious, peppery little man'.[37] But Potts was just letting off steam; he was equally frank when writing about himself. The grumpy sharpness of these comments is in marked contrast to his occasional expressions of delight at the natural surroundings, as on one day in 1855 when he could think of nothing more beautiful than native clematis:

> … spreading its beauties over the dark green foliage in wild profusion, with fantastic elegance, now clinging to the tender sprays of its supporting tree, and anon it droops its spiry garlands to seek some help-mate amongst the strong ones of the wood, and deck his lofty head with her glorious crown.[38]

Potts observed and admired the indigenous biota, and his diaries also record the introduction of an exotic fauna and flora to Canterbury. The settlers and their stock were exotic fauna, and both reproduced rapidly. At the end of 1855 Potts noted, 'we have had fifty calves this year, 24 bulls and 26 heifers'.[39] Cats, rats and rabbits arrived along with people and stock.[40] Stock also brought disease: Leach's sheep were declared scabby in 1856.[41]

As an active gardener Potts grew a broad range of vegetables and experimented with many kinds of fruit trees: in 1855 this included 15 varieties of apple and more than 12 varieties of stone fruit. He planted other trees and shrubs as well, such as 'sycamore, ash, maple, holly and pine', and 'oaks, pineasters, brooms, etc in the shrubbery'. He also grew mulberries and currants. In 1866 when visiting Christchurch he 'called on Dr Barker, who kindly gave me some cuttings … [of] elder, honeysuckle and gooseberries', which he heeled in at Valehead. And, like so many early Canterbury settlers, he planted gorse for hedging.[42]

But Potts also cultivated native plants collected from the bush, and gathered native berries for food.[43] Ribbonwood and rātā blossoms were picked simply for their beauty – young Donald Potts duly presented some to his grandmother.[44] Some native flora were considered a nuisance: flax intruded on a paddock near the cottage at Valehead and had to be cut back, and toitoi was burned.[45] Thorny matagouri and speargrass were simply an impediment to both man and beast, and a few plants were dangerous: one of the boys became ill after eating poisonous tutu berries.[46]

Tussock, however, was a useful plant. Stock could not digest old growth, but when tussock was burnt off tender young shoots appeared and other plants sprouted between the clumps, and together these became the primary source of food for sheep and an important one for cattle. Like every other settler, therefore, Potts periodically torched the tussock.[47] The sight delighted Lady Barker when she became a neighbour to the Phillips family – her description of 'the exceeding joy of burning' is one of the more famous passages in New Zealand literature.[48] Increasingly, where closer settlement, clearing, fencing and stock rotation were practical, more nutritious 'English' grasses such as cocksfoot and ryegrass were sown.[49] Potts noted in 1857: 'English grasses taking the lead.'[50]

As with the tussock, getting rid of native forest involved the total destruction of a local ecosystem in preparation for its replacement with the exotic plants and animals that provided more income for European settlers. Potts' 1856 concern – that nearby treefelling would 'destroy much of the ornamental character of Rockwood' – is an early intimation of where his future concerns would lie.[51] Where it had not been removed to expose the bare earth as a *tabula rasa* for pasture, the forest was a crucial source of timber and firewood. In his diary, Potts describes trips into the bush to fill the dray with wood for the fire, or with logs to split into slabs for wall cladding and posts and rails for fencing.

Although he noted native insects, native birds always captured more of Potts' attention.[52] As with native plants, he viewed different species in different lights. Anything that to his English eye seemed like game might fall to his or his neighbours' guns for food: one day he and Seal 'bagged some teal, [native] quail, etc', and he recorded killing kākā, weka, pūkeko, kererū and tūī.[53] Some birds he killed because they were considered pests, including the grass-eating paradise shelduck, and others he shot as specimens on account of their beauty or rarity.[54] One day he 'heard the whistling bird [shining cuckoo] for the first time', probably the same species he later 'had a shot at'.[55] In 1858 he killed a white heron which he and Emma skinned.[56] To the modern reader his account of 'obtaining' rare kōkako as specimens, which hunger then forced him to eat, is even more harrowing.[57]

A few small native birds he simply observed, such as the rifleman.[58] One day in 1856 when he and Donald were out shooting ducks and kākā to turn into 'Rakaia stew', they saw for the first time some 'beautiful little birds' that looked like 'golden tears'.[59] This was an early sighting of the silvereye, which had recently arrived in New Zealand from Australia, evidently without human assistance. Although he did not kill small bird species, Potts regularly took their eggs to add to his collection; near the end of his life he collated and published all that he knew about New Zealand birds' eggs – their number, their dimensions, their colouring.[60] From 1855 he also kept a 'nest book' in which he detailed the nests he and his children found.[61]

Even in 1855 as a recent arrival or 'new chum', Potts showed awareness of the frequently competing interests of introduced livestock and native birds. A lengthy diary entry about weka illustrated not only the conflict of interest between a native species (the weka) and an introduced species (the hen), but also the ways in which both were adapting to changed circumstances – hens by laying more eggs, weka by learning to eat hens' eggs.[62] The settler himself was adapting, too, and by adding new foods to his diet he often tipped the scales in favour of an introduced species by killing a native one.

One day Potts spotted some quail, 'an unwonted [unusual] sight now … when we came here they were quite common, but the great fires have most probably diminished their numbers so rapidly'.[63] Despite his observation of their decline, Potts later 'spent a cozy evening – pigeon and quail roasted for supper'.[64] These were endemic quail, now extinct; the fires were those deliberately lit by settlers to burn off tussock.

*

Perhaps his increasing differences with Henry Phillips led Thomas Potts to discount the idea of having a run of his own in the immediate neighbourhood. The best opportunities for runholding lay in the occupation of entirely 'new' land, more remote still from Christchurch. To pursue this goal it was necessary to identify an unclaimed area with sufficient potential to support stock. Once a settler had registered his interest in the area at the Canterbury Land Office, won out over any counter-claimants and paid a fee, he was handed grazing rights to the land. These rights were confirmed by driving stock – cattle or sheep – onto the land and establishing the run or runs as a working station.[65]

With this goal in mind, in 1856 and 1857 Potts made two significant expeditions into the Upper Rakaia. On the first of these journeys he and his companions skirted round Lake Coleridge then went where no European had been before – up the Wilberforce River.[66] There they passed a prominent rock which they named Sebastopol in celebration of Britain and her allies' recent siege of that Russian port, a defining moment in the Crimean War. While the weather held they explored up the Wilberforce far enough to glimpse a likely pass between the mountains. Thirty years later when writing about the journey Potts reflected that this must have been Browning Pass, as it was later named, a negotiable route to the West Coast. Potts found land that he liked near Lake Coleridge but was beaten to it by one Cyrus Davie.

The second expedition is better known because Leo Acland described it in *Early Canterbury Runs*.[67] This time Potts, Harry Phillips and their neighbour Francis Leach of Snowdon Station rode up the Rakaia River beyond its junction with the Wilberforce and discovered Lake Stream flowing into the Rakaia from the south. The course of this tributary led them into a large, treeless area of rough and swampy pasture surrounding a lake with 'white herons … standing motionless on its stony beach' (Lake Heron). This, as they rightly guessed, brought them close to one source of the Ashburton River. Further exploration confirmed that similar land extended southwards past smaller lakes, also new to Europeans, to known territory on the northern banks of the Upper Rangitātā. Around these new lakes, Potts said, he preferred 'Clearwater and South of Ashburton for a run, Leach the opposite side of the river by Lake Heron … and [we] thought we would apply for 20,000 to 30,000 acres [8000–12,000ha] each'.[68] Striking south then east they were easily able to regain the Rakaia River. As they passed through John Oakden's Acheron Bank Station on the south side of Lake Coleridge they chanced upon his cadet, Matthew Morris. In his diary Morris recorded giving them 'a good portion of chaff'; he was concerned the men would be 'in a tolerable mess before they get back, as they have taken no meat with them'.[69]

Soon after reaching home Potts made haste to the Land Office in Christchurch and successfully lodged his claim to the land. He then bought and borrowed enough cattle to stock, and presently increase, his landholding. As he proudly announced in his diary in April 1857, he had 'taken and stocked the most Westerly run yet discovered in about the shortest time on record'.[70]

The initial 27,000 acres (11,000ha) he acquired in 1857 were Runs 181 and 189, later combined and redesignated as Run 113 (Hakatere No. 1 block). This was the origin of his Upper Rangitātā station known as Hakatere. In May 1858 Potts took up the adjacent 10,000 acres (4050ha) of Run 256, which included Mt Potts, as its salient feature became known, and by 1860 had also added Run 350.[71] The two runs were soon amalgamated to become Run 114 (Hakatere No. 2 block).[72]

In his diary from April 1857 onwards Potts dwelt increasingly on his improving prospects.[73] In early 1858, however, he acknowledged that while he could generate good income in the remote high country, his family's wellbeing – in particular his sons' education – required better access to civilisation.[74] His stock would thrive but his family would have no social life whatsoever if they resided in the Upper Rangitātā. Potts adopted an expensive solution. On a trip to Christchurch he viewed William Sefton Moorhouse's 255acre (91ha) estate in Governors Bay, which he subsequently bought in February 1858 for £2500.[75]

Sarah Courage, the wife of a Canterbury runholder, wrote:

> New Zealand has great attractions to the man of large capital, who can buy his estate, stock it with sheep and cattle and settle down to the amenities of a pastoral life. His outlay on the improvement of his land will be a good investment, while he will yearly see greater beauties surrounding him as his plantations grow … With a safe and good return for his money, he may enjoy a fine climate and have leisure for any studies he may be inclined to.[76]

This was precisely what Potts was aiming for, but he chose to develop his family estate in a less remote location than his runs. When his diary ends in April 1858, Potts and his family are poised to leave the Rakaia and move, holus bolus, to Governors Bay, leaving their income-earning stock to roam over distant pastures under the eye of a hired station manager. Those early years spent in the high country taught Potts not only the nuts and bolts of colonial settlement, but also the cast and character of New Zealand's natural history.

Governors Bay, 1858 to about 1870

Governors Bay was home to the Potts family for 30 years. Thomas Potts set about building and feathering a nest there for the next generation, complete with house, school and church. His 1865 diary shows how his activities diversified once he was closer to Lyttelton and Christchurch, and clearly details his preoccupation with acclimatisation and horticulture. He was also close to Banks Peninsula, and an account of the bush fires that raged there in 1863 suggests why native forest conservation became particularly important to him.

The move to Governors Bay also brought Potts closer to the ideal lifestyle he had sought in England. In 1850 he had lived in the countryside near Croydon, within reach of London and his business concerns. By 1860 he was living as a 'countryman', close to Christchurch but also near enough to the Upper Rangitātā to keep an eye on the high-country station that provided the family's income. It was a division of interests that only those colonists with a great deal of capital could aspire to. Emma's sister Adelaide and her husband, Grosvenor Miles, owned a large townhouse and farmlet on the outskirts of Christchurch where they were raising their growing family; conversely, Emma's father Henry Phillips had sold his house and sections in Christchurch, thereby rooting his sons' upbringing firmly in rural Rockwood. Only Potts was wealthy enough to pursue an approach that might enable him to give his family the best of both worlds.

Today the trip from Governors Bay to Christchurch involves a 13-kilometre drive along a narrow harbour-side road to Lyttelton, through the Lyttelton tunnel and into the middle of the city. In 1858 Port Lyttelton was best reached from Governors Bay by boat, and the shortest route to Christchurch involved a stiff journey on horseback up into the Port Hills and over Dyers Pass. Nevertheless, it

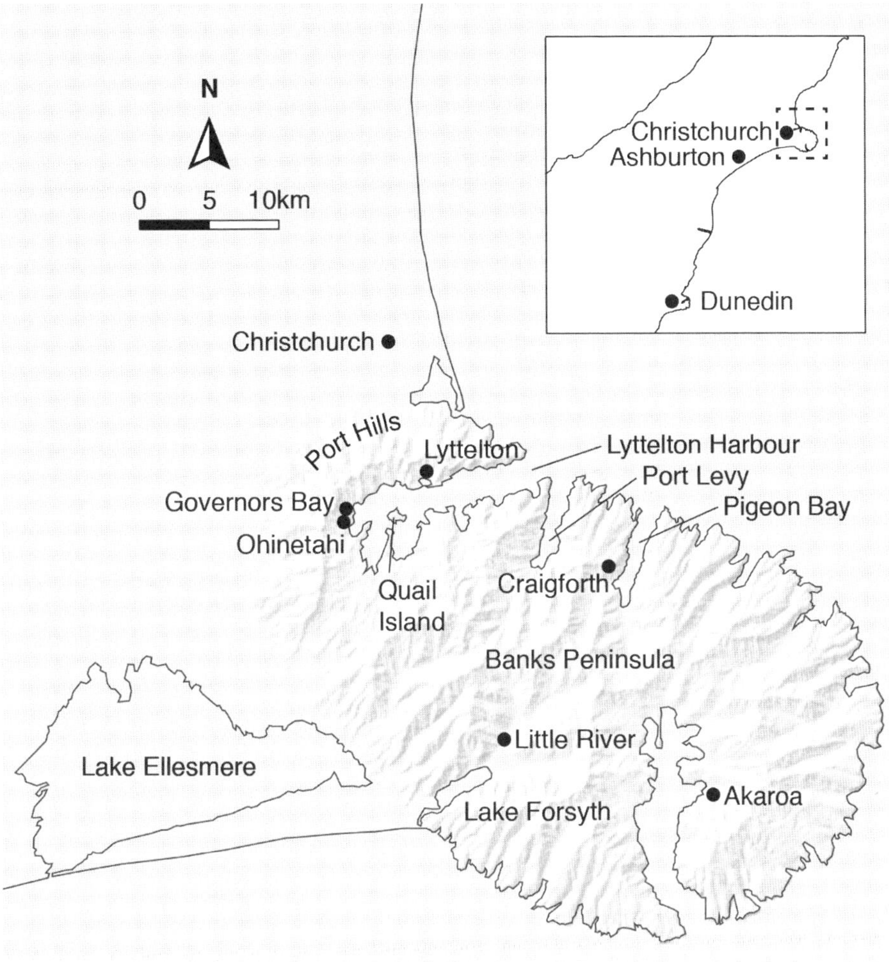

Map 3. *Jeremy Star. Contains data sourced from the LINZ Data Service licensed for reuse under CC BY 4.0.*

was possible to get to town and back in a day, whereas a return trip to Christchurch from Rockwood had occupied the best part of a week.

Canterbury was still in its first decade. The estimated European population of the entire province in December 1860 was 15,370.[1] It remained a tiny society compared to the one Thomas and Emma had belonged to in England a decade earlier, when London's population was 2.3 million and Croydon was home to about 30,000. Christchurch offered Christ's College, where four of Henry Phillips' sons attended as boarders between 1857 and 1860, and where Thomas and Emma's boys could also now receive a decent education. Since it was too far to travel to and fro on a daily basis, the boys boarded in town and returned home for two days each month. It is likely that Thomas and Emma's daughters did not receive any education beyond primary level, since the first secondary school for girls in the district, Christchurch Girls' High School, was not established until 1877. For his part, Potts was able to attend to business in Christchurch, to visit friends and, increasingly, to pursue various political, religious, horticultural and scientific endeavours.

When Potts first approached Lyttelton Harbour from the sea in 1854 he saw a a landscape that was different to most of lowland Canterbury. To the east of the harbour's entrance were the mouths of Port Levy and Pigeon Bay, the peninsula hills rising steeply above them. The area promised a considerable supply of timber but little suitable land for arable farming. In contrast, the vast expanse of the Canterbury Plains was mostly flat and treeless with ample land fit for agricultural purposes.

On his journeys inland from Rockwood up the Rakaia and into the Rangitātā catchment, aside from the presence of rats, wild 'porkers' and occasional stray stock Potts had experienced a seemingly untouched environment. As a naturalist, this was his 'standard' for mountain and high-country habitats. In the late 1850s when he looked east across Lyttelton Harbour, from Governors Bay towards Banks Peninsula, he was presented with a different standard: a low-country landscape with extensive tracts of native forest. Although much of the Port Hills had been cleared to the west behind Governors Bay, significant pockets of the indigenous flora and fauna still remained. Potts described this local environment in an evocative retrospective essay written in 1887.[2] While he always retained a sentimental attachment to the remnant 'wilds' of Britain, his generation's relationship to these New Zealand environments became his major theme.

In 1854 Lyttelton still had a larger population than Christchurch, but the steep terrain immediately behind the port made it an unsuitable site for a major town. The future of Canterbury Province depended upon the expansion of Christchurch, and as settlers moved over the hills to the plain and its hinterland the need to improve access between Christchurch and the harbourside settlements, such as Lyttelton and Governors Bay, became imperative.

Soon after moving to Governors Bay in 1858 Potts stood for Canterbury Provincial Council – perhaps simply because it was expected of him – and he continued as member (MPC) of his own district, Port Victoria, until 1861. He was never particularly active at provincial council meetings. One of his few interjections came in 1858 when he tried to have the budget for a bridle path to Governors Bay tripled to £1500, arguing that 'a good road in this direction' would benefit not only the bay 'but also the inhabitants of the South Christchurch district, who would make use of such a road for the purpose of transacting business in port'.[3] He was informed that the expense was too great.

The cost of this proposed road, however, was as nothing compared to the proposal by Superintendent Moorhouse a couple of years later for a railway and tunnel through the Port Hills from Lyttelton to Christchurch.[4] Its practicability was strongly asserted by both the provincial geologist Julius Haast (later von Haast) and the provincial engineer Edward Dobson. These men were among Potts' closest friends, and it is no surprise that he joined the majority of MPCs who expressed their approval. Once the contract with builders Holmes & Co was signed in 1861, Canterbury province was committed to borrowing £240,500 to fund the project.[5] With the future of the province depending on the venture's success, there was a strong incentive to shield Holmes & Co from any impediment to their completion of the task.

Potts' resignation from the council at the end of 1861 coincided with his decision to travel to England the following year, possibly to attend to his finances. While there he visited London's International Exhibition, and in the New Zealand Court noted 'some splendid articles of furniture made of kauri wood sent from Auckland' that were 'very highly valued indeed'.[6] Canterbury province possessed no kauri, but there were other workable and durable woods such as tōtara among the well-established podocarp species on Banks Peninsula. Potts returned to New Zealand in January 1863 with an enhanced appreciation of the value of the peninsula's forests, so clearly visible from the windows of Ohinetahi, his house in Governors Bay.

By this time the construction of the Lyttelon tunnel and railway had commenced. Holmes & Co had purchased the large and heavily wooded Craigforth Estate in Pigeon Bay on the northern side of the peninsula and planned to 'immediately establish two powerful sawmills in the forest', where heartwood tōtara and mataī could be milled into railway sleepers.[7] Ten days after Potts' return settler James Hay tried to drive his father's cattle away from scrub in Pigeon Bay by setting fire to the 'wild Maori grass … as high as the knees and just as dry as powder'. The fire spread into forest on adjoining properties and thence across much of Banks Peninsula, where it continued to burn for months. It reached Craigforth Estate in early February, where some of the tōtara the fire destroyed were 'six feet [1.8m] thick'. By the time fire reached Holmes' house on the edge of the estate, an estimated 200 hectares and about six million feet of timber had been burnt over.[8]

Farmers saw their future in terms of pasture rather than native forest, so the danger of a burn-off becoming a bush fire was not necessarily a major concern. After all, trees needed to be removed to make way for pasture, and doing so involved an enormous amount of work. Never before, however, had settlers on Banks Peninsula witnessed fires so extensive, and never before had the commercial potential of peninsula timber been so close to realisation. The destruction of a sizeable portion of the timber Holmes had intended to mill for use on the railway and to help his cash flow was not just a blow to him: it also threatened to stall the construction of the railway and tunnel.

In a Supreme Court hearing that August, Holmes sought recompense from the Hay family for the loss of his timber. His lawyer William Travers ably represented that the fire on his client's land resulted from James Hay's action. The jury decided for the plaintiff, and the Hays were ordered to pay Holmes £3000 in damages.[9] The large award ensured that the tunnel and railway project was not delayed by any unexpected dip in Holmes' capital.

But money was not the only thing that was scarce or had been lost; so, irretrievably, was the timber. Nevertheless, enough must have remained on Holmes' land for the main project, since by 1868 'the thirty miles [50km] of railway already constructed in Canterbury was derived from that single forest'. The statement came from Travers who, like Potts, became a proponent of native forest conservation.[10] For these two men, this sequence of events had a significance that grew with time. Both recalled the Pigeon Bay fire in 1868, Potts saying it had been of 'a most destructive character', adding that he had 'seen Banks' Peninsula covered for weeks together, with thick and lurid smoke'.[11] The evidence of tragic waste was clear, but less clear was the question of how it might have been prevented.

*

Potts' 1865 diary (in the form of a typescript copy), detailing his eighth year at Ohinetahi, is the only surviving journal from his years in Governors Bay. It describes a busy life involving a wider circle of contacts than Potts had upcountry at Rockwood, and a more managerial role for himself. His concerns were more with his family and the local area than with Christchurch or New Zealand as a whole. Aged 40, he was regarded as a gentleman of wealth, morality, energy and talent, and was under pressure to take on wider responsibilities.

As with his early diaries, the 1865 volume provides a portal into his principal concerns. 'English packet of newspapers very imperfect. News unexciting.'[12] After 10 years in New Zealand Potts now made few references to his home country. His sister Jane, his only close relative in England, had died in 1860. He mentions just one letter to his brother-in-law Hubert Lloyd, and one from his former business partner Hunt.[13]

Thomas and Emma's main focus was their rapidly growing family. Edith, their sixth child, was born in Rakaia in 1857. Walter was the first born at Governors Bay (1859), and Beatrice (1860), Freeman (1862), Jane (1864), an unnamed stillborn daughter (1866), Thomas (1867), Millicent (1868) and Randall (1870) followed – a total of 13 living children. In her old age Emma would quip that she 'thought no more of giving birth than of changing from a winter to a summer petticoat'.[14]

Like the English birds who raised more broods per season once introduced to New Zealand, it seems many among the first generation of European settlers sought to populate their new habitat as quickly and as thoroughly as possible. Dr Barker had 'the average family for a Canterbury pioneer, six sons and two daughters'.[15] James Edward FitzGerald, Canterbury's first superintendent, was father to 13. He humorously remarked, 'We were sent out not only to subdue the earth but to people it; and I cannot but think that in whatever else we may have fallen short, we have not been unmindful of our duty in this respect.'[16]

Potts' children were ever present.[17] His three older sons would achieve celebrity as members of the Canterbury rugby team on its first tour of New Zealand in August 1876, but at Christ's College in 1865 they were yet to display any sporting prowess.[18] Donald (10) and Ambrose (9) were enrolled in 1861 and Geoffrey in 1862. Their first cousins, the four Miles boys, also attended the college, the older two enrolling in 1865.[19] At the time, Grosvenor Miles' fortunes were collapsing after his unwise investment in a proposed Little River tramway. Potts loaned him at least £1000 and later stood surety for him over a £6000 bond.[20] Despite this Miles lost everything, his health declined, and he died on 17 December 1865 aged 43. Miles' early involvement in the church, the museum, the domain board and the horticultural society had set a precedent that Potts felt inspired – or perhaps obliged – to follow.

Of Emma's siblings, young Harry Phillips visited Ohinetahi in 1865 and irritated his brother-in-law.[21] Her eldest brother John also visited during the year; he had become an alcoholic and would die in an asylum in 1869 aged 40. Harry fared little better, dying in 1876 aged 41, and James died in 1875 aged 38. Thirty years later in a somewhat romanticised recollection of his 1856 exploration of the Upper Rakaia with John and Harry, Potts recalled their passing with sadness:

> these two mates brought bitter grief and sorrow to the household; their little whares in the happy valley too soon became tenantless. In the very prime of early manhood, one by one they slipt away into the silent darkness of the great Shadowland.[22]

Rockwood would pass out of the hands of the Phillips family soon after 1877, when the patriarchal Henry Phillips died aged 72; his son Tom retained ownership of the neighbouring run, The Point, until 1911. Since 1973, both The Point and Rockwood have returned to the ownership of Phillips descendants.[23]

Thomas and Emma travelled to Rockwood from time to time. Thomas took his three oldest boys there in July 1864, and the following December Emma went with four children.[24] The 1865 diary mentions further visits.[25] From 1868 onwards the older boys visited on their own, drawn to the station life they had experienced as small children. Donald spent more time there than his father; for several years he contributed to the management of the family's station at Hakatere and farmed at Ashburton Gorge. In later life he farmed at Katikati, north of Tauranga. In a similar pattern, Ambrose was manager of Waimate Station in South Canterbury in the 1870s before becoming a farmer in his own right in the Hokianga. Geoffrey managed the Clayton run near Fairlie in the late 1870s, then he also moved to the North Island to start his own farm at Kai Iwi, north of Dargaville.

Visits to Rockwood and Hakatere provided Potts with ongoing opportunities to observe native birds, but the frequency of his visits after 1865 is unclear. A journal kept by Tom Phillips at The Point frequently recorded Donald and Ambrose in the area in early 1871 but never mentions their father.

Rockwood and The Point were also ports of call for Ferdinand George Cradock.[26] After initially employing Harry Phillips to manage the stock on Hakatere Station in 1858, Potts appointed Cradock as his station manager through to the early 1870s.[27] A solicitor's son, Cradock had arrived in New Zealand in 1860 and went straight to Hakatere as a cadet, and was manager there for about a decade before buying his own farm at Ellesmere. He oversaw the extension of Potts' station into new pastures and increased the flock of sheep to replace cattle as the main source of income. Potts referred to his youngest brother-in-law, William Phillips, as manager of the 'cattle-station' at Hakatere in 1872.[28]

In March 1865 Potts recorded a visit from John Studholme, his old neighbour from the 1850s, who was leaving for England in charge of 'the most valuable cargo that ever left our Port – about 7,000 bales of wool'.[29] Unlike Studholme, Potts engaged in large-scale pastoralism at one remove: Cradock made the day-to-day decisions at Hakatere. There are minor references to Cradock in the 1865 diary, but in contrast with his hands-on management of the farm in Governors Bay, it seems the station rarely gained Potts' close attention.[30]

By this time he also had Quail Island to consider. The island was roughly equidistant from Governors Bay and Lyttelton. Potts bought about 100 acres (40ha) of it (including a five-roomed house) in February 1863 for £2000. While at first he leased the property to William Phillips, who advertised the island for shooting parties, later he had Harry Phillips stock it with sheep. Potts acquired the remaining 85 acres (34ha) of Quail Island from the Waste Lands Board in 1874. In 1875 when a scarlet fever epidemic broke out at the quarantine station on nearby Rīpapa Island, he offered Quail Island as an alternative site and sold it to the government for nearly £4000.[31]

Thomas Potts' activities in Governors Bay in 1865 were primarily agricultural and horticultural rather than pastoral, and so were more in line with the mixed farming that Wakefield had envisioned for New Zealand. He grew wheat, barley and peas, and his pigs – a source of income – fed on pea stubble.[32] Potts sought out the finest poultry, which he valued both for their eggs and their appearance.[33] He continued to breed Cochin chickens, his old speciality in England, and in November he judged the poultry exhibits at the Christchurch Show.[34] Fruit-growing, horticulture and tree-planting became his consuming passions. The family dined on their own apples, pears, apricots, plums and mulberries and sold their surplus in Christchurch, along with vegetables, fruit and eggs at the Lyttelton market.[35] Potts had delighted in growing things around Kingswood Lodge and at Valehead, but in Governors Bay the scale of his enterprise and extent of his experimentation increased dramatically. He employed up to six gardeners at a time: the most valued was William Gray, a former landscape gardener to the Earl of Wemyss in Scotland.[36]

Horticulture was a common pursuit in early Canterbury and there was serious competition for prizes at the local shows. Potts was particularly proud of 'an extraordinary specimen head' of asparagus, '14 inches in length and 3¼ inches in diameter' (35 x 8cm), which he grew in 1863.[37] Acknowledgement of the quality of fruit and vegetables not only gave the grower satisfaction but also improved their sales at the local market. According to the *Lyttelton Times* Potts regularly displayed exotic fruit and flowers at Christchurch Horticultural Show, and his submission to the 1865 show of a 'Rockwood lily' (*Ranunculus lyallii*) and native grasses and ferns was considered noteworthy.[38] He was somewhat miffed that his roses and most of his vegetables were only placed second at the March 1865 show, even though all his fruit entries won first prize; in November he took first prize for his roses, bulbs, peas, carrots and turnips. According to his employee Trounce (who became a grower in his own right), 'great regret was expressed that [Potts] did not take the Chair at the Horticultural dinner'.[39] In 1866, however, he agreed to become president of the Horticultural Association, and he continued to exhibit successfully at shows into the 1880s.

To get the best available plant materials Potts initially relied on pioneer Christchurch nurseryman William 'Cabbage' Wilson. In 1865 he ordered pears and currants from William Hale of Nelson; dahlias, ixias and gladioli from Coleman, also of Nelson; herbaceous plants from Yarra Nurseries in Melbourne; and bulbs from Baptiste in Sydney.[40] He also experimented with forest trees. He planted three Wellingtonia seedlings that Henry Phillips brought from Rockwood, and Donald planted a Norfolk Island pine on the occasion of his fourteenth birthday.[41] Potts and William Gray spent two days in August planting conifers in the gully by the house and 'on the slope of the hill opposite [the] entrance gate'.[42] This pinetum marked the start of his large-scale and long-term investigation into the growth potential of various exotic forest trees in New Zealand conditions.

Nevertheless, Thomas Potts valued native bush. He jealously guarded what was left on his property, and he and Gray collected seedlings and shrubs from the bush and transplanted them to the garden at Ohinetahi.[43] He also began to develop Fernbrook, a native fernery on the edge of his property that the pioneering Deans family – who were equally enthusiastic gardeners – came to inspect in October.[44]

Diaries often emphasise novelty and change, but by the time he moved to Governors Bay many native plants and birds were no longer 'new' to Potts. He recorded far more about the exotic plant species he introduced than the indigenous species already present. In his 1865 journal there are only eight short references to native birds: two of shooting pigeons and a stilt, two of taking pūkeko and grey duck eggs, one of snaring waders, and one of clipping the wings of paradise shelducks to prevent their escape.[45] There is little in this diary to suggest that, within a few years, Potts would be publishing detailed and informed articles on the habits of New Zealand's birds.

With birds, as with trees, his emphasis was more on exotic, mostly English species and their progress, and in his diary he chronicled their deliberate 'acclimatisation' in the garden. A pair of his greenfinches made a nest and produced young; and although one of the blackbirds he ordered from Melbourne was killed by a hen, he obtained more and recorded two nests with eggs in the spring.[46] He bought a chaffinch, a thrush, budgerigars and a pair of Californian quail, and was delighted when he 'heard and saw the skylark' in July.[47]

Early legislation protected introduced birds in New Zealand, but it came much more slowly for native species. However he viewed his own role in the extinction of native quail, Potts still encouraged his sons to shoot many other native birds. When Donald won a school prize in 1865 his father rewarded him with a gun, which the boy used to shoot oystercatchers, dotterels, sandpipers and stilts.[48] The following month Potts reported that Donald and his friends had shot 'some pigeons and other birds, having enjoyed themselves very much'.[49] Potts – who, after all, had been a gunmaker – clearly approved of this, but would have been appalled if Donald had shot his English blackbirds.

*

Adherence to the Anglican faith was fundamental to Phillips, Potts, Miles and most of their associates. For them the great attraction of the Canterbury Association would have been its provision for planned settlement primarily by Anglican English emigrants. It was important to these men that their children should attend Anglican worship and receive an Anglican education. Canterbury College – forerunner to the University of Canterbury – was founded in 1873 as an extension of the Anglican school Christ's College. Potts became an inaugural member of the board of governors, a position he retained for the remainder of his life, even though none of his children attended Canterbury College or indeed received any university education.

When the family lived by the Rakaia the rare presence of an Anglican cleric ministering to the more isolated members of his flock had been a major event: on one occasion in April 1856 when the Rev William Willock, the 'Iron Priest', visited Rockwood, a number of local babies were mustered for christening.[50] Potts was most likely referring to Governors Bay's first venue for worship when he recalled:

> For a year or two, at least, service was performed in a small single-roomed cottage, in a place where large numbers of poultry were kept … When the voice was raised at all, the whole of the imprisoned poultry seemed to join in a most vigorous sort of chorus of their various notes and calls.[51]

An early concern in the bay, therefore, was the construction of a church for local Anglicans and the appointment of a regular minister to lead services.

In pursuit of these objectives Potts became an active member of the church laity. Both he and Miles were lay trustees for Governors Bay from January 1859, elected to the Committee of Management as church property trustees.[52] Potts attended Christchurch's first Diocesan Synod mid-year and became synodsman for Governors Bay, Charteris Bay and Pūrau.[53] In 1860, as chair of the building committee, he was present at the laying of the first stone of St Cuthbert's Church, the fine building that still graces Governors Bay.[54] Potts also established the wooded churchyard.

Members of the family (Emma rather more often than Thomas) attended services at St Cuthbert's every Sunday in 1865.[55] The church had no minister until Edward Lingard, who was also a master at Christ's College, was appointed that August.[56] It remained to build a ministerial residence, and it fell to Emma to organise the fundraising. A bazaar was held in December.[57]

The bazaar coincided with the opening of the road over the Port Hills, when 'For the first time Cobb's Coach passed along the new road over the hill, and through Dyer's Pass.'[58] Construction of Dyers Pass Road had begun in 1859 and sped up in 1864 once Potts became chair of the Port Victoria Road Board.[59] The project was a major preoccupation for him in 1865 as he personally measured and pegged out the line of the road and chose the sites for culverts and bridges.[60] As much as the church and the parsonage (which were complete by July 1866), the road was testimony to Thomas's enterprise and Emma's co-operation and support.[61] Thomas would also donate land for a school in 1868 and funding for the Governors Bay public library, which opened three days before Christchurch Public Library in 1874.

He now turned to the less spiritual, less communal duty of improving and expanding Ohinetahi to better suit the needs of his growing family and his ideal of a gentleman's residence. Using rock from Little Quail Island, he set about replacing the central wooden section of the house with a solid and imposing stone construction.[62]

Of all his numerous activities it is hard to determine which Potts relished and which he undertook as his duty. Some things he could not escape, such as the occasional summons from Christchurch to attend the Grand Jury. He agreed to remain as a synodsman in 1865 only, he said, if 'they can get no one else'.[63] He headed the local road board presumably because he thought he was the best man for the job and because he wanted improved access to Christchurch. Along with his election to the Christchurch Club in 1859, these roles increased Potts' involvement with Christchurch society and marked him as a man capable of fulfilling an explicitly political role.

A Brief Role in Politics, 1865–70

In the first years of European settlement the provinces of New Zealand were largely left to provide their own governance, independent of the governor of New Zealand. National parliamentary assemblies (the Legislative Council as the 'upper house' of appointees, the House of Representatives as the elected 'lower house') were established in 1854 and met irregularly until the seat of government was moved from Auckland to Wellington in 1865. Even then there was a lengthy battle, before the national House of Representatives emerged as the principal decision-making assembly at both regional and national level. The various provincial councils were finally abolished in 1876.

Potts was a member of Canterbury Provincial Council from 1858 to 1861, at which point he departed for a visit to England. Upon his return in 1862 he dodged serving on the council again, and he was still resistant in 1865 when Ben Moorhouse visited Ohinetahi and asked him, without success, to stand for Ashburton.[1] Three months later Potts was asked to stand for the Port Victoria seat, and once again he demurred.[2]

William Sefton Moorhouse, Ben's brother, was Potts' political mentor insofar as he had one. Late in 1857 Potts had travelled from Rockwood to Christchurch to join in the triumphant election campaign for Moorhouse as Canterbury's second superintendent (effectively its prime minister). Moorhouse remained in office until 1863, and although proud to be 'amongst those that helped on to the broad stage of public life, Moorhouse, the statesman', Potts appears not to have imagined anything beyond a supporting role for himself.[3]

Completion of the Lyttelton tunnel and railway was the main plank in Moorhouse's successful bid for re-election as superintendent in 1866. With his mentor back in the ascendant, Potts finally agreed to further political service and rejoined the provincial council in 1866 as member for Port Victoria. At the same time Moorhouse – whose own ambitions extended well beyond provincial politics – found himself elected to the House of Representatives for two different constituencies, Westland and Mt Herbert. An unsympathetic *New Zealand Punch* cartoon portrayed him 'fallen between two stools'.[4] Moorhouse resolved the situation by relinquishing Mt Herbert (which included Governors Bay) and persuading Potts to replace him there.

Potts was elected unopposed in July 1866 just as his building projects neared completion. This was fortunate, since as a member of the House of Representatives (MHR) he was required to attend Parliament for lengthy stints in Wellington.[5] For the next four years Potts spent weeks on end in New Zealand's capital city before retiring from national politics after the 1870 parliamentary session. His sojourns in the capital would have placed a strain on Emma, who was left to care for the children: their eleventh was born in 1867 while Thomas was in Wellington.

Potts declared that he never felt naturally drawn to 'the tangled web of politics, which those gifted with ability, and those more richly endowed with self-esteem only, tried to weave for the benefit of the country'.[6] In this respect he differed not only from Moorhouse but also from John Hall, who owned Terrace Station that bordered Rockwood, and who was active in Canterbury politics before Potts even reached the colony. Potts and Hall shared a passion for tree-planting, however, and their families remained in contact over the decades; Thomas and Emma's daughter Millicent married Hall's son Wilfred in 1896.

Hall served in every official capacity open to him, including a term as New Zealand's prime minister (1879–82). But whereas Hall 'went into politics as a matter of both inclination and duty', Potts went only with the latter, although his inclination may have increased as he witnessed threats to the orderly advance that Wakefield and his followers had planned, such as that which followed the discovery of gold in the mid-1860s.[7] In his 1865 diary Potts expressed dismay when not only his workers but even a brother-in-law abandoned useful employ so they could search for gold, only to return empty-handed.[8] Disorder sometimes led to violence, particularly on the South Island's West Coast and among those hungriest for wealth. In May 1866 Edward Dobson's son George was murdered on the track to Greymouth by the so-called Burgess Gang, who believed he was carrying gold.[9] Potts was well aware of the presence of criminal activity in New Zealand through his role as a Justice of the Peace, and his comments in the Trial by Jury debate in the

House of Representatives in 1870 displayed his intimate knowledge of court work.[10]

In a frontier society in which neither long life nor even daily sustenance could be taken for granted, the fate of birds and trees was simply not a consideration for the majority of people. But for Potts, the senseless cutting down of a life – whether of man or tree – signified a loss of order. In the face of such raw behaviour, as a gentleman he felt it his responsibility to do what he could. He made regular visits to prisoners in Christchurch and Lyttelton gaols, where 'all matters affecting the interests of … inmates were carefully noted and attended to'.[11] In his opinion, a code of values showing respect for persons, property, and even the flowers of the field and the birds of the bush, needed to be developed for New Zealand.

Potts had the right background to be in the House of Representatives but perhaps not the right temperament. Though he looked forward to spending time in Wellington with new friends, and to involvement with the incipient New Zealand Institute, he considered the role of MHR to be that of a sacrificial victim. Daily sittings of the House were long and arduous, and when conscientiously supporting a move for even longer hours of debate, he commented wryly that 'he would like to see that slaughter of the innocents commenced at once'.[12] He was not a vocal politician – indeed, in his first year in Parliament there is no record of him speaking at all – and he later wrote bitterly of the time wasted by politicians on trivia, their waffle immortalised in Hansard.[13] His own observations were usually brief. One contemporary journalist described him as 'a short gentleman with a lengthy beard. He speaks but seldom, but always to the point'.[14] He voted independently, and not always on Moorhouse's side.

The issue to which Potts most often referred in the House was wastefulness, the opposite of conservation. The waste of money and of men through excessive alcohol consumption disturbed him as much as the waste of wood.[15] The same attitude was apparent in his penny-pinching financial conservatism. His time in national politics coincided with the 1869 transition from the Stafford to the Fox–Vogel government, and although the industrial, scientific and educational endeavours that Potts promoted would benefit from the financial optimism Vogel generated, he opposed Vogel's expansionism for its heavy dependence on borrowed money, fearing 'that, under their new Government, they were beginning a course of borrowing which, without great watching, would lead the country to ruin'.[16]

As a corollary to his disquiet about waste, however, Potts also called for the productive and responsible use of both natural and human resources. Goldminers should be encouraged to settle into regular employment; Māori should be set to 'peaceable pursuits' rather than alienated by further confiscation of their lands.[17] (This latter suggests that in the 1860s Potts already had a relatively liberal approach to Māori.) Although exceptionally alert to the need for forest conservation, he was typically acquiescent about the destruction of wetlands: he thought the drainage of swamps should be compulsory since 'it would add much to the areas of rich agricultural land'.[18] This support for conservation and encouragement of resource use contributed to his strong promotion of local industries.

Potts advocated for the creation of order, and initially thought an orderly approach would avoid any undesirable consequences of acclimatisation. In Parliament the same impulse encouraged him to support a fuller classification of imports and exports and influenced his proposals for public libraries and a copyright system.[19] Opposed to provincial separatism, he also advocated for centralised government in New Zealand:

> He had … for the last ten years been connected with Provincial Councils, and during that time he had seen very little to admire in Provincial Institutions. In fact he had seen so much to condemn, as to cause him to hate the very name of Provincial Government … which interrupted the proper working of government.[20]

In 1870 Potts voiced his support for extension of the franchise (which at the time excluded women and some Pākehā men) – not because he believed others should have the right to vote, but because it would help to sort out the tangle surrounding registration.[21] This was tepid support at most and suggests Potts was no great champion of democracy. Although he had the blind spots of a Victorian man assured in his position at the apex of the pyramid, he did have a concept of fair play: he once opposed some pre-emptive rights to land purchase even when these favoured runholders like himself.[22]

In Potts' last contribution in the House he supported the repeal of the 1866 Canterbury Thistle Ordinance. This legislation sought to stop the spread into pasture of Scotch and nodding thistles (although not of Californian thistle, which later became more troublesome). In typical style, Potts opposed the ordinance on the grounds of futility and financial waste, since it compelled landholders 'to clear their land of thistles, while the neighbouring Crown lands had been covered with them'.[23] The debate ended when the Māori member Tāreha Te Moananui (Ngāti Kahungunu) voiced frustration at what he considered a trivial debate:

> Why is time wasted in talking about thistles? There are very important matters to be attended to by the Assembly. These thistles were introduced by you – by the

> Europeans – into New Zealand. You, the Europeans, are also in New Zealand. Remain where you are, in New Zealand, along with those thistles. I have only to say to the assembly and the Government that it is not the thistle that has taken possession of my land. No, it is the European.[24]

Like Te Moananui, Potts also often found parliamentary debate frustrating. One contemporary in the House of Representatives, Donald Reid of Otago, recalled Potts being 'impatient for the session to close in order that he might go camping in the bush during the nesting season at which period observation of the native birds could be more successfully carried out'.[25] While others approached him in Parliament about matters of state, Potts, Reid said, came to ask how New Zealand's native thrush, the piopio, was faring on the Taieri. Clearly politics was a duty for Potts; natural history was his passion.

Natural Science and Scientists, 1860–74

Julius Haast's development of Canterbury Museum, which he founded and then directed for 30 years, chimed with Potts' efforts to give his own study of nature a more scientific footing. Potts' intellectual journey blossomed as his association with James Hector of the Colonial Museum grew, and resulted in the publication of his bird notes in New Zealand's first scientific journal. Some of the resulting fruit was bitter, however. As Haast engaged in scientific controversy with Hector, so Potts and Walter Buller argued over the classification of New Zealand's birds. Potts retreated from academic dispute and ornithological in-fighting in the late 1870s to write more for the general reader.

Proposals for a college and a museum – the latter perceived as both a scientific and educational institution – gained increasing attention in Canterbury Provincial Council sessions. When they finally took shape the two institutions, along with the public library, shared the same governing body. Potts was among its members.

Haast was a tall man whose booming voice could have led to a career in opera rather than geology. He was a German romantic, an unusual presence in New Zealand. Potts, decidedly shorter, was as full of life as Haast but unflamboyant. The two of them got on well as their interests generally coincided but their personalities did not compete.

In the years when Potts was still collecting birds' eggs in Britain, Haast was travelling around Europe trading in minerals. He arrived in New Zealand in 1858 and participated in geological surveys of the North Island and Nelson before reaching Christchurch in 1860. As Canterbury's provincial geologist he explored the headwaters of the Rangitātā from Samuel Butler's station at Mesopotamia, just across the river from Potts' station at Hakatere.[1]

Haast founded the Philosophical Institute of Canterbury in 1862 to advance scientific study and debate in Christchurch. Potts joined the institute in 1869 and was elected vice-president for 1873, although distance and family commitments meant he attended only one meeting. Nevertheless the institute had value for Potts: it was a scientific body before which the scholarly papers he had begun to write could be officially 'read' prior to publication.[2]

In 1863 at the age of 41, Haast married Mary Dobson, who was 19. The couple honeymooned around the bays near Lyttelton, spending a week with the Stoddarts at Diamond Harbour and a fortnight with Thomas and Emma at Ohinetahi. Decades later their son Heinrich retained vivid memories of this special place:

> ... fine trees and shrubs, a violet bank on the side of the hill, a small maze, a great mulberry tree with luscious fruit ... We not infrequently spent our Christmas holidays at some cottage at Governor's Bay that took in boarders, and became playmates and companions of the younger members of the Potts family.[3]

Against this background of increasing social interaction, Haast wove Potts into his schemes for a great museum in Christchurch. To begin with, Haast kept his geological specimens in a room in the provincial buildings; the provincial council members, including Potts, were opposed to giving him much space or money for his collection.[4] By the end of the 1860s, however, there was a growing mood of optimism in Canterbury and New Zealand in general. Heralded by the appointment of Vogel as colonial treasurer in 1869, it resulted in an extensive programme of public works. Approval for the purpose-built Canterbury Museum, which opened in 1870, was one early expression of the changing mood. Haast's collection formed the core of the museum. The greatest attraction, the 'moa room', displayed the museum's most spectacular acquisition: skeletal moa remains, dug out of Glenmark Swamp in North Canterbury and articulated in elongated splendour.

Haast received thousands of other specimens, including much of Potts' collection of 765 British and 272 New Zealand eggs and nests. In 1873 Potts also contributed the remains of a pygmy sperm whale that washed up in Governors Bay, which Haast overconfidently described as a new species and named *Euphysetes pottsii*.[5] But Haast's vision – and that of Potts, insofar as he fostered it – extended far beyond displays of eggs and bones: a museum should serve a utilitarian function in promoting local industry and stimulating higher education.

In 1870 the provincial council appointed a select committee to investigate ways of maintaining the museum, a public library and a school of technical science on a permanent basis.[6] It was chaired by the energetic John Enys of Castle Hill Station, an amateur naturalist, entomologist and geologist and the 'gentleman of science' most closely aligned with Potts.[7] His committee's recommendation led to the gazettal of thousands of hectares of provincial waste land as educational reserves to generate income for the proposed Canterbury College. Shared scientific interests had always lain at the heart of the friendship between Enys and Potts, but by this time they were also allies in local politics. One of the educational reserves created, presumably with backing from Enys, was at the junction of the Rangitātā and Potts rivers and right next to Hakatere Station.

In parallel with these provincial developments, the House of Representatives (again including Potts) passed an act in 1870 to establish the University of New Zealand with an annual grant of £3000. The Canterbury Museum trustees were keen 'to provide for scientific education in connection with the Museum and desired to affiliate, and to secure a part of the spoil'.[8] Canterbury Collegiate Union – the alliance of Canterbury Museum and Christ's College – resulted in 1872 and was the forerunner of Canterbury College, which in turn became affiliated to the national university. The government funding usefully boosted the provincial council's contribution.

The college board initially had 23 members, but it is hard to identify the significance of anyone's part in this. Haast's contribution was clearly significant, although as a provincial employee he was never eligible to serve on the board. In his history of the University of Canterbury, W.J. Gardner stressed the role of Henry Tancred and other 'well-educated runholders', but only named Potts twice.[9] Potts probably played a greater role on the museum committee established in 1874, whose meetings he attended regularly.[10]

Potts became a Fellow of the London-based Linnean Society in 1872, which gave him some prestige among botanists at least. Though he was never a professional scientist, his close association with Canterbury Museum confirmed the importance of his contribution as an amateur. It also meant that anything concerning birds in the province was channelled to him via Haast and the museum.

*

Potts had strong links in Canterbury, but this is only half the picture. His long stays in Wellington to attend Parliament between 1866 and 1870 provided opportunities for him to meet men from other parts of New Zealand who shared his scientific interests. In particular he became acquainted with the director of the Colonial Museum, James Hector, and the small handful of state-funded professional scientists who worked for him.[11] As a university-trained medic and the government-appointed geologist, Hector pushed for the professionalisation of scientific practice. He valued the systematic collection and classification of biota as distinct from the 'natural history' approach that came more easily to Potts.

The late 1860s saw the establishment of the New Zealand Institute, later renamed the Royal Society of New Zealand. Through publication of its journal *Transactions of the New Zealand Institute*, this association pooled the findings of members of the Auckland Institute, the Wellington Philosophical Society, the Philosophical Institute of Canterbury, the Otago Institute and other provincial scientific bodies. Aware that recognition of his observations would be achieved if they were published in the *Transactions*, which was edited by Hector to conform with scientific standards, for the next few years Potts strove to tailor his articles about New Zealand birds to suit the journal's style. The aim, after all, was an orderly, systematic approach to the study of nature – something Potts approved of.

Natural science in the colonies in the mid-nineteenth century was typically about collection, not analysis. It was the first step only in the classification of flora and fauna into different species, families and genera, for which the Linnean system provided the necessary cartology. In Bruno Latour's terms there were 'cycles of accumulation', with colonial pioneers doing the groundwork before passing their finds on to London and other 'centres of calculation' to be compared and categorised.[12] However, this did not characterise all such scientific endeavour even in the 1830s.[13] By the 1870s a hegemony that could accept, for instance, a compilation of the standard Australian flora from an English botanist who had never visited Australia was widely challenged.[14] Increasingly, inter-colonial exchanges (both of objects and ideas) and colonial calculation were also practised.

*

In 1987 American anthropologist Jacob Gruber used the narrative of moa discovery to exemplify the growing independence in colonial natural science and scientists.[15] The first moa bone reached London in 1839. Richard Owen at the Hunterian Museum was the person to whom all such items were sent, in the same way that botanical specimens usually landed up with the Hookers at Kew; the moa bones that Potts saw in the Great Exhibition in 1851 came from Owen. In 1867 Haast sent him a larger collection of bones from various species of moa that had been found in Glenmark Swamp in North Canterbury. From these Owen identified and named the giant moa (*Dinornis maximus*), but by this time he no longer possessed the key to all further research. This now lay with Haast, who by the 1870s could claim to be a scientist in his own right. Haast retained many more bones in Canterbury: he had learnt how to exploit the 'tyranny of distance' by separating these objects in New Zealand from the experts in London, to his own advantage. He had established 'links with other colonial museums … without reference to any imperial centres', and now had gained both the intellectual independence and the audacity to review any new evidence himself.[16]

Haast's bid for independence from Owen's determinations on moa was echoed in Potts' disputes with German ornithologist Otto Finsch. Long before visiting New Zealand, Finsch pronounced upon the classification of the country's surviving birds from examination of skins sent to him in Europe. Potts' conclusions centred on observations 'out in the open'. He was particularly upset by the refusal of 'cabinet ornithologists' to grant separate species status to 'the dashing little Sparrow-hawk [of New Zealand, which] has received scant justice from many ornithologists, some of whom profess not to believe in it'.[17] Today, Potts' 'quail hawk' and 'sparrow-hawk' are still regarded simply as variant forms of one species: the New Zealand falcon or kārearea.

Similar rebuttals confronted William Colenso in the North Island, whose names for presumed new species of New Zealand plants were consistently rejected by Joseph Hooker or, as in the following example, by Hooker's colleague at Kew, J.G. Baker. In a letter to Hooker, Colenso protested:

> I *know* my N.Z. ferns … to be very distinct from those long known, & which he supposes them to be … had I but *dried spns.* [specimens] *only*, as you have had there, I am pretty sure I should have made the same, or greater mistakes.[18]

By the 1870s scientists in New Zealand were arguing not just with their supposed betters in Europe but also with one another – ironically an indication of increased scientific 'maturity'. Haast fell out with Hector, a disagreement precipitated by the discovery, by Alexander McKay, of moa bones and neolithic tools, side by side, in Sumner Cave near Christchurch in 1872. Their juxtaposition did not fit well with Haast's theory of a paleolithic moa-hunter culture that had killed off the giant birds before the arrival of Māori. Haast, who had employed McKay, remained silent about the find. Frustrated by the lack of any announcement from Haast, Hector publicised it himself in 1874. Haast considered Hector's action unethical, and acrimony ensued.[19]

Potts' one and only attendance at a meeting of the Philosophical Institute of Canterbury in November 1874 was an attempt to dampen things down. He sought to reverse the unanimous decision of the previous meeting (dominated by Haast) to voice 'emphatic protest' against Hector's publication of the find. The November meeting passed a compromise motion to request instead that Hector 'be good enough to give his opinion' on the institute's previous decision. Haast, however, still felt affronted, and would not be quieted.[20]

Potts himself never wrote about moa, save for one reference to bones he had seen in the 1850s on the surface of untouched land – the inference being that moa extinction was relatively recent.[21] This is now the accepted view, contra Haast. But like Haast, Potts drew away from Hector and the New Zealand Institute. He wearied of Hector's editorial support for ornithological judgments that dismissed Potts' own work. In 1878 while trying to write a further paper for the *Transactions*, Potts complained privately to Haast about Hector's practice, comparing Hector to the hypocritical character in Dickens' *Martin Chuzzlewit*:

> I did pretty well till I read the rot and misrepresentation in Vol. 8 once more. I think it useless to write for the Trans. when the editor allows the insertion of such papers – why should my work require the stamp of any Pecksniff?[22]

In the 1880s G.M. Thomson of Dunedin launched a challenge to Hector's domination of New Zealand science.[23] Thomson's *New Zealand Journal of Science* (1882–86) was a conscious rival to the *Transactions*. In a series of biographical studies of scientists, Thomson discussed Haast, Hutton, Hooker and Owen – but not Hector. Potts' choice of this journal as the vehicle for his 1885 articles on birds' eggs, 'Oology of New Zealand', implied support for Thomson.[24]

In Potts' opinion, Hector showed too much respect for the opinions of Walter Buller, a North Islander with whom Potts differed – not just over the classification of various birds but over the very nature of ornithological research. By the late 1860s Potts and Buller were recognised as New Zealand's foremost experts on the country's native birds, but had quite different attitudes to collecting and conservation: Buller's approach was scientific and studious, whereas Potts always trusted more to field observation. He wrote *in situ*, 'amongst the birds themselves when the leisure hour permitted'.[25] His published remarks on individual species demonstrated his skill as a birdwatcher and his ability to write good prose, but ultimately earned him less respect as a scientist.

Buller in 1872 described his wish to 'collect and place on record a complete life-history of these [New Zealand] birds before their final extirpation shall have rendered such a task impossible'.[26] His seemingly passive acceptance of their decline and involvement in the trading of skins of threatened species suggest (in biographer Ross Galbreath's estimation) that he was never more than a 'reluctant conservationist'.[27] He continues to be perceived by some as 'the villain of nineteenth-century New Zealand ornithology'.[28] In the same year Potts wrote with evident passion of the threats facing kiwi. He observed that women of the time wore not just kiwi feathers in their hats but entire bird skins as part of their 'plumage', and feared 'female vanity' might result in 'the extermination of an ancient race of insect eaters, usefully employed as preservers of the forest'.[29]

Buller was born in New Zealand and was initially neither rich nor an Anglican gentleman. Galbreath considered him insecure on the basis of his background and his habit of deliberately seeking honour in order to raise his status – Buller once published a collection of favourable reviews of his own book. Various biographers of Victorian scientists identify a desire for improved social standing, similar to that felt by both Sir Julius von Haast and Sir Walter Buller (as they became).[30] Potts, however, had little need for such enhancement given that he was already rich, British, an Anglican and a gentleman. In his case it seems more legitimate simply to stress his delight in nature and in science. But he did also care, at least in his middle years, about his standing as a scientist – which Buller and others questioned.

As early as 1862 Buller had corresponded with Haast about his self-appointed task to make a complete account of New Zealand's birds. He gained attention with his preliminary work, *Essay on the Ornithology of New Zealand*, which he produced for the New Zealand Exhibition in Dunedin in 1865. Potts began reading his own remarks, entitled 'On the Birds of New Zealand', before the Wellington Philosophical Society in July 1869, and these were published in the *Transactions* from 1870 to 1874. The articles represented the fruit of his observations over nearly 20 years. He modestly 'begged' to offer his 'small budget of information concerning the mode of nidification [nest-building] and breeding habits of several species, many of which are rapidly becoming scarce'. He said he looked forward to Buller's complete work, and proffered his own notes in the interim.[31]

In writing his *History of the Birds of New Zealand* (1872–73), Buller benefitted from the generosity of several men. Observations from Haast, Enys and others proved useful, but the greatest augmentation of his records came from Potts. Buller's introduction acknowledged his collaborators and named Potts as 'a most careful and experienced observer'. But although the book included 36 references to him, Potts grew to consider his contribution insufficiently acknowledged. It is unclear when he became antagonistic towards his colleague, but he criticised him in a letter to Walter

Mantell in 1872 and expressed opposition in later articles in the *Transactions*.[32] It must have been irksome when Buller showed up to a meeting of the Canterbury Philosophical Institute in 1874, on Potts' home turf, to detail his 'disallowance of Mr. Potts' *Himantopus speciatus*', the black stilt.[33]

Potts scarcely received a mention in the second edition of Buller's *Birds*, published in 1888. Buller had made disparaging remarks about Potts long before then, calling him 'our field ornithologist' – a two-edged phrase – and complaining to Hector and Haast in 1871 and 1872 about Potts' proposed new species that failed to pass the tests of science, and his literary style that failed to read like science.[34]

Potts had one enduring triumph when his paper describing and naming *Apteryx haastii*, the great spotted kiwi, appeared in 1872.[35] Finsch in Germany adjudged the bird a mere subspecies. In response Potts poured scorn on Finsch in his third article, 'On the Birds of New Zealand' (1873): 'In the words of a man experienced in mounting the skins of *Apteryx*, the two species could be separated with one's eyes shut.'[36] One hundred and eighteen years later *Apteryx haastii* was still considered the most handsome of the kiwi and 'the greatest prize of them all', and Potts' identification of the species as 'the climax and the end of kiwi discovery'.[37] It was not in fact 'the end' – a further species was differentiated in 2003 – but the rest of this assessment remains true.[38]

In 1874 in the fourth part of his survey, Potts distanced himself still further from Buller. In discussing Buller's *Birds* he wrote that he now felt 'compelled to refer to some mistakes … or else he [Potts] might be thought to concur therein; as to theories, they are the property of anyone to shape according to fancy'.[39]

Perhaps after 1874 Potts realised he had become as petty as others when describing and claiming new species. His taxonomic activity tailed off and his bird notes became more fully devoted to habits and breeding, the areas of study in which he felt most at home. By 1878 Potts had in effect reasserted his goal, 'faithfully to record incidents of bird life'. Instead of writing for the rather elitist *Transactions*, he began to publish in journals that targeted a broader audience.

The Forest and the Trees, 1868–74

Potts may have come to think that both political debate and taxonomy were a waste of time, but he remained troubled by the waste of trees and timber and continued to write of it in his essays. He drew attention to this most famously in 1868 in what is the only speech of those he made to the House of Representatives that is often recalled. His concern at the improvident destruction of New Zealand's native forests, a subject never before mentioned in Parliament, explains Potts' continuing significance in the twenty-first century.[1] His retirement from Parliament precluded him from handling this political hot potato, but allowed him more time to plant exotic trees, an undertaking that he hoped would be widely adopted in order to reduce the pressure on indigenous timber resources.

The Banks Peninsula fires of 1863 had affected Potts greatly. They not only spoilt his view and destroyed a fine forest; they also threatened to set back the development of Canterbury's infrastructure. Given the accelerating demand for timber in Canterbury and the rapid depletion of the province's remaining stands of native forest, he foresaw problems ahead. British anxieties about the sufficiency of their coal supply may also have encouraged him to consider the ongoing supply of wood in New Zealand, where it was the principal fuel source as well as the main construction material.[2]

Settlers envisioned three ways of tackling timber shortages. It could be imported from elsewhere – but for a young cash-strapped colony this was a costly and makeshift solution. More trees could be planted – which might provide a solution if they would only grow fast enough. Third, greater control could be exercised over the exploitation of native forests by discouraging wasteful consumption and conserving key areas, so that some native timber at least would remain available in the long term. In the nineteenth century, 'conservation' generally implied a measured and (arguably) rational use of resources rather than complete preservation against every kind of exploitation.

Potts had resumed his duties as a member of the provincial council in 1866, but there is nothing in the records to suggest that he brought his concern about forests to the council's attention at this time. As a member of the House of Representatives, however, he took the opportunity to raise the issue in Parliament. If forest conservation could be achieved through legislation, this was the most important audience to convince. On 7 October 1868 Potts moved in the House: 'That it is desirable Government should take steps to ascertain the present condition of the forests of the Colony, with a view to their better conservation.'[3] More than five years after they had witnessed the bush fires on Banks Peninsula, Potts and Travers (both now MHRs) would refer to these conflagrations in the ensuing debate on 'the forests of the colony'.

For Potts, two documents placed the fate of New Zealand's forests within an international and intellectual context. The first, *Man and Nature*, was written by the American George Perkins Marsh, who had been a lawyer, politician, sheep farmer and timber dealer in Vermont where, as David Lowenthal noted, 'he had occasion both to observe and to feel the evils resulting from an injudicious system of managing woodlands'.[4] Marsh moved to Italy where he combined his duties as American ambassador with wide-ranging scholastic pursuits that enabled him to set the environmental degradation of Vermont alongside examples of similar events in classical times and in modern Europe. He wrote up his insights in *Man and Nature*.

Lowenthal has called this work 'one of the nineteenth century's two seminal books on the subject its title denoted', the other being Darwin's *On the Origin of Species* (1859). It was published in New York in May 1864 and over a thousand copies sold within a few months.[5] New Zealand newspapers soon after quoted Marsh's stated intentions:

> to indicate the character and, approximately, the extent of the changes produced by human action in the physical condition of the globe we inhabit; to point out the dangers of imprudence, and the necessity of caution in all operations which, on a large scale, interfere with the spontaneous arrangement of the organic or the inorganic world; [and] to suggest the possibility or importance of the restoration of disturbed harmonies, and the material improvement of waste and exhausted regions.[6]

Marsh provided evidence that the increased incidence of flood and drought was often a consequence of forest clearance. It was a powerful reason, above and beyond the prospect of timber shortages, for a more measured and restrained approach to the exploitation of forests.

One reviewer in the *Otago Daily Times* in 1866 – who made no mention of conservation and mirrored none of Marsh's concern about 'imprudence' – displayed a colonial mindset that was fairly standard in the 1860s. If New Zealand were to make any progress, he wrote,

> ... the growth of centuries has to be cleared and supplanted by vegetation of another kind. In place of the primeval forest, fields of corn are to be raised. In lieu of ferns and mosses, pastures are to be prepared ... Such is the mission of colonists ... The earth has to be subdued, and rendered subservient to human will ... The tangled bush must then give place to the hedge-row and the road, and to plants and animals producing material for food and manufacture.[7]

Both Marsh and Potts would have subscribed to this vision up to a point, and indeed pursued it, but what troubled them both were the untempered consequences of its pursuit.

Charles O'Neill, MHR for the Otago goldfields, supported Potts' motion in 1868, and quoted at length from the report of the board appointed in 1867 in Victoria, Australia, 'on the best means of securing the permanency of the State forests of that Colony'.[8] Potts also referred to the report, stating, 'The mischievous results from the cutting down of forests in a wholesale manner has called for the attention of the Legislature of Victoria.'[9] It is clear from his letters to the *Lyttelton Times* early in 1869 that Potts had studied this document with care.[10] The report's recommendations provided both the precedent Potts needed and a blueprint of what might be done in New Zealand. It called for the establishment of new plantations, the abolition of the existing system of timber-licensing within state forest reserves, and the appointment of commissioners to enforce regulations to 'prevent within such reserves the felling of trees under a certain size ... [to] compel the removal of the hewn timber within a reasonable time ... [and to] prevent the destruction of trees for sake of the bark only'.

When speaking in 1868 Potts made no reference to similar Otago proposals that had been voiced by William Murison and William Mosley, and earlier by William Lauder Lindsay.[11] Although Canterbury and Otago were neighbours and faced the same problems of timber supply, the conservation efforts in Victoria appear to have influenced their actions more than these provinces influenced one another.[12]

Once the House of Representatives in Wellington had agreed to Potts' motion, Hector was instructed to gather information on 'the present condition of the forests'. As the head of New Zealand's Geological Survey and of the Colonial Museum, he was deemed the best state employee for the job. Hector sent a questionnaire to provincial superintendents and their officials, and superintendent William Rolleston asked Potts who else he should approach in Canterbury.[13]

One key question was how forests might be better managed so that they remained a source of timber but were not destroyed in the process.[14] A licensing system permitted the felling of timber on specified areas of forested Crown land, but this was poorly regulated and resulted in waste. The system had raised questions since the first days of settlement: in 1851, just three weeks after his arrival in New Zealand, Henry Phillips had 'introduced the subject of the indiscriminate licences granted by the [Canterbury] Association … and complained that the purchasers of land were injuriously affected by it'.[15]

The diverse responses that were supplied in 1868 provide a panorama of contemporary opinions on native forest. Nelson surveyor Thomas Brunner called for 'actual reserves' in which no timber would ever be cut: 'the tops of many of the mountain ranges should be reserved on either side for a certain distance from their summit, and … reserves should be made at the source of all rivers and streams'.[16] His environmental arguments for these reserves would prefigure the 'climatic forest conservancy' proposed in 1877 by New Zealand's first conservator of forests, and the 'climate reserves' introduced under Vogel's State Forests Act of 1885.[17]

Canterbury's chief surveyor Cyrus Davie had no such vision in 1869. 'We have now brought the fire into these forests,' he wrote, 'and I believe it will be utterly impossible to preserve the remaining forests for any length of time.'[18] Forests should 'be allowed to pass into freehold, as the only chance of their ultimate preservation'. Davie lived in an area already largely stripped of native forest; like many Canterbury men, he saw little future for what was left. Yet it was precisely because the timber shortage was so evident in their province, and the area of remaining forest so clearly finite, that a handful of other Cantabrians (notably Potts and, by the 1890s, Leonard Cockayne and Henry Ell) were alert to the need for its protection.

Potts would have been encouraged when both the parliamentary debate of 1868 and the resulting questionnaire elicited expressions of concern in line with his own. There were, however, no further parliamentary outcomes during his last year in the House of Representatives. In 1870 he bemoaned the lack of progress following

Hector's report on the condition of forests. He reminded the House that he 'had seen the whole [of Banks] Peninsula covered with one mass of smoke', and warned there were now 'only two places in [Banks Peninsula] … where there was timber left that was worth preserving'.[19]

After his retirement from the House of Representatives in 1870 Potts could no longer push directly for parliamentary action, but O'Neill remained in the House and kept up the pressure for conservation until upstaged by Prime Minister Julius Vogel.[20] Vogel was alerted to the forest issue late in 1873 while touring the South Island and used Hector's estimates of deforestation in presenting his Forests Bill of 1874.[21] Six years after Potts' motion the ensuing New Zealand Forests Act would finally provide some measure of forest conservation.[22]

*

Cyrus Davie was of the opinion that 'legislation should lead rather to the encouragement of the new plantations than to the very doubtful attempt to preserve the old forests'.[23] In the few histories we have of conservation in New Zealand, Thomas Potts' motion of 1868 is highlighted and approved while the scepticism of those like Davie is ignored. Potts himself increasingly doubted the effectiveness of any legislative cure. By the 1870s his response to timber shortages no longer centred on political actions to save native forests. He still valued the forest, but at a practical level he focused more on the potential for exotic tree-planting – as already stressed by Davie, among others.

Years earlier, in 1856 John Hall had promoted the establishment of private plantations in Canterbury.[24] This had led to a Canterbury Provincial Council ordinance in 1858, 'to encourage and promote the planting of Forest Trees on Rural Sections in the Province of Canterbury' through their proper registration as land improvements. The ordinance had little impact.[25] Fifteen years later in 1871 Hall steered a Canterbury Forest Trees Planting Encouragement Bill through the House of Representatives in Wellington. The resulting Act granted two acres (0.8ha) of free land to any settler who planted one acre of their land in forest trees. Hall's dogged support for private plantations ensured the approach received a significant trial through the 1870s and 1880s, but the 1871 Act failed to generate the volume of timber production required in the rapidly expanding economy.[26]

Potts did not personally take advantage of the terms of these tree-planting encouragement Acts: as we have seen, he was already planting trees anyway. And while he disputed the popular belief that native trees were hard to transplant or establish outside forest conditions, he agreed that in general they were too slow-growing to be suitable for timber plantations. But plant them he did, and in 1870 he read a paper entitled 'On the Cultivation of some Species of Native Trees and Shrubs' to the Wellington Philosophical Society.[27] The paper summarised what he and his gardener, William Gray, had learned from their 'experience of several years' about the hardiness, beauty and potential practical value of many indigenous plants. He noted that:

> Many persons show almost a prejudice against planting native shrubs … [while] bushfires … and the wasteful management of the once magnificently timbered forests, threaten at no distant period the almost entire destruction of many interesting and valuable species, before time has been afforded to ascertain their real position as a portion of the economical resources of the country.[28]

The article concentrated on the value of native trees and shrubs as ornamentals rather than timber, with occasional reference to other possible uses: baskets and ships' fenders, for instance, could be made from the stem of the supplejack vine, and native shrubs were useful as shelter plants for young exotics.

As Potts later recorded, there was a sequential enthusiasm for different exotic tree species during the 1850s and 1860s. He himself planted Australian blue gum at Governors Bay in the late 1850s. He trialled the Monterey pine from 1862, known then as *Pinus insignis* but familiar to us as *Pinus radiata*. Canterbury led the introduction of this species, which was first imported by J.B. Acland to Mt Peel Station in 1859.[29] Experimentation also began with the Monterey cypress or macrocarpa, another Californian tree that by 1863 had been planted in Christchurch Domain, elsewhere in the town and on Banks Peninsula.[30]

Although Potts participated in early government-funded arboriculture in Christchurch Botanic Gardens, he was more closely involved in his own planting efforts at Governors Bay.[31] From 1866 onwards he experimented more broadly with exotic pines (he had 18 different species by 1870), as well as cedars and cypresses. Assorted pinecones from his private plantation won a prize at the Sydney exhibition of 1880, then were donated to the Canterbury Museum. In a conscious attempt to ascertain which conifers held greatest potential for future timber supplies in Canterbury, Potts regularly assessed the growth of his trees, tabulating and publishing the results until 1885. He was able to demonstrate conclusively that, under local conditions, radiata grew the fastest.[32]

Christchurch initially led the way in public plantings in New Zealand. In 1864 the nursery of Enoch Barker, Canterbury's first provincial gardener, extended over four acres (1.6ha) and included 'five thousand varieties of native shrubs and trees ... ten thousand oak plants, one thousand Spanish chestnuts, and a very large number of elms, box, and laurels'.[33] In Wellington, planting activity accelerated following the Botanic Garden of Wellington Act of September 1869, which received support in the House of Representatives from Potts. The garden's principal founder was Alfred Ludlam; Potts had visited his private garden in the Hutt Valley and Ludlam had also been to Ohinetahi.[34] Under the management of James Hector, Wellington's public garden was intended as a storehouse and laboratory for indigenous flora and introduced plants. As a living assemblage of native specimens it made an important contribution to conservation.

Hector appeared before the parliamentary Committee on Colonial Industries in 1870, where he acknowledged that 'the rapid destruction of the native forests ... [is] most wasteful'. But rather than prescribing a conservation approach, he called for 'the immediate planting of large portions of the Colony, from which the natural forest has been denuded, with the most profitable class of introduced trees'.[35] Instead of promoting this by the 'land laws encouragement' system that Hall championed, or with some kind of public plantation such as Potts had proposed, he suggested the government should 'provide machinery for the distribution at a moderate price of the best varieties of trees'. These would be 'raised from seed on a large scale and distributed when they have reached the proper time for transplanting'.[36]

When the government reviewed the condition of native forests in 1868, it also agreed to trial exotic tree species. Hector took receipt of 200 species of seed from Kew Gardens and, by 1875, 127 species of coniferous trees alone were growing in Wellington Botanic Garden. This became the centre of a network of exotic tree-planting endeavours throughout New Zealand. In the 1870s and 80s Christchurch Botanic Gardens also received and distributed many tree seedlings, belying any suggestion that 'the only botanic gardens in Victorian New Zealand worthy of the name was that in Wellington'.[37]

But Potts wanted the government to do more than supply seeds and seedlings or encourage tree-planting: in his opinion it should actually be planting trees. He acknowledged the existing ornamental plantings in Hagley Park and elsewhere, but was now proposing something quite different. In a letter to the *Lyttelton Times* in February 1869 he suggested the government 'devote a certain proportion of the amount realised from the sale of timber land for the purpose of public plantations':

> Let us take into consideration use, as well as ornament, and extend our operations. There are many localities where extensive plantations would provide a great climatic benefit, and it does not require any very long journey across the plains of Canterbury to appreciate the value of this provision for the future supply of valuable timber.[38]

Potts envisaged 'special reserves for plantations of useful forest timber', and 'planting on portions of the reserves that are at present set aside for educational and other public purposes'. The cultivation of timber trees was the action of 'faithful stewards, looking to the future well-being of the community'.

In the context of 1869 New Zealand, Potts' idea was challenging to many. His friend Mark Stoddart thought it was 'surrounded with many practical drawbacks and difficulties, besides the important one of expense', and proposed instead to 'make a few suggestions as to planting, and urge them upon freehold proprietors, with whom the planting movement should begin'.[39]

The idea of public plantations ran counter to the ideology of the time, since it questioned early Victorian preferences, still strongly held, for a laissez-faire approach, private enterprise wherever possible and minimal government. A leader in the *Otago Daily Times* in July 1869 agreed that 'wise and liberal legislation might greatly promote … the planting of timber trees', but suggested it was 'no part of the proper business of the Government to undertake such work itself'.[40] Public plantations would eventually become a reality, three decades later, following the creation of a forestry branch within the Lands Department.[41]

*

It is easy to forget that Potts, the former gun manufacturer, had himself been an industrialist. To his way of thinking, New Zealand required both local industry and overseas income in order to develop; the conservation of native forest and planting of exotics would foster future industry and support the economy through the development of 'local manufactures', thus reducing the need to import essential items like building timber and furniture. The export of surplus resources or goods would provide income to import those items that could not be produced locally, such as railway engines and cotton goods.

Canterbury never had sufficient tracts of forest to countenance the export of native timber: in the 1850s the province's ability to purchase depended on the merino wool clip. It was economically unhealthy, however, for a province to have all its eggs in one basket. The situation was relieved in part by the discovery of gold in 1864 on the West Coast, which at the time was part of Canterbury province. But workable gold was a finite resource, and settlers sought more long-term sources of income.

By the early years of the twentieth century it was clear that sheep (by then the source of both wool and meat exports) would continue to be the mainstay of Canterbury's economy, and indeed of New Zealand's economy as a whole. But settlers in the 1860s had no way of knowing how exports would develop, or what – if any – new mineral resources might be discovered. Would the population even expand enough to support local industries by providing labour and increased local demand?

In 1868, while on the provincial council, Potts successfully moved that the provincial government should 'offer premiums for tweed cloths, blankets, and beetroot sugar manufactured within the province'.[42] In Parliament he suggested that native timbers would be 'appreciated by manufacturers of ornamental furniture' in Britain or onshore, and that 'the forests would furnish bark for dyeing and tanning purposes'.[43] In 1870 he was a member of a parliamentary joint committee that gathered ideas on possible 'colonial industries'. Their first six recommendations related to the exploitation of mineral resources and drew on information from their star witness, Hector.[44] Predictably, government encouragement – although not its direct involvement – was once again proposed for tree-planting. Other recommendations related to sericulture and the production of sugar beet, and free passage to New Zealand for Welshmen and Yorkshiremen versed in cloth manufacture.

During the nineteenth century harakeke or 'New Zealand flax' (*Phormium tenax*) was considered the indigenous species with greatest export potential. As early as the 1830s it was being processed in London and promoted as a suitable raw material for sails and ropes for the British navy: it would see 'Neptune new rigg'd'.[45] In 1868 the industry seemed to be taking off at last: a flax-dressing business at Halswell near Christchurch employed 40 people, and was one of many in the area.[46] Potts was not alone in thinking in 1869 that 'if they could once be put in possession of a machine which would spin flax, the fate of New Zealand would be no longer doubtful'.[47] Aware that 'most of the wild flax that is easily accessible will soon be used up', in a letter to the editor of the *Lyttelton Times* he proposed the idea of developing flax plantations – although it is not clear whether he meant public plantations. His idea that Canterbury's provincial gardener should undertake experiments in the culture of flax was taken up; in 1870, when the government set up a Flax Commission under Hector, Potts became its Canterbury representative.[48]

These local industries would have used native resources, but by the 1850s Britain's imperial history included numerous examples of species with resource potential, such as tea – which had been transported not only from Britain to the colonies but also between colonies. Most people's thoughts focused not on what existed naturally in New Zealand but on what might be introduced to grow there.

Introduction to Acclimatisation, to 1874

In nineteenth-century New Zealand, 'acclimatisation' focused on the introduction of exotic animals, birds and fish. Although Potts remained committed to exotic tree planting as a response to timber shortages – the introduction of exotic flora – in the 1870s he gradually withdrew from his earlier support of faunal acclimatisation.[1]

Potts recognised early on the paradoxical nature of European settlement in New Zealand. In remodelling a land to suit Western culture, settlers like himself threatened to destroy the very aspects of nature that they were beginning to appreciate:

> As the country became occupied, the more remote districts rendered accessible by means of roads, as wide-spreading swamps were drained and brought into cultivation, extensive tracts of country stocked with cattle and sheep, above all, as the whole face of the country became changed by the repeated bush fires, it can be readily understood how these various incidents of civilization should so soon have effected such considerable changes in the condition of our feathered tribes.[2]

In this passage he was describing his own actions as much as those of anyone else: as chairman of the Port Victoria Road Board he had supervised the re-routing of Governors Bay Road through land rich in native ferns; as a member of Canterbury Provincial Council he had promoted the drainage of wetlands around Lakes Forsyth and Ellesmere; and as a station owner he had introduced stock into areas of high-country tussockland.[3] Acclimatists exerted a similar influence when they introduced exotic fauna that took advantage of, and in some instances hastened, the decline of native fauna.

The first 'acclimatisation societies', founded in Paris in 1854 and London in 1860, concentrated on bringing non-European species from the colonies to the centres of empire. People were more fascinated by the new species being discovered than on transfers in the opposite direction. By 1865 the London society was moribund, however, and initiative within the British sphere passed to societies in Melbourne, Sydney, Auckland and Dunedin. Settlers there went about introducing the farm and game animals that they knew, along with cereals and and many useful and familiar plants and crops. These primarily European species were considered assets, to be introduced or 'acclimatised' as part of an ongoing programme of gap-filling and enrichment. In the colonial context, these introductions were the 'exotics'.

An editorial from the *Otago Daily Times* in 1862 reflected the common underlying presumption that New Zealand was virtually 'tenantless' and needed new species: it was a place where 'both land and water are prepared to support life, but are as nearly devoid of it as if creation had not done its work'.[4] In an article that was unusual for the time, William Travers suggested the objects of the acclimatisation movement should include 'the spread of indigenous animals, etc., from parts of the country where they are abundant, to other localities where they are not known' and 'the cultivation and preservation of all indigenous natural products, which are likely to be permanently useful to mankind'.[5]

In 1872 Potts also called for acclimatisation societies to 'expend some energies in the re-establishment of the most valuable of our native fauna'.[6] Both the local and the alien interested him, and at first he saw little conflict in promoting both. In fact, he saw an overriding reason to do so: both could help New Zealand's development. Given that God had created every species, it followed that every species had value. Since native species had only recently been identified, in many cases their value to Europeans was yet to be discovered; if destroyed, any potential use would be lost with them. The conservation of native species was crucial, but acclimatisation was equally important since it introduced exotics whose potential had already been realised in Europe.

Canterbury Acclimatisation Society was founded in April 1864 at the suggestion of Mark Stoddart, a man more interested in acclimatising fish than birds. The initial line-up included Potts, Travers and Haast as vice presidents. Potts was also on the sub-committee that planned the aviaries and ponds of the accclimatisation grounds in Christchurch Domain.[7] At an 1867 meeting of the society, which he chaired, he claimed he had 'stocked the bay [Governors Bay] with greenfinches. He began in October 1864 with a single pair, and the birds could now be numbered by scores.'[8] His diary also indicated how well other introduced birds were faring in his garden in 1865.

By 1868 Potts had growing concerns about the way acclimatisation was going. He feared the acclimatisation gardens were 'becoming merely a poultry depot'. Disturbed by the unsystematic releases, often of species that were not beneficial, he suggested, 'In case of any more birds being sent out from England, care should be taken to import some of an insectivorous kind.'[9]

Potts left the society around the end of 1868, but in 1870 he still put some positive spin into his judgement of acclimatisation. If it were 'impossible to avert the impending fate which threatens the existence of many species of our native birds, we must endeavour to find some compensation for so great a misfortune, in the success which has attended the introduction of foreign birds.'[10]

Potts received blackbirds and thrushes from the society's shipments in 1867, and as late as 1873 he accepted about 30 goldfinches and other insectivores.[11] When he criticised acclimatisation in 1874, one anonymous correspondent in the *Lyttelton Times* accused him of duplicity. Potts replied:

> When I left the Canterbury Acclimatisation Society, some six or seven years ago, I did so in the good company of other early supporters of acclimatisation, because it was patent to us, that whilst we bore our share of the responsibility, we were without any control in the proceedings of the Society.[12]

He saw no reason to similarly end his involvement in horticulture and continued to belong to the Christchurch Horticultural Society, judging and competing at their shows. Many of the flowers and all the fruit and vegetables that Potts grew were exotic species; contained in his garden, they would not have appeared to threaten the indigenous environment. The exotic tree planting he was involved in centred on land that had already been cleared or was treeless to begin with. Potts would have seen nothing incongruous in his own planting practices, and did not live long enough to witness the way garden escapees and wilding pines spread into open country to become the severe environmental problems they are considered today.

Potts frequently mentioned the presence of introduced livestock and remained reliant on the income they produced for him. His personal situation reflected the rarely acknowledged dilemma at the heart of New Zealand's development as a whole, which rested largely on the export of agricultural produce. Given the interconnectedness of all species, it became extraordinarily difficult to preserve an indigenous environment in national parks largely on the western side of the country while fostering exotic-based agro-ecosystems elsewhere. Ecological science has provided us with tools to analyse this problem more systematically than Potts could, but not to solve it.

A Fascination for Birds, to 1872

Birds always lay close to Potts' heart. He had already observed New Zealand's native birds for a decade and a half when he published his first notes about them. By the late 1860s he had examined numerous species of birds in detail, had pondered their decline and was anxious for their protection. His support of bird protection Acts was significant in that he argued not for the exotic species for which the Acts were framed, but for native birds. Through his examination of these species he developed a wider understanding of what we now term environmental transformation.

In 1895 farmer Herbert Guthrie-Smith read a paper before Hawke's Bay Philosophical Institute on the varying fortunes of native and introduced birds on his central Hawke's Bay run, Tūtira.[1] It was the first report on his lifelong endeavour to observe and understand the transformation taking place around him, much of which he himself had precipitated. In 1921 he published *Tutira: The story of a New Zealand sheep station*, which historian Michael King in 2003 referred to as 'our first ecological book, and still our best example of this genre'.[2] Thomas Potts' essays, written decades earlier and demonstrating a similar fascination with the environment, are equally illuminating. Both men in the first instance published their observations about birds, and these developed into more in-depth records and analyses of environmental change in New Zealand.

Potts was never comfortable as a politician. One journalist remarked, 'On the upper row of seats, next to the wall, you will see Mr. Potts … not much given to oratory in the House, but remarkably good I am told at ornithology.'[3] What saved Potts from a purblindness to New Zealand's indigenous environment, of the kind that afflicted many acclimatists and politicians of the time, was his acute naturalist's eye. Of all the things he observed, he valued native birds most. From 1869, once his papers 'On the Birds of New Zealand' had been published, his knowledge of the colony's birdlife was recognised as second to none. Alfred Newton, arguably the greatest English ornithologist of his generation, wrote to Hector expressing his delight that there was 'in your country an observer so well qualified as Mr. Potts'.[4] But Potts was not content simply to describe native birds: he also wanted to protect them – or most of them.

To many modern eyes there is something very contradictory in the way Victorian ornithologists related to their subject matter. Potts was brought up as a hunter and shooter – his fortune was amassed through gun sales – and he continued to shoot ducks until at least 1882. In the 1850s he had shot white heron (kōtuku) and kōkako, but when he visited the white heron colony near Ōkārito in 1871, in an effort to preserve the long-term viability of the breeding colony he selectively removed only a few eggs and nests, and no actual birds.

Sportsmen hunted and fished for pleasure, rather than from necessity like the pioneer, or for commerce like the whaler or the skin-collector. And they went into the bush for pleasure, unlike the saw-miller who went there to cut it down, or the farmer who went to burn it. In the days before trampers and mountaineers discovered the beauty of the bush, sportsmen were really the only ones who could regard it with generosity. Not only was it the necessary context of their sport, but the study of the inhabitants of the bush made them better hunters – and turned many into naturalists. In some it fostered a support of conservation, as it still does today.[5] Hunters saw no inherent conflict between hunting and conservation, viewing selective shooting in much the same way as foresters once viewed the 'selective logging' of native trees. (Nor would it have entered their minds that they were identified in gender-specific terms as 'sportsmen' and 'huntsmen', for at the time these were exclusively male activities.)

In the 1860s, Pākehā sportsmen and settlers were careful to preserve any introduced species. Protection for native birds, on the other hand, was considered only as they acquired sporting significance (ducks were first), or their economic value as insect eaters was recognised (such as kiwi), or they were promoted as icons of the new nation (such as the huia).[6] New Zealand's first animal protection Acts were passed from 1861 onward, and were designed to provide protection for species considered useful to humans, such as pheasants and deer which provided food and sport. There was no reference to native species.[7] Many politicians opposed the idea of extending the legislation to include native birds: there was much emphasis on the right to hunt and little appreciation of what would be identified, a century later, as 'biological diversity'.[8] Progress was therefore slight: the Protection of Animals Act (1867) allowed the governor to proclaim, 'from time to time' and in a particular locality, the protection of any native bird species.[9] To Potts' dismay, however, only those native birds considered as game featured on the 'protected' list.

In describing environmental changes to inland Canterbury since the 1850s, Potts bemoaned the fact that 'instead of the varied cries of birds we have the bleating of flocks'.[10] While he recognised the concomitance of declining native bird populations with settlement, in 1870 he still had no firm view on the primary causes. He accepted human activity was key to the fate of some species, but also referred to the impact of introduced stock, rats, cats and bees, and the destruction of forest habitat through 'repeated bushfires'. He was also at least prepared to consider the common view that native species were innately 'feeble'. It is possible to trace precisely the stages and limitations of Potts' understanding as he gradually refined his examination of native bird decline and formulated ways to respond.

*

In 1871 Potts examined and described three new species among bird specimens received by Canterbury Museum.[11] Only one of these designations was accepted by his fellow ornithologists: this was the 'new species of Apteryx' already referred to, the great spotted kiwi, two skins of which had been obtained in the summer of 1870–71 from the remote Ōkārito region of Westland.

Relieved of his parliamentary duties, Potts now had time to view Westland's birdlife himself near the end of 1871. He left Governors Bay in the last week of November, proceeding first to his station at Hakatere then east until he reached Porters Pass, where he took the new road over Arthur's Pass to the West Coast.[12] While travelling between Ōtira and Hokitika he noted the native thrush (piopio) 'frequently' in the forest, but this changed as he neared the coast. Piopio had been abundant in the area only three years earlier; now he 'searched one of their former favourite haunts, a large island in that river [the Arahura] more or less covered with scrub-bush, dotted with ti-trees, and two or three specimens only were to be seen; they have been driven away … by the clearances for paddocks to supply the requirements of the West Coast cattle trade'.[13] Piopio remained numerous further south: he called on a hermit living in a tree-fern hut up the Waiho River south of Ōkārito, where the piopio were so tame he could feed them until they came inside. Potts himself had eaten this species in earlier times and found the flavour 'not at all bad'.[14] Piopio became extinct soon after 1900.[15]

On an expedition in 1868 Haast had employed William Docherty as his guide in Ōkārito. Though his equal as a character, Docherty was not as literate, nor is he as often remembered, as Charlie Douglas, who was also on the expedition – but he had his uses. According to Haast, Docherty

> had a great experience in kiwi and kakapo hunting, [and] had a well-trained dog for that purpose with him. In this district, so seldom disturbed by man, these two night-birds were still abundant, especially the Apteryx [kiwi], of which, sometimes in one afternoon, we secured as many as ten. I was thus able to study their mode of living, observe their holes and hiding places and, moreover, could, with the assistance of my companions, whom I taught skinning, prepare a large number of skins.[16]

Docherty had knocked around the West Coast since 1864 in search of gold, coal or copper, but only made a decent income once he began supplying bird skins to Haast, an activity he continued until about 1879. For his own visit to Ōkārito in 1871 Potts also employed Docherty, who informed him that, to date, he had obtained about 2200 specimens of kiwi. Together the men saw several little spotted kiwi but no great spotted kiwi, although Docherty pointed out places up the Ōkārito River and east of Lake Māpōurika where he had procured the specimens whose skins Potts had examined in Christchurch.[17]

Kākāpō proved similarly elusive, but a visit to the white heronry on the Waitangitaona River north of Ōkārito Lagoon was thoroughly rewarding. The men 'reached the secluded home of the kotuku by boat passing through forest scenery of wondrous beauty'. They observed about 50 kōtuku but did not shoot any, being 'mindful to excite as little alarm as possible', and noted some 25 nests. One heron, which Potts sketched in amateurish fashion, had built its nest on top of a tree fern.[18]

Potts returned to Governors Bay in January. On 2 February 1872, with memories of the West Coast trip still uppermost, he wrote a letter to the editor of *Nature* identifying 'the collector, the provider of rarities for museums' as a major threat to the future of the kiwi and the kākāpō through their lack of discrimination: 'If spring or summer plumage is interesting, so also is that of winter; eggs, young, the adult, alike he preys on all.'[19] He went on to compare the anomalies surrounding the destruction of native forest and birds:

> We encourage planting, the labour and capital therein may yield returns after the lapse of generations; we, at the same time, allow timber, the growth of ages, to be swept by fire by any one who owns a box of matches, and look on firing as the best

> means to subdue the wilderness. We import with great difficulty insectivorous birds, and allow the Apterygidae [kiwi] and other insectivorous genera to be destroyed without mercy.[20]

As with the modern environmentalist who argues that biodiversity is crucial since many threatened species may have potential benefit for humanity, Potts stressed the untapped value to settlers of native forests and birds. Then, as now, it may have seemed more promising to highlight economic gain rather than beauty or magnificence. But the tone of Potts' letter, in calling on those in Britain to 'help us save our birds', indicates that after 18 years in the colony he now valued New Zealand's flora and fauna for more than just their utility. Despite the parallels drawn between forest decline and bird decline, however, his analysis still lacked any clear statement on the interrelationship between the two.

In a paper entitled 'On Recent Changes in the Fauna of New Zealand' which he arranged to be read before the Philosophical Institute of Canterbury 10 months later, Potts wrote more of the changed habits of native birds than the reduction in their habitat. He focused mainly on harrier hawks, kingfishers, silvereyes and grey warblers, all of which had successfully adapted to European presence and profited from the new food sources presented. He called again for 'the preservation of our native fauna', noting that forest removal by fire was 'quickly rendering whole districts comparatively mute'.[21]

Although well able to record his observations eloquently, Potts struggled to put them within a scientific context. Marsh's *Man and Nature* had provided him with an intellectual framework in which to place his own thoughts on forest conservation, and Gilbert White's *The Natural History of Selborne* (1789), which Potts loved, confirmed him in his appreciation of natural history, but beyond his own observations he had little to guide him to a full understanding of how the flora and fauna of a particular habitat functioned as a whole. Eugenius Warming's *Plantesamfund* (1895), which inaugurated plant ecology, Frederic Clements' work on *Plant Succession* (1916) and Arthur Tansley's introduction of the 'ecosystem' concept (1935) all lay well in the future.[22]

*

Potts continued to cast around for new means to save native birds. In 1870 he suggested that 'the re-establishment of some of our rarer species (many of which are excellent as articles of food) [would] form a worthy, if not a noble, object of ambition for our Acclimatisation Societies', and pointed out that the Paris society had adopted this role in 1864.[23] In the final paragraph of his 1872 letter to *Nature* he went further:

> Could we be persuaded to try and avert … the destruction of so many species of our feathered tribe, D'Urville's Island might be found most useful. Wingless species, and birds of feeble powers of flight, might there find a refuge for some of their representatives. Resolution Island might be placed under tapu from molestation by dog and gun.[24]

This approach linked the problem with firing guns rather than firing forests, and with dogs but not other predators. There is no mention here of habitat loss, or of competition from introduced bird species that were so much better equipped for life in the new environments created by European settlement. Nevertheless, Potts' idea implicitly promoted faunal preservation in insular locations where vegetation remained relatively unchanged and unthreatened. It both signalled and influenced an important direction taken later with nature protection in New Zealand.[25] When the 're-establishment' of native birds on island reserves was finally attempted in the 1890s, acclimatisation societies gave their support and, in doing so, at last demonstrated a concern for native species that Potts had pressed for since 1870.[26]

Potts once referred to 'the dull epoch of Maori conservancy', suggesting he viewed the pre-European period as one of steady uneventful stewardship of the native environment.[27] He wrote of the 'slumbering wilderness' being 'awakened … from the silent trance of ages' by the European settlers' lack of regard for 'virgin forests … in all their pristine beauty'.[28] Like all of his generation, Potts was unaware of the impact Polynesian settlers had had on New Zealand's environment, but he did have respect for their Māori descendants and was aware that European settlement was disrupting indigenous people's lives.[29] In later years he would remark that the 'drainage of swamps and other improvements have put an end to their duck-hunting', and that 'the rapid disforesting of this district [Banks Peninsula]' had made the custom of hunting 'woodland birds … a thing of the past'.[30]

The word 'taboo', an anglicisation of the Tongan 'tabu' (meaning something which may not be used), entered the English language as far back as 1777. In his suggestion that Resolution Island be 'placed under tapu', Potts made use of the te reo word for the Māori concept of restricting access or setting apart. In the same year John Enys also used the word when he noted that, behind Wellington, 'part of the ranges have been rendered tapu by the natives, for the last seven years, so as to protect the Huia from being killed off'.[31] This may suggest that both men had learned something from Māori approaches to conservation.

Whatever Potts gained from 'traditional ecological knowledge', or indeed from his own local experience in New Zealand, the decline of the flightless great auk was also influential in leading him to the concept of island reserves.[32] The great auk was the species of the northern oceans whose evolutionary development most closely mirrored that of penguins in the southern hemisphere. The last British specimen was killed on the remote Outer Hebridean island of St Kilda in 1844, and the last sighting anywhere was off the Newfoundland coast in 1852.[33] It was the only British bird to become extinct in the nineteenth century.

We gain a sense of this bird's continuing significance to Potts from a paper he read before the Wellington Philosophical Society in 1870. In it he remarked that there was 'no *close time* or *fence month* observed for the Great Auk'; he hoped nevertheless that the species still existed 'on some of the surf-beaten Skärs and Skerries [of Iceland], where a frightful surge almost perpetually rages, and denies access to the boldest explorer'. In New Zealand, he added, 'would that some of *our rarer* birds could be sheltered from impending extinction by a barrier as secure, and thus be saved from the destructive attacks of the mercenary plunderer'.[34] The idea of a 'fence month' originally referred to the fawning-time of deer, a period of about 30 days when hunting was forbidden, and later applied also to a 'close season' for fishing. Men in the hunting tradition were well used to thinking both of metaphorical 'fences' and 'enclosures' of time and season, and of closed-off land fenced against predators – after all, England had had game reserves for centuries. In a new country, less densely populated and with fewer legal and social controls, Potts' thoughts had turned to natural barriers, in particular that presented by the sea.

Botanist Thomas Kirk would later claim that he and Frederick Hutton had suggested Little Barrier Island as a native bird reserve in 1868, but the idea of island reserves in the South Island at least belonged to Potts.[35] There may also be a link between Potts' letter in *Nature* in 1872 and Alfred Newton's 1877 call from England for a 'people's park' for kākāpō.[36]

*

At the time that Potts was considering island reserves, the colony had an overall human population of about 300,000 (an 1871 estimate). In the South Island most people, both Māori and Pākehā, lived on the temperate eastern side.[37] Clad in dense bush and subject to high rainfall, the majority of southwestern New Zealand was a wilderness where dense native forest stretched right down the sides of steep fiords or 'sounds' to sea level. It was a picturesque but inhospitable area. In 1873 John Enys wrote that the fiords 'exceed anything that can be imagined in beauty'.[38]

Potts' visit to the west of the South Island at the end of 1871 in search of kiwi had been rather disappointing. In May 1872, still with the West Coast in mind, he donated 56 British birds' eggs to Hector for the Colonial Museum; in return Hector sent Potts a copy of his catalogue of New Zealand fishes. Potts then despatched more eggs and announced that he planned 'to illustrate my paper this year with a few sketches of rare nests'. He mentioned his 'great desire to make a journey to … Sound Country' and hinted that Hector might lend 'some assistance in the matter'.[39]

As the chief state scientist, Hector had access to the government steamship and the authority to invite others on official expeditions. But despite these privileges, his position also constrained him. In his biography of Roderick Murchison, Robert Stafford depicts scientists throughout the British Empire as cultural imperialists whose role was 'to engage and transform the physical world in the interests of perceived social needs'.[40] In fulfilling his role, a government employee like Hector was expected to regard indigenous environments in a utilitarian manner, as a prospector rather than admirer. His capacity to do precisely this was already evident when, as Otago's provincial geologist, he visited the West Coast in 1863. Hector was there to look for new resources. Like Enys a decade later he found the scenery in Milford Sound 'quite equal to the finest that can be enjoyed', but Hector doubted the area could be settled: the flat between the Arthur and Cleddau rivers was 'the only land at the head of Milford Sound that could possibly be made available for any purpose', and the hills to the north of the Sound were 'too steep to be of any value'.[41]

In 1872 as national director of the geological survey and director of the Colonial Museum, his role was even more strongly defined by his position. Nevertheless, Potts' request produced the required result. When Hector embarked on a trip around Fiordland at the end of 1872 he invited not only Potts but Enys, who had also contributed gifts to the museum. They boarded the government steamer *Luna* at Lyttelton and headed down the east coast then up the southwest coast to Preservation Inlet; later they camped overnight under an old sail on Resolution Island in Dusky Sound.[42] Hector was looking for exploitable fisheries and mineral deposits, but Potts had a different quarry in mind: in the morning he walked to the north of the island, hoping in vain for a glimpse of the fabulously elusive takahē.

The *Luna* steamed next to Milford Sound where it ran aground, forcing the men to remain ashore for four days while the boat was refloated. Potts recalled that they wandered 'from dawn to eve, clutching at daylight greedily, hour by hour, as a precious boon, that disclosed to our wandering gaze, the grandeur, the sublimity of Nature'.[43]

Later in life Potts often romanticised his earlier experiences, but his retrospective records of this trip in particular repay close analysis. From frequent literary allusions throughout his essays we know that he read deeply into the works of major novelists, dramatists and poets. He described himself sweating long over his own prose, carefully considering every phrase. In 1881 he characterised his stop in Dusky Sound as 'a holiday trip, hunting for the takahe'.[44] Potts was quite literally a huntsman; as a churchman the word 'holiday' would still have retained for him some sense of 'holy day'. In keeping with a scene from a medieval tapestry, he described their journey against a background of the rich colours of crimson rātā flowers and white olearia. It was a quest for a *rara avis* – comparable perhaps to a knight's religious quest for the Holy Grail.

Potts' 'ramble' contrasted and, to some extent, conflicted with the search for the takahē. The word 'rambling' implies wandering about without definite aim or direction and was a favourite with Potts, who employed the unsystematic method of rambling to glean his knowledge of natural history – and who, when writing, increasingly made his points during a scarcely syntactic rambling within his paragraphs. Perhaps the style of his later essays was deliberate, an idea substantiated by his use of 'Rambler' as a *nom de plume*.

In a retrospective essay concerning this trip, published in 1880, Potts reflected on an event that occurred during the Milford Sound stranding. He began by exactly repeating his formal narration of the event as first read before the Philosophical Institute of Canterbury in 1873:

> whilst exploring the bush that fringes Milford Sound, the writer was so fortunate as to find five nests [of the orange-wattled crow or kōkako], at heights varying from ten to seventeen feet above the ground. The first specimen we found placed on the extended limb of a totara (*Podocarpus*) that overhung a deep, ferny gully ... The parent bird on the nest allowing a very close approach, was found to be covering two nestlings as yet unable to see.[45]

The bird was the South Island kōkako, now probably extinct.[46]

In 1880 Potts then described what he had written seven years earlier as 'a matter of fact description of this interesting find', but one which:

> fails altogether to convey the least idea of one's sensations on sighting an object that had been so long, so far, and so often hunted for. At last there was the nest, together with the bird ... for years the search after the nest of the kokako had been carried on as opportunity offered ... After taking notes of the structure and its surroundings, one was obliged to disturb matters so far as to learn whether

> the nest contained eggs or young; as the parent bird slowly quitted her charge, two downy mites were disclosed that afforded matter for careful observation … Mr Enys, who was on board our vessel in the 'Basin' close by, was fetched to have a look at the kokako's nest *in situ*, and as Dr Hector wanted the young for the Colonial Museum, at the next visit to the lovely ferny dell, the home of the wattle-bird was rendered desolate, the young were carried away from their snug quarters and offered as victims on the altar of science. At the institution thus referred to, probably to this day, they may be observed by the curious, dangling in a jar of spirit.[47]

Potts had clearly felt torn in 1872; he saw the destructiveness of their action, yet could not unbind himself from the practices of his day.

In this passage we see again the imagery of a quest: for Potts the undertaking is a holy one, and he is acutely aware of the sanctity of the treasure. Instinct tells him to disturb the nest as little as possible: his observation is 'careful', his intervention minimal. The context in which he finds the nest is as significant for him as the nest itself. Enys appears as the willing intermediary between Potts the protector and Hector the plunderer. Finally Hector himself, as the symbolic bearer of science (given quasi-religious status by reference to its 'altar'), is ritually involved in the slaughter of nature. The nestling kōkako, subjects in their native habitat, are rapidly reduced to objects of science, dead but immortalised by their preservation.

The 'literary criticism' approach I have taken here includes interpretations that should be subject to debate. However, it is undeniable that in this passage Potts specifically contrasted his scientific and emotional responses to the find. In 1873 he had provided a scientific lens only, as was appropriate for publication in a serious journal. By 1880 he was writing for a more general audience and felt free to express his emotions.

The jar and its contents have since disappeared.[48]

*

After his own experience of Parliament, by 1870 Potts had limited faith in the power of legislation over individual greed, whether in relation to trees or birds. 'The Parliament of New Zealand has taken steps to protect some of our birds,' he noted, 'but however well legislative enactments may be framed, the people themselves can alone determine what shall be allowed to exist.'[49] Writing of kiwi and kākāpō, he expressed his hope that 'our paternal Government [might] interfere in behalf of these interesting aborigines, for we believe there are those who would shoot the Cherubim for specimens, without the slightest remorse'.[50] In 1872 he called for protection of the kōtuku (achieved in 1885) and its one New Zealand 'breeding station' at Ōkārito – in effect an early demand for a native bird sanctuary.[51] Kiwi, kākāpō and kōkako would finally receive protection in 1896.

In 1872 Parliament again considered extending the schedule of protected species. Potts wrote to Hector, urging him to 'stick out for the preservation of native birds'.[52] He also approached Walter Mantell who, as a member of the Legislative Assembly since 1866, had some influence:

> Besides the apterygidae [kiwi], the kakapo and other ancient indigenous forms, the extinction of which would be a lasting disgrace to us, many of our grallatorial birds [such as herons] should come under the preservation act … There are yet other birds which are more difficult to protect, for the unenquiring settler drives them to destruction and a howl of indignation would I suppose greet anyone rash enough to speak a word for their preservation – I mean our few raptorials [birds of prey] – they are so mercilessly slaughtered as to destroy the natural balance of race. Rats, mice, the larger insects increase and multiply accordingly.[53]

Potts understood that, contrary to popular belief, native owls, falcons and swamp harriers were useful as pest destroyers.

He may have become less sceptical of legislative protection upon learning of a Wild Birds Protection Bill before Britain's Parliament, which resulted in extensive legal protection for British wildlife in 1873 and 1876.[54] This was probably a factor behind his letter to *Nature* in 1872:

> We raise a cry for help in behalf of the mass of birds that yet remain *near* us (we had almost said *with* us), in the hope that the attention of naturalists in Europe may be called to the peril of extermination that hangs over many interesting indigenous species … For the preservation of our birds we require some assistance from abroad.[55]

With New Zealand's Protection of Animals Bill of 1872, debated a few months after Potts wrote these letters, we begin to see an old crock being recast to hold new wares. In one astonishing speech the member of the Legislative Council G.M. Waterhouse even suggested that whales might be protected by international law, but this idea gained no traction.[56] Alerted by Potts, Mantell made it known that 'on the west coast of Middle [South] Island a very useful, insectivorous bird, the kiwi, was being slaughtered in hundreds'.[57]

It lay with William Rolleston in 1873 to provide Parliament with the final incentive for native bird protection. He claimed to have seen

> bundles of tuis hanging up for sale in shops, and heard of people dining off kiwis, which seemed to him to be a gross abuse of the present privilege to kill birds; and he would like to see some clause introduced into the Bill which would have the effect of preventing the loss of birds characteristic of the country.[58]

Here was the stirring of a new idea, the sense of a new national identity for which native birds would become a symbol. This bore first fruit with the patriotic protection of huia – too late – in 1892.

After 1870 Potts could only affect parliamentary legislation indirectly, but he could still influence the policy of Canterbury Museum. According to Haast's son, 'it was while Wheeler was collecting kiwi and kakapo for Haast that the Museum Committee of the Board of Governors woke up to the fact, probably prompted by Potts … that, if the New Zealand birds were slaughtered in this wholesale way, they would soon exist only in Museums'.[59] In July 1878 when Haast requested authority to spend a further £50 on bird skins, the committee opposed him. They were 'very much averse to the destruction of the New Zealand fauna for the purpose of exchanges with other Museums, and would call his attention to the fact that there are objects such as fossils, which might be available for the purposes of exchange'.[60] Haast was forced to toe the line.

Musings in Maoriland, 1876–78

Before the late 1870s Potts experienced good fortune twice over. Not only did he inherit wealth, but the prime of his life coincided with a buoyant colonial economy in which he was able to spend freely. The early 1870s were boom years. New Zealand society remained optimistic at least until late in 1878, when the City of Glasgow Bank collapsed and much colonial investment with it. As a sheep farmer Potts would have noted a decline in wool prices from 1873, but this had been manageable in a way that a further fall of one third, between 1878 and 1886, was not.[1] These later years would be identified as part of the 'Long Depression' that dragged on through the 1880s.[2]

During the 1860s Potts established a routine. A trip to Hakatere Station in the early summer for discussions with his station manager and bird-watching would be followed by a family Christmas at Ohinetahi, with outings to Lake Ellesmere and elsewhere. There were frequent parties at Ohinetahi. Haast attended one such event in 1868 at which 'Potts of course took the chair and gave a couple of humorous readings.'[3] As the summer waned he would attend to writing and other business. This routine continued into the 1870s with the addition of lengthier expeditions to the west and north of the country. These were his golden years, when neither the state of the country nor the profitability of his runs took centre stage. Released from political duties, Potts devoted more time to what interested him most.

The first homestead at Hakatere Station was built beside Potts River in the heart of the station. Potts acquired further acreage on the true left bank of the Lawrence River (Runs 374 and 384) in 1867, and around 1870 the homestead was moved to a more accessible site in Ashburton Valley.[4] He gradually expanded his holding until it comprised seven runs covering 81,000 acres (32,779ha) – though one third of that was barren hilltops and shingle slides with little farming potential. He continued to run cattle during the 1870s while gradually switching to sheep; in 1873 he still only had 3000 of the latter.[5] Thomas Scott Johnstone took over from Cradock as station manager in the 1870s and remained in the role until after Potts' death; development of the station rested mainly with Johnstone until the 1920s.[6]

Thomas and Emma Potts and their family had a glorious Easter in 1876. Thomas's friend Edward Chudleigh, owner of the largest sheep station in the Chatham Islands, stayed at Ohinetahi for the week and took their daughter Mabel and two of her sisters to Christchurch to see Blondin, the century's greatest acrobat, performing his 'chair and bicycle feats'.[7] In April Thomas, Mabel and Walter sailed from Lyttelton to Wellington where they made social calls on various families with Canterbury links – the Moorhouses, the Olliviers, the Richardsons and the FitzGeralds. They also visited families with links to the Colonial Museum – the Mantells, the Kirks and the Gores. One day they walked to Lyall Bay to watch sandpipers and collect seashells; on another they walked up Karori Road to the gully for 'a short scramble after ferns'.

The group then sailed to Auckland where Potts spent a couple of days at the city's museum with director Thomas Cheeseman. They wandered in the Domain Gardens where Mabel, now 21 years old and trained to employ a naturalist's eye, noted a prickly pear in fruit and an impressively tall magnolia. At Riverhead they sampled pineapples and bananas and watched Fijian sailors at work, before sailing on to Tauranga and travelling south toward Ōhinemutu on the shores of Lake Rotorua. Along the way they noted 'blue gilled crows', the North Island kōkako. Near Oropi they rambled in the forest, 'busy with our fern boards and bibulous papers to cull off the choicest specimens for pressing'. At Lake Rotomahana they paddled across to the Pink and White Terraces, a popular tourist destination until destroyed in the eruption of Mt Tarawera in 1886, for 'a leisurely stroll of admiration'. The White Terraces disappointed Potts; he was more 'excited and much gratified by noticing quite an abundant growth of that fern so rare and local in this country, *Nephrodium unitum*'. The adventure was still fresh in Potts' memory when he wrote a series of articles a decade later entitled 'To the Hot Lakes'.[8]

While in Auckland Potts left his card at the house of Sir George Grey, who at this time was superintendent of Auckland province and a member of the House of Representatives. Potts looked up to Grey, who was older than him both in age (by 13 years) and colonial involvement. In fact, Governors Bay was so named because Grey, who was governor at the time, had anchored there in 1850 to await the arrival of the first Canterbury settlers.[9] Grey caught up with them just before they sailed for Tauranga and was 'very anxious' that they visit Kawau, his island home.[10] Potts reached there later in his travels and gathered a further trove of native ferns.[11] Kawau has since been called 'an ecological disaster', its native flora and fauna all but destroyed by the wallabies, possums – even zebras – that Grey introduced.[12]

In May 1878 Potts and Grey, the latter now premier, sailed from Wellington up the east coast of the North Island. Potts' hastily scribbled notes of their conversation on board have survived.[13] Much of it concerned bird-watching and gardening, subjects that interested them both. Off the coast near Gisborne Grey 'recommended wood ashes to be applied to the sickly looking lemon tree', and he spoke of 'skylarks singing over the sea some distance from the shore' and 'the abundance of birds on Banks Peninsula in old times'. Potts was disturbed to learn that his friend 'kills the native owl which is quite against my practice'; two days later he noted that Grey was 'in favour of forest reserves'.[14]

Grey invited Potts to join his imminent trip to the King Country, soon to be described as 'the heart of Maoriland'.[15] Potts leapt at this 'rare opportunity of studying from life the social aspect of a large section of the native race, which had for many years, with persistent firmness, withdrawn from intercourse with Europeans'. Grey and his large retinue camped beside the home of Tūkāroto Matutaera Pōtatau Te Wherowhero Tāwhiao, the second Māori king (Ngāti Mahuta). Potts later wrote that his time at 'the mountain home of Tawhaio [sic]' proved to be 'one of the pleasantest episodes of my colonial experience'. The event did much to confirm his respectful attitude to Māori.[16] As Michael King once noted, few early Pākehā observers of Māori displayed such a keen anthropological eye as Potts, who now described in minute detail the village, activities and feasts that took place. For instance:

> Amongst the edibles was a preparation of the roots of the pohua (*Convolvulus sepium*), the favourite food of the pheasant in this district, it is as flowery as a potato with a slightly bitter taste; boiled sow-thistle often appeared in the same basket ... Mamaku – this esculent appeared in junks [sic] of about a foot in length; it is the mucilaginous pith of the black tree-fern (*Cyathea medullaris*). It was presented ready dressed, was soft, with a very sweet flavour.[17]

Potts provided no account of the politicking during a great kōrero that took place on 9 May 1878, simply describing it as 'a meeting from which an unprejudiced observer might learn much as to the social habits of the retired natives'. He did however note:

> these people, so great a proportion of whom *lived entirely without the pale of Christian teaching* [Potts' italics], received their visitors with unbounded hospitality; [and] treated them with a courtesy which showed that the Maori was 'to the manner born', for nowhere could he have learnt it from experience in his intercourse with Europeans.[18]

King Country, as described by Potts in 1878, sounds rather like a national park in which Māori were the endangered and protected species. In the same way that he had come to realise that native flora and fauna had intrinsic worth, distinct from European species but of equal value, Potts now began to learn of the strength and validity of tikanga Māori. He considered the Kingites, left to self-organisation and self-discipline, more commendable than the majority of Europeans they encountered. Though himself a devout Anglican, Potts noted their 'Christian' conduct was independent of Christianity.

The Kingites were markedly different to the Māori he had observed at Ōhinemutu two years earlier, where government officials did little to discourage the sale of rum to Māori. Potts observed, sarcastically:

> The vaunted robes of civilization with which it was pretended the native race had been covered looked very much soiled, befouled and tattered when flung over these wretched inebriates ... But this state of things was under Christian rule and therefore should be held as satisfactory, for, had it not uprooted the wickedness of heathenism, with its wild entanglements of old legends and traditions of a war-loving race?[19]

While in the King Country Potts reflected on the standing of Māori in his own community. 'As one talked and listened,' he wrote,

> visions of Kaiapoi and Raupaki [between Governors Bay and Lyttelton] rose up again and again; then came awkward questions – What had been done to elevate the social status of their people? Had Maoris, either in Christchurch or Lyttelton, a resting-place they could call their own – their home? These disturbing reflections soon received their quietus, as one reflected, Canterbury had indeed exhibited her sympathy for the aborigines, for had she not erected a Maori house – a structure the like of which is not to be found in New Zealand?[20]

It is unclear whether Potts is resorting to irony here, or whether he genuinely considered the erection of the 'Maori House' at Canterbury Museum (the wharenui Hau-te-ana-nui-a-Tangaroa, which was tapu to a northern rather than a southern tribe) a significant gesture of respect to Canterbury iwi.[21]

The acquisition of the wharenui in 1874 had excited debate. In a letter to Canterbury's superintendent, Potts contrasted the resolution passed by the museum trustees – 'that it be built so as to have as far as possible the character of the original house' – with the consequent non-compliance. He expressed his view, that:

> if any alteration takes place in the erection of the Maori House, other than what is *simple restoration*, such a departure from the original building will only be accomplished at the costly price of losing a valuable and most interesting ethnological study, illustrating the old manners and customs of so many of our fellow subjects.[22]

Potts' comments are similar to William Morris's response, around the same time, to the intrusive restoration of English churches by Victorian architects.[23]

Potts also wrote in 1876 to Minister of Native Affairs Donald McLean about the large waka (canoe) he had seen lying 'high and dry, exposed to all the changes of weather' on the shores of Lake Rotoiti. He considered it 'lamentable that such a fine specimen of Native workmanship, so interesting to ethnologists, should be allowed to perish from neglect'.[24] In the same year he raised the idea of making a photographic record of individuals from every Māori tribe, a project he probably still had in mind in 1879 when he published a photograph of a Moriori man, Te Karaka Nga Munanga Pawa (Timoti Tara).[25] Such a project would now be considered culturally insensitive, but Potts is unlikely to have felt this.[26] Many Māori regarded the camera with suspicion, some calling it 'taipō', an unwanted supernatural visitor not of human origin.

In a significant late essay Potts reflected on a group of Māori that he saw on the steps of Lyttelton Post Office:

> [Since] we enquire into the doings of rabbits or sparrows, and record the feats of dogs and horses … may we be permitted to devote a few lines to the state of living of the former owners of all these fertile lands … changes in the manners of Natives are as evident as that the stately black pines [indigenous mataī] have given place to the Australian bluegum trees which dot the slopes that lead down to the [Raupaki] pah.[27]

His ensuing account of changes to the Māori diet, forced upon them by European colonisation, was not unlike his observations on new food sources sought by kea. But while he compared the fate of Māori to that of native birds and forests, Potts was perhaps less capable of objectivising the position of his own race: he never compared European settlers to introduced animals or exotic pine trees.

Near the end of his life Potts was strongly affected by the comfortless death of his Māori neighbour at Raupaki. 'Old T' was a chiefly man whom Potts respected greatly, whose belief that he was haunted by a 'dread maleficent spirit' (taipō) proved stronger than the 'glad tidings of the Gospel' to which he had been exposed.[28] Potts' estimation of Māori resembles that of the missionary James West Stack who, after decades ministering to Canterbury Māori, declared them 'a truly civilized people … more to be trusted to act honestly and rightly than the majority of his own countrymen'.[29] It is in stark contrast to the opinion of Potts' friend Mark Stoddart, who considered that 'greed and selfishness are at the bottom of their character in a much greater degree than is generally found among wild tribes'.[30]

In God's Own Country, around 1880

Potts took his Christian duties seriously and was deeply versed in theology. His religious views supported both his utilitarian and his conservationist attitudes towards nature. His Christianity was not narrow, however: it left him free to question the evangelisation of Māori and to support the Sunday opening of museums, and did not preclude his espousal of evolutionary theory.

The belief that God gave humankind dominion over the earth and its creatures sustained many European settlers in their efforts to 'improve' New Zealand and other colonies by changing the natural environment. In other words, 'dominion theology' sustained 'ecological imperialism'.[1] But Christianity also embraced the idea of stewardship, of treading carefully on the earth. Around the end of the eighteenth century a number of works were published about 'natural theology' – the deduction of God's existence through the observation of nature.[2] Key works in this vein on Potts' bookshelves included Gilbert White's *The Natural History of Selborne* (1789), Paley's *Natural Theology; or, Evidence of the Existence of the Attributes of the Deity Collected from the Appearances of Nature* (1802) and Burke's writings *On the Sublime* (1757).[3] Their approach specifically encouraged men and women to treat nature with reverence since it was the handiwork of God.

The relevance of natural theology to conservation lay in its emphasis on interconnection. All of nature was seen as part of God's purpose, even when its use was not immediately apparent. While awareness of this 'web of life' could prompt support for nature – and there is a sense of this in Potts' later articles – such an approach to religion and nature could also discourage political or social radicalism. If God had created everything, the role of the scientist was to better understand the natural hierarchy rather than to change it. Nature, ordered under the Linnean system and then ranked according to evolutionary theory, functioned in the same way as European society: it confirmed as natural the idea that Potts and his fellow gentlemen should be where they were – at the top.

Pioneering countries in the late nineteenth century had fluid, rapidly shifting economies out of kilter with the planned long-term management necessary for conservation of resources. Leisure and surplus wealth were the privilege of the genteel in colonial society: only those with personal security were free to conserve or to initiate projects that only produced financial benefits in the long term, such as extensive tree-planting. This may explain why conservation began as a politically conservative movement but grew into a popular movement once more people had access to leisure.

*

Nearly all of Potts' friends, including the scientific-minded, were practising Christians. Historian John Stenhouse has remarked on the relative rarity, among Victorian New Zealand's 'men of science', of the anticlericalism so evident in T.H. Huxley, Joseph Hooker and other supporters of Darwin in England.[4] Haast's successor at the Canterbury Museum, Frederick Wollaston Hutton, was an 'ardent evolutionist' and a 'devout Anglican' who argued that 'Scripture and nature must ultimately agree because God was the author of both.'[5] Potts' position sounds similar.

As much as dominion theology, a narrow interpretation of Darwinian evolutionary theory could have served to thwart conservation efforts in Victorian times. Scientists who believed in the survival of the fittest were more inclined to observe and explain extinctions than to seek their prevention. Before any action to counter the decline of a species could be meaningfully pursued, it was necessary to acknowledge that sometimes humans and not the laws of nature are the cause.

If Potts was not so fully a Darwinist as many more professional scientists, he was freer to consider actions that a more professional scientist might think denied 'natural selection'.[6] Potts would have been aware of Charles Darwin long before *On the Origin of Species* was published in 1859 – after all, from 1842 Darwin lived at Down House, just five kilometres from where Potts resided until 1853 – but Potts' particular version of evolutionism may have lain closer to Lamarckism (named after French biologist Jean-Baptiste Lamarck), which maintained that adaptive genetic change could be induced by environmental factors.

Potts' forays into evolutionary biology are fragmentary but suggestive. He wrote in *Nature* in 1872 on 'the retention and colouring of eggs, and the protective mimicry of sounds'. In this article he explored to what extent birds responded to their environment rather than the dictates of their evolutionary programming, and began by asking, 'Is it known for how long a bird possesses the power of retaining its egg?'[7]

He observed that the silvereye in New Zealand often did not build a hanging nest, while its Australian counterpart always did so. That the silvereye still sometimes adopted 'the instinctive precaution of a foreign land' suggested to him that this recent 'colonist' from Australia was 'not yet so thoroughly acclimatised as to be fully aware of the immunity it enjoys from the ravages of snakes'. Over the years he recorded a declining proportion of hanging nests, confirming his idea that there might be 'a change in the style of architecture as this bird, season after season, experiences the comparative safety of the breeding-places in our own cooler latitudes'.[8]

Interbreeding between black and pied fantails, forming a 'union nest', also fascinated Potts. He observed in 1885: 'for the last three or four years the two recognised species have become inextricably mixed. Who shall say which is really a pure *R.* [*Rhipidura*] *flabellifera*, or which is a legitimate *fuliginosa*?' He took a nest and eggs and sent it to the Royal Zoological Society in London 'for the purpose of bringing the fact of hybridisation more prominently before ornithologists'. If the breeding habits of supposedly distinct species and the boundaries between them were so susceptible to environmental change in the short term, any 'law' of evolution became debatable. As a consequence, anything inferred from the laws of evolution could be more readily questioned.[9]

One such inference was the 'displacement theory' adhered to by many biologists, from Darwin onwards, who contemplated the changing environment of the colonies. The theory stated simply that European humans, animals and plants were superior to their indigenous counterparts in colonising and competitive ability; therefore the indigenous would inevitably decline and often die out altogether.

Leonard Cockayne challenged this theory decisively when considering New Zealand plants early in the twentieth century, arguing that this 'doctrine of biological faith' in the superiority of introduced species was wrong. Introduced plants did not compete with and displace indigenous ones in 'primitive' plant communities: they would only do so if humans first prepared the way for them. Cockayne drew attention to the aggressive nature of some indigenous plants, and suggested that if modifying activities such as burning and grazing were removed, the native species could well resist the advance of the 'adventive'.[10]

It followed that human-induced environmental change lay behind the declining populations of many native species. This realisation was an essential prerequisite to the idea that positive human actions – creating reserves and parks, protecting species or banning grass fires – could dramatically alter the situation. Cockayne made this clear but, as we shall see, it had been implicit earlier in Potts' ideas for national domains.

*

A fuller understanding of the role of human activity had already led Potts to distance himself from the acclimatisation movement in the 1870s. His 1872 paper 'On Recent Changes in the Fauna of New Zealand' still supported the introduction of pheasants, but juxtaposed remarks on 'the introduction of foreign birds' without 'some general plan' alongside observations on 'the increasing destruction of many native species'.[11] In March 1873 the acclimatisation society told Potts he had been 'allotted a number of [exotic] insectivorous birds to be turned out in your grounds'.[12] Presumably he accepted these, since the society's secretary wrote to Potts again in August asking him to take 12 Australian magpies.[13] He may have reasoned that if he did not accept the birds someone else would, and would perhaps take less note of their progress.

By the mid-seventies acclimatisation societies were being widely criticised for having brought in rabbits, house sparrows and greenfinches, whose worth as food or consumers of insect pests was less than the nuisance they caused by eating grass and cereals. It had proved impossible to control not only the acclimatisation societies but also the acclimatising species. When Potts republished his 1872 paper in 1882 he added a note affirming that 'efforts in the direction of acclimatisation ... will require the most vigorous treatment, in order to check some of the evils arising from the too rapid increase in the numbers of several introduced species'.[14] It is hard to guess what he felt when the acclimatisation society elected him as a 'supernumerary member' of their council in 1883.[15]

By this time the blackbird was the bane of every fruitgrower in Canterbury. Potts wrote: 'The charm has so faded in the progress of events that one has to think over the condition of matters then [in the 1860s] which could have made the melody of this songster appear so enchanting.' Writing about this most successful of avian colonists in 1882 he weighed up the case for its acclimatisation, balancing its 'attacks on several kinds of crops' with a concomitant decrease in 'the ravages of the caterpillar'.[16] In 1887 he adjudged the house sparrow a liability but the rook an asset; the Australian magpie, though admittedly invasive, was efficient at eating insect pests. He also remarked on 'the very considerable amount of trouble and expense which attended their introduction'. As so often, it was waste that upset Potts most.[17]

*

Potts remained on Canterbury Provincial Council until 1876. This meant he could attempt direct action in support of native conservation, as in 1874 when he tried too late to thwart illegal timber-cutting on railway reserves near Little River.[18] But most of the influence he exerted in the later 1870s and the 1880s stemmed from his position as a respected landowner who continued to correspond with leading politicians and government servants. Increasingly, however, he exerted the most influence through his journalism.

In parliamentary speeches in 1874 and beyond, Vogel and others lauded Potts' initiative of 1868 in directing the government's attention to forests – but only in brief opening remarks. Forest historians likewise have passed on quickly to Vogel's Forests Act of 1874 and the recommendations made by Captain Inches Campbell-Walker as New Zealand's first conservator of forests (1875–77).[19] Potts knew Vogel, but they did not belong to the same set; nor is there any indication that Campbell-Walker ever met Potts, though the former expressed regret at not seeing him during his inspection of Canterbury's forests.

Large-scale national state afforestation did not begin until the 1890s when fears of an approaching 'timber famine' had gathered pace.[20] At the local level, however, central government had already approved a Canterbury Plantation Board in 1879, which supervised existing public reserves and extended the plantations on these. The board's afforestation was limited in extent and was initally geared more to shelter-belt creation than timber production. Its significance lies mostly in its precedence. As one of seven board members, Potts attended many of the 19 board meetings held before his death, and fully supported the concept of public plantings.

Climatic reserves – which protected indigenous vegetation in order to stabilise the climate – were included within the terms of the 1877 Land Act. The value of forest conservation to limit damage from both heavy rain and drought was stressed only by a few, however, and remained an arcane line of reasoning to many.

A new set of ideas now surfaced – of scenic beauty, health and tourism and, from America, of 'national parks'. In 1858 American philosopher Henry David Thoreau referred to the European tradition of hunting preserves for nobility, and pondered, 'Why should not we have our national preserves in which the bear and panther, and some even of the hunter race [American Indians], may still exist?'[21] Soon after, George Perkins Marsh suggested that 'some large and easily accessible region of America should remain, as far as possible, in its primitive condition, at once a museum for the instruction of the student, a garden for the recreation of the lover of nature, and an asylum where indigenous [plants and animals] … may dwell and perpetuate their kind'.[22]

Ten square miles (2.5km^2) in the Yosemite Valley were reserved in 1864, but the first true national park was Yellowstone, established in 1872 on two million acres (800,000ha) of northwest Wyoming. Since Wyoming was not yet a state, the land was placed under the custody of the Department of the Interior as a national rather than a state park.[23] In 1874 – two years before Potts' visit to the area – New Zealand Premier William Fox suggested the thermal districts around Rotorua could be likewise reserved and sanitary and hydropathic institutions established.[24]

In 1878, boosted by Grey's support for the concept of forest reserves and refreshed by his visit to the King Country, Potts married the new ideas on health resorts and national parks to his earlier ideas about forests, penning a striking new article on (as he called them) 'national domains'. This appeared in July 1878 in the *New Zealand Country Journal.*

There was a fluidity in terminology at the time as the English language was adapted to describe new situations in colonial contexts, something Potts himself commented on a decade later in his paper 'On Recreation Grounds'.[25] The English word 'domain' derives from an Old French phrase meaning 'belonging to a lord'. In New Zealand in the 1860s it acquired the unique meaning of 'land reserved by the Crown to be used as a park or other public purpose'.[26] Potts was a foundation member of the Christchurch Domain Board in 1872.[27] Following an Act of 1877 he personally took charge of an area, above and between Corsair and Magazine bays, to be 'fenced and planted for the purposes of a public garden and domain for the Borough of Lyttelton'.[28] One local protested in the *Christchurch Star* after being denied entry to the area by the custodian, who had instructions from Potts to 'refuse permission to grown persons because children might follow' – and children might damage the young trees. 'Reluctantly we turned our backs on this second Eden,' the writer complained, and sarcastically suggested a notice be erected: 'Sacred to the memory of Mr Potts'.[29] The reserve is now dominated by 'old pines in a great state of neglect.'[30] Given his involvement in the Lyttelton Domain one can see why, in 1878, when considering reserves with a national rather than local purpose, Potts proposed they be called 'national domains'.

Potts differentiated between three kinds of preservation in 1878 – of health, trees and birds – for which he proposed three types of national domain. The first he called 'sanitaria', reserves for human health. He noted that 'a large-hearted philanthropist … [had already] devised a notable and important scheme, having for its object the institution of a great *sanitarium* in the celebrated hot-lake district'.[31] (This likely referred to Grey's 1848 proposal, never pursued, for a sanatorium at Tikitere near Rotorua.[32]) Potts used the sanitarium concept as a hook to draw readers – Grey among them – to his ideas on other 'national domains, parks, or reserves' that could be created: for forests and fauna. All three types of reserve would require state intervention in the form of lasting protection, and all three were a celebration of national assets.[33]

As in the past he argued for conserving native forests, his second category, on the grounds of their utility, but he did so now with greater subtlety: 'Do not let us become restless, and sweep away native timber whose qualities have been proved, either because their cultivation has been attended with difficulties, or the ready way of rearing them is yet imperfectly understood.' These forest domains 'would to a great extent become the nurseries and storehouses (so to speak) of the indigenous flora of New Zealand'.[34] In effect this would give native forests, 'which form so valuable a portion of the estate of the country', a role in the development of nationhood. Recognition of the worth of native forests to science was rolled in with their worth to the nation: they should be preserved as 'indigenous objects which illustrate the province of natural history'.

Similarly, the country should not 'suffer the indigenous *fauna* to be exterminated without such further efforts for its preservation', given that 'biologists have made New Zealand a special province on account of its very peculiar forms of life'.[35] For this reason there should also be domains 'where animals should not be molested under any pretence whatever'. He had visited Kawau Island, which Grey had already turned into a kind of fauna reserve – albeit for acclimatised species. Now, as in 1872, he mentioned Resolution Island as an appropriate sanctuary or 'camp of refuge', and added 'small islets off the N.E. coast of the North Island'. In the wake of his relinquishment of Quail Island to the government in 1875 for use as a quarantine station, he now compared island reserves with 'quarantine grounds'.

The identification of New Zealand as 'God's Own Country' is associated with Richard Seddon who, as its premier in the 1890s, used the phrase so often that Tom Brooking in 2014 entitled his biography of Seddon *King of God's Own*.[36] As a description of New Zealand, however, the phrase was popularised by Tom Bracken, whose poem 'God's Own Country' appeared in 1890.[37] Bracken's first verse described New Zealand, 'framed by Nature in her grandest, noblest mould … where the forests are the greenest' and the mountains are 'landmarks of a nation free'. By implying that indigenous species and landscapes were the essence of what made New Zealand special, Potts' recommendation of national domains would help to pave the way for an overt assertion of New Zealand's identity and nationhood by Bracken, Seddon and others.

Later Writings, Last Years, 1880–88

And so to Potts' final years, when his fortune diminished but his writing flowed. Preferring to be out in the open rather than up in arms, he continued recording environmental changes and reflecting upon them. While New Zealand's population was growing larger, younger and more complex, Potts was growing older, poorer and perhaps more tired. In 1880 he was 56, and in some respects his life was already winding down. His remaining public capacities were all in local affairs. Some, such as his participation in the governance of Canterbury Museum and Canterbury College, involved catching the train to Christchurch for committee meetings; others, such as his appearances as a JP in Lyttelton and his contribution to church bazaars in Governors Bay, were even more circumscribed in their impact. Perhaps he enjoyed such parochialism.

By the 1880s Governors Bay had become a tourist destination for the people of Christchurch, with the usual blend of positive and negative consequences. On Easter Monday 1886 the *Press* reported, 'just before the departure of the last steamer load of excursionists, some evil-disposed person (or otherwise booby) set fire to what may be fairly accounted the garden of the bay – a piece of bush, the property of Mr. T.H. Potts who has done much to preserve the natural beauty of the spot, which is really the finest specimen of old New Zealand within easy distance from Christchurch'.[1]

Thomas and Emma's youngest child Randall was nine in 1880, so even though their older children had long since become independent, parental responsibilities remained a daily fact of life. Many runholders went under in New Zealand's 'long depression', and Potts' financial situation had deteriorated dramatically. Ownership of Hakatere Station would pass to the New Zealand Loan and Mercantile Agency Company in 1883.

His retreat from wider affairs meant he had more time to write, however, which may have provided a small income. In these final years we see some of his finest natural history pieces – articles that were mostly directed at a broad Canterbury audience rather than the more select national readership of the *Transactions of the New Zealand Institute*. They display a deeper relaxation into his inimitable style and include frequent draughts of nostalgia. There is often a sadness in his later essays, where he wrote wistfully of 'old times'.[2] He regretted that 'the young folks now growing up will be quite unable to realise the grandeur, the loveliness of the forest glades, which we barbarians so ruthlessly destroy'. The cost of such a 'rough style' of bush clearance 'can scarcely be ascertained, for it is not of to-day only, but the account lies in the future also'.[3] Native bird numbers continued to decline in the Port Hills behind Governors Bay. Of the 31 species recorded there in the 1850s, by 1900 ten species would have disappeared altogether and another six had become rare.[4]

The *New Zealand Country Journal* began publication in Christchurch in 1877 to 'supply persons engaged in Agricultural and Pastoral pursuits in this Colony with information upon rural life generally', and by 1885 had about 450 active subscribers and a large readership through library collections.[5] Although half or more of its followers were in Canterbury, the periodical obtained a wider audience by including contributions from throughout New Zealand.[6]

The *Country Journal* became Potts' outlet of choice. His first contribution was a long series of articles entitled 'Fern Leaves', a descriptive account of his observations of New Zealand ferns that he later presented more methodically as a 'Classified List of New Zealand Ferns' (1881–82).[7] These are his most important botanical essays. When publishing his own early work on ferns in 1882, G.M. Thomson named Potts, William Colenso, Thomas Kirk and Thomas Cheeseman as 'botanists who have done much to bring about the present well-advanced state of scientific knowledge in this young country'.[8] J.F. Armstrong of Christchurch Botanic Gardens thought sufficiently highly of Potts as a botanist (and perhaps as a patron) to name the daisy-like *Senecio pottsii* after him.[9] In the 1950s, the early contributions to the gardens of both these men were recognised with the naming of 'Potts Lawn' and 'Armstrong Lawn'.[10]

In England botanists were the first to recognise the damage done by overzealous collectors and the first to press for conservation. They were shocked by the consequences of 'pteridomania', the 'fern craze' of the 1850s and 1860s, when commercial collectors stripped whole districts of ferns to grace fashionable drawing rooms.[11] As a Fellow of the Linnean Society (the London-based botanists' association) since 1872, Potts would have understood the problem all too well. In an important late essay on the indigenous flora of the Port Hills, he recorded the destruction of its shrubs and ferns. To the 'fern grabber', he wrote, the filmy todea in particular had been 'so great an attraction as to be irresistible': it was 'torn up in a most merciless manner'.[12] Although the protection of native birds had received some attention by the 1880s, in 1885 Potts still wondered, 'When shall we ever take up the question of the preservation of native plants?'[13]

Recent scholarship sees nature as a concept in transition, the perception of its objects (both flora and fauna) dependent upon who is regarding them and when.[14] In the nineteenth century New Zealand's birds, viewed in Britain as 'curiosities and commodities', in their homeland became 'cross-cultural landmarks entangled in notions of locality, identity and industry', according to Molly Duggins.[15] While the kiwi in England was a novelty at London Zoo, in New Zealand it became a national icon; Potts' emphasis on its uniqueness and endemism contributed towards the developing vision of a new and distinct land. At the same time, thanks to 'fern fever', many of New Zealand's newly identified and more 'mobile' plant species were transported around the British Empire. Here also Potts played a role through his published catalogues of ferns. Duggins has argued that the popularity of the country's ferns meant 'the New Zealand landscape was transformed into a worldwide phenomenon in the latter half of the nineteenth century'.[16] Within New Zealand, the endemic silver tree fern became an icon second only to the kiwi in importance. Paradoxically, as the components of New Zealand's flora and fauna became known, classified and celebrated, they also lost something of their uniqueness by receiving Latin name tags and a place within the overall Linnean system of nomenclature. Their physical relocation to zoos, gardens and museums had a similar levelling effect.

Around 1880, at a time when he could ill afford it, Potts acquired one of the individually hand-produced albums of *Darjeeling's Ferns*: a collections of specimens dried and distributed by Phoebe Jaffrey, wife of the curator of the Lloyd Botanic Garden in northern India.[17] This volume was contemporaneous with the commercial production of albums of New Zealand ferns. Its presence in Potts' library reminds us that the transfer of plant and other matter occurred not only between Britain and her colonies: it could also be an intercolonial activity in which New Zealand was as much a gatherer of curiosities as a supplier of them.

In the introduction to his second series of fern articles, Potts consciously addressed the ordinary citizen. He had described the ferns in 'plain and simple words', he said, because 'the everyday toil and employments of colonial life have not permitted many the necessary time and leisure for the attainment of scientific accomplishments'. Potts chose simple language and metaphors to explain technical terms, charmingly noting that cryptogamic plants are so called because they have 'secret marriages'. By aligning himself with the everyday reader he was in effect stating that the New Zealand environment existed for everyone's enjoyment.[18]

Following his fern essays, Potts wrote a series of articles called 'Out in the Open', which appeared in the *Country Journal* from 1878 until his death in 1888. Many were about birds, and the first, on the white heron, set the tone. Referring to 'the insatiable greediness of a collector', Potts condemned indiscriminate shooting of kōtuku by the 'sporting new chum' and the 'ardent naturalist' alike, and made a plea for legal protection of the white heron, at that time 'classed with vermin'. His second article, modestly entitled 'Something About Hawks', condemned the way New Zealand falcons and swamp harriers were vilified for taking lambs and poultry when instead they should be valued for killing rats and mice. In 'Farmer's Friends' he updated his observations on native owls, portraying them as birds that also did more good than harm.[19] And in 'The White-eye, or Blight Bird' he championed the silvereye as a valuable insect-eater that should be allowed a 'portion of fruit' as an appropriate reward.[20]

On the advice of Sir George Grey Potts published these and other articles in book form in 1882 as *Out in the Open*, which he dedicated to Grey.[21] It became a 'New Zealand nature classic', and confirmed Potts' reputation as the 'New Zealand Gilbert White'.[22]

*

He had a different attitude to the kea, the subject of an article in the *Country Journal* in 1880. Potts had became familiar with kea during the late 1850s in the high country 'far above the Gorge of the Rangitata' where he had his station. His initial notes on the 'Green Mountain Parrot', published in 1871, acknowledged its 'indulgence in mischief' but considered this evidence of its intelligence and adaptive ability:

> … the European has been the means of corrupting the simplicity of its ancient habits; the meat-gallows of the back-country squatters attracted the attention of our mountain-parrots in the winter season. To them they became points of interest in their wanderings, and furnished many a hearty meal torn from the dangling carcass as it swung in the frosty air … [and] our *educated* bird now tears his food from the back of the living sheep.[23]

Similarly, in a contribution to *Nature* in 1872, Potts described the kea as 'interesting in the face of the destructive influence commonly exerted by *introduced* upon *native* life. Here we have an indigenous species making use of a recently imported aid for subsistence [sheep] at the cost of a vast change in its natural habits.'[24]

By 1880, however, Potts had grown hostile to the kea. While the bird was still primarily a herbivorous species, its new habit of attacking sheep by then extended over a wide area of Otago and Canterbury high country. Potts had reached the point where his financial future as a station owner assumed greater importance than the future of an endemic species that appeared to be undermining it. He now wrote of 'the mischievous influence of this savage bird on an important industry' – the production of wool. He suggested acclimatisation should concentrate on destroying kea rather than misguidedly killing native falcons.[25]

Through correspondence with shepherds and station owners Potts gathered anecdotal evidence of the kea's 'destructive habits'.[26] By the 1880s the problem was judged sufficiently severe that some station owners employed men specifically to hunt the birds. And whereas the painting of a kea in the first edition of Buller's *Birds* (1873) depicted vegetation as a backdrop, in the 1888 edition Buller had J.G. Keulemans illustrate it with a second bird attacking a sheep in the background.[27] In a final article on the kea published in 1883, Potts remarked that these 'merciless' birds had 'learnt to follow their victims to a lower level' – onto land farmed well below their original mountain habitat – and called for public expenditure to remove 'an enemy whose attacks entail such heavy losses to the mountain sheep-farmer'.[28] He wrote this at the very time a mortgagee was taking over his high-country sheep station. In 1886 his son Donald, now a station manager, lobbied Ashburton County Council for financial assistance in destroying this 'serious pest in the back country'.[29]

Potts' article 'Lost Game' (1886) was on the New Zealand quail, and provides a counterpoint to his unsympathetic observations on kea. He describes wistfully how, 30 years earlier, he had 'enjoyed the pleasure of putting up bevies of quail, which at the time seemed so plentiful'.[30] To his regret the bird was extinct by the 1880s, and it only remained for him to record what he had learnt of the habits of a 'most valued' species. This article has a similar value to his extensive notes on laughing owls (whēkau) published in 1871, which recalled a night spent in the Ashburton Valley in 1857 when he was 'constantly disturbed … by their doleful yells amongst the rocky mountain gullies'.[31] The last known laughing owl was found dead in 1914.

*

Some of the many articles that Potts wrote in the 1880s are included in the third part of this book. In several he reiterates proposals for forest conservation that he first voiced in the 1870s, and these have a touch of melancholy, perhaps reflecting his loss of faith in the realisation of this project. One stresses the inadequacy of research into the exotic trees that were supposed to replace natives; the Scotch fir, a valuable timber tree in Europe which had failed to thrive in New Zealand, illustrated this well. He urges readers to 'avoid trusting altogether to exotics in planting, to give some attention at least to the reproduction of the valuable native species before they are entirely destroyed and lost to the world'.[32]

The concept of native forest reserves had enjoyed some popularity in the 1870s and was an intrinsic part of the forestry legislation of 1874. By the end of the decade, however, in tandem with the approach of economic depression, native forest protection was rebuffed; all funding for the proposed Forests Department was withdrawn in 1876.[33] Potts was now writing against a background not only of national and personal financial decline, but also of governmental retreat from issues that were dear to him.

The last of Potts' natural history essays in his 'Out in the Open' series described flora more than fauna but often dealt with both, implying the links between them. In one of these, published in the *Country Journal* of March 1886, he began by discussing garden flowers in spring time:

> Amongst native plants the climbing shrubs claim our attention not only from the early flowering of some species, but also because they furnish with their succession of blossoms what may be termed a floral chain, that entwines spring throughout its changeful length and links it on to summer. Almost curious as an instance of neglect, is the inattention these interesting shrubs have met with from cultivators; this will likely be amended soon, as the plants are becoming scarce, a charm which to most things gives more value than either usefulness or beauty.[34]

Potts made his way through a floral chain, describing in turn the native clematis, parsonsia (kaihua), muehlenbeckia, convolvulus and bush-lawyer. Remarkably, he then turned to consideration of the strawberry, pondering the origin of the word and deciding it referred 'not to the manner in which it was planted but to the straggling habit of the runners or offsets'. He referred to the 'strawberry preacher', defined as 'a temporary help who wanders from pulpit to pulpit'.

Potts was himself something of a rambling strawberry preacher, whose lines of thought were like the runners of a strawberry plant.[35] There is every indication that he consciously threw off the shackles of academic conformity. 'As it is not intended to present a purely scientific treatise,' he wrote in 1880, 'the writer may be permitted perhaps to become rather discursive now and then.'[36] In 1883 he remarked that, when 'rambling through woods, crossing mountain streams and fern-clad gullies, eager for attainment of further insight into nature's ways, devious is our course!', and asked, 'May one be allowed some such liberty and freedom in writing of our birds?'[37] In another essay composed while 'rambling through a large garden', he flitted from the consideration of Christchurch poppies in 1885, to Rockwood rātā in 1855, to an earlier memory of pear trees in the English Channel Islands. The end of the essay saw him back in 1885, remarking on how environmental change (the sowing of cocksfoot) on Banks Peninsula had led to social change (the arrival of 'swaggers' to harvest it).[38]

This discursiveness is perhaps tacitly acknowledged by the absence of any reference to a particular animal or plant in the titles of almost all Potts' later articles. The titles identified him as 'a countryman in town' (1887), as one who 'rambles in the Chathams' (1888), or as an observer of 'the pulse of spring' (1885). He concentrated more on a variety of species, and on changes in habitat, climate and season.[39]

Potts' understanding of the relationships between species, while notable, does not appear to have advanced greatly in his later years. In 1871, for instance, he explored the link between the kākā, insects and forest regrowth: 'in its persevering and laborious pursuit of this favourite food, the kaka doubtless lends his assistance in hastening the fall of decaying trees'; this would 'materially affect the economy of the timber forests it inhabits.'[40] (Here he meant 'nature's economy', now referred to as ecology.[41]) In 1880 when he again put pen to paper on the subject of kākā, he simply reiterated what he had said in 1871.[42]

Nor did Potts amplify his thoughts on the dwindling population of the South Island kōkako or 'orange-wattled crow'. By the time he found a kōkako nest in Milford Sound in 1873 the species was already in rapid decline. Potts identified links not only between failing numbers and a modified habitat, but also between habitat modification and local changes in climate. In 1880 he recorded what had happened to the kōkako near his own home:

> Banks Peninsula … where the crow once abounded, is now divided into sheep runs, or dotted with dairy farms … It is not a matter for surprise that the wattle-bird is no longer to be found in its old haunts; it seeks shelter amongst the higher parts of the bushy gullies – a refuge at once precarious and temporary. It may be thought that the bird has attained a secluded habitat, but the condition of the

> forest is rapidly changing under the effects of clearings and constantly recurring bush fires. There is not much doubt that the climate of the district has become modified; at a certain period of the year weeks of drought prevail.[43]

These insights were published in 1880 but, as with those on the kākā, were based on work he had published earlier, in 1874.

In the 1880s Potts did extend his observations on the changing 'habits', of both indigenous species (like kea) confronting human-induced change to their habitat, and exotic species (such as house sparrows) that had been translocated to New Zealand. What he did not identify were changes in ecological conditions over time, such as cyclical climatic variation and natural erosion, which were relatively unaffected by human agency. He never addressed where the border might lie between natural variables and changes resulting from 'the effects of colonisation' and 'the agency of civilisation': a further century would pass before this issue received serious attention.[44] He did believe, however, that in some measure at least, 'the climatic change which has overtaken the place [Canterbury Plains] during one's recollection' related to 'the presence of extensive and efficient shelter, partly owing to improved drainage'.[45] More specifically he noted 'how great a climatic change has been effected on some parts of the once bare plains by persistent planting' of exotic trees, enabling even exotic succulents like variegated aloe to be grown there.[46] The actions of European settlers, in other words, had contributed to alterations in both climate and habitat.

If the decline of species was not some sort of biological inevitability – if even climate variability had a strong anthropogenic component – Potts' evidence might have confirmed for him that some changes (though not extinction, of course) could be reversed.[47] He certainly thought that a degree of 'indigenous regeneration', as we now term it, was possible. As a member of the Canterbury College committee in 1882, for instance, he advised Lincoln's School of Agriculture to 'collect and propagate Native grasses and forage plants', noting that 'many of these, which were of great value, were dying out in some places'.[48]

Two late articles demonstrate the interest Potts developed in entomology. In 1886 he recorded the appearance of 'the humble [or bumble] bee, the grazier's reputed friend, with a mission to fertilise red clover flowers', and the insect's gradual spread across the province.[49] Its progress was being watched with interest in Canterbury following three earlier failed introductions.[50] Potts observed some on Banks Peninsula in late 1885; in January 1886 J.B. Acland recorded one in his garden in Mt

Peel some hundred kilometres to the south; and in February Enys reported them at Castle Hill a hundred kilometres to the west.

Potts also studied the habits of the stick-like native mantids. He kept some in a room at Ohinetahi and spent hours observing their steady traverse of window-panes in pursuit of house-flies. By early 1883 he had prepared a paper about these mantids and their 'almost inexhaustible power of "masterly inactivity"', which was read before the Philosophical Institute in Christchurch and later published in the *Transactions of the New Zealand Institute*. It is a masterpiece both of observation and description.[51]

*

As Potts was observing the courtship of stick insects, the more subtle courtships of his own children were taking place around him. Details of one appear in the diary of Edward Chudleigh, a man historian Michael King characterised as having 'tremendous energy, furious temper, strong will and high principles'.[52] Chudleigh was already a good friend who moved easily within the Potts' social circle. He was a gentleman with land and money, and while not such a keen naturalist as Potts or Enys, he knew his birds. By 1880 Chudleigh had been farming in the Chatham Islands for 14 years and was approaching his fortieth birthday. On a trip to Canterbury that year he went to Mt Peel to visit Acland, with whom he had worked in the early sixties, and called at the adjoining station, which was managed by Ambrose Potts on behalf of Ben Moorhouse's widow. He stayed at Castle Hill with Enys and at Governors Bay with Thomas Potts and his family. On his return the following year he proposed to Thomas and Emma's daughter Mabel, who accepted: 'The old old story was told and two lives became one,' he recorded. 'Happy happy happy pair.'[53]

The marriage took place at Governors Bay at the end of June 1881 with Bishop Harper officiating. Mabel subsequently became ill in the course of their peripatetic honeymoon, prompting the attendance of an 'old Granny' who was 'wise in these things'; if she had become pregnant she did not remain so, for the couple never had children. Mabel and Edward lived in the Chathams until 1907; they then moved to Orongomairoa in the Waikato.[54]

Thomas and Emma's daughter Clara had married Robert Dobson in 1876 and moved to Napier. Robert was the son of the provincial engineer and brother-in-law of Julius Haast. Heinrich von Haast recalled, 'Governor's Bay was a favourite place for my mother to take her brood; and consequently the relations between the Potts's, Dobsons and Haasts were close and intimate.'[55] The creation of family links like these was as much a part of the acclimatisation process as the pairing of blackbirds released in Potts' garden.

Jane Potts married in 1883, as did Geoffrey, who farmed near Wanganui. In 1884 Edith wed Robert Fitzhugh Garbett, the vicar at Governors Bay; the church was 'beautifully decorated with white camellias and maidenhair from the famous fernery in Mr Potts' garden'.[56] The following year Beatrice married Robert Dobson's brother Edward, and in 1886 Freeman, who would later become mayor of Akaroa, married Climee Le Clerc of Duvauchelles Bay.

A letter from Thomas to one of his daughters in 1884 is a window upon his delight at the arrival of grandchildren: 'My dear Clara,' he wrote, 'Ralph is so well and much improved in appearance that he scarcely looks like the same little shrimp of a fellow as when Bob brought him down … He is particularly fond of jam tarts.'[57] He compared children to seedlings: 'Let us ever remember that the mirth and joyousness of children should be respected; to their soft, smooth hands has been confided happiness, a tender plant too many of whose blossoms fade and fall away full soon under the shadows of "the tree of knowledge of good and evil" that grows beside life's pathway.'[58]

The Potts family had blossomed, but their finances had withered. Potts was already in obvious difficulty by 1883 when he lost control of his high-country station.[59] In 1887 the family was obliged to give up their home in Governors Bay and moved to rented accommodation in Christchurch. Bankruptcy was narrowly averted. Ohinetahi remained listed under Potts' name until sold along with 572 acres (231ha) of land to William Cook of Lyttelton in 1896.[60]

Mark Stoddart, whom Potts had met first at Rockwood 30 years earlier, died in 1885; when Julius Haast died in 1887 Potts was a pall-bearer at the funeral.[61] In his writing Potts increasingly looked back, describing himself as an 'old timer'. In 1886 and 1887 articles in the *Canterbury Times* he recalled his early days in the colony: the journey out to Canterbury, catching eels with his young brothers-in-law near Rockwood, exploring inland Canterbury with Studholme, and campaigning for a young and politically unseasoned Moorhouse.[62] For the most part, these 'recollections' and 'jottings from an old notebook' were light in both vein and purpose.

*

Potts' natural history observations from his final years are of greater interest than such 'jottings'; they also display a change in focus. No longer a resident of

J.G. Keulemans' painting of the great spotted kiwi, *Apteryx haastii*.

Lithographer T. Walter, 1876. Alexander Turnbull Library: PUBL-0035-1-054

The best-known image of Thomas Potts was first reproduced as the frontispiece in Hutton and Drummond's *Animals of New Zealand* (1904).

Photographer unknown, c. 1875. Canterbury Museum: 19XX.2.5316 [2a]

Below

This rather sorry-looking example of the great spotted kiwi, still held in Canterbury Museum, is likely the one included in the photograph of Potts. Along with the holotype (AV2829), Potts used this specimen to differentiate and name the species in 1871.

Canterbury Museum: AV2828

The South Island kōkako.

Otago Museum: AV742

Below

While the South Island kōkako nestlings 'dangling in a jar of spirits' have been lost, the nest collected by Potts in January 1873, at Freshwater Basin in Milford Sound, is still held at Te Papa. He described his excitement 'on sighting an object that had been so long, so far, and so often hunted for. At last there was the nest ...' (Potts, 'Notes on rare and little known birds', 1880).

Museum of New Zealand Te Papa Tongarewa: OR.029158

'Saw ... several quail – an unwonted sight now and when we came here they were quite common.' (T.H. Potts, 15 October 1855). The New Zealand quail or koreke was presumed extinct by 1875.

Canterbury Museum: AV33171

Emma Potts' father, Henry Phillips of Rockwood Station. Photographer and date unknown.

Canterbury Museum: 19XX.2.2052

Below

'In the afternoon we all went up to Rocky Hill to see the rata and gather some of its flowers.' (T.H. Potts, 26 January 1856). The view of Rocky Hill from the garden at Rockwood.

Photographer and date unknown, from the collection of Bryony Macmillan

Emma Potts. John Enys wrote of her, 'I was down a few days since at a place called Governors Bay and had as many apricots as I could eat and helped find a number for jam. The lady of the house made about three hundred [jars] out of it on that day' (John Enys to Jane Enys, 18 January 1872). Photographer and date unknown, from the collection of Bryony Macmillan

'Sheep Attacked by a Kea', the lithograph that accompanied Potts' 1880 article, 'Kia, Kea, or Sheep-killer'. (T.H. Potts, *Out in the Open*, facing page 184)

Above
Julius Haast explored the headwaters of the Rakaia in 1866, travelling along the Wilberforce Valley as Potts had done a decade earlier. J.F. Julius von Haast, *View of Lake Coleridge from the Valley of the Wilberforce near Cascade Peak.* Alexander Turnbull Library: A-149-009

Opposite
J.F. Julius von Haast, *View of Brownings Pass from the Valley of the Wilberforce.* Alexander Turnbull Library: A-149-006

Overleaf, top
Haast explored the Upper Rangitātā in 1861 and called in at Potts' station beneath Mt Potts. His uncompleted sketch, drawn looking across the valley towards the Two Thumb Range, includes Potts' farm buildings in the foreground. J.F. Julius von Haast, *Mr Potts' Station, Two Thumb Range.* Alexander Turnbull Library: C-097-004

Valuable native forest was destroyed on Craigforth Estate in Pigeon Bay on Banks Peninsula during the fires of 1863. Remaining timber was used by Holmes & Co in building the Lyttelton–Christchurch railway. This photograph, from about 1881, shows one mighty tōtara left standing. Photographer unknown. Parliamentary Library: Photograph albums. Alexander Turnbull Library: PA1-f-186-19-2

Governors Bay, 1867. Emma and Thomas Potts' home, Ohinetahi, is on the left; the parsonage and St Cuthbert's Church are to the right above the road. The Ohinetahi stables and farm buildings are visible directly above the parsonage.

Photo D.L. Mundy. Auckland War Memorial Museum Tāmaki Paenga Hira: PH-ALB-86 –p143-2

Ohinetahi in 1867, soon after Potts had completed the central stone section of the house.

Photo D.L. Mundy. Alexander Turnbull Library: PA1-f-039-35

The author (left) and Paul Ensor examine a large macrocarpa in Potts' pinetum, Governors Bay, 20 February 2019.

Photo Jane Robertson

Potts' sketch of a white heron on its nest in a tree fern near Waitangituna Stream, Ōkārito, South Westland, in December 1871: '... in one instance a heron's nest occupied the top of a tree fern with the bird crouched over her charge ... this specimen was voted the gem amongst all the abodes of the heronry' (T.H. Potts, 'Out in the open: White heron', 1878).

From the collection of Bryony Macmillan

Potts thought a silvereye's nest suspended from bracken 'bore a striking resemblance to a swinging cot or hammock', and indicated the bird was a 'recent colonist', not yet 'aware of the immunity it enjoys from ravages of snakes'. T.H. Potts, 'Nest of *Zosterops lateralis*. On *Pteris aquilina*', lithograph John Buchanan. *Transactions of the New Zealand Institute*, vol. 3 (1870), plate 12

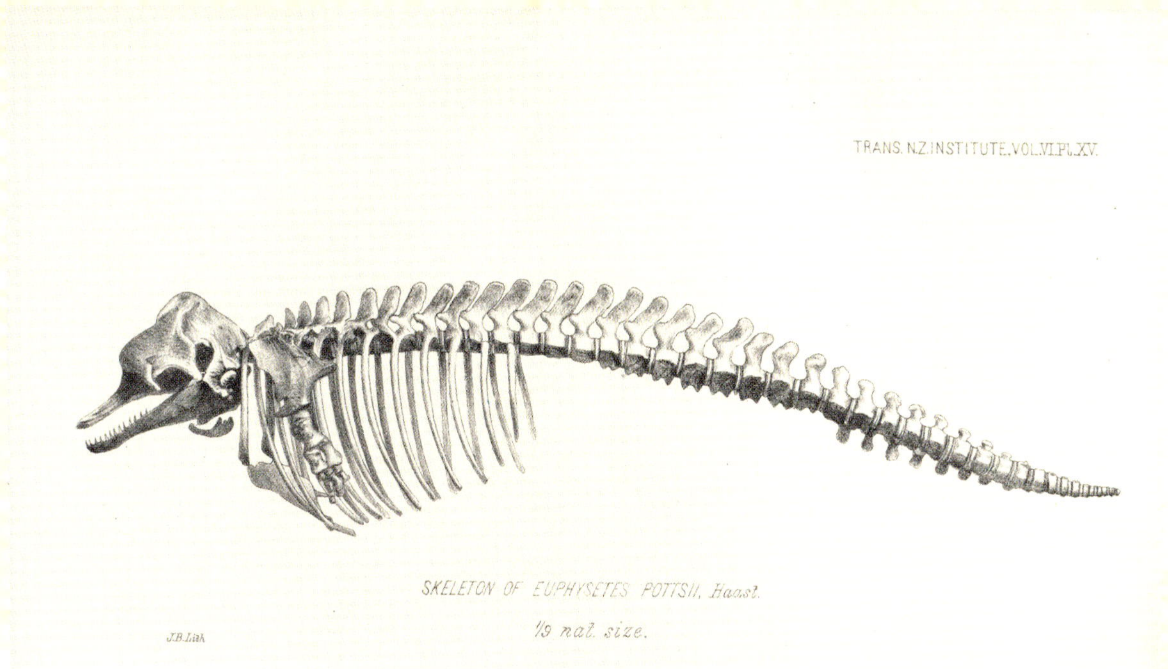

This unusual small whale was stranded on the rocks at Governors Bay and secured by Potts for Canterbury Museum. Julius Haast declared the whale a new species and named it after his friend. 'Skeleton of *Euphysetes pottsii*, Haast', lithograph John Buchanan.

Transactions of the New Zealand Institute, vol. 6 (1873), plate 15

By 1870 Potts had cultivated several native species of olearia in his garden at Ohinetahi. The visiting Auckland botanist Thomas Cheeseman noted that two species had crossed, and the resulting hybrid was named *O. haastii* – the 'New Zealand daisy bush'. It is now a common feature in European gardens.

Auckland War Memorial Museum Tāmaki Paenga Hira: AK9563 001

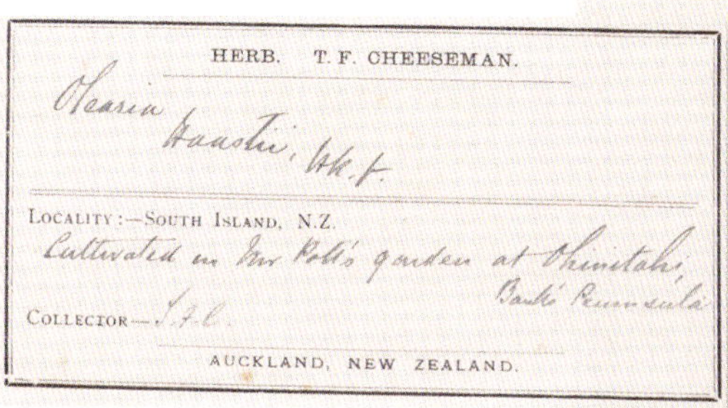

Celmisia angustifolia, collected in the Ashburton Mountains by T.H. Potts. Potts gathered many examples of New Zealand alpine flora, some of which he passed on to Thomas Kirk at the Colonial Museum in Wellington. The specimens are still held at Te Papa.

Museum of New Zealand Te Papa Tongarewa: SP046568

The Chatham Island forget-me-not *Myosotidium nobile* (now *M. hortensium*). 'One cannot pass silently the azure flowers of the giant Forget-me-not, the Chatham Island lily ... a gentleman taking hold of a leaf of the plant, not then in flower, expressed his admiration of the beautiful *rhubarb*.' (T.H. Potts, 'Out in the Open: The pulse of spring' (1885): 473).

Lithograph John Buchanan. *Transactions of the New Zealand Institute, vol. 7 (1874), plate 12*

In 1888 Potts regarded remnant bush in the Chathams as a 'temple of Nature as yet unscathed ... It was like a dream of old New Zealand over thirty years ago.' (T.H. Potts, 'Out in the Open: Stock in the Chathams' (1888): 373). Chatham Islands landscape of a waterfall and bush area. Photograph probably by Samuel Delabere Barker, 1873. Alfred Charles Barker collection, Canterbury Museum: 1957.13.587

Governors Bay, his essay 'A Countryman in Town', written in 1887, recorded what he saw while walking around central Christchurch at dawn.[63] He made the most of his new circumstances, comparing how exotic birds and plants had fared and what flowers people now grew in their gardens.

In January 1888 Potts left Emma and his financial problems in Christchurch and took a steamer, the *Kahu*, to the Chathams, where he stayed for six months at Wharekauri, Mabel and Edward Chudleigh's homestead in the north of the main island.

As a naturalist Potts had long been interested in the Chathams. Located 750 kilometres east of the Canterbury coast, the Chatham Islands were settled by Europeans later than New Zealand's mainland. The flora and fauna, though similar to those of New Zealand, were intriguingly distinct. He was also fascinated by the indigenous people of the Chathams, the Moriori. In January 1879 while walking in Lyttelton he was struck by the appearance of a man he saw among the Raupaki Māori. This was Timoti Tara, a Moriori who was an authority on his people's lore and a major claimant for his people at the Native Land Court in 1870. He had been tattooed when in slavery to Taranaki Māori who had invaded the Chathams and subjugated its inhabitants. Potts arranged for E. Dossetter of Christchurch to photograph Tara, then reproduced the image in the *Country Journal* in 1879. He was not at all optimistic for 'the doomed Moriori', and described what he called this 'rapidly failing race' in a manner disturbingly similar to his notes on some native birds: 'It may be thought fanciful, but their usual or settled expression conveyed the idea that they were patiently waiting for what was to happen; as if they might have belonged to some animal, which though not yet attacked, was preparing, or prepared, for defence.'[64]

Now, in 1888 Potts had the chance to see the Chathams for himself. He described his arrival in the first of six articles about the islands. The ship was moored at the port, Waitangi, until late afternoon – long enough for him to note introduced black swans, skylarks and, in particular, European sparrows, 'bold and audacious as elsewhere, foretelling much mischief to be done in the future'. Yet 'it seemed so short a time since the first of that dreaded pest had been noticed on the island'. Across the bay at Whangaroa he observed 'the rich growth of [introduced] grasses and clovers that flourished in the neighbourhood of the shipping place'.[65] At Te Raki Bay he noticed akeake and karaka, and 'looked about in vain for the sight of a single plant of the beautiful Chatham island lily, [since] the stock depastured on the runs and farms had devoured it in the places one had as yet visited'.[66] Finally the

Kahu rounded Cape Young and dropped Potts off at Wharekauri, where Mabel and Edward welcomed him into their home.

In the ensuing months Potts divided his time between helping on the station and going for walks in the north of the island. One ramble took him around Mt Wharekauri, through the karaka glades where the Moriori had sculpted 'mystic symbols' on the tree trunks, and on to Kohimata. The state of the flora struck him most: 'Native herbage is eagerly eaten by stock, more especially by sheep.' He noted that, apart from the matipo, 'they severely punish most, if not all, other species of trees.'[67] At Maunganui Beach he observed: 'Native growth that formerly covered or checked the inroads of the drifting sand was eaten to insignificance.'[68]

Potts' final article on the Chathams, found among his papers after his death, provided a clear account of the conflicting interests of European farming practices and the native environment.[69] 'Stock in the Chathams' described the rapid advance of sheep on the islands after their introduction in 1841, how they multiplied and profited their owners. More than anyone else at the time, however, Potts realised: 'There is the other side of the medal to be looked at, so as to arrive at a fair story of the sheep and their doings: What has it cost to keep them?' He pointed to the irony of the sheep's destruction of akeake, 'unrivalled as supplying lasting material for posts', and bemoaned the 'woeful decrease' in the numbers of many native birds and their threatened early extinction.

When at last he discovered an area of native forest that had not been 'desecrated' he likened it to 'a dream of Old New Zealand over thirty years ago'. His tone became almost biblical as he wrote of 'general destruction' brought about by the introduction of European stock and the resultant 'sand plague'. But Potts was no innocent, observing and condemning the sins of others: he had run stock on the mainland, and the Chathams sheep were those of his son-in-law at whose table he sat. He ended with practical suggestions on how the settler might combat the encroachment of sand.

This essay is the closest Potts ever came to a concise environmental history of the profound impact of exotic humans, animals and plants on an established indigenous ecosystem – what we now call an 'ecological catastrophe'.[70] Written at the end of his life, 'Stock in the Chathams' exhibits both the expanse and the limits of Potts' environmental understanding. While a few people possessed greater knowledge of the names and physiology of individual species, no-one in New Zealand at that time displayed a more complete comprehension of 'nature's economy' as a whole. This continued to be the case until 1899, when 44-year-old botanist Leonard Cockayne read, before the Philosophical Institute of Canterbury, his analysis of localised plant life 'from an oecological point of view'.[71] A decade later Cockayne successfully argued for the extension of Tongariro National Park on ecological grounds. He was increasingly acknowledged as the leading New Zealand botanist and ecologist of his generation.[72]

In January 1888, shortly after Potts had arrived at Wharekauri, Chudleigh left to attend to matters in New Zealand. On reaching Christchurch he met with Emma and purchased the family's silver and jewels from her. 'It was settled,' he recorded: 'I took the lot at £300 subject to redemption at interest by either Mr. or Mrs. Potts but no one else … the jewellery I leave at my wife's death to the members of the Potts family who have behaved well to their parents.'[73] In the same week Enys paid the Potts' rent for them.[74] The financial embarrassment of Emma's brother-in-law Grosvenor Miles had precipitated his death 23 years earlier. Then, Thomas and Emma had lent assistance; now they were the ones in need.

Chudleigh travelled on to Wellington where he called at the Colonial Museum to see Hector 're. Mr. Potts' – he probably hoped (in vain) that Hector would buy the remains of Potts' egg collection. In Napier he stayed with his brother-in-law Walter Potts and the two 'went into family affairs re. £600 owing to me and about my keeping the silver and jewels'. They calculated that Potts' assets, once so substantial, now amounted to a mere £320.[75] Many of Thomas and Emma's belongings, including 'some of the choicest furniture ever imported into Canterbury', had been sold in 1887 following their move from Governors Bay to Christchurch, and Potts' library was auctioned in Christchurch in March 1888 while he was in the Chathams.[76] These brought in little: when Potts died his estate was worth just £70.[77]

In April Chudleigh returned to his station in the Chathams where he faced – and weathered – his own difficulties: 'I never saw the country so bare of food, and the fern is covering all the good swamps, the run deteriorates as fast as the plough improves the home backs. I see no future to anything.'[78] Potts stayed on for another three months, helping out when not off on his rambles. On one day he burnt the bush at Glencairn for Chudleigh, and towards the end of June he cut 'piles of supplejack'. Chudleigh wrote that his father-in-law 'works all day as few men of his age could even if they would'.[79]

Potts, now aged 64, left the Chathams on 12 July and was soon back at Lyttelton. He joined Emma in Peterborough Street in Christchurch and began to write up his Chathams notes. On 27 July he set off to visit the public library and the post office before going to Mrs Sharland's fancy goods shop on the corner of Armagh and Colombo streets to buy a ribbon. There he collapsed, his head striking a toy gun as he fell, and within a few minutes he was dead. Dr Hanon conducted a post mortem and concluded that he died from natural causes, 'the result of advancing brain disease'. His family quietly buried Thomas Potts in Linwood Cemetery at a cost of £1 4s 6d.[80]

Isolated on the Chathams, Mabel and Edward learned of the loss of her father in October: 'The *Kahu* arrived this morning bringing the worst of news for myself and my dear Mabel,' wrote Edward. Three days later as they worked side by side in their garden they found themselves constantly reminded of his presence: 'I mowed grass and she raked and we ran against dear old Mr. Potts at every turn, this came from Ohinetahi, that he grafted, and so on, there are no thorns about his memory.'[81]

The Legacy of Thomas Potts

Emma Potts lived on in Christchurch until her death in 1919 aged 86.[1] It is hard to gain a sense of what she was like from her husband's journals, beyond her industry and her love for her family. When Thomas took his only trip back to England in 1862 she gave him the *Book of Common Prayer*, in which he noted the religious services he attended while absent from her side.[2] It is evidence of their affection for one another and their shared religious faith.

Part of Thomas Potts' significance to us today lies with the buildings and properties he once owned or was involved with. One of these is St Cuthbert's Church in Governors Bay. A few years before Emma died the addition of a bell tower as a memorial to her husband was proposed, but the Great War intervened and the idea was forgotten.[3] The church in its original form continues to stand as his memorial.

Ohinetahi, the family home for 30 years, is considered 'the most impressive historic residence in Governors Bay' and one of the finest in Canterbury.[4] When Lord Lyttelton, who helped to found Canterbury, toured the colony in 1867, he visited Ohinetahi and declared it:

> a very excellent and spacious house a little way up the hill and looking down the harbour and belonging to a magistrate and a man of importance named Potts. It was the best and largest house that we had yet seen.[5]

Ohinetahi retains the character of 1866–67, when Potts replaced the original central wooden part with a three-storey stone structure and remodelled the wooden one-storey wings at either end. A wide verandah surrounds the whole, and a curved stairway of Baltic pine remains a notable feature. The upper floors of the house were severely damaged in the Canterbury earthquakes of 2010–11, resulting in removal of the third storey and a transformation of the roofline by the architect owner Sir Miles Warren, who originally bought the house with his sister Pauline and her husband, fellow architect John Trengrove. Sir Miles gifted the house and gardens to the Ohinetahi Charitable Trust in 2012, and the Heritage New Zealand category one building and award-winning gardens are now a tourist attraction. St Cuthbert's and the school building also have heritage status.

The gardens that surround the house today are largely the creation of Sir Miles and the Trengroves and date back no further than 1977. Many features from Potts' day had already disappeared when they took over the property: Sir Miles referred to 'an extensive wire-enclosed cherry orchard up behind the house which collapsed in the huge snowstorm of 1945' and 'a ruined orchard of plums, medlars, cherries and greengages [which] ran up the slope towards the road'.[6] He retained some large trees, including a magnificent Queensland hoop pine, but little remains of the extensive planting undertaken by Potts.

The Ohinetahi property incorporates only five hectares around the house – a fraction of Thomas and Emma Potts' original property of 240-odd hectares, which once included the backdrop of the Port Hills up to the crater rim. Nineteenth-century photographs show the land cleared right to the top. While the lower hillsides are still farmed, the upper reaches have now reverted to a cover of native vegetation, in particular on 150 hectares of covenanted land above the 150-metre contour. This has become Ohinetahi Bush Reserve, acquired in part in 1992 and managed by the Summit Road Society.[7] The continued presence there of a few mataī and mature tōtara would have delighted Potts. Farm buildings that Potts erected across the road from his house were bulldozed within living memory, but evidence remains of two or three farm labourers' cottages, and there are several large English oaks and other exotics, all on private land. The once extensive orchards are now represented only by some magnificent old pear trees fenced off from browsing stock.

Potts' pinetum, once the focus of his experiments in the relative growth of pines and other exotic tree species, still exists. At present it is on Paul Ensor's land immediately below the road that leads from Governors Bay to Teddington. Many of its larger trees fell or were felled in the 1970s or 1980s; three cuttings along the hillside, still referred to as 'Potts' tracks', provide access to those that are still standing. Perhaps the best remaining example of Potts' exotic plantings is a row of trees on the other side of the road.[8] There is also a remnant of native bush behind the Ohinetahi homestead, accessible via a footbridge and within Sir Miles Warren's property. The famous fernery has long since vanished, destroyed by a flood.

Quail Island in Lyttelton Harbour, so named when native quail were found there in 1842, was sold by Potts in 1875. It had an interesting later history as a quarantine station, a leper colony and a training ground for Antarctic expeditions. Since becoming a recreation reserve in 1975 it has been maintained by the Otamahua Quail Island Ecological Restoration Trust in co-operation with the Department of Conservation. In an effort to re-establish indigenous ecosystems on the island the trust has planted 100,000 native trees and shrubs, provided nesting boxes for white-flippered penguins and re-introduced bellbirds and kererū.[9] It should be said that when Potts owned the island his focus was on stocking it with sheep.[10]

The Mt Potts area in Canterbury's high country, in the heart of what was Hakatere Station, is also now under the stewardship of the Department of Conservation and has had an equally varied history.[11] In 1891 the station was divided into two: the land facing Ashburton retained the name Hakatere, while the area lying between the Potts and Rangitātā rivers became Mt Potts Station. In the 1960s part of the latter became Erewhon Park and the woolshed was 'transformed into a well carpeted and delightful restaurant and the homestead into commodious bunkrooms'.[12] Erewhon Park Ski Field opened in 1996 on the slopes of Mt Potts.

The rest of the property continued to be run as a sheep station until 1998 when, following tenure review, the 9700-hectare property was divided into 1200 hectares of freehold land (the present Mt Potts Station) and 8500 hectares of conservation land (Hakatere Conservation Park). The park has become a popular tramping area and is crossed by Te Araroa Trail, a long-distance walk that runs the length of New Zealand. There are also established shorter walks to Ō Tū Roto, Te Puna a Taka and Kirihonuhonu – or, as Potts named them, Lakes Heron, Clearwater and Emma. Although many visitors to the area never learn the origin of the name 'Mt Potts', they do know that film producer and director Sir Peter Jackson and his crew chose nearby Mt Sunday on which to build the filmset for Edoras, the fortress city that featured in *Lord of the Rings: The return of the king* (2003).[13]

*

Like his properties, Thomas Potts' ideas have often been refurbished or redrawn. His term 'national domain' did not catch on, though in 1883 the Bishop of Nelson thought there might be 'government lands which could be leased by, say, one thousand acres [400ha] to this [Nelson Philosophic] Society … which might be our Yellowstone domain'.[14] The term that endured was the one A.K. Newman used in Parliament in 1884 when he asked the government to 'reserve Ruapehu, Ngauruhoe, Tongariro, Rotoaira, Tokano and the hot springs in the district as a national park'.[15] Although the government did not respond to this call during Potts' lifetime, the Māori chief Horonuku, on behalf of Ngāti Tūwharetoa, donated mountain land to all New Zealand's people in 1887 which became the core of Tongariro National Park in 1894.[16] By the end of the twentieth century, 30,000 square kilometres – more than one ninth of the country – had been granted 'national park' status. In the century after Potts' death this term came to be applied only to large reserves of public land of scenic and environmental significance; smaller areas with similar values were usually called 'scenic reserves'.

Potts was well aware of the transformation of the English language that occurred, alongside the transformation of English social patterns and of the environment, as New Zealand/Aotearoa evolved.[17] He had no influence, however, on the word usages that finally won through. Cashmere Hills Domain was established in 1884 at the foot of the Port Hills on the western side and comprised '188 acres 3 roods 11 perches' (about 76ha).[18] Potts thought the word 'domain' had 'a smack of grandiloquence' about it that was inappropriate for such a small area, but felt the term 'village green' was not right in the New Zealand context either: 'to the man who proposes to create a township, whose prophetic soul dwells on visions of future cities, the term would seem objectionable'.[19] He preferred to call such an area a 'recreation ground'.

In 1888 the Dunedin and Suburban Reserves Conservation Society – the first New Zealand organisation with 'conservation' in its title – was founded to develop open spaces in the city, many on former rubbish dumps.[20] Since then, conservation has been a contested word in New Zealand, sometimes conflated with 'preservation'. When the Department of Conservation was founded in 1987, some who opposed what they considered its role in 'locking up' land against exploitation or development (other than tourism) complained that it should be called a department of 'preservation'.

When Potts first called for the conservation of New Zealand's native forests, he envisaged limited exploitation of most of what remained. Increasingly, however, his emphasis moved to the preservation – complete protection – of some areas. A century later New Zealand was embroiled in public campaigns to protect the likes of Lake Manapōuri or West Coast beech forests, orchestrated by groups such as Forest & Bird and the Native Forest Action Council.[21] Potts' record of direct action may appear relatively meagre in comparison with the activism of protestors in recent times, but in his day there were no environmental organisations to which he could contribute.

A 'scenery preservation' movement arose in New Zealand in the 1890s, in tandem with the rise to political power of Liberals who increasingly accepted state involvement in town and country planning as much as in economic and social matters. This opened up the possibility of a broad-based lobby for environmental protection, altogether absent in Potts' time.[22] It precipitated the Scenery Preservation Act in 1903 and the formation of a Scenery Preservation Board, leading to the gazettal of 'scenic reserves' throughout the country.[23] These have remained the counterpoint in miniature to New Zealand's national parks.

Potts' idea of island reserves also bore fruit in the decade after his death. In 1891 A.P.W. Thomas and G.M. Thomson proposed Resolution Island and Little Barrier Island as island reserves.[24] Resolution Island gained this status within a few months, Little Barrier Island in 1894 and Kapiti Island in 1897. Caretaker Richard Henry's activities on Resolution Island from 1894 to 1908 are among the earliest and most dramatic attempts at bird preservation in any country's history, and there is evidence that Henry had close knowledge of Potts' writings.[25] In recent years native bird relocations on several islands along the Fiordland coast, including Resolution Island, have been made in full cognisance of Henry's earlier efforts, but with limited awareness of Potts' role in first raising the idea.[26]

The most recognised of the country's early ornithologists is Walter Buller, although continued interest in his *History of the Birds of New Zealand* has as much to do with its frequently reproduced illustrations as with Buller's text: artist J.G. Keulemans, who created the illustrations, only received his full due in 2012 in Geoff Norman's new edition of the work.[27] Norman's 2018 collection, *Birdstories*, makes frequent reference to Potts, describing for instance continued acceptance of his differentiation of kiwi species and the rapid dismissal of his claim for a new species of tern.[28] But while Norman often mentions Potts, he seems not to doubt that Buller, whatever his faults, contributed more to ornithology.

Several native birds have become extinct since Potts' death, such as the huia, so familiar from Keulemans' painting. Some species could have been saved, or not become so severely threatened, had more attention been paid to Potts' concerns about birds and their habitats. There is some irony to the 'birdstory' of the kea, however. As we have seen this was the only native species that Potts wished to see destroyed. Continued ambivalence about its impact delayed the kea's full protection until 1986, yet it maintained a sizeable population.[29] High-country station owner Jerry Aspinall's 1990 booklet *Keas* demonstrated that the amount of harm they did was still hotly debated a century after Potts' death.[30] Conclusive photographic evidence that kea attack sheep appeared in 1992, but the species has never constituted a major threat to sheep farming.[31]

In recent years the kea population has decreased, along with many other native species. Aerial application of 1080 bait (containing the poison sodium fluoroacetate) by the Department of Conservation, with the intention of killing exotic pests, has also resulted in the deaths of some individual birds – most controversially of kea. However, all sides now wish to 'save our native birds' – as Potts phrased it – though with some disagreement on how best to attempt this. Most people accept that the use of 1080 increases overall native bird populations in the long run.[32]

Thomas Potts' role in the establishment of exotic birds is uncertain. Probably many of the British passerines (perching birds and songsters) in the Governors Bay area are descended from individuals that he introduced, but unless these are subjected to DNA analysis we will never know how far their genes may have spread.[33]

The distribution of Potts' own descendants is much clearer. Among his grandchildren, Donald's son Norman (1886–1970), who practised as a solicitor in Ōpōtiki in the Bay of Plenty, was notable for following pursuits similar to those of his grandfather. As chair of the management committee of Hukutaia Domain he supervised the restoration of a two-hectare remnant of native forest to create 'a living museum of New Zealand plants'. He distributed native seed and plant material to public gardens and individuals throughout New Zealand, and two or three plants that he discovered were named after him. In 1944 he received the Loder Cup, awarded annually to 'lovers of nature in New Zealand to encourage the protection and cultivation of the incomparable flora of the Dominion'.[34]

*

Thomas Potts' unpolished impressions of the Canterbury high country and of station life in the 1850s follow in Part 2. His final reflections on natural history and environmental change, made 30 years later, remain equally interesting and relevant. The 11 articles that constitute Part 3 are a selection from among the more literary 'rambles' that he wrote between 1882 and 1888.

This introduction to Potts began by referring to the best photo we have of him. In fact, the photographer – probably Peter Schourup – took two consecutive shots.[35] The one that caught a serious expression on Potts' face is well known and often reproduced, and has contributed to how he is remembered. I prefer the cover photo, however. In this one Potts has relaxed; he no longer looks stern and there is a twinkle in his eye. It is an image to be kept in mind, now, while reading his words.

PART TWO

Seeking a Stranger-Land: *Selections from the diary of Thomas Potts, 1855–58*

Six swift wing'd years, my Love, have fled
And in their train such changes brought,
Since that bright day when we were wed,
Fancy her rainbow-future wrought …

Since then we quit our well-lov'd home
The treach'rous ocean-wave we dare.
And from our friends, our feelings, roam
Seeking a stranger-land afar.

In our new world life's path we find
With thorns and briars overspread.
Hope gives these illweeds to the wind,
And fruits and flow'rs plant in their stead.

Thomas H. Potts, 2 April 1856

The originals of Potts' diaries have long been lost. The following entries are a selection – about 40 per cent of the total – from a surviving but unpublished typescript of his diaries for the years 1855–58. The unidentified transcriber left occasional gaps in the typescript, presumably where Potts' original text was illegible. These are noted within square brackets, as are any simple corrections or clarifications of the text. A few lengthier remarks appear as endnotes.

Dramatis personae

Thomas Henry Potts (THP): the diarist, runholder (Rakaia Terrace lease from 1855; Hakatere from 1857), son-in-law of Henry Phillips
Emma Potts (EP, Mrs P, the Mistress): wife of Thomas, daughter of Henry Phillips
Donald, Ambrose, Geoffrey, Mabel and Clara: children of Thomas and Emma Potts
Henry Phillips (the Governor, HP): runholder (Rockwood from 1852–77; Rakaia Terrace lease from 1855; The Point from 1862), father of Emma Potts
Mary Anne Phillips (Mrs P): wife of Henry, mother of Emma Potts
John, Harry, Jim (runholder, Mt Algidus 1857–59), Charles, Tom (runholder, The Point from 1877), George and William: sons of Henry and Mary Anne Phillips
Grosvenor Miles, Christchurch: son-in-law of Henry Phillips
Adelaide Miles, Christchurch: wife of Grosvenor, daughter of Henry and Mary Anne Phillips; sister of Emma Potts
Ted and Fred Phillips, Christchurch: nephews of Henry Phillips
Henry Richards (Mr R, the Doctor): medic living at Rockwood, employed by Potts
Mrs Richards (Mrs R): wife of Henry Richards
Nurse, William Seal, Eliza, Jack and Maria: Potts' employees
Neighbouring runholders:

Justin Aylmer (Hororata, Snowdon)
John Cordy and his son Jim (Homebush, Hororata)
Tom Hall (Terrace Station, Blackford) and his brothers George and John
Francis Leach (Snowdon, Clent Hills)
William Norris (Acheron Bank)
John Oakden (Acheron Bank, Mount Algidus)
George Ross (Mount Algidus, Lake Coleridge)
Mark Stoddart (Terrace Station until 1853)
John Studholme (Terrace Station) and his brother Michael

Sir William Congreve: visitor at Rockwood
Mr Tomlinson: tutor to Henry and Mary Anne Phillips' sons
Dr Alfred Barker, Christchurch: medic and runholder
Cyrus Davie (Mr Davey), Christchurch: surveyor and runholder
William Dampier, Christchurch: Potts' agent
Charles Edwards, Christchurch: shipmate and friend of Potts
Henry Harper (the Bishop), Christchurch: Anglican minister
Rev William Willock (the Iron Priest), Christchurch: Anglican minister
Thomas Hunt: Potts' business partner in England
Frederick Catling, Tom Dutton: friends of Potts in England

*

1855

11 April. Mr R morticing posts. Nurse making cote. THP pottering about in a purposeless manner, accompanied with much grumbling about everything in general and New Zealand in particular. He attributes it in some measure to Mrs P [Emma Potts] having risen this morning from the wrong side of the bed. At tea-time the clouds were dispersed. Jim came in the evening. (On the conversion of a porter barrel into two wash-tubs, EP broke into a blaze of sunshine.)

29 April. Sunday. A day not soon to be forgotten. Last night the wind increased with strong gusts, and towards midnight raged with a violence that was perfectly astonishing. Our roof soon felt the effects of the storm, the walls rocked, windows blown out, and we had to pass the whole night in barricading the doors, whilst the rain poured in torrents through the open roof, damaging most of our effects. At dawn we got ready for a start to Rockwood for shelter, as own dilapidated cottage was rendered untenable. Mr Phillips and Seal came as we were about to start, and we all returned with them. Great numbers of trees were uprooted, our fences very much injured, some rails were blown from the posts to an almost incredible distance. The stable roof blown down, and much other damage we suffered from this terrible tempest. On our arrival at Rockwood, the ravages of the storm were most conspicuous in the multitudes of fallen trees that were lying in heaps on every side.

31 May. Mr R and Nurse at the watering place fence – ground very unfavourable for the work, wet and very stoney; hindered also by the creek. Six panels finished, they having to hump the rails from the bush. THP and Seal at the cross fence north of the calf paddock, which was so much damaged by the tempest of 28th ult. Have to take down all the posts and refit the rails. Fifteen panels finished by this evening. THP took his telescope when he resumed work after dinner, but Emma [who was visiting Christchurch] did not appear to comfort him, so he left off work at dusk and turned home disconsolate.

1 June. Saw a large mob of our cattle the first thing this morning on the flat beyond the Washpen Creek, but a very thick mist from the South East soon hid them from view, or should have sent Mr R to head them back to the Waikerri [Waikirikiri].[1] Nurse and Mr R at work at the watering place fence. Seal and THP same work as yesterday. After dinner weather got round to the South West and rain increased so as to compel us to leave work. The watering place was complete and ten panels of the cross fence finished. If the weather prove fair, we may be able to have the calves paddocked by Wednesday or Thursday next. Since the chimney was fresh cobbed, it smokes so much that we cannot bear the room with the door shut. It is anything, tonight, <u>but pleasant</u>, as it pours with rain and the air is very raw and cold, and there the door stands wide open. THP can scarcely see to write through the tears in his eyes which the smoke <u>will</u> extract, although he sits in a corner. He is wet through, and his pipe won't draw. Who wouldn't be an emigrant? After thirteen unsuccessful attempts to accomplish the very appropriate game [...] of Patience, he is resolved if EP does not return <u>tomorrow</u> to start for Christchurch next day – weather permitting, and now retires cold and comfortless to his solitary bed.

2 June. This morning the whole face of the country is changed – the snow lies six inches deep, so we must not expect much work done today. I must question if anything will be attempted, as emigrants seem to be particularly careful of their delicate persons. Saw the cattle again on the same flat as yesterday. Sent Mr R to head them back. He brought word they were all right. About two o'clock Seal and THP began morticing the posts for caps as the snow stopped all other work. At three o'clock saw Mr Phillips and Emma over the Washpen Hill. They arrived quite well. THP and Seal going down to Rockwood to meet them. Seal and Nurse brought up a wether. Willy came for flour.

7 June. Mild weather, rather misty, with showers. Mr R nailing pales – in the afternoon filling caps on the bank fence. Nurse digging potatoes and cutting wood. Seal to Rockwood for milk; afterwards with THP splitting palings (200). Saw two drays on the track over the Washpen Hill. Harry came in the evening, and brought some newspapers that came by Cox's dray. Seal killed a kingfisher [kōtare]. Played a rubber in the evening. Very dull night with rain.

9 June. Rain very heavy – river high. THP went round the paddocks to look at the ditches. They answer very well. It was too thick to see further than the first high ground from the fence, so he could not tell what had become of the dray for Richards. Nurse to Rockwood for milk. He found the creeks and river very high, indeed, our stream has swollen so much as to flow over Seal's bridge. It rained from the South West all day. Everything looks rather miserable – more particularly the fowls. The poor things are glad to rush indoors for shelter when they shake and preen their feathers. These damp and uncomfortable visitors are evidently looked upon as unwelcome intruders by the Mistress. Their presence only tolerated on account of the weather.

14 June. Heavy mist this morning. At six o'clock from SW increased to heavy rain. As there appears no chance of out-door employment THP proposes to write letters, an occupation that is always deferrred as long as possible, and everyone here looks upon it as a task they would gladly omit altogether. It being wet today is exceedingly provoking as Mr R was to have gone to Cordey's from the river-bed [and] collected all the cattle together, and they would have been yarded tomorrow, and the calves drafted out. Now we have the delightful prospect of being confined indoors for two or three days with three of the noisiest and most tiresome little boys that ever disturbed any father's peaceful meditations. Mr R Knight with Seal called at tea-time, but did not stop as they were going to Rockwood.

18 June. Harry left this morning for Christchurch and took Buxom with him to try her in the dray. THP on Beda after the cattle. Found most of them on the hills near the old warri [whare]. Called at Rockwood on the way. Received a letter from Mr R intimating that he did not consider himself bound to work, and proposing a fresh arrangement in looking after the cattle. Nurse cutting wood. Seal finishing capping and backing up turf walls where the earth had settled. Wrote to my friend Dutton, and sent the letter to post by Harry. Gave Harry £5 on Seal's account. Saw Mr Norris' man at Rockwood, and told him that any of his dogs found here should be destroyed. Fine day, unusually cold, the snowy range quite white. Wind rising rather strong towards evening. Brought up 69 heifers, one cow, one bull and seven calves.

27 June. Geoffrey's second birthday. Fine morning, wind in strong puffs and bitterly cold. A large fire last night and today across the Rakaia spreading easterly. THP on Beda early this morning taking away heifers to the mob over the Gap. Seal at work at his job of the garden fence. Nurse cutting wood, and hanging meat etc in the morning. In the afternoon THP setting up outside fence of the top paddock. Jim and Tom went to Round Top after five of the Governor's calves, but did not bring them up. Fine clear night, very clear and inclining to frost. The fires over the Rakaia are burning more to the West.

1 July. Sunday. Sharp frost last night, and this morning Georgy dined here. Jim and Tom came in to tea. They had been to Pullwool to the calves, which they found all right. The weather changed at mid-day, a Nor'Wester springing up. Georgy stopped here – It is worth entering here that Charley and Georgy fetching the cows one day last week saw a large hawk rise from a shag which they found still warm. The feathers strewed about for twenty yards shewed [showed] the fierce struggle the shag had maintained for its life.

4 July. Strong Nor'Wester this morning, Harry went home. Nurse cutting wood and at the close bails. Seal at garden fence – in the afternoon with THP planting fruit trees from Bayfield's.[2] They are good-sized trees (30) chiefly plums with some pears and require pruning. The wind has been piercing cold all day, so much so that THP has retained his coat and waistcoat for the first time for months. Chimney smoked most unpleasantly. Little Mabel unwell – most likely teething.

5 July. Mild Sou'Wester this morning. Heavy rain at day-break. Seal at the garden fence when the weather cleared. THP planting fruit trees training, pruning and marking:– memo of apples:

3 Carlisle pippins	I	5 Winter pearmains	VV
3 English "	II	3 Loan's "	IV
3 Paradise "	III	5 Hawthorndean	V
5 Brandy "	IIII	5 Nonsuch	II
3 Stone "	X	10 Yorkshire greening	II
5 Ribstone	XI	3 Flower of Kent	I
5 Orange pearmains	VI	3 Royal Somerset	II
		5 French Codling	I

The trees trained last year are generally of pretty good shape, although the wood made is of small size. The new trees make quite a show in the orchard. Jim and Georgy took tea here. They had been after the calves, but did not find them. Mabel is much better.

6 July. Sharp frost. Nurse cutting wood. Seal at garden fence. THP training fruit trees, etc, and forking up ground where the crops had been cleared off. Fine day. Memo of fruit trees planted:

	8 Peaches	3 Quinces
	2 nectarines	3 Kentish cherries
40 {	Damsons	3 Mayduke cherries
	Greengages	3 Biggereau "
	Plums – various	3 White heart "
	4 Pears	3 Black " "

20 July. Fine day. Donald to Rockwood with THP. Breaking in Mike. Ploughed with team of three bullocks, very fair work today. THP's first appearance between the stilts of a plough. Seal planting raspberry canes. Nurse returned from Christchurch. Brought a March 'Observer' from Miles, containing an account of the death of Emperor Nicholas.[3] Heavy fall of snow at night.

24 July. Harry attained his majority. General holiday at Rockwood. Some went pigeon shooting, others played quoits, singing and cards in the evening till a late hour. Sir W Congreve, Mr Richards, Seal, etc, present. A most beautiful day.

28 July. Weather dull. THP after Earl [a bullock] the first thing, and took him down to their stockyard. He stood roping very quietly, and was placed next the plough, Mike in the middle and Tommy for leader. The team worked well – far better than we expected. Earl apparently has been worked before. Emma rode down to Rockwood on Beda. The quantity of tuis flying about today was extraordinary. There was distant rumbling thunder all day, and between four and five it began raining sharply from the South West. Nurse and Seal planting out gorse round the inside of the garden fence. Kept the 23 heifers in the paddock all day, and most likely they [will] be there tomorrow as well.

3 August. Frost. THP collecting and planting native shrubs including the scarlet flowering shrub (rata). Seal and Nurse as yesterday, and cutting rails and charring posts. Saw grasshoppers and lizards.

10 August. Mild weather. Jim to Pullwool after the calves. THP at the shrubbery. Georgy came to see after Jim who brought word he had found the calves, and that Earl was with them. THP and Nurse went directly to the Pullwool and rode out Earl and put him in the calf paddock. Seal at the fence. Nurse with him in the morning. Jim went home. Three of the Dorkings laid today, but could not find the eggs as they lay in the bush, so a house must be made for them. The boys set fire to the hill in the further side of the Gap. All the calves seemed in good order. Truant's calf better than when last seen. Finished reading 'The Talisman'.[4]

16 August. THP to Rockwood to plough. Tried that tiresome brute Billy again, and so pulling and knocking us all about, and smashing two panels of the Rockwood paddock and doing other damage – we got him into harness after breaking away twice. Worked very badly, and the day's work most unsatisfactory. Nurse cutting flax [harakeke] on the old barley piece. Seal sowing carrots (Early Horn), bed 45 feet by 12 feet. Beautiful and very warm weather. Burning paddock. At night the hills towards the Gap afforded a splendid sight in a perfect blaze of fire, the flames distinctly showing the outlines of the hills and every gully and spur rendered visible. EP saw a butterfly.

17 August. A strong wind from the North West. The weather almost as fine as ever, although the strong gusts of wind made it less agreeable. THP pottering about in the forenoon. Nurse cutting wood. Seal putting in peas and beans, and after dinner with THP sowing onions; the bed 54 feet by 7 feet, rows 9 inches apart. The parsnips and carrots were drilled in 12 inches apart. Cherry's calf died. THP almost recovered from the fatigue of yesterday. The warm days this week have brought out the blow flies who are actively engaged in their disgusting habits. All the Dorking pullets hatched towards the end of November have begun to lay, so that we are now well supplied with eggs – a luxury which is well appreciated.

18 August. Heavy Nor'Wester during the night, gradually subsiding towards morning. Seal and THP planting American early potatoes – the ground turns up in capital order. After dinner Seal helping Nurse to cut wood. Harry came up in the evening. Very fine day, but rather windy. The children are looking all the better for the long spell of fine weather, and THP and EP have left off grumbling about the New Zealand climate, and actually begin to think this winter would bear comparison to an English one.

21 August. Charles, Nurse walked off over the Gap to look for Cherry, he said, and went further than Hall's crossing-place. Cherry was in the paddock, and THP had milked her before Nurse's return. THP, Harry and Jim ploughing same as yesterday, and finished about the same quantity. EP and Tom rode after Earl and brought him in before dinner. The wind still very high – fine dry weather. Seal yesterday put in four rows of American early potatoes, and today finished the garden fence, pricked out cabbage plants of various kinds, and sowed lettuce and radish seed. Nurse as yesterday, cutting flax. Our little Donald, both yesterday and today, was busily employed as a bullock driver, and left off very tired. Saw another butterfly at the stockyard resembling Vanessa Atalanta [red admiral] in the British Fauna. Mr Richards came and looked at the ploughing this morning. Jim came in for some cribbage.

24 August. Frost. THP, Harry and Jim ploughing, got through over 2,000 yards. Nurse to Rockwood to fetch the wether from which Jim's dog had abstracted a shoulder. Nurse afterwards cutting wood and fixing hen's nests. Seal in the garden at sundries, and also sowing Altringham carrots, 15 inches apart in the rows, bed 51 feet by 9 feet. Removed a large tumour or excrescence (the size of an egg) from the thigh of a Cochin hen. The Governor proposed sending someone to Lake's to borrow his dray to fetch up the seeds, instead of waiting till the team of bullocks could go down next week – this he supposed would save time: but this opinion was not shared by THP, who thought that as the ploughing would be finished tomorrow, in all probability, and that it was likely Lakes' [sic] dray might not be disengaged, it would be better to send our own team next Tuesday; a further inducement to do so would be derived from the consciousness of our independence from adventitious assistance in managing our own traffic from Christchurch. On this subject there was considerable discussion carried on nearly all day. Seal said the peas were showing.

26 August. Sunday. Frost in the morning, but at about 10 o'clock the temperature rose very suddenly, and the day has been quite mild, with gentle showers about noon. Cows fetched home very late. EP made a tremendous junket. Billy dined here. Mr and Mrs Phillips came to tea. The Cochin hen which underwent the operation seems to be doing well at present. Our hens lay so well that we were able to use 16 today, without exhausting our stock. One Dorking lays in the nursery, at which act of presumption EP grumbles, rather.

28 August. Wrote to Mr Hunt by Seal. Seal and Harry started for Christchurch with the cart, and three bullocks. Gave Seal £5/10/-. THP assisted Charley planting out cape brooms, laburnums, roses, lilacs, privets, acacias, etc, in the shrubbery.

Nurse planting out currant bushes between the fruit trees top of the orchard. Planted out willows on the river bank. THP returned to Rockwood in the evening. Very fine weather for the journey down to town. Wind rising at sunset.

7 September. Fine morning. EP returned home. Seal brought up cabbage plants, seeds and some of the white mulberry plants from Mr Dampier's garden that we sent out from England. Seal put in the mulberry trees, cabbage plants, etc. THP at the shrubbery. Nurse cutting wood. Rain in the evening turned to a heavy fall of snow. Polyanthus in bloom.

10 September. Fine day. The Gov'nor, Charley, THP and Tom up to Cherub's Rock collecting ratas and other native shrubs. THP returned in the afternoon and planted his treasures in the shrubbery. Harry came and left a wether. Seal planting out eschalots and sowing brocoli [sic], cauliflower, seakale, etc. Nurse transplanting currant trees and killing wether in the evening.

17 September. Fine day. THP and Donald at the shrubbery. Jim came up in haste to borrow Emma's saddle for her mother to ride down to Aylmer's as Mrs Aylmer is practising domestic multiplication. Manuka and violets in flower; small green wren or regulus [rifleman?], building in a tei palm [cabbage tree] by the river. Turkey laid yesterday. Peas up that were sown on the 17th ult. Nurse fixing bail stocks etc.

26 September. Wet again in the morning; heavy showers prevailed all day from the South West. THP crop cutting with Nurse in the morning. Sweet briars just appearing, sown last autumn. The river is much higher than it has been for months, and the lagoons are full. We perceive the benefit of the drains as our garden is not suffering in a single place from wet, so although draining was last year a long and very expensive job, I cannot regret the time or cost expended thereon. Cauliflower and brocoli seedlings are coming up very thick. Two pairs of Paradise ducks (putangitangi) have affected our orchard very much lately. Beautiful birds they are, and would be still more welcome were they as quiet as the grey duck (parerei) [pārera] […] one pair of which variety are building near their old nesting place of last year. I saw some beautiful trading [wading?] birds on one of the lagoons last Sunday.

28 September. A fine day, though there was a very thick mist over the Rakaia which reached Rockwood, but did not visit us – it came up towards the Gorge. Seal returned to Rockwood this morning. THP put in plants of thyme, sothernwood [*Artemisia abrotanum*] and a ribes [currant] the Gov'nor sent up yesterday: earthed cabbages etc. After dinner EP and Mabel, Donald and THP went a ramble to find some of the plants of the lovely white flowering clematis. What can be more beautiful than the appearance of those graceful wreaths of snowy white which festoon the topmost boughs of some of the highest trees, spreading its beauties over the dark green foliage in wild profusion, with fantastic elegance, now clinging to the tender sprays of its supporting tree, and anon it droops its spiry garlands to seek some help-mate amongst the strong ones of the wood, and deck his lofty head with her glorious crown; how beautiful is this state of dependance [sic] for she blesses and is blessed. Well, we had a charming walk to the second little bush up the stockyard gully, and the sight only of the waterfall is worth a long walk, as it dashes over the large masses of moss-grown rock, shaded from the glare of day by a gigantic laurel [broadleaf]. How much we should have thought of even that morceau of romantic beauty in England; here almost every gully can show equal claim to admiration. We must at least allow that 'our time has been cast in pleasant places';[5] but we miss the familiar faces of our friends. Jim and Mrs Phillips came, and Mr Richards in the evening. Barley is up, raspberries and cherries in leaf. A cochin pullet laid two eggs today – one in the morning and one in the afternoon. Two Dorking pullets hatched on the 9th April last laid today.

4 October. A fine day. Set the turkey on 12 eggs. THP and Nurse pulling litter. THP to Rockwood in the evening. Several kingfishers have appeared; they seem very much annoyed by the tuis and bell-birds, who constantly follow them in their short and rapid flight from some prominent dead branch to another perhaps 150 yards off, uttering a sharp irritable sort of note quickly repeated at intervals. Remains of small birds have several times been found in specimens shot here. On one occasion one of the boys discovered a dead robin [toutouwai] still warm lying beneath a branch from which a kingfisher had just been disturbed. Tom came up to take care of the children in THP's absence.[6]

12 October. Rain pouring again this morning. Everything wears quite a soaked appearance, in fact we have lately had quantum [...] of wet. Jim's little heifer calved last night in the stable. Set a Dorking hen on 15 eggs. Talking of eggs reminds me

I ought to record the great number laid by the fowls here, quite surpassing my experience of their proflicacy [sic] in England, and I have observed also the fact I have not known one instance in which the period of incubation has not exceeded the usual term by from 24 to 48 hours. Killed another weka this morning; it goes much against my inclination to wage exterminating war against these amusing and confident birds, but they are so partial to fowl's eggs and so persevering in their visits to the nesting places, that one is reduced to the alternatives of weka or eggs – we decide for the latter. They are so familiar (or, rather, were) that they come to the door, enter the house and curiously examine everything about the floor; nothing seems to escape their prying eyes. The brown plumage barred with black at a little distance bears some resemblance to that of the hen pheasant somewhat shorn of its due allowance of tail; but on closer examination the distinctive features of the weka are at once marked; its powerful bill adapted for digging for its food amongst the partially decayed roots of trees, its equally powerful legs and feet, its small weak wings and tail composed of soft, flexible feathers which debar flight; the legs and feet dull red, iris reddish brown. Good eating when stewed. Its oil is much esteemed for various purposes. Of this useful article it yields a large quantity in proportion to its size, which is somewhat less than that of an ordinary hen. The cock bird is the largest and of the brightest colour; the eggs are white spotted with red, about the size of a pullet's. I have found them four in number, the nest placed under the shelter of a thick tussock of high grass, sometimes among a cluster of young birches [native beech], the nest being formed of rough grass and showing but little pains taken with its architecture. Its note when alarmed is a shrill squeak, but generally it sounds something like 'tweedle dee, tweedle dee, tweedle dee', which is sometimes accompanied with a booming noise, but whether this proceeds from the male or female I know not. They appear to breed throughout the year. One that was tamed used to kill rats by securing them with its feet, and driving its wedge-like bill through its victim. When running swiftly it elevates its wings to assist its movements in turning sharply, and frequently jerks its tail upward. EP came up from Rockwood, having sent Ambrose by Nurse, who had been there to fetch a wether [for mutton]. Mr Leach called: gave him an order on Miles for our half of the bullock.

13 October. Rain, rain, rain, when shall we have a change. THP cutting firewood and carrying out some slabs for the fowl house. It is worth while to take a walk in the bush (even though you do get wet through) and notice the lichens with which every tree is most profusely decorated; the late rains and constantly moist atmosphere have brought out in perfection those beautiful parasites. The rugged stems of the lofty birch trees are adorned with these curious vegetable germs of every tint and shade of colour, and of forms as various. A fine starlight night quite refreshing to look at, for from the 22nd September we have had but five tolerably fine days. Nurse said the proposal to live at the cottage would not suit his views, so that matter is ended.

15 October. Another beautiful day. THP after the heifers; found some near the head of the first chasm round the Point, and the others beyond Fighting Hill. Put them all near the Rat Rock. Did not get home till dark, eleven hours on horseback, and came hungry. Saw wild violets [hāka] in bloom; several quail [koreke] – an unwonted [unusual] sight now and when we came here they were quite common, but the great fires have most probably diminished their numbers so rapidly. One piece of burnt ground on Leach's run for some yards was quite blue with the multitude of blue terns [species unclear] closely packed together – a most beautiful sight. Early potatoes up. Nurse at the fowl house.

17 October. At a quarter past one a.m. EP gave birth to a daughter [Clara]. Mother and child are doing well. Mrs P and Mrs R called and Harry in the evening; lent him my telescope to aid his search for the sheep. A very fine day. THP and Donald planted some more potatoes. In the afternoon rodding the fowl-house. Nurse finished slabbing. Set pullet on 13 eggs.

23 October. Fine day. THP on Buxom after the cattle directly after breakfast: brought up most of them to the paddock. Called at Rockwood coming home for a wether and brought it up and a sitting of Spanish and Polish eggs for Harry. Jim and Harry came up. Jim and THP drafting out heifers. Nurse thatching at the cowshed. Set cochin pullet on 15 eggs. Emma walked to the middle paddock to see the heifers. The Paradise ducks do great injury to the peas: today they have devoured the tops to the extent of several yards. Our cat had a family of six at an early hour this morning. A red heifer looks very bad: left her with some others outside the track. THP gave EP Telltale's calf for Wave's bull calf 'Captain'. Tonight Welcome gave extraordinary trouble before she would be bailed up. Yesterday shot a weka minus a leg.

31 October. Rain and heavy mists all day from the South West. THP sowing peas, lettuces, radishes and white stone turnips. In the afternoon the mist gradually thickened. Could not find all the cows and heifers although Nurse and THP searched almost every gully, the latter going over to Leach's side of the Gap. Altogether 8 away, of which three are close to calving. Upon my word, these South Westers are quite enough to try the temper of anyone less patient than Job! Churned 8 lbs.

1 November. Sou'Wester as bad as yesterday, if not worse. What can be the end of it – rain, rain, rain. Everything is soaked, slushy and miserable. Six more heifers gone today, and the mist is so dense it is impossible to find them. His old friend and companion, his meerschaum, is THP's only comforter. Harry came in the evening.

4 November. Sunday. The ground was covered with snow early this morning and we soon had rain as usual, which lasted all day, getting worse towards nightfall. THP and Nurse after the missing cows – went by the Manuka Hill by the calf bush to Mr Phillips' mob on the other side the Washpen creek, thence round the valley to THP's mob on the low hills and across the river through the Gap home. None of the cows to be seen. What a pleasant way of passing the Sabbath! Peculiar to Colonial bush life, I suppose. Tom dined here and afterwards John and Harry and Mr Richards called in the afternoon. Tom ran in to say that Beda had a foal. After a refreshing half-hour with his merschaum THP went out to reconnoitre and sure enough there was Beda below Stony Peak with a stout chestnut foal trotting by her side. The sire is Mr Packard's 'Joe Miller'. A cochin hen commenced hatching today, her time being up on the 30th ult. In the garden at Rockwood considerable damage is said to have been done to apple and currant blossom by weka, tuis, etc. EP seemed more pleased with Beda's foaling than with anything else that has happened since we have been here. Found a yewtick [fernbird] nest today with three young ones. Outside bents of soft coarse grass lined with feathers and wool carelessly placed in a tussock of fine grass at the edge of a wide creek.

5 November. Cold with frequent showers. Nurse and THP resumed the search for the missing cows, the former went to the little bushes and the latter went up the Gap in the direction of Leach's run. On reaching the summit looking at the glorious prospect of range over range of hills intersected by countless valleys at every angle backed by the snowy mountains like our first parents when excluded from Paradise, he felt 'the world was all before him'.[7] After going over the same line of country as on Friday last he returned home without seeing the 'absconded party'. Nurse also came back without having seen the 'ghost of one'.

6 November. Cold, raw, misty and showery and as THP feels rather tired about the legs, he intends jobbing about the garden by way of a rest with the full purpose of making a long circuit tomorrow for the lost cows. The heifers and young cows I can forgive for wandering, but why that quiet demure old cow Wave, should take it into her head to travel I am quite at a loss to understand. She has seen the world both in England and here, and was not the voyage hither (boxed up in a little case like some unfortunate curiosity in a menagerie) a journey long enough to satisfy any cow since the time of their ancestress in the ark? Nurse cutting wood. THP earthing up early American potatoes, hoeing onion, parsnips, etc, clearing strawberries, sowing sweet-peas, planting out cauliflowers and brocoli, training currant bushes. Also trying to shoot the Paradise ducks which infest the garden, but after walking up the river continued to miss them.

10 November. This morning we saw some blue sky and the sun broke out quite cheerfully. Mystery had a fine light roan bull calf. Cox fetching up his load. Nurse assisting with the bullock. THP getting litter for the calf-pen. Besides sugar and other sundries, the dray brought 19 hundred [...] of flour, four of which Mr Phillips borrowed. Found a Dorking pullet sitting up in the bush on 9 eggs. The cows have, fortunately, regained their usual quota of milk. The job of milking is most disgusting from the extreme filthiness of the yards, and which the weather has precluded any attempt at improving. Literally up to the knees in thick sticky muck, and as several of the milkers don't condescend to enter the bails till they have been pursued round the yard half a dozen times with a long pole, their coyness is anathematised till every known curse is worn threadbare by constant repetition. What a contrast to old times at home [England] where Charles, whose placidity was only equalled by his cows', went through his lactatory duties innocent of bails and leg-ropes and took the foaming buckets to the dairy almost as clean himself as his spotless pails; where the petted favourites, when you strolled about the garden, followed you with wistful eyes in hopes of a treat of cabbage leaves; here go to see the cattle and most likely at first sight of you they trot off, change the pace for a gallop and go perhaps two or three miles, only stopping when quite out of breath, leaving you, if on foot, ample time to reflect on England where 'The lowing herd winds slowly o'er the lea',[8] and at close quarters in a stockyard the way in which these playful creatures knock and kick you about in spite of your activity is, as the Yankees say, 'a caution to see', and only duly to be appreciated by those who have felt it.

12 November. Peas in bloom. Lovely weather – fine refreshing breezes and glorious sunshine. Emma went to Christchurch by Cox's dray to seek a servant as the Nurses leave this morning. She took the baby with her, and left Mabel at Rockwood. The dray left at an early hour, and EP, the Nurses and their luggage, Cox and his boy altogether made up a good load. Mr R called and Henry brought home four cows and heifers, one of them (Daystar) with a white calf. Now we shall have an opportunity of trying what the life of a colonist really is having to work with our own hands for everything that is done, and nothing very dreadful, nothing so very discouraging appears to depress us in the fact of our living thus entirely alone, but on the other hand we have certainly the comforting reflection that we no longer pay most exorbitant wages for most ungracious and unwilling service. Now for instance, we paid the Nurses £70 per annum and their living at the rate provisions cost would cause an equal outlay. Now the man was never satisfied: at whatever work he employed himself you were certain to hear him grumbling; his wife certainly was by many degrees his better half, but her time was mostly occupied in attending to their own matters, so that my wife in reality received but little assistance from her, although of course, having a man and his wife sounds well, as an absolutely necessary appendage to a station. Harry was quite a propos in his arrival today as EP's departure was so suddenly arranged that I must confess to feeling somewhat bewildered when contemplating the various duties and household cares devolving on me. In the first place there were seven cows to milk, calves to feed, pig also, and the poultry, then bringing down the milk, and seeing about breakfast. Upon dressing the children found Geoffrey with a black eye and a bad cut on the same unfortunate optic. Harry set to work, baked the bread, roasted a leg of mutton, baked a pudding, washed up the cups and dishes, scalded the tins etc, and helped to milk in the evening, and as we had a very heavy thunderstorm came down and put the children to bed, so that today I have got on quite comfortably, and 'tomorrow is a new day'. Georgy came up and took tea here. The children and I had our dinner al fresco on the bank, which pleased us all very much. Potatoes up planted on 16th October.

19 November. THP at daybreak fetched the cows and commenced the day by running a pitchfork into his side against one of his ribs. After breakfast availed himself of Mr Richards' kind offer of taking care of the children for the day, and then THP took Mischief with Fashion's calf, Darling and Earl and left them by the Washpen creek on the flat, then across to Rat Rock to one of the heifer mobs; found Comet, Cheerful, Mushroom and Rapture had calved. Captain and Cherry looking very well. Then close to the Point to another mob and found Elfin, Sandfly, Bounty, Spot and Logic had calved. Thence back to Rockwood; dined there. Both Mr and Mrs Phillips seemed rather out of spirits about the wind which was very strong indeed, hard work really to walk against it. Brought home the cows and then to the Richards' for the three boys who were said to have behaved very well. Fine day. Seal left directly after breakfast. The wind has made sad work with some of our pans of milk, but we must not grumble after taking a peep at the Rockwood dairy, where those disgusting blow-flies seem to luxuriate. We were glad when bed-time came round again. About 10 o'clock it set in to rain.

20 November. Wet – very wet. Mystery's calf looked very dull. Churned and stored 13 lbs. In the evening was glad to see Jim on Buxom coming over the Gap. He brought a letter from Mr Hunt dated 2nd July last. In the river-bed he saw that Amber, Lightfoot and Ruby had calved, and Madcap at Cordey's, where also were some of HP's and THP's weaned stock. The account sales of the cattle he took down to Christchurch exhibited a very unremunerative return, I am sorry to say – little more than their cost 17 months ago, without deducting commissions and other expenses. So great a fall has taken place in this settlement in the value of stock. Emma is to return via Aylmers', as Mr S Percival has very kindly arranged to bring her up that far on her way. Today the weather has been miserably wet, but now at night the stars are shining brightly, and there is a prospect of a fine day tomorrow. Seal came in the evening – brought a forequarter of a sheep and Vic's puppy, whose howling is at present almost incessant, and added to the moreporks and the roaring of the river, completes a most unmelodious lullaby. My ancient pedagogue was wont to say that all natural sounds were sweet and beautiful, and if that revered Dominie has not yet 'shuffled off his mortal coil' I think a night of this rough music would change his ideas on the subject. I wonder if his proneness to inflict corporal punishment was at all influenced by any partiality to hear our 'pipes clear and shrill'.

21 November. Got milking over early as possible in order to have a long day with the cattle. Jim left after breakfast, and Seal also. Troubled Mrs Richards with the boys again. Lent Mr R Buxom to fetch his cows in with, and then started over the Gap to the river-bed to get in Amber and Ruby, but as they had planted their calves and could not find them, left them and crossed the river-bed and low hills where found Vampire with a nice red and white calf. With much trouble took her to the calf mob by the Pyramid and left her there: went to other mobs. At last came home quite wearied and footsore, did not finish work till candlelight, and then turned in. Saw Mr J Studholm [John Studholme], his dray and his sheep which are brought up, I believe for washing. Fetched the children from the [...] and took tea there before milking time. Fine day. Jim borrowed the cart.

23 November. THP's birthday. He was obliged to lie down directly after milking, and got up to fetch the cows. Mr R came and helped to milk. Georgey came for some tea. Seal came in the evening and hoed up some of the beds in the kitchen garden. We have had a perfect blaze of sunshine today. THP's throat and rheumatism are less troublesome tonight. The day before yesterday Mystery partially shaved THP by poking her horns in his throat and carrying off beard enough to fill a pincushion – an unusual method of operating and to be avoided as decidedly unpleasant. Heard that most probably Emma will return on Sunday with the Aylmers.

2 December. Sunday. Misty early this morning, but turned out a fine hot day. Madcap had gone back in the night with the two heifers and six yearlings. Jim, who slept here last night, helped THP to milk and bail up Amber and after putting most of the yearlings together on the hill near Long Bush, went off with some cattle to the herds; over the Gap and across the river to the lagoons, out to the Woolshed flat almost to the Point. Brought up Columbine and calf. Spot (HP's) to calve, and some yearlings. THP bailed up Columbine. Madcap back at night, tethered her calf and yarded her. Tom and Jim dined here. Saw some large dragonflies. The manuka is now beginning to look extremely beautiful, it being almost everywhere in full bloom. The green beetle which last year at this time and for two months later almost covered the manuka has again appeared. Terns are setting on five eggs. Rhododendron in flower. Mr and Mrs Phillips came in the afternoon.

11 December. Fine with now and then a smart shower. THP storing butter, fetching down the horses and headed back the cows with calves, taking down the partition in the kitchen and clearing away rubbish. Up the hills again after milking looking to the calves. A most glorious sunset – a scene far too glorious for description. Who could help feeling thankful for the blessing of sight who witnessed the wondrous beauties of the sun's departure this evening?

19 December. Fine day. THP earthing up potatoes. Shot a pigeon and some kakas. EP moved the chickens to Seal's old warri, as they are becoming quite a nuisance here from their predacious habits. Mrs P for tea. In the evening went fishing, caught enough for a fry for supper. Strong Nor'Wester set in at evening.

22 December. Fine day. The sow did a great deal of mischief last night, quite spoiling our crop of early potatoes not leaving one row untouched; killed a cochin hen and a pullet and six chickens including the only Poland. Mr Phillips coming back from eeling saw the potato piece [patch] and sent Seal up, who killed the brute. Jim came up with some calves. In the afternoon Seal hoeing potatoes and afterwards with THP to fetch half the sow. Cut up, skinned and salted it. Seal left at night. Very warm.

23 December. Sunday. Fine day. Harry and Charley dined here (strawberry cream amongst other good things) for dinner. In the evening Mr and Mrs Phillips came up for an hour or two. Kakas very noisy tonight.

25 December. Christmas Day. Rain pouring down all day. The idea of wishing anyone a Merry Christmas seems too ridiculous – the thought altogether is extravagently absurd to us new settlers, and can we help feeling something like a pang of regret for the good old times and customs of home; but, however sad the recurrence of this National holiday would make us, we must not look back. We have changed summer for winter, we have fragrant nosegays and clusters of roses for the holly and mistletoe, but old associations, which 'busy meddling memory musters up'[9] makes the exchange a bitter one. We cling to dear old England still. Jim breakfasted here. We were to have dined at Rockwood, but the weather was too wet, so we went down after dinner and spent a pleasant evening.

1856

2 January. Fine day, warm and rather cloudy. THP turned away Fashion and two calves, and walked to the cattle. Found most of them on the burnt feed on the plains beyond the Gunyah. Called at Rockwood coming home. It is amusing to notice the efforts of Paradise ducks (both male and female) to divert attention from their young ones, feigning lameness and incapacity of flight, only just flapping their wings in the shallow river a few yards distant, till you have passed the lurking places of their offspring: then, their fears at an end, they give a loud call or two, stretch out their powerful wings, and soar high above you in triumphant circles, evidently delighted with their strategem [sic]. Some of the fowls almost get their entire living by devouring the manuka beetle, whose beautiful green ornaments at this time the manuka in great numbers, shining in the sun like glistening emeralds. At Rockwood they were very busy preparing for the shearing, which they expect to commence on Friday next. Saw in the river-bed numerous specimens of a butterfly, resembling one of the English frittilaries. The cuckoos have just made their appearance again.

3 January. Beautiful day. Churning 19 lbs, stored 15 lbs. The cows away. THP on Buxom after them. Found them 12 miles down the river-bed. Gave them a good warming home. Geoffrey poisoned himself by eating tutu berries. Gave him copious draughts of warm mustard and water, milk and oil, and kept him awake for several hours. Mrs Phillips came up and stayed the night. Charley and Tom came and hoed the potatoes.

8 January. Rain, hail and very cold. Charley came up. Killed two couple of fowls. A weka killed a cock Spanish chicken, above seven weeks old at two blows. Sowed lettuce and radish seeds.

26 January. Fine day. THP in the garden. The boys weeding. In the afternoon we all went up Rocky Hill to see the ratas and gather some of its flowers. It is a most beautiful shrub, its shape generally so compact, and the glowing scarlet blossoms almost concealing its dark green leaves, contrasts most happily with grey rocks amongst the clefts of which it seems to delight. Rain in the evening.

29 January. Mr Richards, Jim, Tom and Charley came up to assist in branding the calves. The weather was unfavourable as it poured with rain. Branded Captain (18) and the heifer calves of the following cows:– Telltale (17), Welcome (19), Fashion (20), Daystar (26), Elfin (28), Mushroom (29), Bounty (31), Sandfly (34), Lightfoot (38), Vampire (40), Silverheels (41), Watchful (42), Pastime (46), Trifle (48), Dahlia (49), Strawberry (50), Playful (51), Comfort (52), Actress (56), Nonsense (61). Branded bull calves of the following cows:– Rainbow (24), Mystery (25), Rapture (32), Spot (33), Comet (35), Amber (36), Madcap (37), Ruby (39), Vanish (43), Fidget (44), Bridesmaid (45), Junket (54), Harebell (55), Eyebright (57), Signal (58), Sobersides (59), Nickname (60), Mistletoe (62), Vivid (63). Branded altogether 40 on the nearside. The calves of Gala and Cottager only cut, being too small to brand, and three calves got away. Finished just about dusk. Very dirty work and what with kicks and rolling over and over in the mud, rough work too. A good job it's over. Yesterday Mr Tripp, Lieutenant Wilson and Mr Acland called. The latter to have the census paper filled up, which was done accordingly. Jim brought with him [...]. The calves all look well and Captain bids fair to make a fine bull. Told Jim he should have Tomboy's calf if he saw after the other two calves joining the mob all right.

20 February. Fine day – very hot. After dinner THP and Donald after the mares, but could not find them. Saw two yearling heifers (Cherry's and Truant's). Visited the gold digger's hut, and saw several of their unsuccessful speculations in the shape of deep holes. The plant we call Riband wood [ribbonwood] is now in full flower. We brought home beautiful clusters of bloom. Charley came.

25 February. Wet. In the afternoon THP with Georgey and Donald up the river gathering corninni [kōnini] berries, and then out of the bush up the hill for chuckiechucks [snowberries] for jam. Charley came up. Georgey slept here.

15 March. Jim, Charley and THP on horseback after the cattle. Took the puppy Rata with us. Near the Gap found Hartshorn's lost calf that got away hobbled on the 29th January. It was at its last gasp. Took it some gruel, but it died almost directly. Did not count the cattle, but there were 52 calves in the mob, including Beeswing's bull calf. One cow (Eyebright) got completely bogged and was got out with some trouble, having almost to lie down to get hold of her horns. The way poor puppy was treated by the cattle was certainly enough to deter him from cattle driving by choice, as we had continually to rescue him from being gored. In his fright he usually ran under the horses and got frequently trampled upon. Donald was with us and rode Buxom quite fearlessly. A large hawk followed the poor weary puppy quite a mile, hovering close over him, and making swoops close to him, although he was but a few yards in our rear. A very fine day.

2 April. We have been married six years today. Very fine, hot day. THP on Buxom to the cattle to fetch up the young bull, Captain, and Cherry. Called at Rockwood on the way. Found the cattle out on the plains beyond the Gunyah hills. Brought the two up and put them in the Rockwood stockyard. Called in and walked home at dusk. EP went down and dined there, returning in the afternoon. The children all went down in the Bull Bush to play and brought home some kindling. THP hopes if EP notices the next few lines[10] she will look over the perpetration in more senses than one. I don't think cattle driving is very favourable to the Muse.

3 April. Fine day. All of us busy getting firewood. Jim called at cow time and took home the large rake, as they have begun harvesting at Rockwood. John came up this morning. Heavy Nor'wester increasing in violence at night. The moon early this morning presented a most peculiar appearance. The cat brought in a rat for her kitten, which measured 18½ inches from end of the nose to the tip of the tail. A very large fire appears amongst the hills near the Ashburton. The children are now dipped in the river every morning, and all the better they look for it. Digging self-sown early potatoes.

13 April. Sunday. Fine day. THP to Rockwood in the morning. Charley dined here. In the afternoon saw some riders coming up the track. They proved to be the Rev W Willock accompanied by Mr Macfarlane, whose attentions and company were necessary to the 'Iron Priest' in consequence of a severe fall from his horse. This long expected (and by the female portion of the valley anxiously longed for) arrival put us quiet folks on the qui vive, and now there seems some chance of the christenings taking place – 'better late than never'. Seal was immediately despatched on Buxom to the Rakaia to warn Mr Studholm and Harry their presence would be required tomorrow. In about an hour's time Mr Studholm arrived having met Seal on his way. In the meantime John came over here and fetched Emma. After Mr Studholm's arrival some little time Mr Aylmer came in sight, so that there's a large party at Rockwood as Mr A's man arrived yesterday. EP and THP returned home by daylight. Very warm and close. Emma was rather faint, and after standing by the door a few minutes, dropped, her head just missing the rock outside the door. A little cold water, sal volatile and the cool air down the gully soon revived her. Poor Donald was quite miserable.

14 April. A Sou'Wester. Georgey came up to take care of the children. THP and EP with the two little girls went down to Rockwood. Eliza went on before. Mrs R's little girl having arrived, they were all christened by the Rev W W Willock, Mabel's sponsors being her Uncle Harry, Jane Howlins and Elizabeth Bethel. Clara's were Mr John Studholm, Mrs Wyld and Mrs Dutton. All passed off well. We staid [sic] at Rockwood all night. Eliza and Mabel returning here in the afternoon.

16 April. Fine day, North West wind. THP, Mr Studholm, John and Harry all left Rockwood on a walking expedition to the West Coast. EP with Clara and Jim returned home in the afternoon.[11] Packed Studholm's horse with some of our traps and walked over the hills to Leach's. Found he was very busy sheep dipping, and consequently unable to join us. We had a good dinner and at night spread out our blankets and slept on the floor.

17 April. We borrowed some flour of Leach and set off for Norris's station, crossing the Acheron about a quarter of a mile below the forks and soon reached the tent which we had seen for some time. Had some cold meat and tea, and marched towards the Lake [Coleridge], leaving Studholm's horse with Norris's. On our way we met Norris who showed us a gully which led directly to the Lake, and after a smart walk came in sight of it. We kept the Northern shore close to the water's edge, and having to ascend the mountain constantly, we found the walking exceedingly rough, and difficult, having frequently to climb with our hands, and now and then so encumbered with bushes and briars that we were compelled to cut our way through with our knives, whilst wild Irishmen [matagouri] and Spaniard grass [*Aciphylla*] paid such attentions to our legs as we would willingly have spurned. After walking till near sundown before we could find a spot sufficiently level to spread our blankets, we camped on the beach close to the water, which broke in gentle ripples close to our feet. We were well sheltered by the thick foliage of some gigantic laurels. A cheerful fire and hearty supper soon made us comfortable enough. John, who carried the tea, reported the loss of the greater portion of it, so that we shall have to use the utmost economy to eke out our scanty stock. Fresh North West wind all day.

18 April. Beautiful day. The lake as placid as a mirror, and the walking far easier than yesterday. We soon reached the peninsula. On the occasion half a pannikin of grog was served out amongst us. Came on fresh pig tracks. Saw some wild dog tracks. Crossed a small stream and camped for an hour on the side of the long low point. After walking on a level beach for some distance the ground became much more rugged in character, the mountains again ascending abruptly from the lake which was now beautifully fringed with splendid specimens of the rata, shooteye [?], ghoi [kōwhai] and the broad leaved laurel. Shot some pigeons for supper and camped close to the head of the Lake under the shelter of some tall tei palms. At night the eel lines were set and three fine eels secured, about 10 lbs each.

19 April. One of the eels more than supplied us with breakfast. The morning was beautifully fine with a fresh North West. On leaving the head of the Lake came on a flat which we found to be about two miles in breadth, much encumbered with Irishmen we now had to cross a wide river bed [the Harper], through which flowed two considerable streams joining the Rakaia from the North. We now steered up the Rakaia [Wilberforce] bed,[12] crossing a swamp which we found boggy. We crossed several streams on our way camping for an hour about noon, keeping as much on the moss-covered stones as we could for the Irishmen here were of a size and thickness as almost to be impenetrable. The scenery was magnificent and romantic in the extreme. The lofty mountains capped with snow, whilst their craggy sides and rocky pinnacles were mingled and relieved with shrubs and trees frequently descending in thick woods to the river-bed. We crossed the Rakaia to one of these large bushes, shooting some pigeons, etc, for supper, and camped on the bank of a wide river-bed which joins the Rakaia from the West. We found water there in a very small stream amongst the shingle. We soon had a roaring fire amongst the trees close to our blankets, and as the weather seemed rather unsettled cut out some poles and laid them across the boughs that arched over our bed. The pigeons were cooked, tea made and after thoroughly enjoying a pipe of the fragrant [...] we turned in pretty well tired.

20 April. Sunday. Early this morning the rain fell smartly, so we jumped up and huddled on our clothes, took one of the blankets and stretched it over the boughs above us to make some shelter which was but indifferent, so we had to sweat it out till daylight. After breakfast we fixed the rods, collected thatch and spreading two blankets, made a comfortable snug hut. Strong gusts of wind and rain all day. The river where we could scarce find water now flows in a torrent of immense volume, rattling over its stony bed with tremendous din. We walked out and looked about. Our river as far as we went presented to the view one continued wood principally of which [sic] birch. In the bush we found wide open glades at intervals, almost denuded of undergrowth. The trees were very thickly encrusted with moss and lichens – very beautiful, but as we thought, evident signs of the humidity of the climate. We saw wattle birds [kōkako] and obtained some specimens. Also canaries [mohua], but were chary of using powder and shot. We amused ourselves with carving our initials on a tree close to our camp, with the date of our arrival here. We turned in soon after sundown rather damped in spirit by remembering we were prisoners fast kept by the Rakaia, whose torrent sounded like thunder as we lay on our cozy bed, for so we might deem it contrasted with the wet grass of last night. Rain at night.

21 April. It pours with rain so we are to keep in our blankets as long as we can to save increasing our appetites, which would be rather inconvenient just now. Agreed our meals are to be two daily as there appears no chance of crossing the river for some time. We had a moderate slice of damper for breakfast and supper. Rain all day. A good deal more snow in the mountains than when we arrived. Singing and telling stories enlivened our hours in the camp.

22 April. Very wet, but weather seems breaking. All very hungry. Ate our specimen wattle birds and found them remarkably tough and bitter, but decidedly better than nothing. After noon a marked difference in the appearance of the sky – soon after the sun broke through. Some birds began flying about, and we got some pigeons and kakas. Made up a roaring fire, dried our things, found the water in our river subsiding and we passed quite a cheerful evening. A fine night the moon shining most brilliantly and giving a charm to the picturesque scenery not easily to be forgotten.

23 April. Fine morning. Went about the bush and shot kakas enough for today and tomorrow having 16 hanging up. These birds are exceedingly fat, and excellent in flavour. After getting our firewood for tonight, we all set out for a walk in the Rakaia bed. The waterfalls were very numerous and from the late rains were most imposing. One particularly attracted our attention and we scrambled through a lovely glen thickly green with majestic laurels woven with the whiplike stems of the clematis. The water descended in one unbroken fall of at least 500 feet. Leaving this, we continued our course till we arrived opposite a mountain of no very great elevation, that stands as it were in the river-bed. It presents somewhat of the form of a depressed cone. This we named Sebastopol.[13] Here the Rakaia [Wilberforce] is divided into five branches, whose sources could not be far distant judging from the size of the streams and the height of the mountains. Of these branches the one bearing to the West is the largest, and at a comfortable elevation on the mountain round which it turns is a boiling spring, which throws up its vapour to the height of about 30 feet. On looking down the narrow valley through which the centre stream flows, there appears to be a pass [Browning Pass] at a very considerable elevation (about 3000 feet), but this could not be ascertained as a fact in consequence of the sudden clouds and mists that were continually enveloping the mountain summits. On arriving at the camp found the water in our river-bed had subsided considerably. In the afternoon heavy squalls of rain again descended, frustrating our plans of attempting to cross tomorrow. The rain continued falling all night and it was exceedingly cold.

24 April. Early this morning the rain cleared off, the day improving in appearance as the sun got higher. We walked about all day, everyone finding something to engage his attention, whether it was a beautiful landscape seen from a fresh point of view, new shrubs and plants and fragments of stone from the shingly river-bed. It froze sharply. The river is going down, so we are determined to attempt the Rakaia [Wilberforce] tomorrow. Baked our last lot of flour.

25 April. Got up at sunrise and having despatched our breakfast in more haste than usual packed our traps and started off down the Rakaia [Wilberforce]. Made in the first instance for a place inspected yesterday, but found it impassable, so we walked down the river trying several places, and crossing many streams, in numerous instances crossing water nearly up to our middles and then finding the next stream unfordable. This we continued doing for 8 or 9 miles, our legs getting very numb as it was freezing in the shade and a strong North West blowing off the snow numbed our hands completely. After many fruitless essays we got safely across, gave three cheers and took a good pull at the rum which we had carefully saved for the occasion. We directed our course North of Lake Coleridge to visit another lake [Lake Selfe] which had been observed yesterday. After much rough walking through many gullies reached the lake which we guessed is about two miles long, and about half a mile broad. We chose a beautiful place for our camp in [a] thick cluster of trees and shrubs on the shore of the lake on which were frolicking scores of wildfowl. At night we set the eel lines and caught a beauty about 20 lbs in weight, serving for supper and leaving then the largest portion for breakfast tomorrow. Frost at night.

26 April. After a hearty breakfast of frizzled eel, started about half past ten and came in sight of a long reedy lagoon or lake [Lake Evelyn?] from which we steered so as to make the Lake Coleridge peninsula. On our way fell in with a mob of fine pigs, among which were two very large boars, some sows heavy in pig, and a lot of suckers. Soon secured one of the latter, which we carried on with us to a creek, and furnished a capital dinner after which we walked on rapidly, and getting on a cattle track we reached Norris's station just at sundown. Had a good supper and spread our blankets in his warri, which is not yet roofed in. A sharp frost. Colder tonight than we have been since we set out as we missed our splendid fires.

27 April. Sunday. After breakfast, Studholm packed his horse and set out for Rockwood round the point. Harry went strait [sic] across, and John and THP called at Leach's and got home over the hills a little before sundown, having spent a very pleasant time during our trip. Almost the only untoward circumstance was Harry breaking THP's gun yesterday. Memo. After leaving Lake Coleridge on the 19th saw no tei palms and very little flax till the afternoon of the 25th.

17 May. Very cold this morning. The children did not relish slipping about over the frozen snow stark naked to have their morning dip. Cold thaw about 10 o'clock, and everything rather slippery out of doors. THP up the hills to look for Elfin's calf, but could not find it. EP very busy baking. Sharp frost at night.

24 May. Some rain last night. Dull morning. THP to Richards'. Nailing up slats. After dinner cutting 40 poles and taking some out of the bush. Mr R in the morning with James Cordey to the dray which was fast in the Washpen creek. Donald and Eliza to Rockwood to fetch parcels, etc. Mr Norris there. That lucky fellow has just had £17000 left him unexpectedly. Killed a fowl.

26 May. Wet and snowy and drizzling rain all day. Mr R came up in the morning. No out of door work today. THP when at Rockwood being asked frequently to sing and as the songs are becoming stale that he knows, has written one today giving an outline of a stockman's duties and introducing the language used by the craft as far as practicable.

1 June. Very fine day. Freezing in the shade. Charley dined here. Axe broken handle. Wood all burnt. Room smoked. THP out of temper and everything very uncomfortable. Frost very sharp at night.

15 June. Sunday. Dull morning – everything very wet. Memo. Donald this morning wore a pair of short drawers or trousers for the first time, and is apparently much pleased with this addition to his costume. Seal came up and EP and baby and THP returned to Rockwood with him. Frost at night.

16 June. Fine day. An excursion to the Gorge of the Rakaia was proposed – the party comprised the Gov'nor, Mr Stoddart, THP, John and Charley. Polly carrying our blankets and provisions. By the side of Terrible Billy swamp found a heifer of Jim's very bad with a dead calf. Got to Watt's cottage about two o'clock. Went down the bank to the water and saw lots of grey ducks, pigeons, etc. Spent a cozy evening – pigeon and quail roasted for supper. Rain at night.

17 June. Rain and snow made our residence rather damp as the ridge had been blown off. Found a fine eel on one line of very light colour. Saw lots of grey ducks, teal, blue duck and another variety, the drake coloured much like the English mallard. Polly went off last night, so we shall have to hump our blankets etc home. Made a hasty meal of a stew concocted by THP composed of fish, flesh and fowl and divers [sic] savoury vegetables. As the grog was absorbed this morning, it became necessary in the opinion of the seniors of the party that we should return home, so parked our things and set off accordingly. Near Fighting Hill THP saw a large mob of his cattle, so took to his heels and rounded them up (amongst them was old Polly). After considerable exertion and much perspiration expended (as blankets are cumbersome) got the mob in travelling order and drove them along Leach's track to this side of Laurel Gully – a good way. Charley came up then and we drove to the Pyramid and left them. The rest of the party being considerably in advance, THP and Charley came home by the swamp and reached Rockwood first. We were all very wet as the rain poured down heavily the whole way. Slight frost at night.

23 June. Fine day. THP at work at Mr R's cobbing partitions, etc. Mr Aylmer called and brought an English letter (from Mr Hunt) which much disappointed us, not containing the remittances promised. Harry spent the evening with us and brought up a sack of flour. Jim's heifer died yesterday.

25 June. Fine day. THP same as yesterday. Governor requested him to take home his dog, Rata, as he caused him to suffer severely from fleas last night. Rata's name to be changed to '<u>Fleabite</u>'.

28 June. Weather as fine as ever – sharp frost last night. Jim and THP on horseback to the cattle. Found them in several mobs down the river-bed, and away out on the plains. Sprightly has calved, but her maternal solicitude induced her to conceal her offspring so effectually that we were unable to discover it. THP and Jim today resolved to see the world or at any rate take a peep at what lies beyond our range of hills, so we purpose an excursion Westward Ho!, over the country visited by the Rockwood party on the 19th, 25th and 26th of April last. We may have luck to find there a little grazing land for cattle. Now we must do this thing quietly or we shall be brought before the Council of Rockwood and have our ears dinned unmercifully with pros and cons. So we leave ostensibly for Leach's to seek for cattle astray, and we mean to use the opportunity by going a little further, Jim to bring sugar, matches, pannikin and chocolate and his blankets. THP to take billhook, fatcake, flour, tea, etc. It will be cold work camping out. We have no grog and can't ask for any, as it would be something unusual for THP to want anything of that sort. Hard frost last night.

[c. 29 June.][14] We crossed to Leach's river-bed by the Copper Cliff, and when [sic] towards the Gorge by the house. Saw a fine gay bittern from a small swamp close to us. After passing the flat in front of Leach's house, went down the Gully on the track that leads to the Acheron, here we soon realised the truth of the adage 'the longest way is the shortest way', for thinking to make a short cut we missed the cattle track altogether and found ourselves threading our dubious way amongst the numerous gullies that lead to one branch or other of the Acheron. This took up so much time that instead of making the shore of the Lake Coleridge, our camping place as intended we stopped at the Pason in the bed a little below the forks. Made a comfortable bed of shrubs and grass, having made a glorious pile of logs of drift wood, we were soon asleep. Frost very sharp.

[c. 30 June.] On waking this morning (Tuesday) found our blankets hard frozen and boots also. Got off by sunrise, and across part of Norris's run to the gully which leads to the Lake. Saw a mob of sheep on Barker's run, and nothing worth taking note of except quail, till we came to the country which joins the peninsula divided by a narrow swift river, and about two o'clock came in sight of the little gem of a lake where we intended to camp. We found a good supply of firewood along the rocky beach. After supper we set eel lines and then having had a quiet pipe by the fire, we went to visit our lines. This was dreadfully cold work, as the lake was half frozen over and we had to wade along shore knee deep to likely looking places, and after all we were unsuccessful. After another visit we turned in, as we purposed on Wednesday having a walk to the end of the run.

[c. 1 July.] The next morning Jim fetched a stock of firewood from the bush and THP baked and then we kept along the Southern shore of the Lake which was lively with the evolutions of hundreds of wildfowl, amongst which were a pair or two of the great crested grebe. We walked on to the [Harper] river which, flowing from the North, joins the Northern branch of the Rakaia; crossing this, we kept down the river-bed till abreast of the flat which lies at the head of Lake Coleridge. We observed several wild dog tracks on the sand of the river-bed. We now waded through the river again and visited the flat and returned to our camp, by ascending the corner of the hill which divides the two lakes and descending the Northern side. On our return we made a snug tent of some flat stalks and a blanket and very cozy we were, although the frost was so severe that our boots placed by the fire had one side quite hot and the other coated with ice.

[c. 2 July.] On Thursday morning we broke up our camp and ascended a low gap between the hills on the North side. The country here was very rugged and full of gullies. We observed a tarn towards the river from the North and kept our course so as to skirt one of the round hills that lies back abreast of the peninsula on Lake Coleridge. We crossed a rapid river which flows into the lake, and which is here bounded by precipitous rocks fringed with bush. We made our camp in a sheltered nook in one of the bays East of the peninsula, the trees being very large. We baked tonight and set eel lines again without success. We made our supper of weka, kaka and quail, which the dog caught.

[c. 3–5 July.] On Friday we walked to the little peninsula. This small rock is covered with manuka, rata and laurels, all of which grow to great size. Here we found the surveyors' camping place, and in a thicket of manuka the old Maori hut and several large eel traps, flax ropes, etc. Returning we put up a fine sow and two pigs but were careful not to molest her, as they may come in very handy some day, and wild pigs are now exceedingly scarce. I ought to record we saw numerous wild dog tracks yesterday. We now put on our best pace and walked to Leach's flat by sundown. Here we saw Phillips who advised us to stay as it would be dark, but we pushed on till when we arrived at the Copper Cliff. It was quite dark and we were evidently out of our road on the hills, so we crept down a slope to the creek at the bottom of the gully and after groping about the creek found a few twigs and bits of tutu, so that with some fern leaves we made our pannikins boil and had chocolate. We rolled ourselves up in our blankets and crept into some high tussocks of grass and enjoyed a few hours' sound sleep. When THP woke up it was so light it appeared near daybreak, so we roused up and walked home, arriving here soon after two a.m. On Saturday we were both highly pleased with our trip and THP most anxious to secure the run.

5 July. Between two and three o'clock this morning THP and Jim returned here, having camped in the Copper Cliff last night, being so dark they were unable to find their way over the hills. After breakfast, THP transplanting and making cuttings of different shrubs. Jim went home and Billy came for us to go down to Rockwood as Sir William Congreve was there. Killed a couple of chickens and took them with us. EP covered a cap for the Governor, and THP assisted him in planning his orchard. Home to tea, and THP began writing his diary of the past week.

6 July. Sunday. Fine day. Seal came up to dinner, after which THP walked to Rockwood to see the Governor, taking Donald with him. THP communicated to the Governor the experience and result of the excursion, begging him at the same time to keep the matter secret, and Mr Phillips behaved like a brick and promised most kindly his assistance in securing the run, so it was arranged that THP should accompany him and Sir William Congreve to Christchurch on Tuesday next.

18 July. Frost – fine day. At tea time in rushed THP [on his return from Christchurch] and nearly frightened us all into fits by his sudden appearance, so after tea we sat around the fire while THP recounted his adventures and detailed Christchurch news and gossip. They had been detained by the weather at Cordy's till Monday afternoon and then got as far as Macfarlane's station, where they stopped that night. The next morning a messenger from Dr Donald, the Coroner, summoned them to attend an inquest on the body of a poor fellow found perished from cold on the Desert Run, so they rode to the body which was supposed to be a man not very favourably known as 'Crankey Bill', but as this was not certain further proceedings were deferred till the body could be brought to Christchurch, to be identified. After this delay, Dr Donald, the Governor, Sir William and THP rode into Christchurch which they did not reach until dark. They called on Mrs Miles and found Freddy very ill. The next morning attended the examination of a bushranger called Ronnage, whose feats during the few days previous had thrown the quiet folks of Christchurch into a state of great excitement. The Court was so crowded that the examination had to be adjourned to the land office on the basement, for fear the building should give way. The accused, who looked a rufffian, conducted himself with the utmost levity and impudence, occasionally threatening not only witnesses but the members of the Court also. The next day on enquiry and examination at the Land Office, found the country THP wished to apply for was taken up by Mr Davey. The maps were not trustworthy, as many important natural features were omitted and others improperly marked out. Mr Stoddart kindly profferred his assistance in trying to effect a transfer of Davey's claim to THP, who felt wonderfully dull on the occasion, resolving to start home again the next day. So next morning THP mounted Buxom riding straight for Vale Head, only stopping at Cordy's. He got there about a quarter past 5. Mr Cordy told him of a steer found dead in the river-bed having its head and horns entangled in some long tohe-tohe grass [toetoe], from which it had been unable to get free.

23 July. A beautiful morning. Tom and THP went out to bring up cattle – paddocked above 200 head. They all look right well and many of the cows are again heavy in calf. Many of the calves are now of large size and ought to be weaned had we any country which we could turn them on. Here we have no boundaries, oh, that we could but have got my favourite run not only by far the most beautiful country I have seen but also the most eminently useful. Mabel's birthday.

25 July. This morning the ground is thickly covered with snow, and it is snowing heavily. THP walked down to Rockwood and saw Mr Ross and Mr Aylmer and their men having come up for the purpose of obtaining timber, and firewood. As Mr Phillips has purchased a section where they used to cut wood they now pay their visits to the Rabbit Bush, and if this is persevered with will certainly destroy much of the ornamental character of Rockwood, not so much on account of the gap left by the trees they throw, as by the effects of these gaps on the bush remaining. We have had sufficient experience of this both here and at Rockwood.

28 July. As the garden is still covered with snow THP and Donald went shooting, calling at Rockwood. Went to the lagoons and found them frozen over, so laid down the gun and had a jolly slide. Brought home a couple of ducks and some kakas. Appetites rather extensive when we reached home. Geoff's chillblains very bad. We noticed today some beautiful little birds [silvereyes] – green, inclining to reddish on the breast and wings, with golden rings round the eyes. They should be called 'Golden tears'. Ross's horse away.

29 July. Plenty of snow about. Walked down to Rockwood and found the Governor returned and Mr Stoddart with him. The latter told me for my peace of mind that the run I wished to take up would be difficult to get transferred, it being in three different hands, but that there still was a chance for me as it was so remotely situated. Emperor of France has a son.[15] Frost at night.

30 July. Showery, cold and inclining to snow. Managed to fork up a piece of ground, but perhaps it would have been better let alone. At any rate it will give it a sweetening. In the afternoon got wood and made a Rakaia stew of fowls, wild ducks, kakas, etc, including ham and all sorts of vegetables. To Rockwood to spend the evening. Played rubbers and picquet. Sharp frost at night.

31 July. Fine day. THP went to see Mr Richards, and had a conversation with him about his charge for medical attendance. THP told him he really could not afford to continue his annual salary, and Mr R then readily offered that no stipulated sum was to be paid, but should his services be required, a proportionate honorarium should be given him. The Gov'nor wants a beast to be killed to save the sheep, but THP does not think he has one fit; however, he said he would see and purposes going through the mobs tomorrow for that purpose, and also bring up some of the

Gov'nor's down [sic] calves, as they are short of milk and butter. Saw Lucy go away with a full bag. Jim and Sidey came up with the dray, so Rockwood was quite full.

13 August. Very sharp frost last night. Fine day. EP very busy putting things in order. THP putting in the cuttings from Dr Barker: elder, honeysuckle and gooseberries. Forked up some ground and sowed short rows of peas. Cut a drain, etc. Billy here all day. Jim came up to borrow a bullock chain. Lent it to him requesting him at the same time not to break it.

14 August. Fine. Getting up carrots for jam. THP forking up ground and sowing onions. Billy here till the afternoon. Killed a fowl and some kakas. For the last six weeks kakas have appeared in blocks at almost every station round this neighbourhood.

15 August. Fine. Preparing ground and sowing carrots. Harry came at dinner time, and brought some letters. One from Mr Hunt, and also one from Fredk Catling. The former enclosing a remittance on the bank for £500. As we are very hard up it comes exceedingly welcome. THP with Harry to Rockwood to sleep there.

24 August. Sunday. Showers of rain and sleet. Seal slept here last night, and went to Rockwood this morning for flour and beef, as we are entirely without provisions, which is exceedingly inconvenient. We supplied Rockwood with flour for some months from our share and if we want any we must fetch it. Equal difficulty prevails as to mutton of which, by-the-bye, Mrs Phillips invariably keeps our share of the fat as well as her own, so we have to use the utmost economy in the consumption of candles. Memo: 28 lbs flour, 8½ lbs beef. First sowing of peas has just appeared. Fine drying wind about noon. Seal left in the evening.

25 August. Fine morning, slight frost last night. Wind fresh from Nor'West. THP, Donald and Ambrose in the garden planting potatoes, sowing peas, etc and planting out sweet briars in the shrubbery. Killed two fowls and also two cats and quite time to do so, for although they have benefitted us by freeing us from rats yet eight cats are rather too many for our little cottage, and such cats, too! Steal anything. Wind gusty at night.

29 August. Fine day. Harry brought yesterday half a sheep, 200 lbs flour, 5 lbs tea, one [...] of fat. EP weighed out 9 lbs sugar on Tuesday. This morning Jim and THP returned to dinner, having slept at Leach's last night, and today were employed tracking the weaned calves. On their way home up the Copper Cliffs the wind which had been blowing from the North West all yesterday and today, increased with such amazing violence that the horses were unable to stand against it, so they dismounted, took off saddles and bridles and sought the shelter of a deep gully along the creek side at the bottom of which they scrambled their way. The howling and roaring of the wind amongst the rocks was quite awful. The two cattle-hunters had often to crouch in the grass to save themselves from being blown over, and came back with their lips cracked and their skins as dry as the parchment of an old deed tempus [from the time of] Henry VIII. The wind continued very strong uprooting several trees in the bush. Jim and Willy slept here. Jim lost his dog, Peter.

30 August. Fine day. Jim and THP walked over the range to Wilson's run to head back the weaned stock. Found them on the summit of the range and drove them back. Went down the Copper Cliffs and humped back our saddles, cloths, bridles, blankets, etc which we found Peter keeping guard over. Brought home the mares. After dinner Jim went home and THP sowed cauliflower and brocoli, and then went up in the bush for firewood. Willy went home and Eliza and Donald went to Rockwood for some things for EP. Within the last few days, gooseberries have come into leaf, several varieties of cicadae have appeared, also lizards, and today saw the first butterfly. EP and THP sat by the fire a long while tonight, talking over affairs, plans and prospects, about buying sheep, living at the Rakaia, and so we sat and talked and talked again of the rough life we had lived, yet hitherto we had been blessed with health and Hope, sole tenant of Pandora's box, led us to imagining, almost to feel, that now a smoother track lay open before us. We gladly pursued it, and (Hope furnishing materials) we constructed quite a magnificent castle – in the air.

10 September. Beautiful. THP was going after the horses when EP asked if he thought she would be able to walk to the Rakaia [from Vale Head]. THP much pleased at her energy. Shouldered the blankets, etc and with Donald and his Mama walked off, calling at Rockwood as we went by. We staid but a few minutes as our reception was so chilling that we felt the sooner we left the better. We arrived at the Rakaia after a pleasant walk (8 miles). Donald seemed anything but tired. Georgey we found there. Harry was absent hunting for the missing sheep. The Ghoi trees are in full bloom and very beautiful they look.

13 September. Rain all last night and today it has not once ceased. Could not fetch Emma of course, so played on the Jew's harp to amuse little Clara, and tried to manufacture some treacle for the children's dinner. Ambrose said 'This is treacle', so I felt flattered accordingly. Mr Richards called on his way to fetch the cows and talked much nonsense about his various schemes. Read Hunt's letter again and felt pretty well satisfied with it. 'Bleak House'[16] I almost know by heart. I like it better than I did. Tonight the South West quarter looks rather clearer.

18 September. All ready for starting for the Rakaia, but a Sou'Wester put a stop to our proceedings. Agreed yesterday to give Jim £50 per annum and to assist as much as I can in getting him a run by taking up country enough for both if I can get it. Supposing I get £50,000, let Jim have £10,000 of it. Mr Edwards came up this morning, having arrived at Rockwood last night.

19 September. EP and Mr Edwards rode to the Rakaia with baby and Ambrose; called at Rockwood on the way. The Phillips' very much put out because of Jim's leaving, and also at our going to the Rakaia. THP and Jim with a load got stuck in the Washpen Creek. Fine day. The Rakaia our home.

18 October. Fine day. Jim and THP to the cattle to bring home Junket and Pastime. Could not manage it. Sir Wm Congreve and Charley came over for some grog. It appears that the inhabitants of Rockwood have been suffereing very acutely during the last few days from being out of spirits. Harry to Rockwood with the bullock dray – 1 bag of flour and the rest of the grog. North West strong.

25 October. Wind towards the afternoon was again most violent. In the morning THP to the cattle on the plains and the Waikerri [Waikirikiri]. Mr and Miss Aylmer over here to dinner. THP picked up some of the fowls that were lying about the paddock rendered quite helpless by the wind. Cobbing the kitchen chimney. Georgey cleaning out dairy. Every thing throughout the house has a thick coating of dust and rubblish and broken thatch. Our bed covered. Sheep camped in the yard.

28 October. In the night we had a heavy shower of rain, followed by hail and snow. This morning the ground is covered with snow to the depth of three inches at least. Our two milkers, Junket and Comfort, gave above two gallons this morning. Very cold and wet. In the afternoon Jim left on Buxom for Cordey's on his way to Christchurch. Gave him a check for £70 to purchase a new mare etc. In the evening reading Macaulay's England,[17] which Studholme has lent us. The boys came in about 3 o'clock without having seen anything of the sheep. At night we heard some sheep quite close.

6 November. Very wet. Turned away Wave with calves (79 and 86). THP and Jim cleaning saddles, bridles, etc. Mr Hall's shepherd the other day found a Maori tomahawk. The side next the ground had still some blood on it. The grey mare is to be called Dora. Mem. It was put to Mr Stace's horse Rodney on the 28th ulto. Found the old turkey hen last evening setting under a tei palm.

7 November. Weather heavy, mists and lowering. THP and Jim to the cattle. Put them together, and brought them up the creek below the Woolshed Hill, about 15 yearlings from Leach's have joined the mob. Vivid with a calf. Trifle, Jenny, Nickname and Dahlia away. After dinner Jim mending kitchen chimney. EP and THP up the bank walked to the great slip and headed the horses and brought them home. Beda still lame. Found the old turkey with seven chicks. Fine afternoon. In the evening we heard the crack of Harry's whip, who brought the cart from Rockwood with thatching, rods and several articles from Christchurch, including a Spanish cock and a shepherd boy. The 'Joseph Fletcher' has arrived with many emigrants for this settlement. The Double corner run had been purchased for £4500. Le Fleming and Jackson's cattle sold at an average of £7 to £7/10/- per head, all calves under one month given in. Mr Beard has had a brand like THP's made (Ace of clubs). As THP had not sheep his brand was not registered.

10 November. Fine day. THP and Jim to Vale Head leaving the dray at Rockwood, where Jim spent the evening. The garden presented a most melancholy spectacle, Mr Phillips' cattle having availed themselves of the damaged panels to make their entrance and help themselves which they appear to have done without scruple. Thank goodness they spared the fruit trees.

15 December. Jim, THP and Donald with the dray to Vale Head for a load of our things. Hurrel there too to see our milk pans, of which he bought 6 at 10d each. We brought home a tin of strawberries and an immense nosegay of roses principally, for the flowers are looking most lovely just now. EP busy making strawberry jam, and churning. Half a sheep from the Woolshed.

1857

2 January. Cold Sou'west wind. On looking over the Herd Book, find we have had 57 calves last year, 29 bulls and 28 heifers. Killed a sheep. Harry unwell. Seal fetching down hurdles and putting up yard. THP and Jim on Dolly and Dora to the cattle. Put them in the river-bed by the old Gunyah. Nor'West in the afternoon. Gala calved.

5 February. Fine day. Nor'West very strong in the night. Blew the window out of Harry's room, smashing the frame. Jim on Dora to the mob for the milking cows. Brought them about half past 12, having found them by the hummocks. The fatting sow was put on new milk last Tuesday. As much as she can consume is allowed her. We want some pigs to put up very much. The wind during the night and today has been very strong – unusually so. Some showers in the afternoon from the Nor'west – changed round to Sou'West and heavy rain at night. John came. We had a rubber. Every part of the house is dirty – I might say beastly dirty, so that anyone may easily see that we have no females in the establishment.

9 February. Dull morning. Cows away. Jim on Beda to the mob to fetch them. Harry and Seal with the cart and bullocks. Mr [Matthew] Morris came with them on his way to Leach's. We passed a very pleasant evening as Mr Morris had visited the Crimea, and had been into Sebastopol. He gave us several interesting anecdotes of the War. Mr Phillips has desired that the lambs be shorn, so tomorrow proceedings will commence. The price for wool would tempt a saint.

15 February. Sunday. Dull cold morning. Drizzling mist from North East. Jim with Buxom, Beda and Dora to Christchurch to be shod. THP rather sick. Wrote to Emma [who was staying in Christchurch] enclosing check for £10. Seal to Rockwood. Harry to the sheep. Donald found one of the turkey hens that had been killed by a dog very likely. Last evening Jim was quite indignant that THP should question the cleanliness of his habits. Children bathed in waterhole.

20 February. Heavy rain all day. Jim away after the cows all the morning till 4 p.m. Found them between the bottom and the Point. Harry to the sheep. Georgey churning. Donald playing with his new knife, and what between the amusement of hacking bits of wood, the excitement of losing it once an hour and joyful recovery of the same, the knife is for the day, quite a treasure. The way the little fellows opened and twinkled their sharp blue eyes at the sight of the lollys [sic] and gingerbread Mama sent them was quite a picture of fun.

2 March. Strong Nor'West wind till late in the afternoon. Jim walked down to Studholme's to see after his dray. Boys bathed. THP washing shirts and writing letters to England. Memo. sent letter to Mr Hunt per Kate Kearney on Thursday last. Boys gathering mushrooms. In the evening wind back to Nor'West again, blew strong. Harry came from Rockwood, and is not to go down to Christchurch with the wool, after telling THP he might go or anyone else, that liked. Another instance of his miserable twaddling. I wish I'd never seen him. Nor'Wester all night.

7 March. Beautiful day. Harry and THP thatching all day. Put on the thatch very thick with a close thick ridge over all. Boys and THP bathed. Jim and M Studholme here in the evening and had tea. They made THP's mouth water at the mention of some very excellent runs in the market in the Otago Province. What a pity it seems so much property as I have in England, that I should be unable to have a little here to play with. Georgey to the sheep. Tomorrow and tomorrow perhaps we shall see the dray with the wife of our [...] and the interesting female pledges. Studholme's wool sold for 16d per lb.

9 March. Fine day. Strong Nor'West. Harry on Dora to Aylmer's. Jim with the dray to Rockwood with the grog, gardening tools, mattress, etc. Charley returned home with him – rather dull as though he had left Christchurch with reluctance. Georgey to Studholme's for some more rams. THP jobbing about. Emma and her maid having a regular good day's work at cleaning. Poor old Bailey used to say 'Cleanliness is next to godliness' and I often tell the boys I think it is before it, for I am well assured there can be no godliness without it. I am inclined to coincide with the old pedagogue. Boys and Mabel bathed, and Emma also.

14 March. Dull morning with a cold wind. Jim morticing posts. Tom went home with the wether. THP made about 20 lbs of candles. Jim fixing shelves, etc. Harry came most unexpectedly in the evening, having lost the bullocks from Paulby's. THP bottling gin. Very unsatisfactory measure. Poor Donald came to our room in the night very unwell, suffering from his throat and making a most distressing croopey [sic] sort of noise. Gave him some nitre and water, and kept as warm as we could.

20 March. THP, Jim and Georgey with Dolly and Buxom to the Waikerri duck shooting. Brought home 4½ couple of Paradise and grey ducks. Killed a large male wild cat. Saw three bitterns. Borrowed some candle cotton from Aylmer. The Bishop had just left for Christchurch. Wind all gone today – rather showery.

28 March. Splendid weather. After breakfast Mr and Mrs Leach, EP and THP walked up the river to the Curiosity Shop[18] and spent about two hours in picking up fossil specimens of various forms. Jim on Buxom to the cattle for Brazen, but did not find her. Charley came. The Bishop arrived at Rockwood yesterday.

30 March. Hotter than yesterday. All of us sitting down doing nothing in the coolest place we could find. In the sitting-room doors and windows open. In the evening Harry returned with a supply of the local papers. Played the game of the [...]. In the smoking hour discussed a scheme for an exploration. Hope Studholme will join, but fear other occupation will prevent him. Perhaps Leach will go. Nor'West wind rather gusty. Sheep rising in value very fast. Many yarns about the Nelson gold-field. Dancey has bought Taylor's run in the Maitangi for £650.[19]

4 April. Beautiful day. Mr Richards lanced Donald's abscess, which gave him great relief. Mr Richards left after breakfast. Harry came back from Rockwood, where it apears a great change in domestic policy is at hand. The new regime will commence on Monday next, Mr Tomlinson, a protégé of the Bishop's, being inducted in the office of instructing the boys, under the style and title of Tutor; Charley is to leave for [Christ's] College in a fortnight. A severe wigging has been administered to the Doctor by Mrs Phillips for his strictures on Rockwood. The cattle are to be got up and John is to look at some sheep the Gov'nor talks of purchasing. Mr Seal, 'the cheerful', is to be at the Rakaia during Harry's absence to superintend the sheep. What next! The house at Christchurch is for sale. Mr Richards' town section is to be put up to auction next week – his rural land is under offer in exchange for sheep. The cattle are to be let for dairying and the bullock, Folly, is doomed for slaughter (what a relief could every other Folly be knocked on the head). Horses are not cheaper. Sheep have risen in value rapidly and extensively. The value of the cattle is more difficult to be ascertained. One commission agent sends word there is no present sale for them, whilst another avouches for the fact he has just known cows fetch £20 per head. 'Who shall decide when doctors disagree?' Talking of Doctors, Donald is so much easier that he was trying to stand on his head this evening. About tea-time Mr Leach and Jim returned and we set out, if all is well, on Monday next on our journey of exploration. Mr O'Neil came with the census paper – small as our family is, the row of Potts's made quite a list. Cattle returned as about 250.

5 April. Sunday. Beautiful day. Sharp frost at night. Jim fetched home the mares. Harry has noticed the wine and grog have been tapped at the woolshed, which was left there for Studholme. The stone jar of whisky was sealed and the box of wine had three or four bottles on the top, which were felt through the slats. This was the state they were in on Thursday as seen by Seal. On Saturday Harry noticed the seal off the jar, or it had been opened and only one bottle of port on the top. Aylmer's men passed up towards the Woolshed on Thursday, seen by THP. Harry planted the wine and jar.

[c. 6–7 April][20] (THP on Buxom, Harry on Dora, Leach riding his mare, Zoe.) We got to Leach's on the day we left just about sundown and spent a pleasant evening, and next morning we started as soon as we could taking the remainder of our stores. Amongst the rest more loaves of bread. We went through Leach's cattle and called at Oakden's. He was away, but Mr Groom lent Leach an old tether rope and quart pannikin, and we went our way merrily, ascending the range of low hills that over look Lake Coleridge. Of this we had every now and then a beautiful view commanding at one glance almost its entire length, with the long peninsula fringed with dark leaved shrubs – the solitary rata island, like some lovely waterfowl nestling in repose. From the little lagoons we passed, we obtained some young ducks and it was within an hour of sundown when we descended the high ground through a deep winding gully to the bed of the Rakaia. We crossed two streams which united from the Northern branch [the Wilberforce] (which we ascended last year) and came on some beautiful undulating country of limited extent, in some places encumbered with Irishmen. Saw lots of fresh pig tracks. Descending again to our river-bed we enjoyed in [sic] a magnificent landscape of the [wildest?] mountain scenery, through which winds the Rakaia, and now glowing with all the lustre imparted by the setting sun. We made for an island and camped under the shelter of a gigantic tussock or tohe-tohe grass. Made a hearty supper and tethered the horses for the night. Amongst the various specimens of bird we saw here were Paradise and grey ducks, widgeon, teal, quail, bittern and white heron, etc.

[c. 8–9 April.] Wednesday: Beautiful weather again. The horses were cast loose this morning, and whilst we were preparing breakfast, they quietly vanished. Harry and Leach after them – they had to return to the stream next the hills before they overtook them. After breakfast we broke camp and packing our swags kept up the river. It was bad travelling for the horses on account of the stones and the smoke from a large fire in our rear filled the valley so completely that our view was quite obscured. We rode on slowly till near sundown. Camped in the river-bed on the stones, and made a jolly fire of drift wood. The next morning we got off rather early, and kept our course to the left or South stream. Got some ducks and wound round the base of a sharp peaked mountain to the mouth of a warm sheltered valley [Lake Stream] winding to the South. The tutu was quite green – evidently untouched by the frost. Here we were marvellously struck by the appearance of horse tracks which we found of all ages. Presently we found a splendid grey mare, as wild as a deer. Of course we had many and divers speculations as to how she came there. We observed a piece of cord round her neck. We dismounted and made a pot of tea to let her see our horses nearer, as we would have liked such a prize to take back, but she was far too wild and wary for us, as she just trotted round at a safe distance. So we were compelled to leave her. Soon after the valley widens as the mountains recede, shutting out the high snowy peaks from view, and we saw an extensive flat with a large lake [Lake Heron]. We kept to the West side of the lake skirting an extensive bog, which we at last headed, after floundering about for some hours. We made towards the lake for the sake of the game, but the bog still was our enemy so we camped in the bed of a small stream that fed the lake from the West. We camped under the shelter of an Irishman. Harry went duckshooting, Leach and THP cooking. Leach gave an alarm and THP ran to see what was the matter. The grass was on fire. We endeavoured to put it out, but in vain – the wind was too strong. We untied our horses, threw our swags on them and ran into the river-bed, saving everything but a waist-coat. We camped in the river-bed, but could get no wood to spread our blankets with. The weather looked bad – very bad, but we were so pleased at finding this plain and a new route home by the Ashburton, that we were happy enough. We turned into our comfortable bed on damp grass lighted by the roaring fire in front.

[c. 10 April.] Towards morning our position was rendered unpleasant by the rain which descended rather smartly. Pulled the blanket over our heads and slept till morning, when we had a council as to our movements. Leach was for waiting until the rain gave over, THP for getting on and discovering, if possible, a bush where we could have a comfortable camp and plenty of game. Harry also voted for going on, so we ate a piece of fat cake and mounted. The country improved as we advanced, the clouds broke a little although it was still very cold, and we kept on till we made for a stream which we knew must be a branch or the commencement of the Ashburton [North Branch]. The pasturage here was of a very favourable character, and we talked about the country we would take up. We camped under a thicket of shrubs in the bed of the river, making a most comfortable tent, as we purposed stopping here for a day in order to explore the neighbouring country.

[c. 11 April.] So after breakfast on Saturday we left our traps and explored that piece of country we saw yesterday lying on our right hand. We saw two or three lakes, one we called Clear Water, as we named the large one we passed yesterday Heron Lake, from seeing many white herons gently sailing over its surface, or standing motionless on its stony beach. We ascended a hill which allowed us to see the Rakaia (South branch), Ashburton and Rangitata, and immense jagged peaks away to the West covered with snow – one of extraordinary altitude we supposed to be Mt Cook. THP prefers Clearwater and South of Ashburton for a run, Leach the opposite side of the river by Lake Heron. The most remarkable feature is the absence of bush, the only firewood we got was drift Irishman. We returned to camp before sundown and thought we would apply for 20,000 to 30,000 acres each.

[c. 12 April.] As the wind changed, we shifted our camp into a more sheltered place and well it was we did so for it came on to rain tremendously heavy next morning, but we were very snug and waited till it cleared off, for Harry said it couldn't last long at that rate, for the supply would run short. We started at last down the river which was on our way home and soon came in sight of some bush on the spurs to our left hand, the straggling ends of Halford [Alford] forest. We camped in a stream of the Ashburton under Mt Somers – rather wet and very windy. River high.

[c. 13 April.] Next morning we kept our course near the Forest and were impeded by several boggy creeks. At last we saw a house (J Brittan's) the first since last Tuesday, and without stopping anywhere we made for the Rakaia, and were hospitably received by Tom Hall and Mrs Hall. Many were the enquiries as to what we had seen and where we came from, to which we gave as judicious answers as we could.

[c. 14 April.] Next morning we trotted on to Lane's and crossed the river to Studholme's, who would have us dine there. We told them our adventures, and John was sorry he did not join us as we had expected. We got home all right quite pleased with our trip, having been the first who have discovered a route from the Rakaia to the Ashburton by the Westward hills, and most likely the plain we found will be a valuable discovery for ourselves.

22 April. THP returned from Christchurch and told Jim to get ready for a start tomorrow across the Rakaia to the new country. He got down on Friday being stopped by rain at Fred's on Thursday. On Saturday rode into Port [Lyttelton] and again on Tuesday, taking [...] with him to rub off some of the ill humour he scented on Monday through his interview with the Board of Wastelands. When we were up the country we all said we would not pay any deposit, but on coming to the point Dudley and Heath paid a deposit on the run they applied for. THP after going through the points with the commissioners declined according to their interpretation of the regulations (citing the cases of Studholme and Harmer), and told the Board he should immediately stock the run. So on Wednesday morning he left Christchurch for that purpose, Mr Miles undertaking to keep his name on the application book.

23 April. Fine day. Horses away. Jim after them. THP on Dolly and Jim on Beda – brought down a large mob of cattle to take away west. Leach here on our return. THP and Jim on Buxom and Dora and Emma on Beda to Studholme's. Said goodbye to Emma and crossed the stream without trouble, then ascending Lane's slip to the plains. We kept on driving until it was too dark to make out Mt Somers, and then we were guided by the stars. Camped on the Northern stream of the Ashburton about 10 p.m. and turned into some high tutu.

24 April. Up at daylight, and soon after sunrise driving the cattle passed near Brittan's station, and thence up the South Branch of the Ashburton. Met Harry and Studholme, who had been exploring near the Rangitata. Camped at night in a thick island. Told Harry I should be home nearly as soon as he would be.

25 April. Driving as soon as we could see, and left the cattle on the run, and turned our horses homewards. We missed a cow and two calves yesterday, but could not see them. We rode on smartly and reached Lane's about 6 p.m. Too dark to cross the river.

26 April. Sunday. Fine morning. Crossed the river from Lane's and reached home about breakfast time. Harry had got home yesterday afternoon. Sent Jim on Beda to Christchurch with a statement that my run was stocked on the 25th enclosing £25 cheque for Miles to pay rent. Harry to Rockwood.

28 April. Fine day. Mr Cordy and James Cordy here this evening, with a note from Miles to say I was just in time, so I have taken and stocked the most Westerly run yet discovered in about the shortest time on record. Emma and THP on Buxom and Dolly to Lake Constance[21] to see Leach's cattle cross, but saw nothing of them. Returned home down the Gravelly Chasm. Tripp has taken up a run next [to] mine.

5 May. Fine day. Nor'West strong. Jim and THP as yesterday. Bullocks much quieter. Studholme left after breakfast. He strongly advised THP to apply for an additional 7,000 acres adjoining THP's run on the Rangitata and that would include all the best country about there. Reading my Novel aloud.

6 May. Rather dull morning. Jim mending his stock whip. THP melting fat. In the evening writing. Watson called on his way home with Leach's dray. He met two men and a pack horse near our runs. This information was exceedingly interesting as at the present time there's much scrambling for runs. THP, Emma and Jim sat by the fire in deep consultation on this portentous event. Resolved that Jim start early for Christchurch, THP requesting and authorising Mr Miles to act for him in his absence. Wrote and sent the following letters:– Mr Hunt, Dutton, F Catling, Mrs Kent, Mr Miles and Rev W Willock. To the latter and Mrs Kent informing them I was desirous of taking cattle on my run at 8/- per annum, or on terms. Enclosed cheque for £10 to Miles to cover outlay. Gave Jim an advertisement to put in the paper about cattle for pasturage.

8 May. North West wind blowing strong all day. THP and Donald returned home on Buxom from Vale Head. THP had a heavy fall whilst galloping after cattle from the girth breaking. A very unpleasant discussion with Harry as to the taking up of this addition (7,000 [acres]) to THP's run. Harry says he told THP he meant to apply for it himself, and referred to Emma as being present when he said so, but this was the first time either of them had heard of it. Jim returned in the night, so Beda has been about 100 miles since yesterday morning – quite work enough considering her interesting situation.

9 May. Strong North West wind. Jim posted the letters all right except the one to be delivered to Mr Miles, which he lost. It contained a cheque for £10, and the boundaries of the country to be applied for, so he will have to be down again before Monday morning. Mr Miles entered my name on the application paper and stopped the cheque. Several cattle owners will probably send their cattle to my run so they told Jim. In the afternoon THP after the cows on Buxom, as they have been away since Thursday night. Came home without seeing them nearly starved with the cold and wet through with hail, rain and snow. A very heavy Sou'Wester has set in and by bed-time the whole flat and back covered some inches in depth. Jim left on Dora, so he will have a bitter cold ride.

13 May. Fine day. THP and the children got two loads of firewood. Jim Cordy left after breakfast. Harry killed a sheep. In the evening Jim on Dora arrived from Christchurch, Leach with him. In consequence of the land regulations with respect to river frontage, Mr Miles had to take up 10,000 acres instead of 7,000 to secure the country I wished for, so the boundaries are as follows:

North. By a line 5½ miles from the Rangitata.
East. By a line drawn from the Rangitata to the head of Clearwater Lake.
South. By the Rangitata.
West. By the second stream running into the Rangitata from the North.

Mr Lee, of Kapaia,[22] has written [to] Leach offering him £20 to deliver the mare to him, which we found on the South branch of the Rakaia. We should prefer having the privilege of putting some mares to his newly imported horse. Mr Tripp is in a soot about our taking up country there, as he says he intended doing so himself.

Someone in the Land Office told Tom Hall of my run and that he had only to pay the deposit which I refused – these are gentlemen – of course. Jim found we might get about 80 head of cattle instead of double that number we expected, as we shall not be able to have Mr Willock's which I much regret, as of course the more stock I get, the more country I am able to apply for.

29 May. Oak apple day. Why our children will require to go through a course of Brand, Hore's [sic] daybook,[23] etc before they realize any of the ancient manners, customs, rites and superstitions of their fathers. Fine day. Yoked up Garland and No 6. The cow was very savage and troublesome, and the treatment received at our hands was certainly of the harshest. Jim on the stray mule for cows, which were away again. Harry went to the sheep with Ugly Jack, but this young aspirant for pastoral happiness did not return with him, so we sat up rather later than usual. Harry passed the evening in lighting up the palms and cooeeing, but although he made a great blaze he did [not?] alight on the lost one.

3 June. Fine day. Jim on Dora to the cattle. Emma and THP on Beda and Dolly across the Rakaia to Mr Lean's. Mr Studholme kindly piloted us across. Emma is, I believe, the first lady who has performed this feat of riding across the Rakaia on horseback. Spent a pleasant day at Lean's.

18 June. Fine day. THP, Donald and Geoff same as yesterday. Jim on Beda to the cattle. Brought home steers 1, 2, 5, 6, and 7. Harry returned from Leach's. Studholme sent up some letters and papers – one from Mr Hunt enclosing remittance for £1,000. Also one from F Catling for £300. Mr Hunt's letter with a satisfactory balance-sheet enclosed. This is very pleasant, and Jim was to start for Christchurch tomorrow to see about getting the cattle I am to take charge of. Now we must begin sheep-farming, to which we have so long looked anxiously forward. And the vision, yes, the vision so dimly seen of £5000 per annum does not look quite so indistinct as it has done. We shall have a busy time, indeed, forming the new station. First comes the house, with a patch of garden ground of course; woolshed, washpen and stockyard; our old friends the cattle put in a claim for a large stockyard, and there ought to be a shed for milking, and a yard and shed for a mare and foal, as I really hope all our mares intend exhibiting the effects of a salubrious climate by each producing a little foal. To this hope they ought not to say 'Neigh'.

19 June. Snow falling lightly now and then throughout the day. THP very busy writing letters, etc. Offered Jim to advance him money to cover rent and deposit for the 5,000 acre run up the Rakaia, which he has desired to have ever since our return from exploring in April last. This offer he accepted with thanks, so this morning handed him check for £40 – also my banking book and the drafts for £300 and £1000 to be paid into my account. Letters for Messrs Hunt, F Catling, Taite and a list of sundry small articles required. He left after breakfast on Buxom. Wet in the evening.

20 June. Dull, raw, cloudy morning. THP after the cows through the mob of cattle in the Woolshed Valley. Harry fixing water-cask to a sledge, so as to command a better supply of pure water. The water-hole for a long time has been far too foul to be used for any culinary purpose, and it is a job to get enough water fetched in buckets from the main stream. Disagreeable weather and trying for the children, as it is too wet for them out of doors.

23 June. Very mild this morning. Harry to Rockwood with a wether. Messrs Lean and Haynes left after breakfast; THP gave Mr Lean the Dorking cock 'Tommy'. We dined early and then THP and Ambrose and Geoff went for a load of firewood. Emma and THP spent the evening alone for the first time for many weeks, I think, so we made all sorts of calculations about sheep and wool, as to the best means of laying out some money in sheep and whether it would be most advisable to buy all ewes or ewes and wethers, as in the latter case you get so many more sheep to shear for the same money, but all this hinges on the supposition that someone is willing to sell – 'First catch your hare' said Mrs Glasse.[24]

3 July. Blowing and snowing till late in the afternoon. All the high ground covered. A strong fresh in the river. Jim on Dora for the cows. Returned just before tea without them. Harry pig-dressing and a very savoury dinner we had. Wild pork is so scarce it is quite a treat. THP all day preparing the room. Emma as usual, which is, of course, busy as one person can well be. Due enconiums are [...] on the road up the slip, so THP feels like Mr Wintle[25] in a state of honour and glory. Hopes to be off tomorrow sheep-hunting, via Studholme's and Dunfords, perhaps to Christchurch. Wrote notes to Studholme and Matson, the former enclosing cheque for £8/15/- for wethers.

13 July. Fine frosty morning. THP making up the journal from Jim's notes. THP's journey to Christchurch has not been successful. There are numerous sheepbuyers in the market, and owners are anxious to hold on till after shearing. Annual notices are issued to various run-holders to stock their runs forthwith, which will, of course, give sheep an increased upward tendency. Two or three small lots may perhaps be secured, but it is a question whether waiting would not be the best policy. Last accounts (14th April) from England anticipate a probable fall of 1d to 1½d per lb in wool. Nelson diggings promise to be more remunerative than we have been led to expect hitherto. Horses are very scarce and dear; dearer, I think, than they have been these three years. For cattle there seems to be no demand at present, but we may expect good prices for beef should the diggings either in Nelson or Otago draw many immigrants, as live stock (surplus) in either place is totally inadequate to sustain any great addition to the existing population. THP papering our room. Charley shooting.

25 July. Fine day. In the afternoon, THP and Jim returned from Christchurch, having bought one imported cow brought out by Captain Simeon, a two-year-old bull, two beautiful shorthorn heifers, one bred from Flash, which Mr Rhodes purchased at the sale for £55. Two well-bred cows, one with a roan bull-calf, by Brother Phil, who was also purchased by Mr Rhodes for £90. Cattle and horses also sheep and produce generally are enhanced in value.

1 August. Change in the weather. Rain from the North East. Mr Gray left after breakfast. Jim on Beda to the cattle. THP on Buxom after the new cows that have gone away. Returned without finding them. Saw Mr T Hall; told him of the man who was here on Thursday, and who was very reserved as to where he came from. Mr Hall said there was a man prowling about, who had murdered his mate in Otago, and who was supposed to be making his way up here, perhaps this was the gentleman.

18 August. Jim on Beda brought home Flirt with a white heifer calf. THP returned from Christchurch – he had been in Port to see some horses landed. Lockhart's run is at present under offer. Mr Waitt up the country so left instructions with Miles about Casterton. Jim here from Rockwood to see if a dray had arrived. THP was offered 1000 weaned ewes to be delivered March next at 12/-.

22 August. Beautiful day. Jim to the woolshed to paint the top of the dray green and thence to Rockwood for a few things, taking with him Vic and Jerry. Harry walked to Studholme's – he found a sand-lark's nest with two eggs; several gulls building; two had fallen victims to a large quail hawk. Jim returned in the evening. He saw a lark sitting on three eggs, and the boys had found nests of the wren and parroquet. Jim Cordy came.

1 September. Beautiful day. Jim on Buxom for the bullocks. THP and Jim with Donald, four bullocks in the dray for a load of firewood. Found a nest of copper bearded sandlark with three eggs. Shot a couple of Paradise ducks. Frost at night. Harry killed a wether.

2 September. Fine day. Jim on Buxom for the young bullocks. THP, Jim and Donald up the river with the dray for firewood. We topped our load with a large laurel and a tough job enough it was to cross-cut it, which from its size we were obliged to do into several lengths. The root, after much axeing and sweating we gave up as an obstinate piece de resistance, which defied our efforts. Harry rode to Studholme's and back. Planting potatoes – red rivers.

10 September. Heavy mist. Knapman[26] came and operated on Tupwood. Studholme left after breakfast. THP and Tom with sledge and [. . .] from Rockwood. Yesterday THP and the Gov'nor to Vale Head to look at the trees and shrubs, which THP exchanged with Mr Phillips for two steers, Timothy and Rodney. Golddigging going ahead at Nelson. Studhome has bought Stewart's run and cattle at the Bluff. Mr Cap [sic] has not made his appearance at Studholme's station as expected. Mr Hall, our opposite neighbour, has been alarmed by the appearance of a stray bullock which answers somewhat in description to a steer which Jim left on the Ashburton, Aug 10. A charge of small shot has been expended on the unwelcome visitor, and Mr G Hall has hastened to his station for ball. Light North East rain at night. Spinach up.

11 September. Drizzling rain from North East. Tom to Studholme's for the sheep. Jim on Buxom to Hall's and brought the steer back, but he broke away, and made across the river for Lean's. Nothing particular occurred today. Children behaved pretty well. House already rather dirty [Emma was at Rockwood] and our living anything but luxurious. When we reached here yesterday, dinner was just finished, consisting of shank bone of beef, with a few gristly knobs on it; today we had a salted round-looking knuckle of beef, not very inviting, but I can hold a few days yet on cheese and bread. The children dined on burnt rice milk, with a strong flavour of the iron pot for relish. Mr Paull only wants £500 for [...] Casterton than we expected. Hall offers Purnell's sheep for sale – 500 breeding ewes and 400 miled [mixed] lambs. Sowed peas, beans, etc. Grass is now springing very fast – English grasses taking the lead.

15 September. Fine morning. Jim on Buxom for the bullocks and Jimmy the bull. Harry came from Hall's. Prunell's sheep to be sold – 550 at 27/- (100 of them in lamb), 200 wethers at 15/-, and 200 mixed lambs at 12/-. Rain set in very heavy in the afternoon from the South East. Changed to snow, which continued falling steadily. In the course of the evening Jim said he thought his time was up tomorrow and asked what I would give him to stop another year, he would not drive bullocks for anybody; he did not care about working hard; if he had to do hard work, he would better work for himself, he did not see how I could keep him, and he thought he should go to the diggings. I said he had given me but little time to think about it. At the worst I can only do as before – Jim engaged with me and look after the cattle myself, keeping the breeding stock on this run. Hens laying well.

19 September. Fine day. Sharp frost last night. THP and Mabel rode Buxom over here from Rockwood. Jim to Rockwood in the afternoon. He appears anxious to make terms with THP, and so it is to be supposed that his journey to the gold-diggings was held out in terrorem [as a threat] over our devoted [sic] to enhance his value. This may have been good policy, but I have my doubts. Jim to take Garland's stock. Harry returned.

23 September. Wind Nor'West. At about 11 o'clock this morning, Emma was safely delivered of a daughter [Edith]. Mr and Mrs Waitt to be god-parents. Much quoit playing in the daytime and rubbers in the evening.

30 September. Fine day. Strong Nor'West wind all day long. Onions coming up very thickly. Seal, Harry and Studholme left after breakfast. THP and little children for a walk. Set 10 turkey eggs under Dorking hen. Nor'West wind very strong, but if the night is boisterous without, at least peace and quietness reign within. It has been warm enough to sit without a fire till within an hour of bedtime; with my book and pipe I have passed a meditative and enjoyable evening.

2 October. Fine day. W N W rather strong. Puppies tiresome at night. Got up to look at the kitchen fire which I heard crackling. Memo. to speak about it. Yesterday practised quoits – could only throw from one end on account of the wind. Looking after the horses, fetching water, milking, a quiet book, pipe, to bed. We found some turkey eggs in a patch of fern. Today Ambrose and THP walked up the river seeking gulls' nests. Wind changed in a moment from North West to South West, and with the change a heavy hailstorm. Made haste home quite blue with cold and hail. Found Seal and his horse here and it soon came on to snow heavily. The ground was quickly covered to a depth of two inches on the flat here, whilst the bank, particularly beyond the Gravelly Chasm, had apparently a thick coating. Fine night, and very hard frost. THP up to keep the puppies quiet. Round Top looked beautifully white in the morning, but Mt Hutt was still shrouded in gloomy mists. Jack and Maria aught [ought] to have the prize for dirt. I have to partake of the same food as they do, to share the same loaf, eat from the same dish, and anything more repulsive than their persons and habits I am at a loss to conceive; their squalid appearance from dirt and filth is most disgusting. Jack never washes; I made him wash his hands today, which is an act I am afraid he looks upon as arbitrary and tyrranical, but as I have to cut my slice of bread off the loaf he uses, why, I hold myself excused under the circumstances. Maria washes or rubs her face and mouth and hair, and now and then disguises herself in a clean frock, but I suppose lest she should be accused of pride, suffers her neck, hands, arms and stockings to remain in status quo. Oh, for the largest engine of the London Fire Brigade.[27] Seal in the course of the evening said he considered Purnell's ewes to have cost but 12/- each, as they were in lamb. That is certainly taking a very favourable view of the situation.

3 October. Fine all day – frost has the snow quite crisp. THP for the horses to the high terrace, and then on Buxom up the river-bed. Saw white heron; found sandpiper's nest, three eggs. Fairly driven home by the piercing Nor'Wester which was not only strong but bitterly cold. Pointed out to Seal the necessity of some new arrangement here, as I find as long as we have things in common, we have to find all the service, and I will not suffer my wife to work for anybody. I said when Harry returns, he and the boy must get their own stores and the things, and cook or pay someone to do it, as I can't stand the unpleasantness of the present system, particularly when there is no occasion for it. Turkey sitting in a fern patch.

3 November. THP returned home on foot, having left Aylmer's this morning. He has been quite occupied with electioneering. [William Sefton] Moorhouse was ahead of Brittain [sic] for the superintending by a large majority on Friday.[28] On Saturday with other electors had an interview with Hazelwood about the Rakaia district, as it was rumoured [Henry John] Tancred was coming in, so that it would appear this district was to be quietly handed over at the eleventh hour to another representative without our being consulted on the subject. Got up a requisistion or letter to Tancred informing him we had been pledged for some time to Hazelwood, and informed of it to prevent the trouble of a contested election. Amongst the signatures Brittain's appeared with a note which gave offence to Tancred, I expect. On Sunday Buxom, having [...], walked to Hazelwood's and slept there. Yesterday morning left Hazelwood at five o'clock for Ross's to attend the nominative – both of us riding lame horses. Mr Tancred having no chances of success in the face of the requisition he consented to propose Hazelwood who was seconded by Studholme. Mr Tancred adverted to the requisition, to which THP made an explanation to the meeting of its intent and purpose. After the meeting THP walked to Aylmer's and slept there.

12 November. Fine morning. Seal left. THP mending thatch and afterwards started for Christchurch on Dora, driving Dolly and Beda to be to [sic] the horses. Soon after we had the most terrible hailstorm with thunder and lightning; the hailstones of immense size broke some windows, stripped the kohi [kōwhai] trees of leaves and flowers, and even broke off the vigorous young flower stalks of the flax plants. THP and the mares got dreadfully pelted; called in at Studholme's for shelter, and came to seek the mares, who made off in the storm. The largest hailstones ¾ to 1 inch in diameter, and weighed 20 to the lb. Tom in the evening.

26 November. Fine day. Much surprised by a visit from a Moari [sic] woman – none of us understood what she wanted. Gave her some food and a box of matches. Mr Studholme left.

4 December. Showery. THP and Donald cutting a strip of bull's hide for tether rope, cut off 120 yards in one length. In the evening EP assisted by THP plaited it into a tether rope 35 yards long.

12 December. Fine day. After milking – watering and changing the horses. EP, THP and all the children up the river-bed to a little hut made of drift wood, where we made tea and had our dinner, spending the whole day. EP was fortunate enough to find the nest of the black [...] which contained two eggs built on some drift wood raised about a foot above the shingle. Help at home yesterday.

23 December. Fine day. Nash here to borrow some sugar. Brought a fine basket of rhubarb with him. THP returned from Christchurch in the evening on Dora. He had been obliged to leave Lady and her foal at Fred's as it was not strong enough to go on. At Christchurch found two letters from Mr Hunt enclosing original and duplicate of remittance for £500, and one for Emma from Mrs Dutton, which gave us great uneasiness, although we were pleased to receive it. Horses are very dear just now. THP was offered £85 for Dora, £25 for Lady's little foal. Mr Moorehouse [sic] and others strongly advised THP to enter her for the Produce Stakes, as the old mare possessed points of well-known excellence. Baby rather uneasy at night, so we sat late talking over all the news. Waitt has bought Carterton for <u>himself</u>. The Spray's cargo of horses were landed in Nelson and driven overland and sold on Saturday last, realizing an average of £57 – weedy things, and unbroken. £500 is to be forwarded to THP on receipt by Mr Hunt of safe arrival of £1,000, which THP received June last.

25 December. Christmas Day. Wind strong and cold. Mr Tomlinson, THP and Emma and baby rode to Rockwood. The two gentlemen much nipped up with cold. THP morose and most disagreeable all day. Emma's good humour as usual invincible. After a cup of tea THP mounted Dora and cantered over where he found Mr C Edwards for whom he had waited for so long on Tuesday last in Christchurch. He left thereon and managing to encounter a variety of adventures and disagreeable contretemps, including camping out last night at the Gunyah in that Nor'Wester. However through the kind offices of Watts he reached here safely this morning, soon after we left. He rode old Dolly, whose foal has grown very much. Heavy thunderstorms in the evening. Lightning most vivid, accompanied by heavy rain, soon passed off. The Nor'Wester has brought down good fresh in the river. Our water hole filled again. Yesterday THP and Emma very busy writing to Tom Dutton, Mrs Dutton and Mr Brenchley, as after Mrs Dutton's description of her husband's state of health, we could only endeavour to persuade them to emigrate after due consideration and medical advice. In the evening Co [company] and THP had yarns of portentous length to unfold and much tobacco passed away like smoke.

28 December. Fine day. Edwards same as Saturday. THP planting cabbage etc, filling the water barrel etc. EP and THP for the cows. The Rockwood gardens look very neat and orderly, but the North West winds have entirely stripped the fruit and gooseberry bushes of all sorts of fruit, there was a promising show of blossom, which makes the top the more vexing. Strawberries have proved unproductive from want of rain. Tei blossoms are now most beautiful and we brought home an immense specimen this evening, of the perfect shape and most powerful fragrance. Strong North West till evening, then gentle showers from South West.

31 December. Fine day. Parritch [porridge] morning. Edwards and THP at the well. Got to water which came in very fast to a certain height. Bailed it out several times, and got some totally clear water for tea. THP watering in the garden. Edwards fixing handle to pickaxe in anticipation of a journey to the Curiosity Shop in the morning, about which he is rather enthusiastic. Heavy rain at night. A quiet rubber at cribbage and a glass of wine was our simple way of keeping the last night of the old year, and to their shame be it recorded, THP and Edwards finished their last yarn before the advent of 1st January 1858.

1858

23 January. At work in the garden. We get pretty well supplied with vegetables now. Vaccinated Clara.

24 January. Sunday. Harry over here. THP to go to Christchurch tomorrow to buy or rent a house either there or in the neighbourhood, as we cannot put up with living here any longer. The boys are getting big enough to go to school, and we think we have roughed it quite enough for nearly four years.

31 January. Sunday. Seal came after sheep that were lost again. Mr Oakden told them at the house THP had bought a place somewhere near Christchurch. Blowing hard all day. Edwards and Donald to get some butter. Vaccinated Mabel from Clara.

8 February. Fine day. THP home to breakfast on Dora. Very much occupied by detailing his adventures in search of a house, of which he has had so many offers in different quarters. He thinks the most eligible would be the estate of his Honor the Superintendent in Governor's Bay, comprising 255 acres or thereabout with several buildings, plenty of wood, good water. Seven miles from Port with access by land and water. Brought up the plan with the offer from Mr Moorhouse to remain open for a fortnight for THP to decide.

18 February. THP started on Dora for Christchurch as the time for giving an answer to Mr Moorhouse's offer expires on Saturday next. THP resolves to give £2500 for it, Mr Moorhouse's offer being £2700.

23 February. Fine day. THP home at night on Dora bringing up Lady and foal and Beda, having left Christchurch this morning about half-past 11. He purchased Governor's Bay on Saturday last, paying down £550, employing Mr Wyatt in Mr McGregor's absence, as his Solicitor. On Sunday his Honor accompanied [THP] in a visit to Governor's Bay and introduced him as the new proprietor, returning to Christchurch in the evening. On Monday attended the Land Board and bought 70 acres of bush land adjoining the estate and making a valuable addition to it.

8 March. Fine day. Emma's toothache very bad, so she rode Buxom to Rockwood to have it taken out. Mr Richards called here soon after she left so he went back directly. THP and the children getting firewood. Made them a raft of some firewood and amused them very much, by towing them across the first stream. Memo. mushroom omelettes we tried yesterday, and found them very good indeed.

11 March. Fine hot day. Emma, THP and Donald along with Jim and Miles to see the latter cross the river – quite a cavalcade through the paddock – eight horses and a foal. We had to assist Jim in getting Tupwood across. There was a good deal of water in the river and EP and THP crossed over by the main stream, getting rather wet, and then we were nearly two hours in driving him into the stream with stones. Jim racing him about over the shingle which made THP rejoice he was not mounted on Duchess and Beda, who are now under Jim's charge for a while. Returning home we met Mr Richards who came home with us, and we reached there just in time, for a heavy squall from the South East soon came pelting down. Jim brought up the intelligence of the arrival of the Rockhampton with emigrants, but as to news he seemed to know nothing, except the sayings, the doings, the fishings, the visitings of sundry members of the great Phillips family[. O]f that distinguished portion of the community, there has been staying at Sumner Mr and Mrs, Harry, Jim, Charley, Ted and Fred Phillips. Very wet night so Mr Richards slept here.

12 March. Rain all day. Mr Richards gave an account of the number of pukekos up the river that THP having plenty of powder and shot intends trying his luck there tomorrow if fine, as we have nothing but very old hung pork and beef to eat. Shot a weka in the peach island. Cleaning gun and looking up ammunition. Lots of mushrooms. Richards left after breakfast.

14 March. Sunday. Dull day. Children bathed. THP shot a beautiful white heron in the water hole. EP and THP down the river with the gun. Got one duck and a fine young turkey.

25 March. Weather changed – cleared up. THP and Donald after the horses. Brought them all home. Roped up Jessie she was very quiet. THP then received a spiteful kick on the knee from Buxom – no damage done. Put the harness on her and fetched home two good loads of firewood. Tethered Dora ready for a start to Christchurch tomorrow – was to have gone yesterday.

31 March. Fine but cloudy. THP home again. He got to Christchurch at breakfast on Monday. Found a letter from Mr Hunt containing remittance for £500 and urging him to send his Colombian Bonds to England to be duly recognized, so he had Dora shed and came back for the Bonds. He left Christchurch this morning. Owen is said to have taken up a large run behind me.

Part Three

Still Out in the Open: *Eleven essays by Thomas Potts, 1882–88*

Many of Potts' essays were entitled either 'Out in the Open' or 'Old Times'. Bracketed words in the title are an editorial expansion to differentiate one essay from another. Simple editorial corrections or clarifications within the text are included in square brackets; a few lengthier remarks appear as endnotes. To clarify a faunal or floral species, a further name (variously Latin, English or Māori) is often provided. A full list of English, Latin and Māori names appears in the appendix at the end of this volume. Potts' use of capitals and italics in Latin names was erratic; where necessary, Latin names have been standardised to conform with modern practice.

1. Old Times [A forest ramble] (1887)

Not a trace remains of the bareness, of the absolute nakedness, which formerly distinguished Christchurch, owing to the entire absence of trees; this was remedied in the space of a few years by the persistent efforts of those who occupied themselves zealously in planting trees and shrubs, causing its desolate and forlorn appearance to give way to its present picturesque aspect. Everything there had to be done. There was no opportunity of supplementing species of the native flora; so to speak, there was a clean sheet to work upon. Besides luxuriant flax bushes, which were abundant, and huge tufts of toi-toi grass; the river banks were dotted with a few native shrubs of small size, such as *Coriaria*, *Coprosma*, two, or at most three species of *Olearia*; scrub manuka in some places retained its hold for a while, but these plants were all far too insignificant in their habits of growth, to produce any effect on the landscape. Of necessity willows and poplars, a case of Hobson's choice, were the first loves of the tree-growers, the choice of plants being in some measure limited to those kinds; they grew apace, side shoots and cuttings from them were eagerly sought for, and together with a sprinkling of cluster-pines [*Pinus pinaster*], they relieved the monotonous level of the place. They soon had their day, as a few seedling gum trees showed such extraordinary vigour and rapidity of growth that they induced a fashion to sow seeds of Australian trees. The blue-gum trees that started up in the gardens of Dr Barker and Mr W.G. Brittan, just opposite the old Waste Lands Office, were objects of general admiration; the dimensions they had attained within so short a time appeared little short of marvellous to Englishmen only acquainted with the slow growth of their own native timber trees. Blue-gum seed maintained a high value. Up to this period Wellington was the chief source of supply for fruit, forest trees, and ornamental shrubs, but communication with Australian ports soon permitted opportunities of much more extensive selections to choose from. The desire of cultivating Australian species in turn gave way before the furore for growing Californian conifers; the pine and the cypress in a great and attractive variety of form and foliage began to elbow the Australians. These changes spread over several years, have been attended with the happiest effects. The present generation has all the advantage of living with a beautiful variety of vegetation, that is not surpassed, if indeed it is equalled, in any other part of the Colony.

Taking into consideration, the scarcity of native timber trees within reach of the large majority of the population, it is a subject for lasting regret that the administrators of the affairs of the [Canterbury] Province did not take decisive measures to reserve for the purposes of a public park and recreation ground, the greater part, if not the whole of the forest of magnificent timber on the Port Hills, so conveniently situated for access by the people of Christchurch, as well as being within a healthy walk for the inhabitants of Lyttelton. In addition to its attractions as offering an ample fold for ease and enjoyment it would have proved an invaluable property for the public as a teaching ground for the rising generation. Children are now being reared in hundreds, or perhaps thousands, who have little, if any, notion of the native vegetation of the land in which they were born, or of the many interesting forms of animal life that exist in the primeval forests. Readily accessible from town, it would have been a priceless boon to working men of every class. There is little room for doubt that valuable discoveries would have rewarded patient investigation into the peculiar properties of the leafage, bark, gums, or even of the lichens and different parasitic growths that so abundantly invested several species of trees. But short-sighted policy prevailed, and official foolery and incapacity permitted the majestic growth of ages to be ruthlessly swept away so entirely, as in some places to have become obliterated, within a less space of time than the years of a single generation.

Years ago a ramble in these woods, a picnic if you will, was about the most enjoyable and charming outing that fell to one's lot throughout the twelvemonth. It is impossible to wander in the solitary depths of a venerable forest without turning over in pleasant surprise a neglected and unread page of natural history, of learning something from Nature that had been hidden because unsought, and which had remained undisclosed and unsuspected, though lying near at hand. The spirit of enquiry thus moved stirs one to fresh researches, which are sure to be rewarded, by affording an insight into some of the habits of the living world, that spreads its riches around us with lavish generosity. What book knowledge on the subject can be so true, so pure, so fresh? The student can read from the original text, without being led with the bias of another's mind, or confused by the explanatory commentary of some theorist. Here one is invited to see for himself the teachings of life; in one view is spread before him, birth, infancy, maturity, decay – the many phases presented in the struggle for existence which is always going on; the curious and most interesting forms or provisions, suggestive of protective mimicry. Can the trim plantation of a few seasons' growth teach us like the primeval forest? The glass case like the fern-tree gullies? Or can the aviary with its cramped surroundings and artificial modes of maintaining the survival of its cooped-up inmates instruct like the breezy shrub-zone of the green woods, revelling with the very breath of life untrammelled and unchecked? Yet natural history, in a great measure derived from such sources, has been dished up and welcomed as wholesome food. One has seen specimens of 'the old man of the sea', the wandering albatross cooped up in a wire-netted cage too narrow for the expansion of its wings; what lesson could be learnt from the wretched petrel enduring torture under such conditions, except from its pining away and its sickness unto death, from which one turns away disgusted with the licensed cruelty. May one be excused for this unwonted digression, and begin a forest ramble as of old. In preference, an early summer's day was chosen, but in a retreat where Nature showed so much of loveliness no part of the year was unfitted for such an excursion. It was a favourite habitat for birds, a resting place and feeding ground between the extensive forests that almost covered Banks' Peninsula and the isolated woods of Papanui, Kaiapoi, Rangiora, or the great fagus [native beech] forests far to the westward. On the way thither, attracted by their notes, one could always count upon seeing small flocks of kakas journeying to and fro, flying high, and progressing so steadily that their visits seemed matters of business or of duty. The brief note uttered at intervals, probably by the leader, somewhat confirmed this fancy; it sounded as in a satisfied tone, like a complacent intimation to the party that all was right. Through the tussocks that clad the spurs, lizards were scuttling away or luxuriating in a sun bath. Thousands of grasshoppers skipped before one's steps with a clicking noise. Sometimes, for a pleasant rest to breathe awhile, the advantage of a leading spur was sought, where an outcropping rock, grey with crisp dwarf lichens, gave an opportunity for enjoying a most extensive prospect of the plain, and the white crests of the snowy Alps. Whilst quietly lounging, the dark compact form of the bold falcon was not infrequently to be observed perched on some rocky eminence, motionless, except the head, which slowly turned, so that the hawk could warily scan all, above and around. Fearlessly, as though scorning any instinct of caution, it allowed a close approach, and when it chose to shift, with a forward stoop of the head and neck, a slow lift of the wings, it launched out into space with rapid flight. Its jarring scream often seemed to hush all other bird notes. This shrill cry was emitted whilst on the wing, either when in search of prey or at an early period in a chase. It was a terror to the feathered tribe, few could outfly it; sometimes the fatal stroke of its horny talons was avoided by a ruse, rather than by strength of wing.

When the outer belt was reached, amongst the thick bushy shrubs which crowded the boundary of the wood, where manuka grew in thick patches, or the wide spreading Broadleaf stretched out its gnarled roots, ferns were met with, though at first somewhat sparingly. It was the custom to collect ferns in those days, friends at a distance thought much of them for their rarity, the beauty of the fronds, and as a memento of so remote a place as New Zealand. Usually amongst the species first to be met with would be the round-leaved *Pellaea* [cliffbrakes], growing amongst the tussocks, very often, in nearly rounded patches; near by, often sheltered by a large stone or rocky fragment nestled the yellow green Rough bracken, *P. scaberula* [ring fern], with its beautiful oblong fronds twice or thrice divided. Among the shrubs or outermost trees, the Common Hard fern [*Blechnum discolor*] was plentiful, with a root-stock often several inches high; dotted about were grand specimens of the Prickly Shield fern [*Polystichum vestitum*] on stout root-stocks, sometimes a yard in height. These species tempted the collector, they were found to be hardy enough to withstand the rough treatment of a hasty removal for a time, and give some promise of being able to survive, not that the promise was at all reliable. It was certain that one's appearance just within the border trees would be the signal for the gathering of a flock of tree-creepers [brown creepers], who noisily greeted every arrival with a chorus of chirping sounds as they fidgeted and moved restlessly around and above the intruder. Far from being a scarce bird, having a very extended range from the coast line to the river beds of the Alps, and the woods that bordered on them, this little insect eater had the art of concealing its nest so skillfully that it was very rarely discovered. One's attention soon became too much absorbed with the magnificent timber to heed the little creepers that still hovered near on some of these trees. The totara bore away the palm from its grand dimensions – from sixteen to twenty-four and twenty-five feet [4.9–7.6m] in circumference. Numbers of them reached this size, and very many exceeded it. On a saddle near the higher part of the forest stood a glorious specimen that was fully 42ft [12.8m] in girth. This tree had grown rather flat in the bole on the side facing the south. Standing on that side, but on lower ground, where the twisted cable of huge roots rose through the mossy covering, looking upward on the mighty trunk with its flaky bark in places roughened or storm-torn, it showed some of the vastness of its size, and appeared like a time-eaten wall of a venerable tower with drooping ferns niched in the seamy crevices. The beautiful flaky bark of the totara often led to its mutilation and disfigurement. What so handy and easy to get for the covering of a bushman's hut; but a few chains distance toi-toi or tussock grass for thatch could be got in abundance. The easily-stripped bark was preferred, though the roofing of a wretched hut despoiled a noble tree.

One remembers it was to point out the mischief occasioned by this destructive usage that led to a fruitless interview with a Provincial Secretary some thirty years ago. It took but a few minutes to discover the unprofitableness of this proceeding; with the utmost urbanity of demeanour, the worthy official showed that he neither knew nor cared a rapp [sic] about the matter. The expensive system of timber-cutting licenses without efficient supervision, remained unchecked.

The black pine [mataī], less in dimensions than its congener the totara, was the next finest species amongst the valuable timber trees; of stately and majestic form, carrying a noble crown on a tall, robust stem that measured a considerable height before a single bough or branch jutted from the trunk, which was clothed with dark-coloured and rather scaling bark. The dead or decaying wood furnished at once the home and the food supply of the fat white larvae of the weta, one of the largest of the native insects. The hard, close-grained wood was perforated and comminuted into particles of coarse, gritty dust by the cutting organs of this soft, podgy-looking grub, whose workmanship was as true and perfect as any auger holes bored by a first-rate carpenter. The drupes of the several species of *Podocarpus*, in their season, offered most attractive food to some of the native birds, which migrated to these trees in their fruiting time. When the large and beautiful wood pigeons [kererū] – true fruit-eaters – flocked thither in their stated time of journeying from one forest to another, they appeared in very great numbers, that could scarcely be credited in these later times, after a whole generation of persecution has so woefully diminished their numbers. The extent to which such sweeping extermination has befallen these useful and perfectly harmless birds may be partly understood when it is stated that years ago a man, single-handed, killed one hundred and fifty pigeons in one day. These were packed off to Christchurch and sold at sixpence a-piece – not a very extravagant price to pay for so good a bird, when one considers its weight is from a pound and a-half to a pound and three-quarters [0.7–0.8kg]. Within a very short distance from that part of the wood where this sample of pot-hunting took place, last year a single pigeon appeared; this was so rare an event that the stranger was treated as one by a number of small birds, which moved restlessly about the bough on which the wood-pigeon was perched; bell-birds which joined with other species in mobbing it, uttering warning cries incessantly. This showed conclusively how rare the bird had become in one of its most frequented habitats. The pigeon was an ornament to the forests; its beautiful necklet of lustrous green showing very plainly above the white breast. It often kept its perch for some time without changing its position; just the noise of the wings gave one notice when it shifted, perhaps but a few trees away from its former resting place. When approached it exhibited no signs of timidity, nor seemed to watch the movements of any one drawing near to it. It was apparently endowed with a contemplative disposition, which perhaps meant it was disposed to indulge in recuperative rest, after a prolonged flight. When the fuchsia [kōtukutuku] berries were hanging black on the trees, pigeons were to be found near the creeks and moister parts of the wood, as the kohnini [kōnini][1] is a tree that loves the neighbourhood of water.

As showing the quiet habits of this game-bird, it may not be out of place to mention that one of the methods made use of by the Maoris to obtain it was by spearing. The instrument reserved for this purpose was made from a very straight growth of supplejack [kareao]. The hunter warily approached a tree on which a pigeon was resting; the spear was then raised. Often great care and skill was exercised when inserting it in the openings between the branches. When the proper distance for a stroke was reached, the weapon was thrust sharply into the breast of the bird. The main difficulty with the hunter was to manage adroitly this very long spear so as to avoid bending it, either when pushing it upwards between the branches or whilst looking for game in the woods; hence it was usually dragged along the ground. A pigeon spear that one had the opportunity of examining, measured rather more than seventeen feet [5.2m] in length. Although the bird was formerly so abundant its nest was not often met with; it is a slightly concaved platform structure; the egg of glossy whiteness is of a perfectly oval shape; it is so rarely found as to remain amongst the desiderata of most collections. It has been said that Maoris had some superstitious objection to taking the egg as bringing down ill-luck on the spoiler. The kaka was so frequently associated with the pigeon, in past days, as one of the woodland game birds, that one's thoughts at once turn towards it; its habits were in strong contrast to those of the last-named bird. The disappearance of the kaka is like the loss of an old friend; its qualities at once so varied, so conflicting, were not to be learnt by a mere casual acquaintanceship on a pot-hunting cruise in the bush. It was bold, affectionate, courageous, wary, subtle, noisy, silent, hilarious, or melancholy, just as circumstances affected its changeful moods. Its broad brain pan was something more for it than a mere ornament. A tolerable familiarity with this fine parrot allowed one opportunities of appreciating many of its more striking qualities. Its subtlety in deceiving one as to the position of the nest was very amusing, and quite made up for any disappointment in being led astray even half-a-dozen times.

In former days, wild pigs were plentiful about some of the Port Hills, and had many camps in the bush, where some people regularly hunted them. Some of the boars had achieved quite a local reputation for fierceness and the number of good dogs they had ripped. A certain black fellow was almost as well known to fame as Terrible Billy used to be in the Rakaia Gorge and thereabouts, of whom there are shreds of tradition that exist even unto this day. One day W–, who had a cottage near the foot of one of the long spurs, went up into the wood to shoot pigeons, and being very near sighted, he probably had not made a very large bag, before he heard the sound of something moving quietly through the thick undergrowth in his direction. As soon as he could make out what this might be, he espied a very large black boar coming towards him. Unfortunately, his gun was unloaded. As the brute advanced nearer there was nothing for it but to climb – for him almost an unknown accomplishment. W– was a dapper little fellow, who had a weakness for wearing long military boots; though, no doubt, as bold as a lion, still, on this occasion, it may be he thought 'the better part of valour is discretion'. Incommoded with his pet boots, he abandoned his gun, and clambering and clasping, raised himself into a tree in some fashion, the quicker perhaps as he could hear quite distinctly, somewhere just beneath his long boots, very suggestive grunts and champing of tusks. When he had recovered breath sufficiently to secure a very uncomfortable seat on a knotty bough, that seemed quite too pliant under his weight, by carefully craning and stretching his neck he could peer through the screening leaves, which gave him a momentary glimpse of a part of the enemy as it champed and moved below. Cramped and benumbed in all his limbs, yet not venturing to try a shift, being mistrustful of the endurance of his bough, that had saved, but now tortured him, it was unpleasant to know from the unmistakable sounds which reached him that the fierce animal was yet beneath. Hours seemed to slowly linger in their passing during his dreary watch, when to his joy he heard the report of a gun, and soon after the sound of voices. Clutching as tight as he could with both hands, he shouted 'Coo-ey! Coo-ey!' in a most frantic manner. This was happily responded to by the appearance of a couple of strangers to whom he called out, begging them to shoot the great black boar that was somewhere near the tree. When this feat was accomplished by his deliverers, he descended from his irksome perch, not only to find his cruel enemy slain, but that his game had been devoured. A few pigeon feathers only were strewed about the ground. Picking up his gun, he hastened home as fast as his numbed condition permitted. He directed his man to take up the sledge and fetch down 'that great black boar', which he had managed to kill at last, after the most tremendous hunt that had taken him hours. Up went the man and a boy with the bullock sledge to the spot described by W–. The man walked round and round the beast, staring at him, when at last taking out his pipe, he said: 'What's wrong with the boss, now. I'm darned if he ain't been and shot our imported prize boar – well, I'm blowed, this here is a rummy go!'

*

Far up the hills, quite on the curving saddles, the broadleaf (*Grisilinia* [*Griselinia*]) attained its largest size, stout and robust of figure, marvellously gnarled in the outlines of the trunk as well as in the branches, neither were the bare portions of the high arching roots that spread in ridges above ground, less elbowed with bulbous swellings. Growing so twisted, it seemed it might fairly claim, as of right, a place in [Gustave] Doré's weirdly landscapes, so full was it of bosses, knobs, and rotund humps, and bulging excrescences, gibbous, and bowed in every part. Framed for the polichinelle [i.e. Pulcinella, a Neapolitan puppet character] of the forest, with its uncouth figure, that, in an uncertain light, well might startle and alarm any wandering company of dryads or fleet-limbed wood nymphs. This fantastic habit was only thoroughly developed in those of ancient growth, whose odd grotesqueness of form so strangely quaint, set them as admirable foils to the majestic trees that neighboured them. On some of these old stems, at intervals, pale, glossy leaves had found a way to force a passage through the rugged bark that showed a world too tough to yield to any tender influence. Lithe and soft of texture, as they displayed their delicate structure, resting unfolded on the ridges of the seamy bark, they were as unlooked for, and seemed as much out of place and keeping as tears dropping down the furrowed cheeks of dried-up withered age. The spreading tufted coronet of the prickly shield fern was not infrequently to be seen coquettishly perched on a hunch of one of these venerable trees, or perhaps snugly niched in some of the many forks and hollows, as though aware that its beautiful fronds acquired a new grace when brought in direct contrast with the homeliness of its crooked support.

On the tangled roots sprawling above ground, has not one often taken a seat gratefully, less for restful ease than through being charmed thither by the loud, melodious notes of the dusky-feathered wood-robin [South Island robin]. Sometimes its lively song was poured forth from a straggling bush of karamu, or from a tarata growing with close compactness, overtopped by waving fronds of lofty tree ferns, fending off all glaring light from moisture-loving ferns and springy mosses, that spread over soil and root and rock, thick carpet coverings that hushed every footfall; in some such spot, on the very edge, on the brink of a mossy dell bordered with rocks and foliage, cleft out of the pleasant shade of over-hanging trees, just where some infant spring first learnt to trickle amongst green-clad stones and roots too shy for a fair view, dropped down in haste to hide itself in leafy tufts with many twists and turns. In such a place in the sylvan solitude oft one's ears drank in the full measure of this untutored carol in all the power of its sweet wildness, and listening, yielded to the ambushed bird the palm for its delightful wood notes. When the wood robin appeared in sight, with his black beady eyes watching everything, whilst he was singing vigorously, it was observable that, except turning very slightly, he forbore all motion. When encouraged to a close approach by remaining still, he picked up a few bread crumbs thrown towards him, but did not swallow them while in sight; he carried them away, returning again and again. What best seemed to please him was to raise some rocky fragments long embedded in the rich, leafy soil, and thus disclose to view the scared insect occupants scurrying away for concealment. On these the robin feasted with voracity. It required the removal of several stones to satisfy him and his attendant mate. She was equally tame and confident, but the pair allowed no other visitors to intrude. When its prime had been past and decay had set in, in its slow decline, the broadleaf was often, perhaps, as interesting as during its flourishing days; as the strength and toughness of the fibrous tissues became sapped, various forms of animal life found shelter in its massive but unsound limbs. The halcyon [New Zealand kingfisher], most laboriously, chip by chip, with its strong bill, picked out its sloping tunnel and chambered nesting place. The titi pounamu [rifleman], the wren of Colonists, the smallest among native birds, sought out some narrow chink or hole, whither it could convey grass leaves, fine sprays, and rootlets, the wherewithal to build its pear-shaped nest. Year after year the same crevice was used, the old structure renovated and the tiny white eggs, like sugared comfits, hopefully deposited. In the dark hollows of the broad trunk or larger boughs, bats took refuge, creeping close together in a companionship sometimes of many scores, till the dim twilight invited them forth to hunt nocturnal insects. Sometimes, though rarely, the beautiful wood lizard, with its deep velvety markings, was disturbed from its peaceful rest amongst fragments of decayed boughs that partly hid the roots. Large black spiders lay concealed under the *débris* of rotting bits of timber strewed around in a jumble of litters, just as it had broken off from the windswept limbs above. For its value, economically considered, the reddish timber of the broadleaf furnished excellent fencing material, posts made from it were durable, though perhaps rather rough in appearance, as the wood does not split very smoothly or evenly; however, it was well appreciated for the purpose, when neither kowhai nor totara was available. It was noted as excellent firewood, where black pine or manuka could not be procured; for these several reasons a big log of sound broadleaf had its admirers. Yet have I heard the same bitterly cursed, which seemed somewhat to verge on the unreasonable, and this by a man who had fired his splendid timber for grass-seeding. There lay around, the charred and mutilated remains of magnificent trees; for the impulse of the moment, and hot lust and greed for gain, had been too pressing for the slower work of converting the trees into useful timber. We were strolling on a saddle where immense broadleaf trees, charred black as coal, stood out stark and bare amidst the general 'abomination of desolation'.[2] Said the owner, 'Curse these confounded brutes o' trees, they won't burn, they'll only scorch, they're so deuced hard it costs too much to fell 'em.' At the thought thereof and in memory of their stubbornness, the pure air winning its way up from the deep gully carried away many a deep oath from the lips of the irate and impatient grass-grower.

On the colder exposures that received and welcomed into the foliage of the straggling wood cool and humid mists as they travelled onward from the far south, the kowhai, small of leaf, tall, and straight of stem, grew into a noble tree, with every part of it of value. The most useful and important species of all the native pod-bearing tribe, springing from an infancy of slender, pliant, yet tough branches growing in an interlocked whirl of green or yellowish-brown colour, it was surprising how straight a tree should lift itself from out the entwined tangle and hold its stem so upright. One could find in places near the outskirts of the wood patches of seedling plants of melicope [*Melicope simplex*], carpodetus [marbleleaf], and sophora (kowhai) growing close together. These at a transient view seemed to bear close resemblance to each other. The growth of the kowhai was very interesting to notice from its period of unpromising tough, wiry scrub. To watch how one of the intertwining branches gradually thickened and lengthened as it waxed stronger, as though it drew to itself more than its fair share of sap; then how gradually the end lifted itself from amongst the mesh of the other branches, establishing a lead, though still flexuous, and ever ready to sway to and fro. Month by month, year by year, the aspiring branch assumed a straighter form and grew out of the twists that marked its length, when this main shoot projected other branches, forming a slight head, a sprinkling of a few old gold coloured blossoms appeared hanging racemes to note the epoch of the kowhai's life. The sweets centred in its winged flowers were much sought after by some tribes of indigenous birds; even the widely scattered blossoms on a young tree just beginning to prove its fertility and capability of reproduction, would be visited by numbers of tuis and bell birds. Perhaps there might also be found another reason for this attraction, inasmuch as the species was a very early bloomer, closely following the flowering time of the large white clematis. A flock of tuis feeding on a kowhai with a large head of golden-coloured blossoms was a sight exceedingly pleasant to watch, but which must now yearly become rarer, owing to the peculiar methods adopted towards anything native. There were the various motions of the birds to notice, creeping, whisking and flouncing about the branches, clinging to the pendulous racemes of flowers that swayed with the bird's weight, thus showing off the metallic lustre of the plumage in almost endless reflections. The most unobservant could note all this play in bird life, from the heavy fluttering of the tui's wings directing attention to their movements. The restless gaiety and cheerful disposition of these happy creatures caused constant interruptions to their feast. There must be time for play, so with sprightly alacrity a sportive chase and pursuit is started, leading these play-mates through the intricate openings between the flexuous boughs, not very unlike darting through irregular meshes of a cord net-work. During this merry making, how quick the shiftings of the green-black feathers with their purplish reflections, and the snow-white chin-tufts tossing in their lively antics, which often ended with an outburst of song irregular and bizarre; then once more to brush with their tongues the honied sweets from the nectaries of the keeled flowers. Legal protection has at length stepped in to save the tui from extermination.[3] May it prove successful, and may flocks of these beautiful birds be allowed to survive for the enlivenment of woodland scenery for generations to come. In the very wood we are supposed to have been visiting a man boasted of having destroyed above seventy tuis in one day's sport?

The tui by no means enjoyed a monopoly of the kowhai blossoms; bellbirds [mokomoko] came for their share of the food, though some of their numbers might be driven off once and again by jealous tuis. But these lively skirmishes were without much real result, for the mokomokos quickly returned quite unabashed, and resumed operations till again chased away. Kakas were particularly fond of this sweet food; the very last time I saw a specimen of this fine parrot was whilst watching it thus feeding in a bye-place protected by a fence. This solitary specimen of one of our old intelligent friends seemed from his discreet conduct to be aware, not only that his race was doomed to destruction in this part of the country, but that his own life depended on his not being observed. He went carefully over the kowhai, threading his way quietly through the branches, visiting in silence the many-flowered pendulous racemes; feeding on them in mute reserve, yet with an eagerness of appetite that told of a long flight. His desolate lonesomeness had affected the bird's habits, the noisy hilarity, the wild screeches, the notes of warning were laid aside as not fitting the times, which for the safety of his life, enjoined secrecy and silence. If the remainder of the race should survive the rapid destruction of forests with their abundant feeding grounds, and the daily persecution that awaits the birds themselves, it is quite possible that many of the kaka's habits will undergo a change. Its congener, the kea, very quickly adapted itself and its habits to an ever-abounding food supply, by which, too, its numbers must have actually increased.

The water-loving konini (fuchsia) with stout trunk and brittle crooked branches, seemed ever to thrive best by a creek. The ragged, papery bark peeling off in jagged strips, apparently preserved the fuchsia from the growth of parasites of every species; it was rarely that one found any kind of fern growing on it. Birds sought the flowers and the berries; in early spring the bell birds visiting its blossoms frequently had the top of their heads stained blue, from the pulverulent substance on the anthers. In the early days konini berries were collected for jam making. A party thus engaged, with hands and faces purple-stained, reminded one of blackberrying in some favourite open wood in the Old Country.

There were many other trees in flower from the month of October, or earlier, even till January, such as the dark-barked mako (*Aristotelia*) [wineberry] with its thin, long-stalked leaves, almost heart-shaped, having a reddish or purple stain beneath, the flowers, in bunches, changing from pale yellowy green, rosy, sometimes to claret colour; the wood white and very light, hence it was sometimes known as cork wood. The ribbon wood (*Hoheria*), the ngaio (*Myoporum*) that so loved the sea breeze, with sticky tips to the branches, speckled leaves and small flowers of palest purplish white; the drupes when ripe were of a rich purple colour; there was also among them the rather locally rare titoki (*Alectryon*), but large specimens were not met with there; the branchlets were covered with a fine woolly down, the leaves shaped out with shallow notches, that reminded one somewhat of oak leaves. When in fruit it was specially attractive, as the rounded seeds were embedded in scarlet covers, which were very ornamental, so that when they could be procured they were used for decorative purposes, or were often sent away to excite admiration in the breasts of distant friends in the old country, as the rare tree was confined to New Zealand.

Titoki berries will persistently serve to remind one of an artless old female, who nearly always managed to introduce the name of this native tree into her conversation. The process might be circuitous, like the narrative of the effects experienced by her and her husband from the exhibition of certain medicines. Although this topic of her ailments might be somewhat embarrassing to her hearers, every detail was dwelt upon without abridgement. Titoki, in a word, was probably used by her to show that she had acquired Maori to a certain extent. As she was a woman of decidedly philanthropic principles, she – perhaps with pardonable vanity – justly prided herself on the civilising influence she exercised on the Natives with whom she was brought in contact. In early days she had established a kind of barter or Native trade on a very limited scale, parting with certain cast-off garments, and receiving in exchange, as equivalent, rolls and pieces of flax matting, Maori kits, &c. These various articles of Native manufacture, it is supposed, in great part were disposed of to her friends and acquaintances for ready coin, as curios. Being very religious, naturally anxious for the conversion of the heathen, she managed her deals in such a way that her swarthy customers received some soul-harrowing tracts, mainly such as contained startling promises, for certain shortcomings, of a long sojourn for the near future in a very warm climate [in hell], where water-races and artesians were unknown. These pleasant and agreeable little works, she in her pretty broken Maori, called 'bookee-bookees,' one of them added to a bundle of old clothes that might be bartered for, she considered ensured her Native customer the best of the bargain, it was such a valuable make-weight. Yet her artless goodness was not always fully appreciated by those she sought to benefit, and this unsatisfactory review of business transactions found expression much after the following manner by old tattooed Wiremu, a discontented purchaser: 'Your shirts no good, too much hole, eh! Old man's breeches, too much wear, eh! No fear, too much old, eh! Spose you give Maori more good shirt, eh! More breeches, ver good, eh! You like the good bookee-bookee much, ver good, eh! Maori sell you good bookee-bookee for one nip of grop, eh!' Thus spake Wiremu, holding up one finger to denote the nip of grog for which he thirsted, and then taking out from his battered old hat three of the precious tracts or bookee-bookees, tendering them in all good faith to his fair 'guide, philosopher, and friend'.[4]

In the earlier days there was but one gardener, and great was his profit, so many folks endeavoured to obtain a supply of plants from the bush. Out of the number who tried the experiment, not very many succeeded, hence native shrubs were said to be very difficult to rear. This non-success was not altogether a matter of surprise, when the rough manner in which they were secured is taken into consideration. Few, very few people, humoured the young things, so that they left their natural seed bed with as little damage to the rootlets as patient handling could ensure. The usual way was catch hold of the seedlings wanted, and tear them up by sheer strength, as though the strong man was the best collector. The belt of various shrubs that environed the timber trees used to be of such interesting character, that perhaps one may be excused in trying to recall something of it. On the south side, overlooking the [Lyttelton] harbour, the common bracken grew immensely strong, and the great wing-shaped fronds lay over each other in dense imbricated masses that one could scarcely struggle through. Olearias which later in the season, in their blooming time, were so attractive to moths and other insects, gave out a peculiar odour that was most pleasant and agreeable. How much of this insect life, that used to haunt these shrubs, yet exists? What portion of it may have perished, probably unrecorded? One shrub the wary avoided carefully, the nettle (ongonga [ongaonga]), a harmless looking shrub, straggling in its growth, the coarsely-toothed leaves profusely decked with stiff white hairs; a mere touch of it raised a blister on the skin at once, accompanied by a sharp sense of pain not readily forgotten. One has noticed the ardour of the green hand as a collector very much eased off after meddling with this plant, which seemed to prefer the drier slopes just outside the bush. Not very far from it used to grow a climbing shrub not commonly met with – now probably rare, if not almost extinct – the *Senecio sciadolphilus* [sic, climbing groundsel]. The aromatic drymis, or pepper-plant, also grew best on dryish situations; it was a handsome shrub, with dark, almost black bark, and bright dotted leaves with whitish under-surface that gave an odd appearance to its very compact form when its foliage was stirred with the wind. The several species, with their varieties of the sticky-seeded pittosporum, were always acceptable to the man who was trying to furnish a shrubbery, their beautiful foliage and close-growing bushy habit making them most desirable acquisitions. The small leaved species, *P. tenuifolium*, (tawhiwhi) [kōhūhū], may probably have some legend connected with it in Maori tradition, which might be worth while endeavouring to trace. When the funeral of Pita te Hori, the chief, (the last in the direct line from Tahu, the founder of the tribe), took place at Kaiapoi several years ago, amongst those who formed part of the procession from the deceased chief's *whare* to the grave, on either side, were some men armed, each one with a mere pounamu, wearing head dresses and mantlets fashioned out of the foliage of the tawhiwhi. The covering partly hid the face; it was said to be an emblem of mourning. But it certainly gave one an impression that these armed and partially concealed warriors might have been intended originally to represent some notable ambush, by which some well known chief had distinguished himself in a remarkable way, which was occasionally commemorated on important occasions, or that some person of note, probably an ancestor of the deceased chief, had been killed in ambush.

In addition to the shrubs, the collector almost invariably busied himself in wrenching up ferns of every species he could find, those of arboreal habit not excepted, because he fancied they would at once make a great show. One of the special charms of the wood was the luxuriant manner in which the Filmy todea [*Leptopteris hymenophylloides*] flourished – a most beautiful object with its oval translucent fronds, as delicate and sensitive as those of an hymenophyllum. To the fern grabber, it was so great an attraction as to be irresistible, the result was this species was torn up in a most merciless manner; the tender and flimsy texture of the fronds caused them immediately to wilt and wither never to revive. Perhaps not one plant in a thousand survived removal. Nor was this much to be wondered at; they would be taken away bound up in a bundle as large as a man could well manage to carry; then they would be planted in a corner of a potato patch, only sheltered by a post and rail fence; such were the usual gardens of the early days before trees and shrubs had grown high enough to make their mark on the landscape.

2. Out in the Open: A countryman in town (1887–88)

The visits of many a countryman to town are usually very brief, and so fully taken up with the transaction of various matters of business, that one returns home quite tired without having had the time or opportunity of noticing many things, the observation of which might be attended with some amusement, if not advantage. The hurried visit drawn out to a few days' stay, affords due leisure for looking about and seeing something of the town [Christchurch] as it really is at other times than during business hours. Perhaps the custom of early rising so confirmed as not to be hurriedly shaken off with a mere change of quarters, impels rather than invites one to stroll through the quiet streets in the fresh hours of the morning, whilst the bareness of the city is exposed during the helplessness of sleep. The unused streets lie so open to observation that the appearance of any living object attracts attention, the motions of a horse, a dog, or of a few birds, one's eyes follow involuntarily, as though the mind felt some relief from a sign of life breaking through the dull lonesomeness of empty throroughfares. The effect is curious in looking along the causeway, where verandahs are tolerably continuous, presenting the aspect of a long vista perfectly deserted, often without a single figure to disturb its solitude. The city seems given up to almost complete abandonment; in the midst of thousands, one is treading as in the privacy of a woodland path. Yet, let but one peal on the alarm bell be sounded, the deserted streets and footways would be thronged with crowds of anxious citizens, now snuggled in the confined air of bedrooms.

At this time of year there is light enough for a brisk walk before the rosy glow in the east points where the rising sun will dart its beams through and over the level fences with dazzling power. With a brief glance at the warming effect on houses nestling in the freshly tinted foliage, one hastens onwards for a view of the mountains. There are places where the Port Hills can be seen, and where they show up grandly. It is no longer so with prospects of the western ranges, open spaces are becoming crowded up with a rapid growth of foliage that shuts out the far distance. One has to go further a-field now-a-days whence to follow the outline of the snowclad mountains and note how their pallid crests become rosy with the greeting of the welcome sun.

A wakeful countryman used only to the crowing of his barndoor fowls, is not likely to sink into slumber for sometime after the outburst of shrill clamour that sets in about the break of dawn. Every poultry pen or yard within ear shot assists in the discordant jangling noise, the crowing of the cocks is as simultaneous as the word given out in the game of 'shouting proverbs'; in the harsh din of mingled and confused sounds it is scarcely possible to detect the note of any single fowl. A few hints may be gathered on natural history, the natural history of the streets during an early stroll, as several species of animals disclose some of their habits of city life. At an equally early hour with the poultry challenges, those familiar pests, the [house] sparrows, indulge themselves with incessant chirping for about an hour, then they become comparatively silent. Notwithstanding the efforts that are made to destroy them in agricultural districts, such attempts must be vain unless means be found by which they can be cleared from their strongholds in the towns, where they find an abundant food supply in the streets and yards. Sparrows are so hardy, with such omnivorous tastes, that their little bills turn almost everything to account in the way of food. I have repeatedly seen them watching the ebb of the tide in some parts of Lyttelton harbour, then immediately descend and pick about in the wet sand and mud flats, amongst bits of seaweed and other small matters that may be left on the flats by the falling tide. In these marine foraging parties, sometimes a chaffinch or two may also be observed equally busy with the bolder sparrows. In Christchurch, some parts of the river [Avon], that most attractive and useful feature that gives so much of beauty to the town, is very ill-kept and cared for, so that mud banks are suffered to form and remain, these often catch or detain masses of fallen sprays and floating bits of weeds, on these unsightly patches sparrows frequently alight and search them over for some favourite food. Birds that show so much intelligence and energy in hunting for supplies will be difficult indeed to destroy. The bold ravaging sparrow will continue an expensive parasite for the farmer, will follow his cultivation, and as he changes the face of the country by his labour, will impudently take its share of the grain without making much return. In the gardens its robberies are yearly shown by the appearance of the cherry trees laden with crops of bleached stones still adhering to the pendant stalks long after the luscious flesh has filled the craws of the defiant thieves, cheerfully chirping and befouling the house eaves with the coolest effrontery. It is too much to expect the hapless fruit-growers to be embued with so much philosophy as to feel

> 'The robb'd that smiles, steals something from the thief.'[5]

Some of the clumps of tall blue-gum trees afford sites for very small rookeries, as may be noticed in Barbadoes and Worcester streets; it is a matter for congratulation, that this valuable and friendly bird has thus shown a disposition to found colonies within the city. Here it is unlikely that their nesting places will become very extensive, like some of the great rookeries, which are highly prized features in many of the great parks in England. The cawing of rooks is among the more familiar and agreeable of rural sounds; it is pleasant to watch the long straggling flight of birds wending their way home towards evening. One's thoughts are carried away to many a cluster of grand old elms that shelter some of the picturesque homes, or are grouped about some of the venerable churches in the old country. Just now they are busily engaged in building, and the rooks may be observed patiently carrying up sticks to some of the higher branches of the trees. They are very social in their habits, the nests being placed pretty close together, at a very considerable height from the ground, where the boughs are sufficiently pliant to yield to the wind. In England where they have such an abundant choice of lofty and full-grown trees, it is the elm which is always reckoned their favourite for nesting purposes, although sometimes tall fir trees are selected; it is by no means an uncommon occurrence for nests to be met with in the precincts of a town. Rooks are exceedingly tenacious of their holdings, year after year rearing their families in the same clump or avenue of trees in a most conservative fashion, in spring repairing the old structures with fresh material. These birds for years to come should be strictly preserved; the farmer should cherish them for the good service they render in devouring wire-worms and the grubs or larvae of many forms of insect life. If they do occasionally help themselves to food of the farmer's producing, they honestly pay for their meal by the industrious and careful way in which they snap up insects in the newly ploughed furrows.

Sometimes one catches sight of a few hedge-sparrows [dunnocks] or shufflewings in the hedges, from their insectivorous habits they are useful friends to the gardener. The skylark whose delightful song may be frequently heard over some of the quieter parts of town, is by no means a general favourite with the farmer, it gives him too much trouble with his turnip crops. The habits of the skylark here are much more sylvan than in the old country, where they affect wide fields and open downs; here I have frequently put them from off paths amongst trees in the garden and orchard. I have seen them perched on low trees, notably the Kowhai, but this infrequently; it is not at all an uncommon occurrence to hear them in full song whilst perched on a rail or stone. At this time of the year very few of the pretty sprightly goldfinches are to be noticed shifting about the gardens, somewhat later they arrive in numbers; they thrive well here, and this gay little songster promises to be one of the commonest birds in the future. The nest is a beautifully made and compact structure, only less admirable in the closeness of its workmanship than that of the chaffinch, and is usually placed in a forked branch of a fruit or fir tree. Apple and plum trees seem to be frequently selected for the purpose; but this fancy need not alarm the fruit-grower for the safety of a portion of his crop. I have seen the nest built where its sides were touched by cherries, not the slightest attempt was made to taste the fruit, which was plucked before the young quitted the nest. Although the goldfinch is sometimes known as the thistle-finch, from its favourite food, it may be observed feeding on many kinds of seeds. Amongst others it shows a strong liking for those of the cabbage. One of the more useful birds that is now well acclimatised, and has become quite familiar from its attachment to our buildings, is the starling. About here, there were very soon after their introduction, quite colonies in some of the old decayed trees of the original forest on the Port Hills. It is very confident and familiar, liking to haunt the dwellings of man; the varied notes of its peculiar whistle are often heard from the roof or chimney top. It has a weakness for the society of [domestic] pigeons, or rather breeds in pigeons' nesting places, herein it shows a strange pertinacity. In a barrel pigeon house, I have taken the eggs and removed every stick of the nests, only to find within a few days the nests rebuilt, and the starlings as busy as ever, going in and out of the barrel. It breeds in holes on the cliffs of Lyttelton Harbour. It is a great insect-eater, feeding on caterpillars and the larvae of grasshoppers and those of many other insects; often it may be noticed on the backs of sheep. A large flock of starlings on the wing is a peculiar sight most interesting to watch, at a distance it looks like a dark cloud, it is seen to be capable of changing its figure instantly, so simultaneously are the movements executed with the cleanest precision, not a straggler out of place to blur the neatness of the evolution so swiftly performed by a vast assemblage. Now one would like to ask what has become of the Australian magpies which were quite numerous but a few years since; did they not become thoroughly acclimatised? Or is it owing to their confident habits, that they are now so rarely seen? One much fears their very boldness has caused their numbers to be so greatly diminished, that they offered temptation for slaughter, which was too much for the destructive propensities of many to resist. It will be a matter for regret should so valuable an insect eater become exterminated, more especially when there is taken into account the very considerable amount of trouble and expense which attended their introduction.

The song thrush has taken more than twenty years to gain anything like a firm footing in the district, that could be accounted as approaching successful acclimatisation. Twenty-three years ago I was able to show the late Colonel Packe and others some nests with eggs, in the shrubberies at Governor's Bay; from some cause which has remained without explanation, the birds very shortly afterwards were no more to be seen or heard. Within the last three years they have again appeared fairly numerous, the sweet and varied notes of these charming songsters may be frequently heard now at intervals throughout the day. Although cautious, they are far less shy than blackbirds, and often take up a more open and exposed position whilst singing. That may be considered as a rule. I saw a blackbird singing whilst it was perched on a sharp pointed finial on the roof of a villa close to the street; that is an exception to the rule. Lately I have seen the thrush here as near to the heart of the city as on the strip of greensward which fringes the river close to the municipal buildings. One may hear the blackbird daily in some of the more closely planted gardens, where it is well screened and hidden by thickly growing shrubs; only early in the morning is it likely to be seen on the ground traversing some of the side paths of the quieter streets, as about Latimer Square, everywhere it seems to be only too abundant for the interests of fruit-growers. On account of its destructive habits in attacking nearly all kinds of fruit grown here, the pale of protection is withdrawn from this old favourite species, and great numbers are annually destroyed. According to my own experience it feeds on strawberries, gooseberries, currants, raspberries, cherries, plums, peaches, pears, apples, and quinces; this list shows that the blackbird – like the sparrow – enjoys an accommodating appetite quite capable of appreciating

> 'A perpetual feast of nectar'd sweets,
> Where no crude surfeit reigns.'[6]

*

Almost the first thing that strikes an old settler in walking about Christchurch and its suburbs, is the climatic change which has overtaken the place during one's recollection. Quite a catalogue could be compiled of plants once considered as too tender for the plains, which now flourish here – plants that certainly could not have survived an experience of the great range of temperature which formerly was recorded for this locality. The spring months of October and November together, form a very favourable time for viewing the gardens and plantations, which teem with handsome flowering shrubs, many of which have been old friends at home. The lilac, known by some old-fashioned folk as the pipe-tree, in allusion to the structure of its branches, this year made a grand display, in some of the older gardens there are specimens about fifteen feet [4.6m] in height. During the luxurious *regime* of the last Empire, it was said that French gardeners had discovered an ingenious plan for blanching this flower, so as to meet the enormous demand for white lilac blooms, which a caprice of fashion had called into vogue. The elegant white lilac is not commonly seen, and deserves for its beauty's sake to be very much more extensively cultivated. The thorns blossomed freely; in some places alterations of garden grounds had left a quick-hedge plant to grow up into tree-like size with a noble head of flower, the scent from which was carried far and wide, so that in some of the streets passengers really could enjoy the walk

'Beneath the milk-white thorn that scents the evening gale'.[7]

With the double crimson thorn, its beauty is followed by the drawback of a very seedy, unwholesome appearance that overtakes it when its blossoms are fading. Of the *Viburnum* genus, the Gueldres rose might be more plentiful; then species such as *suspensum*, *lucidum*, and others, all attractive from their bold foliage or excellent habit, might find their places in most shrubberies of any extent. The *Cytisus* laburnum, introduced into England nearly three hundred years ago, still represents the genus in most collections, although there are several species quite as deserving of cultivation. It may not be generally known that the seeds of this favourite tree are poisonous; a mysterious and in the end fatal occurrence, that befell some very young children a few miles from Christchurch, was attributed to their having eaten seeds of the laburnum tree beneath which they were playing. Sycamores and oaks bore an unusual quantity of blossoms this season. The same remark will apply to many hollies, one of those two at the gateway of the Public Library was crowded with flowers, the scent of which spread to a considerable distance.

The appearance of many of the gardens gives one the idea that the contents are too much crowded together for the due display of the distinguishing habits of most of the various shrubs and trees. It may be that some of the owners are endeavouring to meet this difficulty with the use of shears; a few evenings since I passed a garden where the occupier was trimming a young oak as nearly into the shape of a ball as his management of the shears permitted. There are unmistakable signs in several parts of the town, that there is taking place a sort of revival of the hideous practice of clipping and shearing trees and shrubs into many uncouth shapes; this new old-fashion might be suitable enough for a Dutchman's paradise, but only produces as a result unseemly and misshapen eyesores, amongst the natural outlines and contours that beautify an English garden.

One cannot fail to notice that in some situations, the favourable soil and climate has urged on trees to make very rapid growth, which is not always satisfactory, this not so much from the fault of the trees, as on account of the situation where they have been planted. Often one may see specimens of the largest kinds of forest trees the world produces, occupying a small plot of ground in front of some neat little cottage. Already the boughs stretch forth their young shoots, shutting out light and air, as they proceed to block up windows, to press and chafe against walls and verandahs, to every passing breeze by creaking they are audibly making known the sufferings they endure from the narrowness of their quarters; these are in the first few years of infancy – seedlings perhaps from the mighty forest giants of the Yosemite – struggling for breath on a garden plot some half-a-dozen yards square. Among the commonest of sights are those of trees interlaced and locked together to their great mutual disadvantage and injury, to the permanent hindrance in most cases, of a necessary and proper development of their natural beauty of foliage and grace of form. Before many years elapse the ornamental grounds about the city and its suburbs will require a forty-Gladstone power[8] to amend their ways, so that 'the axe is laid upon the root of the trees'.[9] These hints might extend beyond ornamental planting, fruit trees are sometimes set without much regard being paid to their future growth; as when one sees eight fine young apple trees occupying a lineal space of not more than twelve paces, or about ten yards, these same trees evidently are grafted on vigorous stocks; not but what this amount of room would have been ample for certain kinds, if worked upon the paradise, and treated to a special kind of culture. Much as one must admire some of the effects of the planting of trees and shrubs about the town, there yet seems to be some little room left for a few suggestions, which are offered with deference, about some ornamental shrubs that might be cultivated more generally with much effect in private grounds. We owe to the South American flora many desirable plants, which prove suitable to this soil and climate, this ready acclimatisation perhaps seems to hint at an intimate connection in former ages. Amongst these shrubs there are the Escallonias, of the very easiest cultivation, of these *macrantha* is an established favourite; but why are not the lovely white blooms of *E. floribunda* or *montevidiensis* more frequently seen? The handsome *Photinia serrulata* with its magnificent corymbs of white flowers, deserves to be encouraged a great deal more than it is at present, if only for the sake of the large bright glossy leaves which, as they decay, change to scarlet and bronze; these are found to be very useful for decorative purposes, the bark of one of the Indian species, in economics, is made use of for obtaining a scarlet dye.

The elegant genus, Magnolia, would in itself furnish quite a number of beautiful showy shrubs, some flowers of which are deliciously perfumed. Few of the species are grown here. The Rhododendrons that one sees are too much alike, being mostly layers of the old-fashioned *R. ponticum*; this grand family of evergreens in various species and their hybrid varieties offer an abundant choice of lovely flowering shrubs to select from. How rarely does one observe the fragrant *Azalea pontica*, with its rich yellow blossoms that come so early in the spring. The immense number of deciduous azaleas of North American origin, and perfectly hardy, are scarcely known here – at anyrate in private gardens; yet they produce flowers of nearly every colour and shade, except blue.

In how many gardens could one see the lovely wax-like blossoms of the Kalmia, or the *Benthamia fragifera*, with its nankeen coloured bloom and large globular fruit of a peculiar yet not unpleasant taste? A fine specimen of this plant stands in the Public Gardens, an inspection of which will prove what an admirable addition this Nepaulese [sic] plant would be to the larger shrubberies. The *Acuba japonica* of either sex, with fine glossy blotched leaves, suffers a cold neglect. *Quercus coccinea* is admirable for autumn effects, whilst the Copper beech exhibits the richest coloured foliage in the spring.

For scent, the *Diosma ericoides* from the Cape of Good Hope, with neat white flowers and heath-like foliage, only requires a trial to become a universal favourite. The *Boronia megastigma*, with its powerful aromatic perfume, is only second to it in its claims for recognition.

The modification of climate, due in great measure to the presence of extensive and efficient shelter, partly owing to improved drainage, warrants the trial of several plants which could not have survived out-door treatment some years ago. For instance, further selections might be made with advantage from the numerous Acacias, Abutilons, and Hakeas; *Ficus macrophylla* [Moreton Bay fig], *Protea mellifera*, *Plumbago capensis*, the dwarf *P. Larpentae*, the ever-flowering *Polygala grandiflora*, are worthy of some trouble. These are all exceedingly easy of cultivation, and, be it remembered, a handsome shrub occupies no more room than a scrubby one. The *Camellia japonica*, in its beautiful hybrids, should soon be accounted among the common evergreens; in another place, I have seen a very beautiful screen fence composed of azaleas.

Why should not native plants be more generally planted? Can there be found evergreens to surpass in beauty and closeness of foliage the native representatives [New Zealand beech] of the genus *Fagus*? Yet these fine shrubs or trees are so rarely planted that very many old settlers know not the blossom. *Brachyglottis repanda* [rangiora], with its masses of large branching panicles of flowers, scented like violet powder; the shrub rata of the sub-alpine country of Canterbury (*Metrosideros lucida*) with its scarlet myrtle-like blossoms, would be most desirable additions to the shrubbery. It seems almost invidious to name but these few species, where so many have almost equal claims, but space will not admit of an extension of the list just at present.

Before leaving the subject of shrubberies and plantations, I should like to say a few words about the strip of evergreens situated above and below the mill-bridge, on Cambridge terrace. The ground lies very low on that part of the terrace and seems to offer special facilities for making extensive swimming baths for the use of persons of either sex. The complaint of bathers is the coldness of the water of the Avon, and some bathers will walk as far as Wilson's bridge to obtain a good bath at a slightly higher temperature. A wide exposed surface of almost still water, that is, still as compared with the flow of the Avon, would show a far higher temperature than the stream of the river, and be more generally acceptable to bathers. To place the means of bathing and swimming within the reach of a large population, would be a very valuable boon, health-giving and exhilarating. Learning to swim, it is needless to say, is an accomplishment that should be almost compulsory with youth in a country like this, a narrow island intersected with dangerous rivers that have over and over again exacted the cruel penalty of death from both sexes. When the mill is removed, very probably great alterations will be taken in hand, which may lead to the increased attractiveness of that part of the city. Enjoyable baths, without having to overcome almost insuperable difficulties, might be dovetailed into such plans, to the comfort of thousands of citizens. To his Worship the Mayor, who has been often perplexed with the proffered aid of the unemployed, I would respectfully point the advice –

> 'Cast they bread upon the waters, for thou shalt find it after many days'.[10]

Whilst taking a peep at gardens early in the morning one has found some apparently excellent instances of animal intelligence, particularly in the horse. One was led to this observation through noticing that whilst feed was very scarce, in several gardens where there were grass plots or tennis lawns, at some late hour of night or very early in the morning a horse has managed to secure an entrance, and apparently done ample justice to the feed before him. The matter of surprise is how so many horses had learnt to overcome the difficult feat of opening a gate, and in some cases shutting it behind them. In one instance the horse seemed to have forgotten his cunning, and, as a modern Lucius, was finishing off a rose-bush, perhaps with the hope of recovering the lost spell.[11] One feared, that like Ali Baba's brother Cassim, lest he should not find his 'open sesame' before the wronged owner of the garden discovered him. Taking down a set of slip rails and replacing them is another intelligent performance that deserves to be recorded. This feat apparently is performed sometimes by two or more horses acting in concert: it displays a degree of sagacity and thinking principle worthy of Honyhnhnms.[12]

The sparrow invariably seems equal to any difficulty in the way of procuring food. A pair having young to feed traversed the corrugations of an iron roof over the edge of which they examined small spider webs fixed there. From these preserves they repeatedly carried away insects up to their nest. To clear out webs that were attached lower than they could reach from the top side, they hovered in front of the webs, vibrating their wings much in the same manner that the grey warbler does when collecting cobweb to felt into the materials of its nest. By this clever scheme they obtained some insect food for their young, already caught; a thick holly hedge supplies them with a fair amount of insect food. I am not aware that they pick off the scale, but they constantly visit the hedge and pick out insects that take refuge there.

About the middle of November, young rooks were trying their wings. Very early in the morning, rooks from the colony in the blue gums in Worcester and Barbadoes street visited some cypress and pine trees in Latimer square, they perched on the very slightest and most pliant sprays, near the ends of the branches; these swayed with their weight, causing the birds to make an awkward sort of flutter which always appeared to end in a very brief flight. Those in Salisbury and Manchester streets, rather later by a day or two, practised on the extreme ends of tall poplars, precisely the same kind of exercise.

The rooks will clear off an immense amount of wire worm and chafer grub, which should help the farmer with his potato crop, and he wants all the help he can get. At the profitless value at which they have been sold this season, there is but small encouragement to continue their cultivation in large quantities. But could not something be done that would afford some measure of relief to the potato farmer? Could not the manufacturer step in to help him, with advantage to himself? What is the amount that is sent away from the colony for the products manufactured from the potato? I believe both in England and on the Continent very considerable industries are carried on in the preparation of delicate food, of which the foundation is the farina of the potato; nor are these the only articles of wide consumption that are manufactured from that valuable tuber. When prices fall so low as to range below £1 per ton is there not margin enough to encourage the establishment of a manufactory of some of the potato products? It almost resolves itself into a question of machinery. The bright hope for the farmers at present appears almost to centre in the success of the Farmers' Co-operative Association – their own special institution for marketing their produce. It seems only reasonable that through the agency of this patriotic organisation, enquiries should be made and information obtained on a matter which might lead to beneficial results to the farmer. The cost of the raw material here being so very much below that ruling in Europe, where a farmer carting his potatoes to a market or station for twelve shillings per ton or even at a lower price, would be happily an unknown experience. A steady price for this kind of produce, even though it should be low, would be a certain relief for the future.

3. Out in the Open [On humblebees] (1886)

The level surface of the Canterbury Plains offers some difficulty in arriving at the results of planting which has been carried on more or less vigorously for many years. This difficulty especially makes itself felt just around and about Christchurch, where the rampant growth of vegetation engirts and shuts in the observer with thick screens of foliage, preventing the enjoyment of any distant landscape. It is true that one's eyes following some line of street may rest on a very limited section of the Port Hills, but such a view is scarcely satisfactory. The bold outlines of the Southern Alps, the magnificent border which befringes and hems the Plains is now almost lost to view, hidden by the rank leafage of thriving plantations and orchards. Any day towards the end of May month, it was quite worth while dragging oneself up betimes, daring the chilliness of early morning, only to mark the effects of sunrise on the snow-capped peaks and ridges, to watch their cold solemnity quickened with glowing blushes at the sun's radiant glance. We owed much to the full prospect of the mountains, the lofty ranges gave us many a forecast of the weather, there was no need of speech, attendant clouds changed their form and outline into signals which the weather-wise had learnt to interpret. Year by year we must go further afield to study the expressive face of the mountains if we care to observe the signs they foretoken.

In gazing around one, it is difficult to look back and recall to mind the appearance of the city and its suburbs in former days when 'the bittour with his bump'[13] frequented the sedges and flax-bushes of the river-banks, and ofttimes flapped his broad wings, steering sedately across the market place. It seems like the sudden upstarting of the enchanted woods, at the wave of the magician's wand, those woods which make such effective scenery in the stories and tales of faery land. Yet, thriving as are the trees in appearance, not all of them will bear close scrutiny; some that have grown apace and mightily upreared their topmost branches, may be hewed down as worthless; to dally further would be to fare worse. To give an example, let us take that noble pine the Scotch fir (*P. sylvestris*) [Scots pine], which may be set down as a failure: after the bestowal of care and attention for twenty years, when giving fair promise that it would even or surpass the growth of the species on its native mountains, suddenly it has been blasted with a blight filthy and baleful.

For the estimation of its value in the old country, we know it would scarcely be possible to select a hardier or more robust species; one that produces excellent timber on the mountain slopes, yet thrives vigorously on level ground. Here in contrast, whether growing close together as in a belt or plantation, or completely isolated, the same miserable fate overtakes them, they become completely covered with aphis. This repulsive insect has entire possession, the divisions of the bark it has edged with whitened seams, it infests boughs and branches to the outmost sprays, not sparing cones or leaves. This disgusting disease, if it may be called a disease, is said to be unknown on this valuable fir in its native habitat. The loss of this useful and ornamental timber tree is a grave disappointment to those who have planted on the Plains, but still worse is it for those who have covered hilly ground with the young trees. In so many cases where these favourite and highly esteemed pines occupy commanding positions, clearing out the blighted trees must cause unsightly gaps that will require years to hide. As the parson says towards the end of a sermon, when he wants his hearers to pluck out the pith of his words, there is a lesson to be learned. Now this lesson, I take it, is this: to avoid trusting altogether to exotics for tree planting, to give some attention at least to the reproduction of the valuable native species before they are entirely destroyed and lost to the world. Many of these species are of great value for their timber, hardy, easy of cultivation, but comparatively are of slow growth; this is a fatal objection with many folk, but their excellent qualities should weigh in their favour, this should be so at least where public plantations are undertaken. What a list of noble and useful trees at once cross one's mind, all of which must eventually be of the utmost value, within a few years' space. Let us suppose public spirit to be sufficiently aroused in this direction to undertake the planting of that majestic and most valuable timber tree, the totara (*P.* [*Podocarpus*] *totara*). Questions, it is likely, would be asked concerning its habits, which could be satisfactorily answered. Would it thrive on the Plains? Those who can remember, or who enjoyed the pleasure of visiting or becoming familiar with the Waimate forest in its glory can answer the query; those extensive woods spreading from the level ground up the rising spurs and slopes produced magnificent totara timber of great commercial value. Is it hardy? Few native trees can surpass it in this respect, it is a marvel of robust sturdiness; it is found of large dimensions on the terraces of the Alpine valleys, thriving under a most trying climate. Within a few miles of Christchurch I have measured a specimen which gave 42 feet [12.8m] round the bole; another on Banks Peninsula exceeded this in circumference of its stem by some three feet [0.9m]. The totara is mentioned by way of illustration, it is but one of many native species of great economic value. If the people had but a desire to have such planting undertaken, the result would prove of the utmost benefit, it would offer useful occupation for the unemployed, remunerative to the whole country, valuable as an endowment for the future. The objection to the rearing of native trees on account of their slowness of growth, after all, is but comparative, how many valuable trees cultivated in Europe, of superlative excellence, might be discarded for this very reason? yet the Englishman has stood by the oak.

There are many reserves that could be rendered valuable by covering them with native forest trees, these should be planted and maintained with the full intention that they should succeed, there should be no perfunctory, careless, or half-hearted work about it. There should be an abundance of nurses in the way of undergrowth, shrubs that produce drupes and berries on which native birds could find a living. For be it remembered, such species would afford to the young forest, just as much protection, attract and preserve as much moisture and cost no more to sow, than other species without the same recommendation.

Many persons may feel grateful to those legislators who, having some care for the preservation of native birds, placed the tui under the protection of the law, and saved this beautiful bird from extermination. It would be a further boon if the schedule was once more brought under consideration, with the view of extending the list of native birds to be brought under the Protection of Certain Animals Act. Why should not the far-famed bell-bird be included? From its tame and confiding habits, but too often it falls a victim to the catapults of thoughtless boys. Before now one has felt ashamed at the sight of a string of bell-birds bunched together, lying in the dusty roadway, just as it has been dropped by some tired youth when trudging towards Lyttelton after a long day spent in the gullies of the Port Hills. The massacre of the Ocean Shag (*P. punctatus*) [spotted shag] should be stopped. One of the handsomest of the native sea-fowl, this characteristic ornament of the cliffs and headlands is now wantonly destroyed in the name of sport, and for what? Much good would probably be effected if steps were taken to secure, on the part of the public, a more general knowledge of the schedule of protective enactments.

The tui during the past season, not only appeared about here in greater numbers, but it seemed to evince some signs of a wish to become sociable, to flutter around and gladden man's dwellings by more freely bringing glances at its gleaming feathers fairly within eyeshot. An interval of peace, a rest from persecution, has heartened it to abide with us, giving forth gleeful notes in the first breath of spring, through the hot summer-time, hunting, gliding, hurrying amongst the rustling leaves of shrubs and trees from rosy dawn almost till the balmy hour when grey-clad evening cools the dew-bent grass and herbage. It pairs early in August, when sometimes jealous cock birds may be seen fighting in the air. This probably unusual sight shows off the green metallic lustre of the plumage with bluish-purple reflections, as turning, twisting in the warm sunshine, the rivals oftimes descend and rise together with strong wing-beats, their curled white chin-tufts fluttering, as the birds struggle for the mastery. Now comes in view such changes of colour in the bright sunlight as if the glossy feathers were shot with varied tints of green, and bronze, and bluish purple. The short-lived contest never appears serious; perhaps it is a kind of high parade for the benefit of some coy female, whose favour is thus disputed in this aerial strife. The chase of the female is well worth watching; for, with noisy wings, the pair start off with great speed, sweeping amongst trees, darting into the open, then for an instant hidden in the depths of some bushy gully, now again they come in sight, fleetly skimming the outer branches; the female just dodges her pursuer, till she drops into the darkling shadows of some friendly thicket. In the first days of last October I noticed a pair often peering about some laurels, close to the dwelling-house; on the 4th, it was with the utmost pleasure one understood from their movements they were about to build. To gather materials for the foundation of their home, twigs were secured and carried off into the laurels. A group of tree-ferns (*Cyathea*) was frequently visited, fragments of decayed fronds selected and taken away. The hen-bird was the busier; she came fearlessly under the verandahs, perhaps for cobwebs. The home was being constructed in a very thick-leaved laurel at nine feet [2.7m] above the ground, about four yards [3.7m] from a door where there was constant traffic all day. The hen was hard at work on the nest, most carefully laying and fixing the materials from the interior, sometimes staying a minute or so at a time, turning round and round, shaking and consolidating the building. This while her mate was apparently engaged on the look-out, whilst he beguiled the tedium of his watch with frequent songs. On the 6th the hen early at the nest; on the two next days the birds did little, if any, work; on the 9th they were taking strong flights from lofty trees, both uttering sharp, quick notes, sometimes together; on the 11th the tui was happy in the perfect enjoyment of her nest. An honey-eater, the bird often displays most pleasing bits in life-pictures. To see it hanging in almost any posture from the long climbing strings of that pretty Peruvian climber, the *Eccremocarpus*, sipping the sweets of the pendant orange-coloured blossoms, swaying, swinging at ease amongst the brown, wind-swept and raveled seed-pods till the whim for a song leads it to quit the dangling bower of sweets, and seek, with quickened movements, another perch, to which it hies, where it can puff out the feathers of its throat and fore-neck, turn its head, and with an air of grotesque gravity jerk its head from side to side whilst pouring forth its loud notes. Often several of these birds will take to flight and follow each other almost in single file, to alight on some particular tree; or many will dart upwards in the bright sunlight, really as if in the very act of adoration of the great source of light and heat; or one may be seen, perhaps, hawking a moth; notwithstanding its somewhat heavy flight, it turns and twists, and often succeeds in snapping up the dodging insect. A few years since it was but seldom seen. It had been well-nigh destroyed in this neighbourhood, where a bird-killer had been known to slay above seventy in one morning. Legal protection has done good in this instance, which should induce further efforts in a similar direction.

The Yellow-head (*Orthonyx ochrocephala*)[14] has remained in a gully near the house throughout the year. The surprising perseverance with which it has continued to utter one call, day by day, week after week, has assumed the aspect of monotony; the oft-repeated sound is very like the distressed cry of a lost chicken.

On the flowers of the abutilons – by some better known as Chinese lanterns – the Blight-birds (*Zosterops*) [silvereyes] feed at times. It is pleasing to watch these active, restless creatures, crowding together and hanging about the round bells of various colours. One needs something of this kind to be reminded that ornithologists have included the genus amongst the honey-eaters (*Meliphagidae*). Most often it forebears tasting such sweets, leaving them for much coarser food.

If one could tire of the presence of birds, their interesting ways and their most useful teachings, there are numbers of insects whose habits would afford plenty of occupation to those who take an interest in the curious pages of natural history. Many native species doubtless have been exterminated, others have become rare, some have accepted the changed condition of things existing under cultivation, and may be considered as likely to remain with us. Of the burrowing insects, one of the most remarkable is the trap-door spider [*Cantuaria dendyi*], not so much for its figure and appearance as on account of the finished workmanship which it bestows on its home. This interesting creature for some time was found only near Oamaru, to the south, and in and about the suburbs of Auckland, in the north; but probably it was overlooked, as the covering to its home is so beautifully contrived that its discovery is not an easy matter. Some time since, a perfect specimen of the nest was found in a plantation here, beneath the shade of a pine (*P. ponderosa*) where the ground sloped gently. The soil had been under cultivation some years before, and afterwards was laid out as a plantation; the aspect was north-easterly. The depth of the cylindrical tunnel was about ten inches [25cm], and the width of the mouth very nearly an inch, all was beautifully lined with tough silky webbing. The most curious feature was the lid or trap-door which, with the hinge, was a marvel of construction; the mouth of the nest or tunnel was beveled, the lid exactly fitting it, so that when shut down all was quite close. The beautiful hinge was so admirably formed and adjusted that it fell to almost with a spring; the underside of the lid was made of web whilst the top had bits of grass and earth interwoven, so that it was a firm close covering, so like the surrounding soil as to be difficult indeed to detect.

The Bumblebee or Hummel or bummlebee, according to older English, in the spring and early summer enacted the part of the distinguished foreigner, the lion of the season; the public appeared so interested in its welfare, that its movements constantly under the eye of the observer were carefully chronicled in the columns of almost every newspaper. Well it carried out the role assigned to it; it buzzed and hurried away from place to place, with all the restlessness that marks the progress of the well known globe-trotter. The Bumblebee as an emigrant is not on its trial however, we know of its use, of its value, we have already settled that only good will follow its introduction here; it is to fertilise the red clover, and tie another string to the bow of the hard beset farmer. Still it will be interesting to ascertain some of the results of its labours, these will be appreciated only gradually, let us say, after the lapse of a few years. It is a bold bouncing creature, blustering and vigorous, as though feeling the spring and gladsomeness of life and joyful that fate had brought it to a new and wondrous land so sunny and so fertile. Heedless perhaps in some slight degree, or it would respect our prejudices and avoid meddling with huge purple-crowned thistles, scarlet poppies, and divers other plants esteemed but as worthless weeds by careful cultivators. Often we must have looked on the harmless thistle-down disporting itself in spreading showers; or whirling onwards in clouds; leaving fleecey keepsakes at every fence and hedgerow; floating light as gossamer, now softly falling, or circling in round dances with each freakish eddy; fanned with a warm breath, now again ascending, till hurried by the fretful breeze into space dimmed beyond our vision.

Now arises an interesting question; to what extent if any will the productiveness of undesirable plants be affected by the working of the bumblebee. At present we do not require any change in this respect, as regards the habit of the thistle, though the presence of that well known plant may be a trusty indication of good soil; we are satisfied with its silent information. 'How large are the thistles here?' said the blind man when *looking* for a farm. Many of the plants to which this bee has been accustomed in its native home are to be found growing luxuriantly; in addition to these, this genial climate affords an ample choice from the variety of exotic plants which have become acclimatised and flourish here. It seems odd to find this insect probing and gathering from such flowers as the scarlet geranium, the native veronica of several species, the tender feathery black wattle, so impatient of frost; the highly scented blossoms of the lemon, or the wide corollas of the delicate fuchsia. What are its relations with the honeybee? Are the insects rivals or must they become so at no distant date? Many species of flowers which till this year were attractive to the honeybee, moths, and some small insects only, have been visited in the past season by the bumblebee. For instance, the broad brown disk of the stately sunflower with its vandyked border of yellow petals affords verge and scope enough for a bevy of honeybees, on it the new chum hath alighted, and with sonorous buzz rather jostled our honey storing friends; the golden chalice of the marrow invitingly upheld for winged wayfarers to sip, often is monopolised by the bumblebee who arrives noisily, sounding his horn of triumph as claiming an indisputable right of possession.

After the honey harvest has been taken, according to the old world notions, at some early hour of murky night; and the rich combs have been set to drain out their luscious yield; it is usual for the emptied boxes, reeking yet with sulphur fumes, sticky, smeared over with wax, honey, and fragments of comb, to be placed so that the reserve stock of bees may get access to them and gather something from this spoil and refuse. This season, on the boxes being exposed, it was seen they were quickly almost in the sole charge of strong parties of bumblebees. Nests of this insect have been found in many places; one situated near here is on the edge of a creek amongst the roots of a tree; it was noticeable that when a person stood in full view of the hole, the home-coming bees wheeled round without alighting, as if to avoid disclosing the position of the nest. On timing those coming home, it was found that in five minutes an average of ten bees would return; the busiest time for arriving was late in the afternoon – March 23rd from 5 p.m. to 5.5 p.m. seventeen came to the nest.

From the extraordinary rate at which this bee increased in so short a time; from observing that it already shares many flowering plants with the honeybee, it seems possible that we shall have quite enough of its company, and may perhaps in time reckon that the consideration paid for the fertilisation of the red clover is sufficiently high priced.

During this summer some interesting forms of insect life usually abundant, have been rather infrequent in their occurrence about this neighbourhood. This remark certainly applies to the Tiger beetles (*Cicindaloe*), the Walking-sticks (*Phasmae*), the Sand-wasps (*Sphegidae*)[15] and a few others. Some of these species show instances of animal intelligence that are remarkable, and will repay close observation.

The Tiger beetle, or Butcher – the last title is the name by which it is known to the children hereabout – is by far the most active and restless of any of the native coleopterous order; it usually occurs during the warmer season in such numbers, that its sprightly movements are doubtless familiar to many. Its customary habitat is on dry clay banks or bare spurs of silt or cob, having a warm aspect; especially does it haunt naked patches, left bald of herbage by ground-slips, the work of some very wet season of past years. Such a spot may be observed to be drilled with numbers of round holes, often rather close, varied in diameter; some are but large enough to admit the insertion of a fine grass stem, whilst others measure at the least three or four times that size. The depth is from two to six inches [5–15cm], rarely is this exceeded; they usually follow an easy angle from the surface; there seems to be no fixed or precise rule as to the direction in which they are excavated, except that they decline from the entrance, often they trend obliquely to the right or left, some few are almost perpendicular, whilst many are nearly horizontal. Sometimes these tunnels have an artificial addition to the entrance in the shape of a circular projecting rim, the width of which varies; these projections would probably divert water from the mouth of the hole; others have the entrance hollowed out neatly, as if the work had been done with a countersink. In some places, where stunted and dwindled grasses straggle over the beetle warren, I have noticed the rims are more produced, being elevated above the surface an eighth of an inch [0.3cm]; widened above, like a trumpet mouth.

The ugly grub, stained of an unwholesome-looking dull yellowish-white, remains in its hole, obtaining food from the chance visits of insects, all unconscious of danger, which rest, perform their toilettes, or sun themselves into renewed vigour on the warm bank

'Alas! regardless of their doom,
The little victims play;'[16]

The larva either keeps out of sight in the tunnel, or shows its big horny head at the entrance or just within it, looking like a crumb of earth, it is watching patiently and stealthily the precise moment when to clutch its unwary prey. How often must this cave-tiger endure the keen pangs of hunger? he must be of necessity a sun-worshipper, for dull, gloomy, or cold weather suits him not, it is keeping away his game. Yet at times he must do well, I have frequently heard the loud interrupted buzz of a fly in distress and have found the hapless insect tightly held by the savage foe. More often the prey thus suddenly captured has been one of those large yellowish-brown flies that love to congregate in numbers on a warm bank, or post, or tree stem. Children have seen this wily grub successful, have noted its ferocious tenacity of hold, for they sometimes amuse themselves and flavour the tasteless hours of idleness, by drawing the Butcher. A straw or grass stem is lightly placed at a hole and gently stirred, it is often seized and held firmly with bulldog grip till the savage 'butcher' itself is drawn from its den in all its naked ugliness.

In the last days of March and early in the following month, larvae may be found lying apparently dead immediately below or about the holes, a close examination shows these are but 'counterfeit presentments'[17] – they are the freshly cast skins from which the late occupier has extricated itself so cleverly that even the hook coverings remain intact; these exuviae afterwards assume a curve, become indurated, and are bleached to a pure lime white.

The Tiger-beetle in its perfect state is a beautiful creature, but the aid of a glass is requisite to enable one fairly to appreciate the quaint markings and the rich and lustrous colours which gem-like sparkle on the head, thorax, and elytra – that is, always supposing it can be induced to remain quiet for inspection. Amongst the native beetles it is restless beyond compare; on bare ground this nimbleness and activity is displayed afoot, but where its habitat lies amongst scanty grasses, the wings are more freely used, usually for short distances only. But temperature has much to do with the employment of the wings, as in hot sunny weather it flies frequently. It shows much fleetness in pursuit of minute flies, turning with surprising ease and swiftness; should the prey be caught it is quickly eaten. They also pry into holes and crannies as if in search of food, this is done by both sexes. In the autumn I have often seen females enlarging burrows, scratching away soil with their feet, some of these holes are widened sufficiently so that a beetle is able to turn.

In fossicking amongst tunnels visited by this beetle I have found a small species of ant; it might be that the larvae of this little insect is searched for and devoured by the Tiger-beetle.

It is gregarious also in the perfect state, but although many individuals may be seen running together, they meet each other with marks of distrust and enmity. The male seeks a mate as late as April, this appears to be a 'catch who can' sort of business, with an entire absence of courtship, the favoured female even seems to partake the general distrust of the species; spry and alert, she nimbly retires, so with virginal coyness protests by a hasty retreat, till overtaken by her pursuer.

The Walking-stick (*Phasma*) [stick insect] whose peculiar structure has attracted much curiosity, is represented here by *P. Hectori* [*Orthodera novaezealandiae*]; these insects are remarkable for their attachment to a particular locality. About thirteen years ago, a portly female having quite the matronly air, I placed on a bush of ake-ake (*O. Fosteri*);[18] in due time a small colony appeared and became established there. The original foundress of the colony was green, but the progeny assumed and retained a light brown hue that very closely matched the sprays of the plant on which they lived. So much was this the case, that it became an amusement for the children in rivalry to detect and count as many phasmae as possible. These insects appear to enjoy a power of approximating their colour to near objects, when drizzling light rains somewhat persistent set in from N.E. to S.E., I have frequently noticed small darkish patches on the insects that so completely matched the sodden sprays of the ake-ake as to render their discovery very difficult. A few tufts of cocksfoot (*Dactylis*) grew beneath the outer branches of the ake-ake; a phasma on a dry grass stem with its fore pair of limbs extended straight forward could scarcely be detected. So much does it resemble the grass-stem that the delusion may be termed perfect. The community has rarely shown us a green-coloured specimen on the ake-ake; the neighbouring tree is a manuka, on it more than once we have found green phasmae well matching the foliage. Is this mere coincidence? or is this utterly defenceless animal endowed with a protective power we can observe and admire but fail to understand? The facts are given as noticed, for the consideration of those who love to investigate the secrets of nature.

On one occasion, about fifty members of the community were removed to a distance, with the view of founding another colony, but without success, owing I believe to the number of birds which preyed on them; it should be mentioned that the community under observation decreased sensibly in numbers after the introduction here of Australian magpies [*Gymnorhina tibicen*], but in spite of all attacks, a remnant more or less numerous has remained.

A marked feature in their habits is the impatience with which they bear deprivation of light; placed in an uncovered basket they preserve their wonted sluggishness, cover it, they stride forward rapidly towards the light that steals in beneath the lid and points to free air. When disturbed or alarmed often they relinquish their hold and drop through the foliage to the ground. As showing their attachment to a place, I noticed another instance with a different species of phasma, on the island of Kawau, these kept exclusively to one tree *(Cupressus)*, on this these insects abounded, but after a close scrutiny, I could not detect any specimens on the neighbouring trees.

Other species are more rarely seen here; one of them of larger dimensions than *P. hectori*, having an abundance of dwarfish spines diverging from either side and also from the underpart of the body. Nor are the limbs left entirely unarmed, as thorny points jut out not far from the flexures. Here is a fine specimen sprawling across some native foliage; it exceeds five inches [13cm] in length, and indeed looks very much more, as the anterior limbs, three inches long [8cm], are held out nearly in a line with the body. An angle is defined as the aperture between two lines meeting at a point; you look on the phasma's limbs, the living embodiment of the acute and the obtuse, and immediately conclude that Euclid[19] may have owed the conception of some of his problems to gazing on the different angles in which it pleases this curious insect to arrange its straggling limbs. It is all angles, of many knees and elbows, as may be seen with a glance at the three sets of limbs; when still, its postures fail to convey any idea of rest or comfort, always excepting the fore pair of limbs. The basal portion of these, it will be noticed, when brought close together, are so shaped as to form a hollow or groove, which just fits and protects the head when required. The other limbs are mere legs, used for locomotion and clasping with clutching foothold; but the fore pair serve not as legs only, they have other important functions to perform. They feel or enquire the way to climb and reach to fresh sprays of foliage, pawing with the small, delicate, and inquisitive feet till satisfied with some clue they are on the right track, when the phasma moves on with careful but vacillating steps, straying now and then for its faithful scouts to make further enquiries. These not only protect the head, but the hair-like antennae, with their numerous articulations, are also frequently shielded and covered by them. Then, as legs, they have at least one exceptional privilege worth noticing. With man, crossing the legs is indulged as a luxurious position of ease and comfort, which indubitably confers at times a sense of power. Look at the bore, just starting his hobby, let him nurse a leg across his knee, then how long may not one expect to suffer? Now, the insect under notice is endowed with the happy gift of being able to solace itself by crossing its legs in two places at once; one long shank, it may be observed, crosses at the part we may term the knee and recrosses nearer the foot.

Sand-wasp or Stinging-fly *(Sphex)*.[20] One individual gave us a good instance of intelligence; its home was in some stone-work at the end of a long verandah, whence we had ofttimes seen it emerge; one day it had captured a large black spider, and was with great difficulty dragging it along a gravelled walk parallel to the verandah; contrary to the usual method, it sometimes pushed its load in front, but pebbles and sand offered continual impediments; still it toiled and struggled with its cumbersome burthen well beclipped, pushing and dragging, but progress was slow and tedious; at last, after a longer pause and stoppage than usual, it altered its course, making across the walk in the direction of the verandah; this reached, it commenced climbing the skirting board. This perpendicular ascent successfully accomplished, it met next with a projecting and rounded moulding, to surmount this curious obstruction and carry its burthen required a supreme effort, that seemed to tax its powers to the utmost. Slowly, inch by inch, with many a pause between, the difficulty was overcome, the persevering insect so heavily laden appeared gradually round the moulding, then gained the top. Its troubles were now almost at an end, it reached the flooring boards, and thus had a smooth road to travel for about thirty-nine feet [12m]. Along this level way it dragged its prey with ease, and slipped down at the end of the verandah to its hole in the stone-work.

This wasp-like insect is capable of inflicting very severe pain by the use of its sting, in a case which came under the writer's notice, the venom caused a painful irritation for several days.

Animal intelligence, as displayed by dogs, is so constantly observed, that I know not whether I shall be held excused for recording an unusual instance that came under my notice last spring. A spaniel of the Spanish breed often keeps me company. One morning I was gathering cherries from a tree close to the fruit-house. Don was lying apparently asleep close by the spot to which I had shifted the garden steps. After filling the basket I entered the fruit-house. Whilst occupied there, hearing a slight pattering noise for which I could not account, I looked through the doorway. Don was slowly ascending the steps; he reached the top, stood there, thrust his nose amongst the well-laden branches, picked and ate cherries till I disturbed him, when he slowly and gravely descended, with an air that showed his satisfaction in that he had added to his various accomplishments by learning the use of a pair of steps.

4. Out in the Open: The white-eye, or blight bird (1882)

Tauhou of the Maoris. *Zosterops lateralis*, Reich.[21]

To this bird belongs the peculiar merit of self-introduction; without troubling any Acclimatisation Society it put in its appearance here within the memory of the older settlers. Like many another parvenu it must depend on its own merits for favour, as it cannot lay claim to ancient relations with the land by coming over with the Conqueror, that is, in having its perch on one of the canoes hailing from the mystic Haiwaki [Hawaiki].

We first noticed this bird on some *Fagus* [native beech] trees in the Rockwood Valley, Malvern Hills, July 28th, 1856. Its numbers, since then, have increased with great rapidity. It very soon obtained the name of the Blight-bird, in recognition of its services to gardens and orchards, from its habit of feeding on the American blight, with which apple trees in this colony are so generally infested; but, although the gardeners noticed with satisfaction its labours in this direction, during the winter months, yet as summer returned and fruits ripened, its incessant depredations on cherries and plums were witnessed with anything but pleasure. From examining scores of nests, we find that out of a considerable variety of materials made use of, moss and grass predominate; the fabric is strong, although frequently slight, in some cases the walls are extremely thin; it is usually suspended, at the sides, by fastenings bound securely over slender twigs; some are almost wholly constructed of grass, amongst which, now and then, may be found a few small tufts of the grey-beard moss, in others the cottony down of plants is neatly interwoven with moss and spiders' webs, lined with fibres, or fine stems of grass, sometimes with hair; some nests are quite shallow, others of deep cup-like form, and measure in diameter 3 inches [7.6cm], cavity 1 inch 6 lines to 2 inches [3.8–5.1cm], depth 10 lines to 2 inches [2.1–5.1cm].[22] In gardens, it has been observed placed in a great variety of shrubs, occasionally in a rose-bush bordering a well-frequented walk; never far above the ground, usually from two to six feet [0.6–1.8m]; we have found it suspended to our common fern, *Pteris aquilina* [bracken]. It has three or four clear-blue eggs, ovoiconical in shape, measuring 8 lines in length, with a breadth of 6½ lines; incubation lasts about ten days. The nest and eggs form as pleasing an object as those of the hedge-sparrow [dunnock] at Home. The gift of song does not appear to be equally shared by these birds; in addition to the quick, sharp note or chirrup, which all seem to have in common, now and then an individual bird is heard pouring forth a low, well-sustained, melodious song; possibly this power may exist in all adult males, though not so constantly exercised as in many species; pretty close observation proves it may be heard through ten months in the year, we have noted this singing habit from August 17 till quite in the autumn (May 4).

September 20 – Crowds of blight-birds in bushes of the *Pittosporum colensoi* [black māpou], busily employed about the woody capsules, picking off the gluten in which the seeds are embedded. In some former notes we described it thus as one of the pensile nest-builders, which seems to be almost equally rare in our temperate climate as they are in the old country. The suspension of its habitation is more accomplished in a different manner from that of *Gerygone* [grey warbler], and more after the fashion adopted by *Regulus cristatus*, of Europe, the kinglet or golden-crested wren [goldcrest], except that the nest is very often formed without any protection or shelter from an overhanging leaf. The rim of the ladle-shaped structure is firmly secured to a forked twig by silky threads of spiders' nests, finished on the outside, round the bottom, with braces of green leaves of grass, crossed and recrossed, which adds much to the strength and stiffness of the fabric.

Now, as pensile nests are peculiarly adapted for ensuring the safety of their contents against the predatory attacks of various egg-robbers, does not the suspension of the habitation of the *Zosterops* – the instinctive precaution of a foreign land – afford an indication that it is a recent colonist, not yet so thoroughly acclimatised as to be fully aware of the immunity it enjoys from ravages of snakes, etc.? will that form of nest which is now sometimes found built in, rather than suspended from, a bush or thicket, become a more common object, and thus show a change in the style of architecture, as this bird, season after season, experiences the comparative safety of the breeding-places in our cooler latitude? Amongst our indigenous genera are there any pensile nest-builders? For years we invariably found three eggs to be the complement to the nest; now in many seasons we have met with several instances where four eggs have been laid, where this has occurred, the home has been built in, rather than fairly suspended from a bush. If the reason, before suggested, for a modification in the manner of fixing the habitation be considered as not altogether too fanciful, may we not likewise be allowed to advance our opinion that the change of climate is also gradually producing its effects in the increased fecundity of our little white-eye. Once we found five eggs in a nest in tutu (*Coriaria*) at Ohinitahi [sic].

Note. – December 4 – Nest in a manuka (*Leptospermum scoparium*), appeared to be completely lined and finished. On the 8th it contained three eggs, the next day a fourth egg was laid, on the 19th one callow nestling was exhibiting its ugliness, perfectly naked, except two or three small tufts of white down on the bald cranium, the body deep yellowish-pink, with dark slatey-coloured marks along the line of the vertebrae, the exterior of wing, and legs. The day following, his ugliness had a companion, on the 23rd feathers had made their appearance where the slatey markings had been noticed; two unhatched eggs remained in the nest, which was only visited quietly once a day.

Young birds, for some time after they can fly well, can scarcely be said to possess any just pretension to the title *Zosterops*, as they are without the circlet of white feathers round the eyes.

From the large number of nests we have observed, December must be the height of the breeding season.

The *Zosterops* is so partial to the berries of the trailing *Cotomeaster* [*Cotoneaster microphyllus*], that we have known it to be taken by the hand, when it has been busily engaged on them; in the early spring we have observed it eating clover.

From observation of an egg taken at Ohinitahi [sic], the writer is in doubt whether this immigrant has not become the dupe of the whistler (*Chrysococcyx*) [shining cuckoo].

A nest was found, built in a manuka bush (*Leptospermum scoparium*) containing four eggs, one of which greatly exceeded the others in size, and was of a deeper blue-green colour. This incident bears upon a very interesting and much discussed question as to protective mimicry by parasites of the eggs of dupes, by approximate colouration. The nest and eggs were deposited in the Canterbury Museum. Some years since, it was far less abundant than it had been, the exceptionally severe winter of 1872 having greatly diminished its numbers. Birds of this species, dead and dying, were often observed after storms of snow-sleet, or even cold rain; this tenderness of constitution is a strong argument in favour of the opinion of the writer, that the *Zosterops* is but a recent settler amongst us.

Perhaps in no other season of the year are they seen to more advantage than in the autumn and winter early mornings, when heavy dews besparkle trees, shrubs, and grass; when the brown earth laced over with myriads of threads of fairy gossamer, is brilliant with the many coloured opal fires that change each moment under the glance of the yet faint sun-rays from gold to green, from crimson to glowing purple, these little rovers gathering in flocks, scatter the glittering tracery of the close-set leaves, as they dart in and out of bushes, seeking the dried pulp of berries that yet cling to the more sheltered sprays. Or, again, in the treacherous frosts of the earlier days of spring, that now and then catch even the careful gardener napping, when all thought of danger to tender plants is over for the season, when the dawn breaks upon a landscape crisp with the white rime that outlines each form of leaf and spray; the garden or orchard skillfully dug with an even roughness that exposes as much surface as possible to the mellowing influences of rain and frosts, is then at times alive with the active movements of scores of busy searchers after insects. Even this pursuit is not all pleasure. There are watchers amongst them that take up their posts on boughs, and with plaintive note give warning of coming danger; the fact of their gregarious habits is fully borne out by the way they settle to the food supply, the first who ventures seems timorous, looking round anxiously for others to countenance its boldness by their presence; these it appears to summon by its calls; or is this seeming fearsomeness misjudged? is this uneasiness rather to be taken as a sign of good fellowship which prevents the enjoyment of a meal till it is shared by others? We doubt it, rather attributing to the instinct of self-preservation this show of careful watchfulness. Soon others follow the leader in lots of two or three together, till scores are busily occupied with their hurried feed; nor is idea of good fellowship quite consistent with the air of intimidation assumed to those who press too closely to some favourite morsel: they do not bicker noisily like sparrows, or fight desperately like the [New Zealand] robins (*Petroica*), they partly spread the wings, which are quivered for a few seconds threateningly, then advance with raised beak towards the offender; the snapping of the bills is also heard. These symptoms, which bode hostility, bid the too greedy beware of what might follow such menaces. Spotted and decaying apples thrown out from the fruit house supply a favourite meal; crowds are soon attracted to the feast, they first peck at the softest part of the fruit, extending their work till the whole of the interior is cleaned out, leaving the framework of the core in its place, with the skin still distended to its proper shape. To secure a better position, one leg is sometimes advanced, the foot placed firmly on the fruit. It is not an unusual sight for an apple to be seen moving and twisting about apparently of its own accord, till the mystery is explained by the appearance of a bird from within. Sometimes a few apples that have been overlooked at the gathering, are seen to hang temptingly on the leafless branches, yet it may be they are but the outward resemblance of the fruit; the pulp has been adroitly extracted, leaving but a moderate sized hole on one side to show the mode of operation pursued by the blight-bird; the ribston pippin especially thus treated often looks a fine specimen, richly coloured with yellow-green, pleasantly veined with russet and streaked with dark red; nor is the feat exposed till the hand that plucks it closes on an empty rind. It is too restless a bird to remain long on any one food supply; a few twittering notes are sounded, then the flock rise and hurry away to another kind of provender; perhaps one or two of the flight, too busily at work to notice the departure of the main body, no sooner find themselves alone, than casting a glance around, with a shrill chirp, they hurry away to join their mates. From watching their proceedings, one is almost disposed to think that a mixed diet is necessary to them, so often do they vary their food. Scarcely any tree, shrub, or plant is neglected in their industrious insect search; they are not apparently affected by strong odours, as we have noticed them very active climbing about rosemary bushes (*Rosmarinus*), that have been beset with scale insects. Of the many receipts recommended by experts for the extermination of the scale on fruit trees (to which it clings with a tenacity that would not shame the leech), one is made up chiefly from a mixture of fat and oil. We have seen these birds quit their feast of apples to pick off fatty particles that stick to the bark of a tree dressed with the greasy compound. Fat is so favourite a dainty that it is used to lure them to destruction. Boys carefully secure and tie a white-eye in a cage, in which are placed some bits of fat; the call of the prisoner quickly attracts attention, and numbers flock around, many of whom enter the cage, and are easily secured. Its gregarious habits have already been noticed, but it must not be understood that it is never solitary; at times a single pioneer may be observed occupying its station for some while before it is joined by its fellows, yet its summons is always responded to without a very prolonged delay. Now the notes uttered – shrill, chirpy, or plaintive – vary much in tone, and probably, by their modulation, convey much intelligence. We have noted the wings are sometimes used so as to produce a fluttering or ruffling noise; this appears only on some of their briefer flights. Then, again, the movements of a flock are not always straight for a given point; often they take wing and pursue a series of spiral curves far from exhibiting any regularity; they ascend and descend, yet in their twisting jerky flight a spiral or zigzag course is followed till the trees are reached on which they pitch. Now in some cases of this kind which came under observation, the trees could be seen for a long distance, and might have been reached in a tenth part of the time occupied by these erratic movements, had a more direct line been followed.

This species can be tamed without much difficulty; we know of an instance in which one of these cheerful little birds has been tamed so thoroughly that it keeps about the room, hopping on the table, and taking money from the lips of one of the younger members of the household.

It is one of the commonest birds in the Chatham Isles.

Prying amongst lowly trailing plants, or it may be ransacking the frost-smitten dwarf *Solanum* [nightshade] for its hoard of black berries lying strewed on the damp earth, with what appears the whim of the moment; uttering sharp trilling notes flocks rise to the upper branches of high trees, perching quietly almost in silence for awhile; they sit with puffed out feathers and muffled forms, as though inactivity and silence engendered moody humours. Sociable are they even at the still hour of night, in company more or less numerous they roost, closely packed side by side we have found them lining out on the boughs of ngaio (*Myoporum*).

In early spring days (August) we have noticed a single pair sedulously hunting together without other company, and, we believe, before the breeding season had begun. Under the warm shelter of a thick gorse hedge, a heap of decaying garden refuse, heated by the rays of a bright sun, seemed to promote a genesis of minute insects, that swarmed in the genial air. The active little couple, feeding on this favourite food, were most restless in their motions to and fro, capturing their prey flying, or as they crept up, when emerging from the almost reeking heap.

It is difficult, from its feeding habits, to assign its true place in our bird system. Placed amongst the *Meliphagidae* or honey-eaters by ornithologists, nevertheless, as we have shown, it displays a very impartial appetite for many varieties of food. According to our observations, this honey-eating habit is but feebly developed. The bell-bird and the tui may be seen glancing through the flower-laden boughs of trees and shrubs, extracting luscious food from nectaries of a variety of blossoms; but the attention of the white-eyes is then occupied in obtaining less delicate fare. In the month of July (midwinter just over) we have observed it in flocks, day after day, on one species of acacia, the flowers of which were just expanding. Those who wish to ascertain if it is frugivorous are invited to watch its proceedings with rich full-fleshed cherries, such as the early Lyons, or on trees of the early South American plum. In the latter end of November and through December the white-eye settles on these trees in family groups rather than flocks, unless the numbers of these family gatherings entitle the whole to be termed a flock. These visits are repeated at such brief intervals as to lead one to suppose these fruits are especial favourites. The young, following the parents, take their places on the boughs near together, as they have not yet cast off the close stowage of the nest, with quivering plumage, piping their feeble, tremulous chirp, await the movements of the elders.

Alas! the little bird, in its educational course, has become our *bec-figue* [ortolan], well-known to those who cultivate the luscious fruit of which we never raise enough. Enough! When you hear that a person does not care for figs, are not the eyes raised in devout thankfulness that a less meagre share remains for those who dote thereon. Doubtless it was through repeated visits to gather this delicious fruit that She who first gave thought to the art of dress [Eve] was led to choose its broad leaves, and arrange them with coquettish grace, thus setting a perennial study, endowed with all the freshness of perpetual change, for at least one-half of the human race. That reminds one that on a visit to the Art gallery of a city acknowledged to be the centre of civilisation, that where such veils for the nude have been considered necessary, a common nail is the means of attachment which secures to the figure 'the counterfeit presentment'[23] of leaves (which probably have been modelled from those of the cabbage). Is not this a somewhat barbarous method of sacrificing to modesty? But to our *bec-figue*. The fruit, let it be the well-known Ischia, the Toulousienne, or white Marseilles, ripe and glowing with a pulpy plumness delightful to gaze upon, the smooth tender skin swollen as if with pride, conscious of the luscious charge committed to its keeping, may too often be found riven and ravelled by the beaks of these active gourmands, which quit their feast leaving a sticky mass of purple-stained shreds.

It may be thought from one of its familiar names that its peculiar mission here is to clear away from our apple trees that nasty plague, the American blight; if so, from the appearance of the trees in many fruit gardens, its duty in this respect now must be very much neglected. To its carnivorous propensities it sometimes falls a victim by drowning in pig-tubs whilst pecking at shreds of meat or fat. Notwithstanding the display of so accommodating a taste for variety in its food, as an insect-eater, it is a very valuable bird, in spite of its love of fruit. We should be very sorry, indeed, to be deprived of the important services it renders us in all parts of the garden. Its apparent craving for variety in its fare is a positive advantage to the horticulturist, which cannot fail to be appreciated by those who work the soil and are disposed to receive the bird as it is, although it may not be as we should choose. In grudging its portion of fruit it would seem that we recognise the value of an active unpaid servant, to be fed from any other stores but our own, yet rates and taxes have become so familiar to us that it does not seem unreasonable that the white-eye should levy an insect rate. Scarcely a bird offers a more interesting study to the naturalist, as since its self-introduction here some of its habits have become modified within one's own observation. In the manner of its nidification, the suspension of its nest seems on the eve of abandonment, as that mode of structure is now of far rarer occurrence than during the earlier years of our acquaintance with it. The attachment of the rim of the wall to a spray is a vestige of the old method of building. We have already pointed out its increased fecundity, a fact ascertained by the personal inspection of so great a number of nests during the last twenty-five years. As it became acclimatised, it gradually advanced the period of its breeding season, at its first settlement, family cares were deferred till the warmth of summer was well pronounced. As to its mode of feeding, more information should be ascertained of its habits in that respect in Australia. Is it a honey-eater there now? It seems possible that its habits, especially as regards food, may yet be considerably modified by the varied influences caused by the more extended cultivation of the soil. This would apply to parts of Australia as well as New Zealand. It should not be forgotten that the kea (*Nestor notabilis*) offers a memorable instance of the development of a change of habit within a brief period, owing to the appearance of a new and ample food supply within its mountain fastnesses.

5. Out in the Open: The kea, or sheep-killer (1883)

Nestor notabilis – Gould.

The merciless attacks of this parrot on some of the flocks depastured amidst the southern mountain ranges continues to excite alarm amongst sheep-farmers on highland runs. With a view of again directing attention to this important subject, some further particulars of the history and habits of the kea are now offered.

Since the discovery, some fifteen years ago, of the mischievous propensities of these mountain parrots, on Mr. H. Campbell's station at Lake Wanaka, the number of sheep that have perished from their attacks throughout the Southern Alpine districts must amount to many thousands. Such changes as have been noticed in the habits of these parrots are not by any means re-assuring to the mountain sheep-farmer, the birds now have learnt to follow their victims to a lower level; in the months of spring and early summer, they may be found harassing and wounding sheep on the flats. They seem to take to the higher ground in the autumn, keeping about the snowline in winter. Now this summer campaign is a new departure, and augurs badly indeed for the welfare of flocks in the range of country it infests. Having received several communications on the subject, a few instances of its method of attack will be cited and the methods at present employed to destroy the bird. One of the keas has been seen to hover about a small flock near a hut, just alight on a sheep, and run it through the little mob three or four times, remaining on the sheep but a few minutes, till the shepherd could get near enough to drive it away, next morning the sheep lay dead. Some of the more experienced and knowing birds just seem to make a dart at the sheep and injure it at once fatally. Sometimes sheep have been brought into the yards or shearing shed with a hole in the side close to the back, through which they passed their excrements, these animals were very poor, and did not seem likely to live. Occasionally sheep have been seen with some of the intestines appearing through the wound, but these were of course sheep that had been recently attacked, as they did not long survive this kind of punishment. Keas have been observed hunting a sheep in company, driving the distressed animal amongst rocks, but the wretched creature's struggles were in vain – unable to escape, it was attacked in turn by the mischievous keas.

Out of a lot of 1300 hoggets placed in a large paddock for a few weeks, 90 were found to have died from the bites of keas; in another instance, a flock of 500 double-fleeced sheep, kept by themselves, lost 200 of its number. Double-fleeced sheep seem to be preferred, perhaps as affording a better hold for the claws of the bird, but sheep in good condition were nearly always selected. In one case where 40 rams were put with ewes, when the time came to remove the rams, but 9 remained alive. In a very bad season, keas have been known to destroy as many as ten per cent of a flock. The most striking incident of audacity was an attack by a kea on a mare in foal belonging to Mr. Campbell of Wanaka, in all probability it would have been killed, but fortunately the stricken animal was observed, the wound dressed, and covered with a plaster of tar; the mare was damaged in the same spot and in a similar manner to the sheep.

The hunting and destroying of these birds was begun in 1871, and on the station just mentioned, from one to two hundred a year were killed; this just seemed for a time to check their ravages, but as they became more frequent, active measures were taken to extirpate them. Men were engaged to hunt them, for the reward of one shilling per head, or two shillings and sixpence per head if the men found their own supplies; shepherds were paid a shilling a head in addition to their wages; in this way, as many as 800 were killed about Wanaka in 1881, the next year some 300 were destroyed.

Kea hunting is an arduous and uncertain employment, some of the difficulties attending it may be appreciated, when it is stated that the wild mountainous country has to be traversed for the most part at night, or before dawn, so as to reach the spots frequented by these birds by daylight. Should a flock of them be met with, and one of them wounded, the remainder are easily obtained – the bond of fellowship appears so strongly developed, that the cries of a wounded bird at once attract the presence of its mates. This habit is taken advantage of by the hunter or fowler who usually stands on the wing of the wounded bird, whose calls quickly summon the remainder of the flock within shooting distance. A shepherd brought into a yard a few sheep for killing, he observed some of them to have been quite recently pecked, (this was winter time), he started at 3 o'clock in the morning, returning about 10 o'clock, having destroyed 19 keas; he managed this by following their cry about daybreak, when he came to the spot, he found a hogget being attacked; it lay on the ground and was dreadfully torn yet still alive; he shot one bird and stood on its wings, by its cries the keas came so close that he killed three with one shot, and six more with three shots. The next evening he was away again, stayed out all night, brought home 25; this same man once killed 41 on one of his expeditions. However, it often happens that a man may be out for days without being able to kill a single bird; some of the most successful hunters imitate the call of the bird and attract them within reach of the gun. Poison has been tried with success, a shepherd knocked over a sheep, gashed it in several places, into which he introduced strychnine; he left the sheep thus prepared, on a rocky precipice; in a few days he returned to inspect progress, and found a very satisfactory result before him, in the stark carcases of 40 dead keas that lay scattered about the dead sheep.

Having now given some information as to the destructiveness of these birds, it may be urged that the subject is worthy [of] the attention of Government, in order that some aid may be given to supplement the efforts of the Crown tenants in their attempts to diminish the number of these marauders. It may be said that the area of country where the losses occur is too limited in extent to call for any assistance in lessening the evil complained of; it is more probable that the official eye has not yet made itself acquainted or familiar with the wide spread of country affected by the kea. Supposing the necessary knowledge is in possession of Government officials, the above argument might be used as a convenient reason for avoiding any trouble or expenditure in the matter, but that does not make it sound. There is money ready for expenditure in this direction; the sheep rate raised specially for promoting and preserving the health and well-being of our flocks, might be made to yield some share of its product for this legitimate purpose. This tax is collected over millions of acres that make up the provinces of Otago and Canterbury. When sheep were attacked by the ravages of another animal plague, very strenuous exertions were made to stamp out the pest; leading articles were written on scab,[24] candidates stood on scab, the time-honoured name of John Hall is intimately associated with Scab Acts and Sheep Bills. This rate is still collected in these provinces, whence the plague has been long since eradicated, its funds for some time past (as far as farmers may judge) appear to be expended in the production and issue of sundry forms and returns, the entry and docketing of which probably engage the attention of, and furnish useless employment for several clerks at Wellington. If there be no longer scab in Otago and Canterbury, why not employ a share of the sheep rate in trying to rid the flocks of an important district, of an enemy whose attacks entail such heavy losses to the mountain sheep-farmer.

To obtain this concession the farmers must bestir themselves, as Government is an institution that usually does not take the initiative except under inducement, which the unfortunate sheep-farmers may not be in a position to offer.

The kea is conspicuous for its courage, not less than for its spirit of mischief; it looks about boldly, with a fearless air that is quite remarkable; it is delighted to have something it can tear and rend, bark or wood flies into chips before the efforts of its powerful beak. In some of its positions, when not on the wing, its outlines are hawk-like; it has an odd way of raising and ruffling the neck feathers, it seems to do this when it is noticing any object, as a horse pricks its ears. Grass, herbage, twigs, bark, flowers, seeds, and fruits may all be entered as forming part of its varied food. The mandibles which can rend asunder the rough bark of a tree can delicately and adroitly extract something edible from a fragile blossom. It uses the foot to hold down the food at times, or employs it to convey the food to the mandibles; the tongue seems to be brought into contact, in a careful sort of way, with such tender victual as flowers or leaves; the lower mandible is much employed in placing its food against the upper one or beak. Notwithstanding its destructiveness, it is a small eater and very slow feeder, it tears, cuts asunder, or pulls into shreds, and wastes much, but the food it swallows is carefully triturated into very small morsels. A very favourite food consists of the sticky seeded capsules of *Pittosporum*; sowthistle (*Sonchus*) with its milky juices; it frequently cleanses its beak whilst feeding, in the same way as does the kaka, by rubbing it from side to side against a hard substance. About dawn, its scream or call is usually heard; one of the cries very closely resembles the rather shrill bark or yelp of a puppy; and one of its habits is to jump with both feet off the ground many times in succession, the beak being raised pointing upwards. When scratching its head, it thrusts up a foot under and behind the wing, the head being slightly inclined downwards.

To the house of a friend, nesting close to the picturesque shore of romantic Te Anau, one day came a kea, unencumbered with any show of bashfulness; he became so familiar and confiding in his bearing towards the inmates of the dwelling as to enlist their kindly feeling in his behalf, he fearlessly hopped or clambered in or out when it so pleased him, he was a cadet of the house. How he managed matters with the cook is not recorded, yet it is certain that she especially favoured him; for reasons, he did not discourage her attentions, he even entered that part of the house where she 'ruled the roast'. But the third day of his sojourn, he privately visited the kitchen on a tour of inspection, in the absence of anyone to admire him perhaps, he amused himself by climbing about the shelves; the result was a fearful smash of glassware and crockery. The domestic cat is usually credited with a good deal of this kind of thing, but the doings of any individual of that much maligned race would be held as feeble or harmless compared with the amount of work got through coolly and cheerfully by this winged demon of mischief – a view of the wreckage that lay strewed around, curiously enough recalled to my friend's recollection that he wanted a good specimen of the kea – and he got one at once.

In appearance the kea is far from being unattractive; as one looks at this wild mountaineer and admires the sober toned plumage, saved from the charge of dullness by the faint lustre of its silvery gleam, one is apt to think it the very bird to set a fashion as to colour. Aesthetic taste might safely adopt it, that is, if shifting fashion yet holds in the same vein but lately obtained, when her votaries were bound to array themselves in unobtrusive colours. This bold bird, with its soaring flight over snow-fields and glaciers, however, is too little known 'to the general'; its day of fashionable glory must be postponed till Mount Cook and its crested ranges are seamed by well-beaten tracks worn by the feet of Alpine tourists, then the world may rejoice in warm soft fabrics dyed *à la* Kea.

Can we call it handsome? The bright black eyes, ringed in yellow circlets, give a certain air of intelligence to every action; they lend a queer droll look too, such as Puck might wear, they seem to let you understand that the owner of them, knows all about it you know, he is not to be taken in, you may just lay aside all blandishment and come to the point; oh yes, he can take care of himself, thank you; in fact, he has his eye on you.

In tearing and rending a piece of timber his form shows off to great advantage, as he twists and turns his head and neck to obtain a better purchase for his strong beak, the body falls into undulating curves and outlines at once easy and graceful. You are tempted to sketch him, he evidently guesses your intentions, his attitude changes each moment, his whim is apparently to make you aware how quickly he can show himself other than he appeared an instant since, the result is that 'the drawing from the life' is an unfinished study.

Through the kindness of Mr. H. Campbell, the writer is in possession of an egg, it is white, with the surface granulated, having irregularly scattered pits, with a few chalky incrustations towards the smaller end, the shell is much thicker than that of any kaka's egg that has come under our observation. Of ovoid form, it measures 1 inch 7 lines [4cm] in length, with a breadth of 1 inch 3 lines [3.2cm]. It is one of four that were taken from an almost inaccessible rocky fastness in a gully called Rough Creek, on the east side of Hawea Lake between that sheet of water and Lake

Wanaka. There are nesting-places inaccessible without tools or iron implements, in the deep fizzures [sic], amongst piled up rocks, on the Clyde, a tributary of the Rangitata.

6. Out in the Open: Lost game (1886)

It seems an early period in the history of the Colony to record the extinction of one of the most valued amongst its native birds, yet can there now exist a doubt as to the loss of that excellent game bird, the native quail? If a doubt remains amongst the most hopeful of ornithologists, it would take this form perhaps, that it is just possible a few stragglers may survive in some of the islands that lie off the north-east; this is improbable, for long since the existence of such survivors would have been ascertained with certainty, for most of these localities have been harried by collectors.

To write down the particulars of its history, one has to look back to the early times of settlement here, to the *Pilgrim days*, to turn over the faded pages of old diaries and journals, 'the small beer chronicles'[25] of that happy period, when roughing it gave a healthy charm to rural occupations on land that in its virgin freshness ever offered something new or strange to the zealous new chum. Such diaries as have been referred to, furnish information that tells us something that throws light upon the habits of the bird. Here is an extract from an old journal which shows how a party of us fared when camping out amongst the hills in the Rakaia district, date June 6, 1857: 'made our supper of kakas, wekas, and *quail which the dog caught*; plenty of wild dog tracks; saw nothing more worthy of notice than the quantity of quail.'

On the younger part of the community it will be difficult to impress an idea of the abundance of this species on the [Canterbury] plains, and those of the earlier settlers who can remember the fact are daily becoming fewer.

It is now more than thirty years since the writer first enjoyed the pleasure of putting up bevies of quail, which at the time seemed so plentiful that it could share with the pipit (*Anthus* N.Z.) [pīhoihoi] the distinction of being one of the commonest species: be it remembered, this period was years before strenuous efforts in the cause of acclimatisation had so successfully furnished this remote out of the way country, with its redundant supply of bird life which now exists here.

Especially was the quail plentiful in the Malvern district, with its long stretch of low and undulating downs, bordering the wide spread plain, on the stony finely grassed Rakaia terraces, and away west beyond the gorge of that great river, on the downs and hummocks that intersect the Acheron, to the hills that confine the clear depths of picturesque Lake Coleridge. When journeying either on horseback or a-foot across the tussock country, the sudden upstarting of a bird, the short whirring flight, was ever a pleasant surprise; then one tried a guess when the next quail would be put up, or to make sure where the quail pitched amongst the friendly sheltering tufts of the great tawny sea of tussocks.

With a dog and gun a fair bag was almost sure to be made by a man fond of good walking exercise, that too without a gunner having any pretension to being dubbed a sportsman, or considered a crack shot.

I have a very distinct recollection how jolly we used to think this sport, with one's lungs filled with pure and bracing air, as we tramped over and through the varied herbage that covered the hills and downs. The ever-present tussock-grass (that we believed gave horses such wonderful endurance), was interspersed with many other interesting growths, tufts of *Celmisia*, the kid plant, with silver linings to its broad pointed leaves; little sharp foliaged heaths (*Leucopogon*); patches of berry-bearing pimelias and gaultherias that seemed to cling flat to the earth. In the hollows of moister soil from whence often came the note of the utick (*Sphenaeacus*) [fernbird] were tufts of curling or crumpled astelias, masses of broad-leaved sweet-scented grass, the weeping leaves of snow-grass, drooping with an easy grace that well contrasted with the light plumes carried high above the sharp cutting edges of the useful tohe-tohe [toetoe]. There was an abundance of insect life, craneflies, grasshoppers, &c., at least were obtrusive; and for some years after European settlement, the quail flourished.

Many theories have been offered to account for the marvelous rapidity of its disappearance. Some professed to believe that stocking runs with sheep caused its destruction, that the nests and eggs were trampled. The bird became scarce long before the country was well stocked, when runholders borrowed sheep not exactly to dodge, but rather to comply with the regulations of the Waste Lands Board. Bush or grass fires in the southern districts have probably been a chief cause for its disappearance; the effect of these extensive fires on the habitat of this prime game bird has come under the writer's personal observation. In the early part of 1857 a large part of the country on the southern side of the Ashburton river, high above the gorge, had been burnt in the previous year; on the opposite or northern side, known as Clint [Clent] Hills, the grass presented no signs of ever having been fired, here quail abounded, they were flushed every few yards; whilst one never saw a quail on the opposite bank, their food and shelter being alike destroyed, at that time not a sheep had been on either side of the river.

There remains to be considered the probability of some fatal epidemic rapidly spreading and sweeping this much prized game bird from the face of the earth; we know how other species of the *Tetraonidae* suffer from disease at times – as witness the grouse.

A very slight nest, composed of a few bents of grass twisted into a depression of the ground, was all the artificial shelter this bird relied on, for the purpose of incubation. The eggs were very numerous, we have been told that as many as ten or twelve have been found in a nest; oval in shape, colour buffy-white suffused with rich brown splashes, with a remarkably glossy varnish; length 1 inch 3 lines [3.2cm], by 11 lines [2.3cm] in diameter. We have not heard its call-note, or seen a bevy of quail, for years. The sheltered valleys around Lake Coleridge, and about the head-waters of the Rakaia, were amongst the last places in which it lingered, to our knowledge, in the central districts. On the flats of the Waitangi [Waitaki?] river it survived for some time after it had entirely disappeared further to the north. In Westland it was found about 'the paddock' on the west coast road from Christchurch to Hokitika. A few stragglers, very few, had found shelter in the more southern river-beds as far down as the Paringa.

They bred more than once in the season, as we have a note of abundance of young quail so late as the 9th and 10th of April (this was in 1857). We have seen it escape the talons of the quail-hawk, by dropping perpendicularly, just when about to be struck, when all hope of escape from its relentless pursuer was quite abandoned. The flight of the quail was low, and it used to be said that it would not rise after being flushed the third time; numbers were killed by sheep and cattle-dogs in the early days, when it abounded. In style of flight our bird must have resembled the Quail of Taberah and Kibroth-hattaavah, that fed the Children of Israel in the wilderness:- 'And there went forth a wind from the Lord and brought quails from the sea, and let them fall by the camp, as it werc a day's journey on this side, and as it were a day's journey on the other side, and as it were *two cubits high* [0.9m] upon the face of the earth.'[26] Our bird is not migratory, as we believe. The young, with the exception, perhaps, of *Apteryx owenii* [little spotted kiwi], undergoes less change in plumage than that of any other bird; the young when it assumes its feathers, exactly resembles the adult female, with the white streak along the shaft of the feathers, which adds so much to its beauty,

The male had the upper surface ferruginous brown, with varied black and dark brown markings, a narrow whitish streak following each side of the shaft of each feather; top of the head rich brown, streaked with very dark brown, buffy-marked feathers intermixed; beak horn black, except at the extreme point; nostril covered with membrane; a line over the eye, cheeks, and throat, rufous, with a faint blackish curved mark just above the line of the gape; primaries dull smoky brown; secondaries edged with pale brown, marbled on the outer web with buff and dark brown; under surface ferruginous; breast marked with black and white; abdomen white; thighs buff; irides bright hazel-brown; tarsi dull flesh colour. Bill from gape 8 lines [1.7cm]; wing 4 inches 9 lines[12.06cm]; tarsus 9 lines [1.9cm]; length 8 inches 3 lines [21cm]; weight 7¾ ounces [220g].

The female was not so rufous about the cheeks and throat, had a darker tinge of colour generally; abdomen almost buff. Weight barely 7 ounces [200g]. The feathers of the thigh light and flocculent, those on the abdomen slaty black, tipped with white, or buffy-white, so closely arranged as to give that part of the bird a whitish or buff colour.

Although the sexes differed but little point in size, yet they were easily distinguishable by their general tone of colour as well as by the rufous cheeks of the male. On the ground their movements were active; sometimes they might be seen indulging in a dust bath as they lay basking in the sun; unless suddenly startled they almost always maintained that plump rounded appearance which characterizes several genera of the *Tetraonidae*.

From tolerably close observation, we are inclined to suppose that their organs of hearing were far less acute than those of sight; they often gave utterance to a low purring sound, that one might suppose to proceed from an insect rather than from a bird. The call was indulged in most frequently during moist or wet weather; it sounded something like 'twit, twit, twit, twee-twit', repeated several times in quick succession. In very stormy, gusty weather, these birds appeared dull and silent, secreting themselves amongst thick tussocks. When flushed, they do not rise perpendicularly, but still rather straight for a few feet from the ground.

In confinement they were fond of picking about amongst sand, and throve well on soaked bread, grain of various kinds, and the larvae of insects; the male was not an attentive mate at feeding time, and where several were kept in the same enclosure, constant little bickerings took place without actual hostilities being indulged in.

The eggs required twenty-one days incubation, and the chicks were mostly active directly they emerged from the shell. They grew very rapidly; at about four months old the young could not very readily be distinguished from adult birds, either by contrast of size or plumage.

Jan. 20, 1856. – Bevy of young quail.

In instances where this bird has been reported as seen, I believe the Australian Brown Quail [*Coturnix ypsilophora*], imported here many years ago, has been mistaken for the native bird.

7. Out in the Open [On Māori] (1883)

Visitors from 'the old country', whether they be young folks thrown off by John Bull in a sporadic kind of way, in the hope that some may light on good ground, or of that class styled rather humorously 'globe-trotters,' here to-day and away to-morrow, usually show a feeling of disappointment because they find everything here [in New Zealand] so English-like. Railways, highways, telegraphs, post-offices, churches, schools, drink-shops, &c., are all so ready for their service, that the romance of travel to the remote Antipodes is swept away; climbing up mountains of difficulties or dangers anticipated at home, is found on the spot to have dwindled down to an occasional stumble against some mole-hill of inconvenience. Dreams of the wild savagery of far distant Maori-land have been dispelled by the common-place aspects of civilization, and so thoroughly, that many of our new friends evince some reluctance in admitting how completely their fanciful expectations have been overthrown.

Some of the first questions by new-comers relate to the Natives: Where are the Maoris? Are there no Natives about here? Now for the opportunity of pointing out a redeeming feature in the landscape of common-place to the new arrivals: squatting on or about the steps of the Lyttelton post-office, or lounging against the wall are a number of gipsy-like people, forming an uneven row, or broken up into small groups; we are enabled to answer, 'here are the Maoris!' The rare untidiness of the garments of some of the elder folk, the colours and the general misfit of their clothing, point out the aborigines almost as surely as the dusky faces; a prolonged stare is answered by the good humoured salutation 'tena koe'; we see the inevitable notebook produced, memoranda are jotted down; we are conscious that these people look as though they were and had been very carefully neglected; we know we cannot answer many questions about them; we need not explain to strangers why these Natives are thus lounging on the footways and doorsteps.

It may be well to find out what may be learnt about them; we enquire into the doings of rabbits and sparrows, and record the feats of dogs and horses; the anxiety we display about the welfare of sheep, cattle, and pigs is most praiseworthy; may we be permitted to devote a few lines to the state of living of the former owners of all these fertile lands, the produce from which causes the busy harbour of Lyttelton to be filled with fleets of ships, and its quays to be crowded with throngs of sailors hailing from so many British and foreign ports.

As time rolls on, changes are surely if slowly taking effect in the manners and customs of the Maoris, that dwell so near to us yet are so distinctly not of us; the cares and occupations of the inmates of a native village will readily furnish us with something to think about. It is intended to steer clear of 'the native question,' leaving that to the curious student who pores over Blue Books, or dips into *Hansard* (that costly tomb raised by a lavish country to preserve from oblivion the garrulous remains of many of our living dead), with the almost certain fate of being hopelessly confounded with the enigmas of native affairs. The said student in the end probably desisting from abortive attempts to master the inscrutable, with the idea that in the choice of a well for veiling her modesty, Truth might have found not only a drier but a more obscure hiding-place.

We find that with the lapse of time, changes in the manners of Natives are as evident as that the stately black pines [mataī] have given place to the Australian bluegum trees which dot the slopes that lead down to the pah. A village has arisen on the site of the old Maori pah; this has come about gradually, till the weather-boarded cottage with its shingled roof has ousted the ancient raupo warri [whare], with low entry, narrow spy-place and thick grassy thatch; the handier whaleboat has superseded the time-honoured canoe.

The Europeanised Natives have undergone many severe struggles to maintain their foothold in the few camps of refuge that yet lie open for them; change of food, clothing, lodging, have each exercised an influence in attacking the health and sapping the old vigour of the Native race; years must pass before they become accustomed to the advantages and the drawbacks of civilization.

Cultivation in former days, only so far engaged the attention of the Natives here, as to ensure an abundant supply of potatoes; in a few choice spots the kumera [sic] was grown, but this favourite esculent required a fine light soil and a sheltered position; Tamatutu was said to be the most southerly place in which this tender plant could be cultivated with any hope of success. Subsequently, patches of maize made their appearance, great care being taken to keep the plants clear of weeds; late in the autumn the cobs were gathered and hung up in huge bunches to dry on trees and rails; the rich golden heads of corn showed plainly at some distance; when well dried the produce was sold, or placed in the wata [whata] or store till wanted for use. At the present time, potatoes, maize, mangolds, vegetables in variety, such as marrows, pumpkins, cucumbers, &c., are grown for sale as well as for their own consumption. The women do a very large share of the work of cultivation, they are especially careful in their attention to the weeding and hoeing of these crops, which are grown in very small patches. The Natives almost seem to work in pairs at home, as you rarely see a man digging or hoeing without a woman beside him, those who go out to work are invariably men, these undertake jobs as shearing, fencing, grass-seeding, &c.

The alterations which have taken place in the character of their food has much affected some of their customs and employments; there is now very little hunting of food, as the means of supply have been rapidly circumscribed or in some cases have almost altogether disappeared before the cultivations of the white man. Drainage of swamps and other improvements have put an end to their duck-hunting; formerly they used to form parties for this purpose during the moulting season in the autumn. The place chosen was in a district where ducks abound, a circuit was formed and the birds were driven into some swampy hollow, where the old moulting birds were secured pretty easily. At other seasons, or in places which did not offer facilities for driving, flax snares were fixed to light manuka rods, which were firmly driven in an upright position into a creek frequented by ducks, a cross rod being fastened to the uprights about a foot [30cm] above the water; as the ducks were alarmed and swam down the stream they had to pass through the spaces between the rods, and thus many were caught by the snares. Some of the elder Maoris tell with much gusto of the manner in which koeke [koreke] (quail) were caught by nooses fixed in the runs amongst the tussock grass. Pigeons, kakas, and some of the smaller woodland birds were also hunted; but the rapid disforesting of this district has made this custom a thing of the past. Wekas (*Ocydromus*), penguins (*Spheniscus*), are still objects of pursuit. The first named is hunted by several individuals in a party, who thoroughly scour a wide area and preserve the wekas for winter use, or to be sent as presents to friends, this oily kind of food being much relished; as many as two thousand of the birds have been taken in one of the hunts. Or, it may be, that two persons will go out searching along the coast-line amongst rocks and caves for penguins; men so employed, we have noticed in the spring month of November, carrying quite a burthen of penguins and wekas tied up in bunches with a bit of split flax leaf or ti palm [cabbage tree]. Eel fishing is still a great resource, and is eagerly pursued, some men going long distances to reach favourite spots for the spearing; they now usually travel on horseback, leaving the pah very early in the morning, and usually returning on the evening of the same day, or circumstances may induce them to remain for some days; when brought home, the eels are split down, hung up and dried for future use, or a portion of the take may be sent on to the towns for sale, in this case they are usually strung on a string of flax, so many for a shilling, or 'herrin' as they call it; for their own use they seem to prefer the very large thick eels. When dried, the eels are tied in bundles and then kept ready for use. Years ago, two of our highest church dignitaries on a tour of inspection round Banks Peninsula, passed a night in a Native warri so bare of all furniture, according to European notions, that the only available pillow was a bundle of dried eels. Sea fishing has in a great measure been abandoned as the old folk have died off, there has been little attempt amongst the younger people to fix the huge flaxen nets for the dog-fish (*scyllium*); this was a work of some ceremony, the net was dropped late in summer when the harbours thronged with schools of dog-fish; the fish were hung up and dried on a rough kind of scaffold or stage made of long poles. Every passer-by was made aware of the success of the fishers, for weeks during the process of curing or drying the air being pervaded by a very unpleasant odour. Fishing for moki, conger, rock cod, &c., also engages attention; lampreys [*Geotria australis*] are held in estimation, along the coast we once came on a large portion of a huge whale in which were immense numbers of lampreys writhing and twisting; a Maori family laughing and shouting, was gleefully engaged splashing and leaping in the water, securing as many of these delicacies as possible.

Shell-fish are eagerly sought after; oysters, mussels, pipis are collected, and quantities are taken into the towns for sale. Much of the work falls to the lot of the women and children, numbers of whom may be seen at ebb-tide prying into the crevices of the rocks as they are left bare by the receding waves. Mutton and beef now furnish a goodly portion of their food, often the men and women returning from marketing their produce, may be seen carrying home joints of meat. Pigs are not bred so largely as formerly, some may be seen tethered just outside the warris, secured in this way so as to prevent damage to their gardens; of late years, the rearing of geese has become in fashion, and rather large flocks may be noticed grazing in the pah; surplus birds are sold, but there is a large demand for them for home consumption; weddings, funerals, the welcoming of friends, all afford reasons for feasting which are not lightly to be disregarded.

8. Out in the Open [On rātā] (1885)

Rambling through a large garden with its surroundings of sheltering plantations, its bosky shrubberies, under such a beneficient climate as we enjoy, is indeed a pleasure; not only are the eyes gratified by the number and variety of the objects to be seen, their different forms and colours, but the objects themselves give us much to think about. At this season, the very commencement of the young year, its birthday in fact, so abundant are the attractions offered by trees, shrubs, and plants, that some difficulty is felt in deciding what to begin with, what is to be looked at first! There are many plants gathered together from many countries, all more or less interesting, and all worthy of attention and notice. Let us take one that is in its perfection of bloom; which one out of the multitude? Here at haphazard is a brilliant flower, with an intensity of colour in its broad scarlet petals that arrests attention at once; but it is a common weed. This common poppy with its frequent neighbour – the corn bottle (*Centaurea cyanus*) [corn flower] troubles the British farmer: let us in fancy stroll down a rural lane in the Old Country, where tall elms ranked along the hedgerow dispense a grateful shade that falls in fitful checquers across the roadway, the busy cawing of rooks is heard from some of the lofty trees, honeysuckle and briars perfume the air. We look over a stile or five-barred gate into a corn-field, what a beautiful picture lies before us in the broad sweep of the growing crop, waving as the breeze stirs, whilst the red poppy and blue corn-flower play at hide and seek amongst the stout stems of the bending wheat. But the farmer does not admire the presence of the bright flowers, they are weeds that tell their tale of slovenly culture, to be eradicated by good tillage. Here in some few gardens, the corn poppy is allowed to live, and so, proudly lifts its head, crowned with its scarlet cap of liberty, a most effective bit of colour that may be used with marked effect in room decoration, but like many another 'bright particular star'[27] it soon fades. The blue corn-flower appears to lose its brightness after years of self-seeding, as white flowers predominate; the scarlet poppy produces some variations that are pretty and nearly always brilliant in colour. It is perhaps worth remarking that the showy Godetia has a very lasting quality as a cut flower; I saw in Christchurch on New Year's Day, blooms that had been cut on the 14th December, they then appeared quite fresh-looking; this is a virtue that should recommend its culture to many whose space for flowering plants is limited. The scarlet myrtle, or rata (that is the rata of the hills in the Canterbury district) is now quite delightful to look at, it pleases the eye only, not being endowed with the perfume of the myrtle; the species of rata are numerous, the one referred to is, *Metrosideros lucida* [southern rātā].[28] This plant which seems usually to maintain a shrub-like appearance, most symmetrical in form, compact, of handsome foliage, is entitled to a place in the shrubbery even without the lavish beauty of its scarlet flowers. Why is it so seldom seen? it is very easy to cultivate, any ordinary loam appears to suit it, yet who has it? beside those familiar with sub-alpine districts, who knows anything of it, except perhaps the name. I have raised it from seed and from cuttings, but the readier method is to procure it from a native nursery; most of mine were obtained thus, and a plant-seeking expedition afforded pleasant, healthy recreation; not unfrequently, this kind of outing was in some way combined with pig hunting, if the Fates were propitious. There were many places amongst the higher lying lands in the more remote parts of the Malvern district; or, in the neighbourhood of the romantic gorges of the Rakaia and Rangitata rivers that furnished such native nurseries to the explorer. The huge rocks that beetled above the western stream of the Hororata, or Rocky Hill, that shuts in one part of the Rockwood Valley, were very favourable spots to search for plants. In the days one used to journey thither, to collect and forage – the gardens and orchard at Rockwood were in themselves a great attraction – the late owner, Mr. Henry Phillips, being almost unrivalled as an amateur gardener, unless by the late Archdeacons Mathias and Willock, parsons who knew what land was and what could be done with it. Let us pause a few moments here; the orchard was famous for the excellence of its produce throughout a wide district, the careful manner in which the trees were trained made them a very interesting sight. Scarcely a spray was to be seen out of its proper position, being part and parcel of a well-formed cup-like shape; no gross wood was permitted an unwieldy profitless growth at the expense of the other branches; the crop, usually a fair one, was pretty evenly distributed throughout the tree. A frequent remark of the genial cultivator was, 'look at the pear trees in the Channel Isles, you might put all the roots of a tree into a bushel.' One of the secrets of his method of culture, so successful in spite of indifferent soil and a trying climate, was an efficient system of root pruning, he kept the wood roots in due proportion to the wants of the tree. But one's interest in this charming spot was not exhausted with an inspection of the gardens and orchard, there were the fish ponds to look at; an immense amount of energy and skill had been expended in so utilising the mountain stream as to form a succession of large ponds and breeding places for the cultivation of several kinds of fish. Trout, perch, carp, tench, might be seen there of all sizes; a handsome dish of perch was a treat not often to be met with; fish of half a pound weight [225g] were considered best for frying. After a day or two devoted in this fashion 'to the lions', the business of plant collecting followed. To secure young plants and seedlings of the rata, it was necessary to undertake a fair amount of scrambling and climbing about rocks and rough places not very accessible. It was usually in the moss-seamed crevices and crannies of rocks that young plants had put forth their tender rootlets, moistened with the damp gathered from the hill mists. Stoutly they maintained their foothold; it was waste of time and labour, and the certain destruction of the plants to tug at them and pull them up by force, the result was sure to be a broken root scraped bare of all fibre that had not the slightest intention of humouring your violence by pretending to grow. The aid of a long bladed knife persuaded these natives perhaps reluctantly to quit their home; but they usually got over the change of quarters, and in course of time, throve well. I say in course of time advisedly, because the rata (as Pitt described confidence in aged bosoms) is a plant of slow growth.[29] It requires plenty of air and exposure and to be away from the drip of trees. If stimulated to extra growth by rich damp soil, the young shoots become so luxuriant that the beautifully coloured blossom is quite hidden in the foliage, but on an exposed, rather dry situation, it puts forth a blaze of colour that repays one for all the trouble of collecting and cultivating. The wood is hard and heavy, in the times when croquet was in vogue I have known capital mauls [mallets] made of this material.

Both kinds of manuka are worthy of cultivation; they are very ornamental when in flower; they are rapidly becoming scarcer; when nearly exterminated probably some bright minded creature will find out their value. *L.* [*Leptospermum*] *scoparium*, the scrub manuka, often may be observed with a pinkish tinge in the petals. The different species of native fagus [beech] are excellent evergreen trees or shrubs, they are always fresh and beautiful, their foliage of deep rich green not to be surpassed for decorative purposes. When the fagus is sufficiently matured to furnish good seed it quickly reproduces its species, as may be seen in any outraged wood that has been subsequently fenced off from the ravages of cattle on the tender seedlings.

A grand looking shrub now just past its best is the strawberry tree of Nepal (*Benthamia fragifera*); it is hardy, a fast and vigorous grower, an abundant bloomer, bearing gamboge coloured flowers, which in turn are replaced by fruit of a not unpleasant flavour. Birds are so fond of these berries that it is difficult to obtain a share of them. [Joseph] Paxton gives the height of the shrub at three feet [0.9m], that possibly refers to dimensions attained in England; here I know a specimen raised from a cutting which is over twenty feet [6.1m] in height. A puff of dust like pollen raised from the roadside is a reminder from a troop of swaggers tramping to the peninsula, that Cocksfoot grass (*Dactylis*) is now playing an important part in the operations of peninsula farmers. The past two or three seasons have remarkably favoured its growth, from moist and cloudy weather prevailing. This valuable plant is spreading over hills and spurs in a very rapid manner, from its possessing a vitality that enables it to overcome difficulties which many other plants are unable to survive. The seeding of the past and present seasons will, no doubt, make a permanent alteration in the grazing qualities of a very wide area of land. Impatient to be at work, to secure the cutting of a 'good bit,' men are to be seen trudging hopefully along the roads weeks before the grass is ready for cutting, some of these leave fair employment in towns in the hope of making good wages at 'seeding'. Some of these get woefully disappointed, finding the work altogether different from what they expected; the toil of ascending and descending steep hill sides, alone severely testing the muscles of those who have been only accustomed to the plains.

9. Out in the Open: The pulse of spring (1885)

Some writer has said that, 'Spring is a shabby excuse for prolonging the winter by three months,' but this smart saying, however appropriate to the seasons in Europe, does not apply fairly to this favoured country. Here, there is no well-marked boundary to cross which separates one season from another; as soon as the middle of the month of August is reached, one can feel the mild incoming of the genial period of growth. We may watch the mercury in the thermometer, we may fidget and tap at the weatherglass, call it a late or cold, an early or a warm spring, but its influence beams upon us gradually, its presence is spread everywhere around us, however ungratefully or churlishly we accept the boon. Spring comes upon us quietly 'doing good by stealth', like pitiful-eyed charity, clothing the naked. She spreads abroad verdure as a garment, causing the face of Mother Nature (like that of many another female) to break into radiant smiles when adorned in the freshness of new apparel.

For the rain-sodden earth during many a dreary day lying benumbed with cold, awakening, feels a reviving power. The pulse of Spring, whose beat at first feeble, is quickened by increasing sunlight, gathers strength with its growth, till its impulsive throb is felt in each element of air, earth, and water.

Now is a good time to look about, to take notice of some of the changes that are gradually but surely taking place around us. Amongst the common and familiar trees, there is the ash, the farmers' tree in the Old Country, see how coaly black are the buds, in a few days these must change to purple as they burst, even now some sheltered boughs are already disclosing the secret that has been concealed through the wintry months. The common oak holds out its branches bare and naked, but there are varieties of it, which at this time are masses of russet-brown leaves, these, curled and crisp, thin and withered, still hang persistent beneath the swelling buds; this tenacity of hold displays a valuable habit; it at least points out a good tree for sheltering purposes, and gives a hint as to a useful kind of plant for a screen that will last through the cold months, how advantageous it might be found on the weather side of a paddock set aside for early lambing.

There is the willow, that almost universal favourite, its long trailing sprays have scarcely parted with the last yellow leaves, ere the young buds, striving for light and air, give a verdant tinge to the long streaming boughs; in the undergrowth of the inner branches a few specks of pale delicate green mark the tender leaflets upward turned, part curled towards the strengthening sunlight, that kindly fosters these, the first-born of the season. Tradition has it, (and in our new world we have reached to the dignity of tradition,) that most of the weeping willows here are descended from the celebrated trees that drooped by and screened the tomb of Napoleon, plants or cuttings were brought to this distant land by the hands of French immigrants, in veneration of their great hero; as relics these may be termed imperishable, so readily can they be renewed with a fresh lease of life, and thus be handed down to the children's children. Who shall say that in this changeful world the willows thus reverently introduced, may not outlive the memory of the Exile of St. Helena – the graceful outlines of their green livery be reflected distinctly and life-like by many a fair stream, long after the tale of the great conqueror shall have become blurred and faded in the mystic cloudiness of fable?

What an irksome prison ground, the ocean girt rock of St. Helena, for a plant so loving of water as the weeping willow! how fondly it showers down its drooping branches, shading deep pools from the glare of sunlight, allowing but slight flecks of golden sheen to peer through its foliage, and glisten fantastically on the trembling waters.

It is a peace-loving tree above all things; it is seen to most advantage in a state of repose, when not stirred into active motion; a breeze distorts its form, the long boughs, under its influence, become irritated into unseemly restlessness; a gale tosses its streams hither and thither in the wildest confusion, they look panic stricken, seeking rest and finding none. – Try a fire near a weeping willow, as the sticks crackle and sparkle in the flame, and the warm smoke riseth, the draught thus caused urges the boughs to toss and writhe as though in pain, or struggling to escape. The beauty of form or outline, the screening and shading of streams or lakelets is so constantly before us that we, perhaps, do not sufficiently appreciate much of its work silently performed. Out of sight, down in the cool moist ground, the pink rosy-tipt rootlets ceaselessly work, insatiable water drinkers; and perhaps the effects produced are most noticeable on a mountain rill or streamlet. Now the cutting or plant properly fixed in its fresh location, grows quickly, and in the robust vigour of its youth develops an unmistakeable mastery of, a controlling power over, the course of its watery neighbour. Rocks and boulders, clad with green mosses or algae, or smoothed or worn by everflowing water, bound the sides or pave the bottom of the stream, where sand-cased caddis worms lurk and lay hid in the sheltered crannies, till fossicked out by the probing bill of the inquisitive wild duck. A few years pass and the old bed of the ravine is hidden away, lost under myriads of small rootlets that have gradually plaited them into a thick massive net, an outwork that intercepts, receives, and catches, sediment and particles that stray into the meshes. All stones or obstacles are overlayed, a smooth bottom is formed, over which the stream glides softly, and its once angry ripples, that fringed obstructive rocks with foam and froth-specks, have given place to a quiet current that gurgles placidly along its winding course. So the willow carries on its work of reclamation, and many an acre the little rootlets of this and other species save from destruction, where well planned protective works confine rivers within prescribed limits.

Notice how simple in form are the tools employed in the work of reclamation; a series of slim rootlets, more or less numerous, emerge from the earth-bound banks and jut into the stream, as they undulate, waving gently with the movement of the water, they bear much resemblance to slender worms; with heads directed down the current they rise or fall with it, and thus influenced by the unstable element, their motion becomes almost life-like. Whilst these pioneers of the root-work thus float unresistingly, their lower parts, at close intervals and at varying angles, throw out an array of infantine pointed rootlets that are destined in their turn to bear increase; additional material for the meshes of the ever-growing net that is to bind and hold the rushing waters at its will. Unheeded, so the pinky worm-like rootlets floating at their ease, in the course of time, accomplish work that would require the employment of a vast amount of human labour directed with great engineering skill. We all know the value of the 'right man in the right place', plant willows in the right place, they know not fatigue, and will work whilst the planter sleepeth. This power and energy properly directed would ensure an amount of work the value of which would be almost inestimable.

This too is a time of year that reveals much to enquiring eyes, the battered nest with its sunken walls of faded brown moss, and rotting sprays, is so openly apparent, that one scarcely believes it could have held its place last summer, when every bough was thought to have been carefully searched. Here too, on some of the outlying boughs, may be noticed slender cones of dark grey, these are the strong tough cases of the larvae of a small moth (*Liothula* [bag moth]); how tough are the silk-lined coverings may be ascertained by attempts to tear them. Though so like a morsel of broken spray or stick, the animal with its conical home, moves about freely enough. Many years since I collected a number from boughs of the black wattle, placed them on a tray in a room, by next morning they had explored all parts of the chamber from the floor to the ceiling, and had even traversed the polished surface of a mirror. The sharp teeth of the mouse can penetrate the tough envelope; some months since we found in a ngaio (*Myoporum*) well preserved, the solid structure that marks the blackbird's nursery, it had been converted into a capital food store by mice. It was filled to the rim of the walls, principally with nuts, there was also a fir cone with its hard scales nibbled and the strong larval case of the liothula bitten through, showed how the insect had been extracted. This provident little rodent utilises the shallow nest of the white-eye (*Zosterops)* as a storehouse, I have descried the structure well supplied with nuts in a filbertbush [hazel]. Amongst the birds that frequent the willow, the flycatchers are conspicuous with their graceful movements and rapid gyrations, as they twirl and flutter after flying insects, pursuing them under, around, or between the long hanging boughs. At this season too the yellow-heads (*Orthonyx*) [mohua] often may be observed on the willows in pairs or in a small family party; it is probable this indefatigable insect destroyer mates for life, so rarely does one ever see a solitary bird. How closely it pries into and thoroughly searches every foot of the bark of the tree as it hops and climbs upwards; when on the wing its course is almost invariably downwards, then its search recommences on another tree; or it may be it starts its quest on the ground, its strong limbs afford plenty of power for scratching amongst dead leaves and mosses, after a close and careful rummage of these insect covers or preserves, creeping and hopping with constant wing-flutters, it rapidly ascends another tree stem. Now watch it amongst a patch of dead leaves that yet remain on a lodged wind-broken bough, each crisp leaf rustles as it is turned and twisted under its keen inspection; see, it takes nothing for granted, but pries and peers with a close and conscientious scrutiny that would do credit to an untipt douanier. Now the yellow-head, or native canary as it is often called, possesses this satisfactory habit, it often takes its insect food *ab ovo*,[30] it fossicks out their nests and devours larvae, the limpet-like holding scale it deftly picks from off the crumpled and blistered leaves it infests and blemishes. During the prolonged food hunt, it utters oft-repeated notes to summon its mate, it is impatient of solitude, and it is only fair to say that its call note does not remain long unanswered. Scarcely does it appear to rest in the day-time, for throughout some weeks' close observation of its habits I but once observed it enduring perhaps rather than enjoying ease and idleness; it was then basking in the hot sunshine on a tangled mass of convolvulus that trailed over and around a lofty ti tree [cabbage tree], even then the call-note was sounded pretty frequently.

On yon hill-side grows a scanty patch of sweet vernal grass, which through the winter has escaped the browsing of stock, and now carries shaggy but trifling heads of seed on its spindly stalks; it is stirring with life; a flock of goldfinches has discovered merit in the impoverished grass – it hath found favour in their eyes. Deserted now, the scattered whiffs and light rolls of down that show where once were held their feasts of thistle seed, the pretty songsters are busy alighting on the slim grass-stalks that sway down and bend to the ground with their weight. Scarcely do the beaks seize the spikelets before they have to relinquish them, so frequent is the fluttering of each bird in its endeavour to maintain its slender foothold and secure a share of food amongst the hungry twittering flock.

When the orchard undergoes its annual transformation, assuming its veil of white, the bridal robe of promise, suddenly butterflies appear in numbers; the dark-winged insect displays his crimson bands, preferably choosing early plum and cherry trees, on and over these, to and fro, it constantly flies, chasing and chased, or rests while basking on their sunlit blossoms. Often now we see the film of gossamer which floats or bears on high the tiny spider traversing aërial space far beyond our range of vision, we speculate on its appliances which afford such ease of transport, and give a share of the freedom of the air to the wingless midget.

That homely, rural sound, the hum of bees, a prophetic dirge that forebodes disaster, robbery and death; yet this 'industrious apprentice'[31] natheless [sic] toils on gathering its store. The treatment of bees, however savage and cruel, is rendered more odious by the use that is made of our knowledge of their diligent labours to point a moral; many a 'wise saw and modern instance'[32] for the guidance of youth is suspended from the gauzy wings of the 'little busy bee'.[33] How many of these goody tales point out that the industrious habits of the bee render it peculiarly liable to pillage and murder? and how many moralists would avoid sticky fingers? Just here in the shade of gum trees, the murmuring is loud and sustained, for some of these huge trees, with their ample limbs, raise overhead a hundred feet [30m] or more of myrtle-like flowers – a grand harvest for bees and moths, which hasten thither in multitudes as soon as the warty lids of the capsules drop, freeing the protected inflorescence. Busy amongst these flowers, too, may be seen the whistler, or bronze-winged cuckoo (*Chrysococcyx*), that welcome visitor of Spring, with distended gape, preying on the diurnal moths right greedily. As in the Spring of last year, but very few of this interesting species have been observed, possibly the long-continued droughts in Australia are in some way responsible for its now rare occurrence.

The appearance of another visitor, or rather immigrant, remains to be mentioned – the humble bee [bumblebee], the grazier's reputed friend, with a mission to fertilise red clover flowers. I have noted lately its presence on Banks Peninsula, burly and strong of flight, looking remarkably alert and vigorous; may it fulfil its mission, and may the farmers benefit from the labours of their humble ally!

In the vegetable world the weak and feeble display mighty powers in responding to the general summons to be 'up and doing', to take their share in the great work before them. Slender grass-leaves of bulbs push their way, pursue their upward course, often penetrating through inches of overlying loam, the narrow green leaves come up straight as wires, although the weight of a few grains bends them. Now on a border of mixed flowers often a mass of earth may be seen upheld by this kind of foliage, especially where a clump of bulbs has sent forth several leaves rather closely. The leaves of half-a-dozen roots of that old cottage favourite, the daffy-down-dilly,[34] lifted up such a lump of soil; this having collected and weighed, I found these few leaves carried on their tender points full fifteen ounces [426g] of soil.

In this country the phenomena of life and death are portrayed with singular sharpness in the habit of that well-known British plant, the Common Buckler fern (*Lastrea filix-mas*).[35] Handsome and bold in the aspect of its outlines, vigorous of growth, its rich green lance-shaped fronds stand up rather stiffly some three feet [0.9m] or so above its tufted scaly crown, a grand ornament amongst the varied occupants of the hardy out-door fernery. Let Spring come fairly in, the tapering fronds but yesterday proudly erect, still deeply verdant, fall flat as though struck down by force, or bashed by heavy gusts of wind. Pluck or handle a frond, the leaflets may be found fresh and green, the numberless chaffy scales not to have lost their crispness, yet on a sudden call of nature, without fading or showing any of their gradual discolouration of decay, prone lie the fronds, disclosing the young growth knuckled and crowded, just appearing and rousing from the thick bed of scales that so closely invest the crown. A plant with such a habit, that forestalls decay in its members, that waits not for the withering faintness of age, but clears all away promptly and at once, leaving a free stage for the young, such a plant should indeed prove vigorous and transmit hardy offspring.

It may be added that a tasselled or fringed variety of this species exhibits a similar habitat; although seen each recurring year, this living symbol of death in life never loses its interest; many to whom I have pointed out these plants at Springtide have wondered at the sudden prostration of vigorous looking fronds that revealed no outward symptom of decadence. Is this sacrifice compulsory or voluntary? it is an act of devotion or bowing down before Spring, a notable example of the prevalence of sun-worship, openly and punctually performed, for this fern in common with a large proportion of the vegetable world holds not

> 'That all the world will be in love with night,
> And pay no worship to the garish sun.'[36]

The Buckler fern is becoming naturalised, inasmuch as unaided it is reproduced here; the habit above referred to does not seem to be acquired by the young seedlings, as yet. Is not this fact evidence that the drooping of the mature fronds is to make way for the new growth in Spring. I do not think it is to further the germination of the spores, as I have not found any seedlings immediately around the old plants which annually have abased their fronds for years past.

Just a word or two of the Hartstongue. This favourite with its long narrow leaves is abundantly reproduced here, scores of young plants may be seen clinging to mossy stones, or affixed in the crevices of roots that stray over a moist surface; the bright green fronds more spear-shaped than those of mature plants, at this season especially, encourage the fern-lover with satisfactory evidence of healthy growth. Then at least one enjoys the pleasure of having fostered the establishment of a very interesting plant in a new habitat, for a grand tuft of Hartstongue with its coronal of long narrow fronds is a pleasing object in any suitable situation; but it must be remembered that the vigorous thrift of the plants rests mainly on this condition being found.

At this season that dainty little annual, the Jersey fern, (*Gymnogramma* [*Anogramma*] *leptophylla*) may be detected shyly peeping forth from crannies and crevices of dented rocks and cliffs by the sea; nowhere have I observed it more thriving than in a little bay in Akaroa harbour. There, a mountain rill sweeping down a small wooded ravine cleft a narrow opening to the rocky shore; on the sea-facings just above high-water mark, this tiny fern flourished with the utmost luxuriance; its pigmy tufts crowded into thick pale-green patches. These seemed to follow a soak caused by a thread-like trickle that slid over slippery rock-ledges drop by drop, encouraging and feeding moss growth. Scattered about were a few stunted ngaios (*Myoporum*) that offered some shade and shelter; these advantages the tiny annual appeared to neglect, as it displayed its tender unevenly-divided fronds to the full light of day. But the Jersey fern, the kindly visitor for a season, soon passes away after its spore-fall or seed cast; as though this lover of sea-girt rocks and beetling crags satisfied with providing successors for the future, like a good fairy, departed for other shores, where barren sea cliffs needed the rare charm of its soft green foliage.

Of the children of the Spring, that universal favourite the common yellow primrose thrives well in this climate, producing luxuriant leaves with an abundance of blossoms. It would be difficult indeed to conceive any arrangement more elegant in its simplicity or more grateful to the sight; to many a grey head a flood of early recollections are called up by this simple flower of the wayside and woodland, fondly grouped by memory with the blue-bell and wind-flower [anemone]. To some it appears unfortunate that so great a favourite, for political purposes, should have been selected as a party emblem,[37] surely there should be no decided love for such a flower; why should the ins and outs of the political arena lay special claim to this sweet wilding? To the English politician might aptly be applied that line of Goldsmith's

> And to party gave up what was meant for mankind.[38]

Still, it is probable this incident of party symbolism will lead to its cultivation or more careful protection as a prevailing fashion – for a time.

Here, placed under much the same conditions as to situation as in its native habitat, I have not observed any seedling plants; a similar experience applies to the blue-bell.

One cannot pass silently the azure flowers of the giant Forget-me-not, the Chatham Island lily (*Myosotidium nobile*), in addition to the lovely tint of the large blossoms it rejoices in splendid shining foliage of deep green. The heart-shaped leaves, traversed by bold parallel veins, reach noble dimensions, over thirty inches [76cm] in length, with a breadth of twenty inches [51cm] at the widest part. This grand flower requires liberal treatment, of which kelp or other sea-weed should form a considerable share; it well repays all trouble and care in this respect, under favourable conditions freely reproducing its species. A time comes when surprise ceases, or probably I should have been surprised on an occasion, when a gentleman taking hold of a leaf of the plant, not then in flower, expressed his admiration of the beautiful *rhubarb*. This goes to show that this lily is not grown, or even known, as much as it deserves to be.

A well grown, luxuriant tuft of this grand Forget-me-not is a gem of the flower border, one is in doubt whether blossom or foliage asserts the prior claim to admiration. Charming are the azure-tinted flowers, eyed with deep purple, closely packed into shapely rounded crowns, these lovely crests dyed of this rarest blue, do not stand erect or tower aloft as seeming self-assured or proudly arrogant, nor seek they to lurk concealed, partly they recline, as rather to screen or foil their beauty in the shadows of the embossed leaves that stoutly are up-reared above. Smooth, soft to touch, with a subdued satin-like sheen, the leaf's pale underside contrasts with the brilliant glossiness of the deeply virid surface. Native of a humid climate, and often washed with showers of salt spray, or bedewed by heavy mists off the sea, the structure of the foliage, gracious in its sweeping curves, appears specially adapted for the collection and rapid transmission of moisture. It is a funnel with the polished surface fluted by strong veins, these are channels that unite together and lead the gathered moisture to the deep groove that furrows the upper side of the stalk, widening at the base to a broad duct. On the underside stands out in its fullness and strength the stoutly ribbed framework that firmly supports this expansive catch-water.

Through the shrubberies, the strong honied perfume attracts attention to the little bell flowers of the *Melicytus lanceolatus* [narrow-leaved māhoe], one of the early bloomers, and worthy to be cultivated even on a limited space devoted to shrubs, because it is so early.

In some favoured spot, may be, the kowhai is flowering, with its rich adornment of 'old gold' coloured blossoms; to the honied feast they offer, hie [hurry] bell-birds, and fluttering tuis with their white chin feathers curled in pleasing contrast to the dark plumage of lustrous metallic green. That now scarce bird the hoary-headed Kaka scents out the kowhai, turns and twists itself into grotesque postures to reach the nectarines with its tongue; rather silently too it gets through its meal, then disappears as suddenly as it came. But the kowhai itself is now rarely seen, its timber so highly prized for its toughness and durability, is but seldom met with, it is being cleared off rapidly like the black pine [mataī] and manuka, in our absurd zeal for disforesting. Many facts might be given showing the durability of the timber of the kowhai; in September, 1882, at Akaroa, there were standing in good condition several pales fixed in August 1840 by one of the original French settlers, who still hale and hearty, was able to dress his vines and cultivate his garden. This timber was highly prized for a variety of station purposes in the earlier days of the settlement, far back up the Rakaia, promising logs were looked for and brought home. The September floods swept through the gorge collections of timber and useless *débris*, from the forests amongst the back ranges, these were deposited on the flats and spits in a chance-medley style, as they happened to lodge coming down. Searching for good sticks of kowhai was not the least agreeable occupation that fell to one's share, albeit at times the sand-laden nor'wester was troublesome enough to encounter. You had a day's work in the grand scenery of the river, with its vast level terraces that stretched away from the deep gorge, seawards. On either hand formal ranks of ti trees [cabbage trees] stood in close array on terrace above terrace; at flowering time their huge branched panicles diffused a fragrance not to be forgotten. Heaps, irregularly formed, of water smoothed boulders lay just as left by some prehistoric flood; over some of these trailed twining plants, and amongst them countless lizards basked in the sun, deadly still all but their eyes, which sparkled like gems, till an approaching footstep caused a general scuttle of the harmless reptiles. Crossing the swift shallow streams to reach the flats, one's presence was at once made known by the shrill alarm notes of the keen eyed red-bills [oystercatchers]. On this, the copper-banded dottrel,[39] perched on some mound or shingle, also watched all proceedings with bowing head, evidently he had family reasons for mistrusting intrusion on his windswept haunts; yet did he possess gifts, such wiles and cunning artifices to mislead any would-be egg-lifter, that it was mere chance generally that led one to the discovery of the hidden treasure. That rarer wader, the guileless crookbill (*Anarhynchus*) [wrybill] was often seen fossicking for aquatic insects amongst stones by the margins of the streams. Where coarse grass in thick tufts bordered some placid backwater, reflecting tall flax bushes and tohe grass, sometimes a family of paradise ducks might be seen together for a moment or two. But the sound of a warning note of danger changed the peaceful scene of domestic ease. The young disappeared, the old birds fluttered along temptingly near, as with crippled leg or wing.

Now whether it was that there were no game laws in those days of Arcadian simplicity, or that the august arm of the law was not long enough to stretch from Auckland to Rakaia, it is said a certain custom prevailed of pinioning paradise ducklings when fit for the operation. This was to render them more readily accessible for future inspection in the autumn, when they would have had time to acquire size and plumpness, and prove interesting subjects for close investigation and discussion. Many glances in natural history were obtained whilst the logs were being collected and thrown together, ready for removal at a future time.

When shall we ever take up the question of the preservation of native plants? In a recent serial appeared some capital suggestions in furtherance of this object, so desirable yet so little in accord with public taste, which appears rather to lean either to entire neglect or active destruction of our woods and forests. In Europe, this matter has awakened enquiry both in England and on the Continent; the Midland

Union of Natural History Societies has appealed to lovers of British plants to save the rarer from complete extermination. Then in Switzerland, the Association pour la Protection des Plantes has its seat at Geneva; this admirable society has a large garden devoted to the raising of Swiss plants in quantities, and the sale of them properly established at very low rates. This Association undertakes this labour to save the native flora from the depredations of the unconscionable plant-hunter.

The unconscionable plant-hunter who despoils without mercy is a nuisance anywhere, and may continue to inflict almost irreparable injury to local flora by overgreed in his perquisitions; but this country [New Zealand] has suffered from permitted excesses in disforesting, which a few years hence will be deemed almost incredible. What unbiased stranger could give credit to the tale of whole forest districts that have been delivered over to the axe, to be swept with fire without reference to the value of the timber thereon? Is not this short-sighted policy still in progress for grass sowing, when flocks and herds are already far in excess of the wants of the population and of the demands drawn upon them for the supply of foreign markets. It seems a question for the Industrial Association to entertain whether they should not use their influence to some further waste of what should be a valuable resource for the nation. The country is killing the goose without permitting it to lay the golden egg. The numberless purposes and economic uses to which the timber and produce of the forests could be converted, the thousands of hands that might be maintained in carrying on the various industries, should be sufficient reasons for at once adopting a policy of real forest conservation.

Planting exotic trees to which much encouragement has been given, is only in its infancy, it is quite experimental as yet, who can tell the issue of a few years? Some of these species that are being extensively grown have already proved failures, many more may lose or retain only in a limited degree the noted qualities that marked them out as valuable trees for planting.

10. Out in the Open
[A countryman in the Chathams] (1888)[40]

Notwithstanding the severity of the depression which so long has afflicted the colony, this season, at any rate, gardens have blossomed as gaily as ever. It may be this bright streak in the prevailing gloom is owing to the cause that so many good people have more leisure to attend to their little favourite plots of ground, than has been the case in more prosperous times. Whatever the reason, the fact remains, that Christchurch with its suburbs does make a very satisfactory display, both in fruit and flower culture. That the love of flower growing is spreading can be seen from the attention that is now generally bestowed on quite a list of favourite flowers. Just notice in what a number of small gardens one may observe excellent blooms of roses quite fit for exhibition; the rose is singled out amongst a crowd of other good flowers, so as to avoid jostling against fashion, it enjoys the privilege of being always in vogue, in despite of the aesthetic pretensions of garish sunflowers, single dahlias, and many other claimants for public favour. In time, no doubt, florists will cultivate more generally hyacinths, tulips, and other early flowering bulbs, with a view to the production of fresh varieties of those charming flowers. In a city of verandahs like Christchurch, one might expect to see many sheltered corners devoted to that lovely tribe of plants, the pelargoniums. There are many odd nooks that could be very satisfactorily occupied with ferns – Mr. Abbott[41] has shown us that, with limited space at command, with a trifling cost, a very beautiful and interesting fernery can be constructed in a manner that would convert an unsightly corner into a most attractive addition to any house or cottage residence in town or country. Such a modest but useful addition to one's garden plot surely holds out to many a temptation to know more of the native growth of this country by seeking out and gathering together a collection of its living ferns, their allies, and the more attractive species of its orchideous and epiphytic plants. This colony with its outlying dependencies, stretching through so many degrees of latitude, including the Chatham group, the Kermadec, and the Auckland Isles, could furnish such a fernery nobly with plants of hardy growth and habit.

Perhaps one is more strongly inclined to recommend such an interesting and economical fernery as hinted at on Mr. Abbott's lines, from rambling in one of the primeval forests of the Chatham Isles. It is but the truth to own this paper would have been considerably more advanced but for the impossibility of withdrawing oneself from the quiet contemplation of so many beautiful forms of vegetation met with in this morning's walk in the wooded heights about Taupapa [Taupeka?] and Rangitehia [Rangitihi]. There are many points of very great interest to be noticed in the flora of this ocean island. Genera one may be familiar with in New Zealand, are represented here by species of very robust habit, this is especially the case with several shrubs or small trees. It may be of interest to some readers to mention a few instances of this difference of growth. That very common native shrub *Veronica salicifolia* [koromiko], which, in Hooker's Handbook of New Zealand Flora, is described as having branches as thick as a crow-quill, may be observed here having the dimensions of a small tree. It may be met with, from thirty to forty feet [9–12m] in height in some places; this morning I put a tape round the stem of one of them, at between four and five feet [1–1.5m] from the ground, the circumference was found to be three feet and one inch [94cm]. Terehine (*Dracophyllum scoparium vel* [var] *urvilleanum*), which we know in New Zealand usually as a small shrub, here attains a height of perhaps forty feet [12m]; one, not selected as of extraordinary bulk, gave a measurement of five feet three inches [1.6m] round its rugged bark, which in roughness somewhat resembled that of some species of pine. The genera *Coprosma* and *Olearea* are represented by large timber trees, the latter being held in much esteem for fencing purposes. In many parts of the island it is the stubborn breakwind against the gales that sweep across the ocean, a natural fence to the 'clears' where cultivation is carried on. The karaka (*Corynocarpus laevigata* [*laevigatus*]), our only representative of the tropical genus *Anacardiaceae*, requires a few words. It is a tree of the very greatest interest to the [Chathams] aborigines, it supplies them with fruit; it furnished timber of sufficient size, from which in past days large canoes could be constructed; often it is to be observed carrying a straight rather smooth stem, bearing a rounded top of deep dark shining foliage. The large berries are rather egg-shaped, now of a deep shining green, being as yet quite immature, these are called kopi by the natives [the Moriori], in consequence the karaka is very commonly known as the kopi-tree. The foliage provides excellent fodder for stock, sheep fatten on the fallen leaves in winter. When dead the karaka, besides the timber it yields, is still valuable, for on its branches mainly grows the crop of that well-known fungus hakeke (*Hoineola auricula judae*).[42] This thin, concave or ear-shaped fungus is one of the articles of export from this island to a Chinese market.

On the smooth stems of karaka trees in various parts of the island are still to be seen some of those quaint figures carved by the Moriories [sic] in former days. I took notice of about a dozen of these weirdly [sic] designs in the woods near the Mairangi pah; but these mystic symbols are yearly becoming rarer, as the timber is felled or dies away, from exposure to the wind by neighbouring clearings, or from the disforesting which seems always to mark the White Man's doings in a new field of enterprise. This interesting tree is worthy of a place in any shrubbery from the brightness of its dark green foliage, it is as handsome as the Moreton Bay fig and hardier. For those who are admirers of variegations in leaves, it may be mentioned that a variegated karaka can be obtained. This sport was discovered by the late Alfred Ludlam of the Hutt; the plant he caused to be propagated, and it was extensively distributed in Europe as a great rarity from New Zealand.

In whatever direction one approaches the woods at this season of the year, a thick carpeting of *Acaenae* must be traversed, called piri-piri or biddy-biddy by the settlers. The barbed bristles of the rounded heads become firmly attached to one's clothes, so that the pedestrian quickly assumes a pair of thick brown gaiters, difficult to be quit of. This burr affixes itself in masses to the woolly coats of sheep, in some of the 'clears' in the woods, sheep, thus disfigured, are constantly met with tufts of burrs persistently adhering to their heads and fleeces, and have a very strange appearance. Eventually this vegetable matter gets thoroughly dried and in a powdered form drops out of the fleece.

In the woods where depastured stock have not destroyed them, the ferns are magnificent, in many places sheep have eaten most of those which are not of arboreal habit. Of these the Black-tree-fern, mamuku [mamaku] (*Cyathea medullaris*), and Cunningham's tree-fern [gully tree fern] (*C. cunninghamii*) are in grand condition. The former attains immense size, both in height and bulk, I have measured specimens with a circumference of above seven feet [2.1m] about two feet [60cm] above the ground. Nor is it very rare to find these great ferns furcated, I came across an instance this morning, where three huge stems sprung from a common root, the area covered by the sweep of their wide-spreading fronds was very considerable, they made a most noble display, many of the old leaves still clung about the group, on which no officious gardener had yet laid hands rashly, under the excuse of making it look neat and tidy. Untouched stood the noble group beneath the shelter of loftier karaka trees, in the profound depths of darkening foliage that over-shadowed it from all but fitful and curious glances of sunlight, it was a meet [suitable] temple for a hermit's worship. Cunningham's fern which is abundant, is of less robust proportions, with the stem somewhat slender, particularly a few feet from the ground. Sometimes these are forked, within a limited space, I noticed two specimens with double stems, whilst another bore three, all of which were of fair height. The slender Dicksonia (*D. squarrosa*) flourishes in dense thickets, it is more robust in habit than those one has been familiar with on Banks Peninsula. In some parts of these beautiful woods, the dicksonias become perfect storehouses (if one may call them so) for epiphytes and parasitic ferns. One specimen carried, rooted between the old stipe bases, *Asplenium falcatum*[43] in handsome tufts, whilst wreaths of *Earina mucronata* [bamboo orchid] perfumed it with panicles of its creamy flowers, and the curious pendulous fronds of *Tmesipteris forsteri* [fork fern] appeared in the clefts or spaces of many old stipes. On some, above a dense growth of *Trichomanes venosum* [veined bristle fern] which clothed the lower portion of the stem, might be noticed *Polypodium* [now *Micosorum*] *pustulatum*, one of the scented ferns, amongst the slender fronds of this parasite appeared tufts of *Asplenium flaccidum* [drooping spleenwort]. On many trees twined the tawny roots of the climbing Shield-fern [leatherleaf fern] (*Aspidium capense*) with its oval, triangular, thrice-divided fronds; in some places dry weather had withered its young growth, but the rain of a few days was inducing fresh fronds to spring forth. In some of the more open parts of the woods, the common Boss-fern (*Nephrodium decompositum*) covered the ground by the acre, one could almost say without exaggeration. *Polypodium serpens* [now *Pyrrosia eleagnifolia*] is exceedingly abundant, and makes a beautiful show on the old karaka trees, when intermixed with great tufts of drooping Earina, and those of the Shining spleenwort [*Asplenium oblongifolium*], which is by no means rare as a parasite. On the outskirts of the woods, a Shield fern (*Aspidium*) attains a height of eight or nine feet [2.4–2.7m], forming some of the grandest coronals of fronds that I have ever seen anywhere. The kawa-kawa (*Piper excelsum*) attains a considerable size with a very bold habit of the foliage, the wood has joint-like swellings at almost regular distances, which gives it a cane-like appearance. The Rautini (*Senescis hunti*)[44] has been flowering grandly this season, its large panicles of golden coloured blossoms make a goodly display, I am not aware that the Natives make any use of this small tree. Just on the edge of a screen of ake-ake I saw a fine specimen of *Gastrodia* [potato orchid]; this tall leafless orchid was about 18 inches [46cm] in height, bearing an abundance of pendulous brownish-green flowers blotched with white. When fresh, these gave out a faint sweet odour, which afterwards yielded to a scent, which I could only liken to that of a freshly scraped potato. I was desirous of being particular about this, as one may read of this plant, that its odour is aromatic but disagreeable. On the open 'clears' I have seen other orchideous plants, but have not examined them. On the swamp there is the *Gleichenia dicarpa* [pouched coral fern] in great abundance, often too, one may see the trailing growth of *Lycopodium volubile* [climbing clubmoss]. The Kikiterihe [*Olearia semidentata*] with its panicles of beautiful lilac blossoms is one of the more ornamental shrubs that is found on the wide moorlands. It has a rival in the Putitere (*Leucopogon Richiei*) [Chatham Island mingimingi] which bears on its thickly crowded branches, spikes of snow-white, pink or rosy-red berries. The white Gentian (*Gentiana* [now *Gentianella*] *saxosa*), which is very common on some clears, occasionally presents a variety, by producing flowers of a pinkish hue. Perhaps the glory of the island, may be that by which it is best known to the world, is the Chatham Island lily (*Myosotidium nobile*). This plant is seen in far greater robustness of habit here than I have observed in any specimens under cultivation in New Zealand. It loves the sea-shore where its broad fleshy leaves are frequently bedewed with the saltish scathe that travels from the open seas. And now, oh gardeners! the heavenly blue flowers that crowd its racemes are in danger of being rivalled, I have seen fine tufts of this noble forget-me-not bearing white blossoms! Here is a chance for those who rush about after novelties. One of the effects of settlement has been the rapid disappearance of this beautiful native, from the fondness of stock for its large fleshy leaves. In its wild unprotected state, for many miles in this direction I have met with but few specimens. Its threatened fate reminds one of that of the mountain lily (*Ranunculus lyallii*), in places where this lovely plant once grew by the acre within fifty miles [80km] of Christchurch, I do not suppose a single specimen could now be discovered.

*

During the past season, equally during the spring and summer months, flowers grown out of doors were remarked upon as showing extraordinary brilliancy of colour. Nor was this peculiarity of the year confined to one or two species only; in an unmistakable manner it was a charm shared as common property by nearly every plant that contributed a part to the rainbow hues of the mixed flower borders.

One is reminded of the enjoyment of this pleasure in visiting several gardens in different parts of the Chatham Islands, where the intense colouration of blossoms does not appear to be affected in any way by local causes. East or west, north or south, every patch of garden rejoices in brilliant colours. Large plants of Crassula of most luxuriant growth are crowned with fragrant blooms of the deepest crimson;

pelargoniums and geraniums trail against and cover fences with irregular, widely-spreading masses of splendid blossoms. In some places geraniums may be seen entwined amongst the boughs of protective ake-ake, decking its downy branchlets with an abundance of scarlet knots and bunches for sixteen feet [5m] or so above the ground, till the dull sombre foliage of the tree fairly beams with the borrowed gaiety of its friendly neighbour. A fence of ponga [*Dicksonia squarrosa*], rough though it be, appears to set off to advantage the blossoms of such plants as be trailed against it, its dark, dusky brown supplies a capital background that is a convenient foil for flowers of almost every shade of colour. Lobelias of many hues and tints are here exceptionally bright. Nowhere have I seen that old favourite of early days, the twining, wreathing, twisting, honeysuckle, hung around with bonnier or sweeter blooms. Splendid in their intensity of colour, are some species of *Amaryllideae*, notably those of the blood-flowers.

If due precautions are taken to guard against winds, the soil and climate here are very favourable for all kinds of gardening. Seeds are grown and matured here with tolerable ease, of very good quality; so that one is justified in believing that seed raising as an industrial pursuit might be followed here with advantage. Not only good varieties of several kinds of flowers have been obtained, but those of excellent vegetables also. Turnips, carrots, parsnips, beetroot, cabbages, cauliflowers, peas, beans, &c., are produced of prime quality. Vegetables grown in a bush 'clear' cannot be surpassed readily for the excellence of their quality. They possess all the luxuriance of those cultivated by Chinamen, without a taint of certain peculiar odours, that sometime distinguish the produce of those industrious men from the East. One may mention, that amongst several delicious vegetables, some lettuces, grown in a kopi [karaka] bush 'clear' at Moreroa could not be excelled for tenderness, crispness, succulence and delicacy of flavour. These lettuces, perhaps the best one ever tasted, were raised by an Irishman, without any assistance from a Celestial [a Chinese person]. How a row of such delicate vegetables would be appreciated by salad makers on the dry plains of Canterbury! In former days these islands were well and favourably known throughout the Australasian colonies for the superior quality of the potatoes. For many years whaling vessels were supplied with pigs, potatoes and other produce; but it was not until the Australian diggings created an extraordinary demand that the cultivation of the potato was undertaken by the natives to any very great extent. Traders and speculators soon caused a great stir in the minds of the natives in favour of the more extended culture of this vegetable. Urged by the prospect of gaining good prices for this esculent, 'clears' were made in the woods in almost all parts of the island from whence produce could be shipped. In the absence of roads the nearness of a convenient shipping place was a material consideration in making a clear. Prices that seem really fabulous now were then obtained in Sydney for wheat and potatoes; in some instances the latter were sold at from £24 to £30 per ton. Very good heavy wheat was grown, but the prices for it suffered somewhat, as the natives seldom were able to offer a very clean sample. Under the stimulus of such a demand for their produce, natives undertook extensive cultivations; money came fast to them, and was lavishly expended in drink and in a variety of luxuries. For a brief time gaudy dresses and ostrich plumes were in fashion, and, with a certain class of jewelry, realised excessive prices. With the collapse of the potato trade many of the clears went out of cultivation.

Among the favourite kinds of potatoes now in vogue are the Kowiniwini and the Kapeta. These are of excellent flavour but of very indifferent appearance, that would not recommend them to those who were not aware of their good quality. When a clear is made by chopping and felling trees, the ground is at once planted, so that the potatoes may have a fair start with the native herbage or weeds that would very soon take possession of the ground. Of these plants not one seems to thrive with more vigour than the piri-piri (*Acaena sanguisorbae*). It is surprising how the coarsely serrated leaves of this much branched trailing herb cover up a garden that is not constantly worked. The rows in a strawberry bed are quickly hidden in a tangled mass of piri-piri. Often it ascends, creeping up and concealing such plants perhaps as the stoutly-growing chrysanthemum, whose whereabouts is marked by a huge dense growth that resembles a tumulus or barrow. Nor are many species of plants its only victims; birds and animals it invests with its barbed bristles, causing them to assume most extraordinary guises. A few weeks since I was working in a garden, when some black object came into view slowly and very gradually, for a time one was puzzled whilst guessing what manner of creature this strange visitor might be. On a nearer approach, as it with troubled air moved wearily yet sedately towards a creek hidden by rich over-hanging ferns, one made out it was a large black cormorant, strangely bedizened, with its legs clad in a very wide pair of brown trousers shaped out of piri-piri. Slowly it paced the uneven way to the little streamlet. One might have caught it without much trouble to biddy it, but there was such an unmistakable appeal in its uneasy glance to respect its defenceless state, that one was bound to let it stalk slowly onward, without causing it further alarm in an attempt to assist it. This large seafowl had probably been tempted to an inland foray by an abundance of inangas (*Galalidae* [*Galaxiidae*, whitebait)] in the upper part of the creek, where it was bordered with a thick growth of piri-piri, with its trailing branches reaching to the water's edge, half hidden by aquatic plants. The word *biddy* requires a little explanation perhaps, for those beyond the island's limits. Piri-piri by the settlers has been converted or corrupted into biddy-biddy; a verb has been formed on it, which is in very constant use for a good part of the year at least. To *biddy* is to rid one of burrs, as 'I'll just *biddy* my clothes before I come in.' Small birds are occasionally found in a wretched state of discomfort, in which they appear a moving mass of burrs. Parroquets, pipets [pipits], and the little whiteyes, have been found victims suffering from these tenacious burrs of the piri-piri, just moving little brown balls quite unable to fly till picked up and released from their bonds. One has not yet become accustomed to the very strange and even comic appearance of sheep in some pastures on the outskirts of the woods where piri-piri usually is abundant. It is said to drop out of the wool so that no loss or damage is sustained owing to its presence. It is esteemed much for the valuable quality of supplying good winter keep for sheep.

Tree-ferns to the settlers as well as to the natives are almost invaluable; for various improvements about their homesteads the ponga is in constant requisition. Strictly speaking, the ponga signified the *Dicksonia squarrosa*, but the word now covers any good tree-fern that can be made of use. Neat houses are built of ponga: these are durable, warm, and comfortable, the inside being often lined with tonga, the dried leaves of phormium [New Zealand flax]. A ponga fence will last for many years if well made originally; this material is used for cowsheds, pigsties, sheep yards, &c. A sheep yard with the pongas well and securely tied and fastened with koriwa [?] has a very neat appearance, which is also a consideration. When one looks back to the thousands of treeferns that have been destroyed by fire on Banks' Peninsula without any attempt to make use of them, it gives one some idea of waste in disforesting in one small item alone. Of the large tree-ferns which give so much beauty to the woods, the genus Cyathea holds the most important position perhaps. In writing of the mamuku and Cunningham's tree-fern, Hooker seems to draw but a very slight distinction between the two species. This perhaps arises from not having seen them in quantities; here where Cunningham's fern flourishes in its thousands, and where the mamuku is plentiful, there is no likelihood of one species being mistaken for the other. The mamuku when pushing forth its young fronds gives one an idea of enormous strength and vigour. From the midst of the broad crown of widely spreading fronds, slightly curving in their splendid sweep, arises the young growth; the sturdy stipes of deep grass green, partly stained with black, is thrust forth with the rachis yet encurled, like a stout arm raised bearing the fingers closed. In addition to the slight points of divergence mentioned by Hooker, the carriage of the fronds differs. The massive structure of the mamuku in all its details is absent in Cunningham's fern. The mass of jagged black-brown scales that invest the crown of the mamuku causes the bases of the fronds to assume an appearance of jutting out from a huge black cup. With Cunningham's fern the scales not only clothe the crown and the space immediately below it, they often cover and almost conceal the bases of old stipes two or even three feet [60–90cm] on the upper part of the stem. To observe another point of distinction make a collection of the spores and note the marked variance that is presented by the sporules of the several species of the genus *Cyathea* which are available for comparison. In colour the sporules of the mumuku [sic] nearly resemble those of the silver tree-fern, whilst they differ completely from those of Cunningham's fern, which again diverges from its near ally the *Hemitelia*. As far as I have observed, the sporules of the mamuku are coarser in grain than those of the other species of the same genus. Although I have not observed that this character has been noticed before, it appears in this case it may prove useful as a test, and a further aid in distinguishing species when they are supposed to resemble each other so closely as those magnificent species of the genus *Cyathea*.

To those who take much interest in ferns, and love to study and note their various habits, the vast number of forked specimens must appear remarkable. This peculiarity a few years ago was considered to be of very rare occurrence, but one is rather inclined to think they only require looking for. It is very probable the furcation was due to the operations of some insect; it is usual to find several instances of this abnormal habit of growth within quite a limited area. In the course of a few hours' rambling in the woods of one secluded bay in Banks' Peninsula, I took notes of upwards of fifty furcated stems of varying heights, nearly all of which were referred to *Hemitelia smithi*,[45] two or three only of the number were found to be those of the silver tree fern (*C. dealbata*). In the beautiful primeval wood that extends from the heights of Wharekawi [Wharekauri] to Kohimata [?], there is a fine specimen of *Cyathea cunninghami* which bears no less than ten heads, all of which are in a flourishing vigorous state of growth. Sometimes one may there enjoy a treat indeed, as when gazing on a gigantic mamuku carrying bravely three crowns aloft; the huge arboreal fern in a perfect state of preservation, all untouched by roaming cattle, unswept by rough winds, its deep green leaflets untinged and unbrowned by the searching salt laden gales that pour inland from the wide ocean.

In some few parts of the forest where there is to be found a sprinkling of Terehine

(*Dracophyllum scoparium*)[46] a singular fate overtakes some of the arboreal ferns; death by strangulation, a slow process, only accomplished after the lapse of many years. Terehine is not of rapid growth; from appearances it may be supposed that the tree-fern flourished scores of years before the long rigid leaves of the young terehine rustled its grass-like leaves against its upright stem. But if slow, the terehine was sure, as summer after summer saw the opening of its spikes of blossom, so its branches grew and strengthened, resting against the fern, clasping it, holding it month by month, year after year with a firmer, tighter grip of the bases of old fronds. As the shrub grew into a tree the pressure of its branches closing round the tree-fern cut off all moisture from below, in some case the struggle was well maintained as terehine branches appear through parts of the fern stem as if the fern tried to secure nourishment from the earth by over-lapping and overgrowing the ridgy constrictive branches that compressed its form. Far oftener indeed the terehine appears to have begun its infliction as a parasite seated from three to perhaps five feet [1–1.5m] or even more from the ground, sending down its bossy rootlets partly through the bases of old persistent stipes, that adhere to the fern stem for years. I have observed a flourishing specimen of the plant as a parasite at about six feet [1.8m] from the ground, the roots of which were entirely concealed from view. In another case of many years standing, at some ten or twelve inches [25–30cm] from its foot, part of the fern stem is visible, then it is hidden and again appears at about five feet [1.5m] higher up with a growth of pendant *Tmesipteris* and *Asplenium falcatum*, jutting out of the terehine with its crowns alive, but putting forth only depauperised fronds.

In accounts that are given of this *Dracophyllum*, scant justice is dealt out to it, either in regard to its size or appearance. I took a few measurements among individuals of a group in the midst of which were several 'fern-stranglers' in the woods at Wharekauri. One was five feet [1.5m] in girth, and certainly over forty feet [12m] in height; another measured nearly six feet [1.8m] round the bole, whilst one that had been overthrown in some great storm was eight feet five inches [2.6m] in girth; it was yet healthy, and bore on its twisted branches and gnarled stem, lichens, mosses, ferns, and orchids in abundance. In a clump of terehine there may be perceived a pleasant aromatic scent from the fallen leaves. To the remarks on the 'fern-stranglers' one instance should be added, where a fair sized terehine had killed a tree-fern and thrust a branch through a neighbouring *Dicksonia squarrosa* as if with the view of annexing another victim.

The Chatham Islands are rich in ferns from the huge mamuku to the little adder's tongue [*Ophioglossaceae*], they are to be found in the utmost abundance, enough to satisfy any zealous admirer of the tribe; even such an enthusiast as the young lady who confessed she hastened the drying of her ferns by placing them between the mattresses of her bed.

Of the various genera, *Cyathea* make a glorious show with enormous numbers of Cunningham's ferns of fine proportions. In certain places Aspidium is scarcely second in the grand development of some of its species, as *A.* [now *Polystichum*] *oculatum* at Wharekauri, *A. capense* at Te Whakaru in the extreme north-east.

11. Out in the Open: Stock in the Chathams (1888)

Many years ago, when settlers here [in the Chathams] very reluctantly found out that the demand had declined for their wheat and potatoes, some of them began to turn to sheep-farming. One who had made arrangements for a flock, at work with a Maori hand, was underscrubbing and cutting a track through a large wood to enable the sheep to get through it: when master and man, who had begun their work at both ends, had the track almost meeting or within a chain or so, the employer called out, 'Well Te Whetu, I think it will do, the sheep will get along that.' In reply, said the Maori, who had never seen a sheep, 'We think it kaipai, when ipi [sheep] come what he think, what he do, eh?'

The sheep has been a factor in so much that has taken place on this island, that it may be of interest to record some notes showing the progress of the sheep-farming industry on the Chathams. As well as one can learn the facts, the first sheep that arrived here, composed a small flock of fifty, which was shipped from Wellington in 1841, and landed on South East island.

In 1846 or '7 sheep were first depastured on the main island, a batch of twenty was then brought over from South East island and landed at Te Wakaru, this little shipment was followed by a second lot of twenty, which were landed at Taupeka. From this modest beginning, the flock now depasturing on the island mainly have arisen. The number of imported sheep being relatively very small in comparison with the size of the flocks at the present time. It is probable that the importations altogether, beside those sheep that were obtained for stud purposes, did not exceed by much the number that have been exported at various times to New Zealand ports for consumption. Sheep seem to have thriven well for several years, flocks greatly increased in numbers. After a while, the natives began to take some interest in animals so much esteemed by pakehas; they became owners of very small flocks – a much envied native has been known throughout the islands as the proud owner of one individual sheep. A case involving some litigation, recently under consideration in the Resident Magistrate's Court, from the evidence adduced, threw some light on the fact of very small flocks existing here formerly.

It is very well known that several kinds of stock, both large and small cattle, suffer greatly from eating an undue quantity of Kopi berries, the fruit of the laurel-like karaka tree (*Corynocarpus laevigatus*). These berries, of a rich golden or orange colour, of a rather agreeable flavour when ripe, bestrew the ground in the woods after high winds in the autumn and winter months from April to July. In the season of 1859 the karaka trees were most prolific, producing an enormous yield of fruit; it is said that the effect on the flocks was disastrous; that year is still quoted as memorable for the large percentage of deaths amongst the lambs.

To give a fair idea of progress in sheep-farming, the following fact may be valuable: in 1867 a settler, after clearing off his original flock, made a fresh start by the purchase of 500 imported ewes; his flock now numbers 6,000. It should be mentioned that he has sold and killed several hundred head during the time occupied in rearing his flock.

There is the other side of the medal to be looked at, so as to arrive at a fair story of the sheep and their doings: What has it cost to keep them? The merchant or middleman knows or cares very little about this part of the question; nor is the flockowner much disturbed till very awkward facts stare him in the face. Amongst other qualities possessed by sheep besides wool-bearing is that of enjoying an almost omnivorous appetite. This can only be held in due restraint by means of judicious fencing; a precaution which, costly though it is, time and experience have proved to be absolutely necessary under the peculiar features of the island. When sheep were first depastured, and for several years afterwards, whilst their numbers were but few, the coast was well sheltered. Fierce ocean blasts and rude gales laden heavily with scathe, broke against the girdle of sandy earthworks, which, in course of centuries, the sea had thrown up around those parts of the island unprotected with lofty cliffs. These sandbanks were thickly covered with a mixed vegetation to which herb, shrub, and tree lent their contributions; of these, the enduring ake-ake (*Olearia Traversii*),[47] that valuable timber tree, formed the more striking feature. The outer belt of trees might be windswept often, as the branches twisted and contorted into fantastic shapes, casting shadows in grotesque forms on the glistening herbage that trailed in tangled masses of luxuriant growth beneath them. This was the home of many species of animal and vegetable life, some of which were known as indigenous and peculiar to the limited area of these small islands. Nearly all this lavish display of nature's bounty has disappeared before the vigorous onslaught of the depastured stock. It is replaced with sand – a perpetual torment – ever shifting, always encroaching, which with baneful effect has assumed the mastery over many miles of the coast line. Huge banks of loose heaped up sand, threatening further damage and loss, meet the eyes of the wayfarer to the north, the east, and the west. Almost every green thing has been devoured, flowering season and seed time have been anticipated equally, and share a common fate. The wondrous and perfect schemes of Nature to ensure the reproduction of vegetation have proved powerless to avert the general destruction.

The botanist may regret that monandrian species with their one stamen, or polyandrian with their twenty or more, with some rare exceptions, have equally suffered. They have not been allowed to mature seed, they have been eaten down to the roots. Amongst the exceptions notably the matipo (*Myrsine Chathamica*), *Pimelia arenaria* [sand daphne], *Euphorbia glauca*; and on the swamps and wide spreading clears, *Olearia semidentata*, *Olearia angustifolia*; Turutu [*Dianella nigra*], *Libertia ixioides* [New Zealand iris], *Gleichenia dicarpa*. This does not establish a very long list of plants distasteful, or rather perhaps it should be put, not relished by sheep; yet one could scarcely extend it, unless the arboreal ferns were added thereto.

The ake-ake, 'For ever and ever', as its native name signifies, is one of the trees that can be least spared – its durability makes it of value to the farmer for so many purposes. The growing scarcity of this fine timber will be severely felt, it is unrivalled as supplying lasting material for posts. This is devoured in the seedling state, even young trees, when a few feet in height, are quickly destroyed. It is of a shore loving habit, and throve well on the sandy soil, whence the best timber for durability was produced. Young plants are now rarely met with in or near unfenced beaches. Posts have to be imported from the timber districts of New Zealand, as ake-ake suitable for fencing purposes is no longer found in accessible places whence it would pay to procure it; it is now admitted that on some stations it is more economical to import this sort of material; the absence of good roads had its due weight in arriving at such a decision. Both horses and sheep are observed to be very destructive to trees through indulging in a habit of biting and eating the bark, one has watched sheep tearing away wide flakes from stems of the white wood trees ([*Pseudo*] *Panax*). Pieces of bark cleverly loosed and torn away were so large that, unless one had seen the animal at work, the feat would have been deemed incredible.

The beautiful forget-me-not or Chatham Island lily [*Myosotidium hortensium*], Kopukapuka of the natives, some years ago covered the sandy shores above the actual wash of the sea with a broad belt of its glossy leaves and lovely flowers, now one may walk mile after mile along the same line of beach land without encountering a single plant; it has become quite rare except on steep places inaccessible to stock. After sheep had thoroughly demolished the luxuriant foliage of the plants, pigs are said to have devoured the roots with avidity.

Veronicas, pale flowered, or delicately tinged with blue, pushed forth their fine fibrous rootlets that permeated and held the sand together. The prostrate leaves of the aromatic anise spread out to the very verge of the unwashed beach. Damp with clouds of spray, often wetted by far-reaching waves, the tough yet useful pingao (*Desmoschoenus* [now *Ficinia*] *spiralis*) thrives on sand mounds or small hillocks, with its harsh wiry foliage gathered up into round masses not far below the succulent yellow blooming beach spinach (*Tetragonia trigyna* [now *implexicoma*]). These, together with many another species of herb and shrub and wild fern growth, fairly representing the littoral flora, have disappeared as shore plants along many a mile of coast line, except in those places where beach fencing has protected and saved them. Among the wind-swept ake-ake trees with sand hummocks half-way up their rugged trunks, the sand has blown where the wild wind listeth, without let or hindrance.

The naturalist and the ornithologist will express regret at the woeful decrease in the numbers of many most interesting species of native birds and their threatened early extinction. The vast increase of cats and rats may have much to do with this serious loss, but it is not the less true that owing to the grazing of stock, there has disappeared much of the thick covert which afforded the requisite privacy and seclusion during the breeding season. What has become of that charming songster, the larger bell-bird (*Anthornis melanocephala*), indigenous to the Chathams. During the past summer and autumn months, I rambled from the wooded Wharekauri in the north, to Te Raki in the extreme west, thence to Te Wakaru in the east, explored the gullies about Onenga [Owenga] and Manukau, without once sighting the bird or hearing the gush of its wild notes. It was only during a solitary ramble in the silent ferny depths of tree-clad Pipitarawai that I met with these beautiful birds, and was able to call down several within the distance of a few feet: now with sudden flutter, with quick flirting of the wings, they perched near and nearer, with quaint motions, shy or confident their mien, as the whim took them, through leafy openings, with bright enquiring glances peered down on the intruder. Then one stood charmed, and listened to the fitful outpourings of their delightful melody. A concert to be remembered, held under the arching roof of spreading boughs, wreathed with drooping bannerols of fern fronds, filmy and translucent, that tempered daylight in the moss flecked aisles of this temple of Nature as yet unscathed in the restless search for gain. It was like a dream of old New Zealand over thirty years ago.

Not song birds alone are sensibly becoming rarer; – the mutton bird [*Puffinus griseus*], so prized by the natives when a nestling fat and oily, covered with its dark grayish down, is now scarce. Sheep have eaten away the tender foliage of the nau [whau?] and other shrubs that screened with their shade the tunnels scratched out of the soft peaty banks. Where are the water-fowl that only a few years since thronged the wide waters of the Whanga [Te Whanga lagoon]? Flax bushes burnt, sedges and rushes destroyed, soon disclosed the down-covered nest to the soaring kahu [swamp harrier], ever on the alert for plunder. This list might be largely extended, showing some light on the rapid decline in the numbers of the native fauna. But to return to the sand plague; some settlers alarmed at the serious outlook are already contesting the ground with this persevering enemy – and none too soon. One man can point out where a road formerly led through a pleasant wood, now buried and utterly obliterated; another may show where some excellent land that produced fine wheat now lies beneath mounds of sand – or perhaps one has to take down and remove his large woolshed out of present reach of this relentless foe.

They are meeting the plague by grass sowing, *Festuca littoralis* [sand tussock][48] being used largely for the purpose; it grows with vigour on the sea sands. But grass growing will not suffice of itself; beach fencing should be undertaken at the same time, or else a similar fate will overtake the new grass plant that has befallen the native herbage – stock will worry it out. Cattle are specially destructive in their grazing, as in taking their bite the young tufts of fescue are often pulled up out of the sand. I have walked over a length of grass-sown beach covered with cattle tracks and strewed with young grass plants torn up by their roots.

In beach sowing, in order to realise successful results, there must of necessity be co-operation amongst the owners and occupiers of lands along the line of danger. Rather an amusing incident took place at a sowing not long since: – A landowner procured from some distance a sack of fescue seed, and directed it to be sown at once, beginning at his own fence. This order was carried out, only the man made this error, through absence of mind, he started at the wrong side of his employer's fence and got through the whole of the seed before he recognised he had been sowing the next neighbour's beach. Some of the more encouraging results of fescue sowing are to be seen at Wharekauri, Monnganui [Maunganui], and Waitangi west, and Kaingaroa. Steel wire has proved a failure at the Chathams, some years since a quantity of it was imported, but it was unable to withstand the humidity of the climate. In two years much of it was rotten, quite unable to bear tightening up or straining; in three years, in some cases, it fell out from the staples. Of this wire I have seen samples. Inferior faulty wire will not answer, one has noticed coils of this stuff hanging from a fence, the owner knowing full well from costly experience that it was not worth the labour of putting up.

Before leaving the subject of beach fencing, it appears worth mentioning, that I have seen a fine growth of such young forest trees as ake-ake, matipo, &c., close to the sea-beach where properly protected from stock; and ake-ake plants thriving on rocks yards beyond where drying seaweed tangle has shown the mark which high tides occasionally reach.

Though the wool growth of the islands is very considerable now, reaching about one thousand bales, doubtless it might be largely increased by the subdivision of runs into smaller and more convenient sized paddocks; together with a general cultivation of introduced grasses to supply the place of the declining native herbage.

Thoughtful old Te Whetu's doubt as to what the unknown *ipi* might do, was not altogether an unreasonable one.

In the first years of sheep-farming here, the flocks were shorn out in the open, and those farmers thought themselves fortunate who had a shed for the storage of their few bales. Shearing was got through after peculiar fashions; in some cases men tied their sheep, and began to open out the fleece at the tail. Diverse were the implements used to get off the wool; razors, scissors, and knives were put into requisition for the purpose. I have been assured by an eye-witness that razors made the best work. A native owner of one sheep was observed on the beach, painfully removing the fleece by means of a sharp-edged shell; in the morning he began his work, noon still found him over the patient animal, it was not till well on in the afternoon that the job was completed, and the fleece gathered up ready for sale.

Appendix

Selected indigenous New Zealand bird & plant names

Birds

Australasian crested grebe, *Podiceps cristatus*, pūteketeke
bellbird (Chatham Island), *Anthornis melanocephala*, kōmako
bellbird (NZ), *Anthornis melanura*, korimako
black stilt, *Himantopus novaezelandiae*, kakī
blue duck, *Hymenolaimus malacorhynchos*, whio
brown creeper/tree creeper, *Mohoua novaeseelandiae*, pīpipi
brown teal, *Anas chlorotis*, pāteke
bush wren, *Xenicus longipes*, mātuhi
falcon (NZ)/quail-hawk, *Falco novaeseelandiae*, kārearea
fantail (pied and black varieties), *Rhipidura fuliginosa*, pīwakawaka
fernbird/utick, *Bowdleria punctata*, mātātā
grey duck, *Anas superciliosa*, pārera
grey warbler/gerygone, *Gerygone igata*, riroriro
huia, *Heteralocha acutirostris*
kākā, *Nestor meridionalis*
kākāpō, night parrot, *Strigops habroptilus*
kea, green mountain parrot, *Nestor notabilis*
kingfisher (NZ)/halcyon/sacred kingfisher, *Todiramphus sanctus*, kōtare
kiwi
  great spotted, *Apteryx haastii*, roa
  little spotted, *Apteryx owenii*, kiwi pukupuku
  North Island brown, *Apteryx mantelli*
  southern brown, *Apteryx australis*, tokoeka
kōkako (North Island), blue-wattled crow, *Callaeas wilsoni*
kōkako (South Island), orange-wattled crow, *Callaeas cinerea*
laughing owl, *Sceloglaux albifacies*, whēkau
morepork, *Ninox novaeseelandiae*, ruru
muttonbird/sooty shearwater, *Puffinus griseus*, tītī
paradise duck/shelduck, *Tadorna variegata*, pūtangitangi

pigeon (NZ)/woodpigeon, *Hemiphaga novaeseelandiae*, kererū
pipit (NZ)/lark, *Anthus novaeseelandiae*, pīhoihoi
pūkeko, swamphen, *Porphyrio melanotus*
quail (NZ), *Coturnix novaezelandiae*, koreke
rifleman, *Acanthisitta chloris*, titipounamu
robin (South Island)/dusky-feathered wood-robin, *Petroica australis*, toutouwai
shining cuckoo/whistler, *Chrysococcyx lucidus*, pīpīwharauroa
silvereye/waxeye/white-eye/blight-bird/golden tears, *Zosterops lateralis*, tauhou
spotted shag/ocean shag, *Stictocarbo punctatus*, pārekareka
swamp harrier/harrier hawk, *Circus approximans*, kāhu
takahē, notornis, *Porphyrio hochstetteri*
thrush (NZ), South Island piopio, *Turnagra capensis*
tomtit, *Petroica macrocephala*, miromiro
tūī, *Prosthemadera novaeseelandiae*
weka, woodhen, *Gallirallus australis*
white heron, *Ardea modesta*, kōtuku
wrybill, *Anarhynchus frontalis*, ngutu parore
yellow-crowned parakeet, *Cyanoramphus auriceps*, kākāriki
yellowhead/bush canary, *Mohoua ochrocephala*, mohua

Plants
akeake, *Dodonaea viscosa*
akeake (Chatham Island), *Olearia traversiorum*, hakapiri
beech/southern beech/birch, *Nothofagaceae* family
bidibid/biddy-biddy, *Acaena novae-zelandiae*, piripiri
black māpou, *Pittosporum colensoi*
black matipo, *Pittosporum tenuifolium*, kōhūhū/tawhiwhi
bracken, *Pteridium esculentum*, rārahu
broadleaf, *Griselinia littoralis*, kāpuka
cabbage tree, *Cordyline australis*, tī kōuka
Chatham Island forget-me-not/Chatham Island lily, *Myosotidium hortensium*, kopakopa
Chatham Island grass tree, *Dracophyllum arboreum*, tarahinau
clematis (NZ), *Clematis paniculata*, puawhananga
climbing groundsel, *Brachyglottis sciadophila*

fern

- boss/trim shield, *Lastreopsis decomposita*
- crown/common hard, *Blechnum discolor*, piupiu
- filmy todea, *Leptopteris hymenophylloides*, heruheru
- prickly shield, *Polystichum vestitum*, pūniu
- ring, *Paesia scaberula*, mātātā

flax (NZ), *Phormium tenax*, harakeke
kahikatea, white pine, *Dacrycarpus dacrydioides*
karaka, *Corynocarpus laevigatus*
karamū, *Coprosma robusta*
kauri, *Agathis australis*
koromiko, shrubby veronica, *Hebe salicifolia*
kōwhai/kohi/ghoi, *Sophora microphylla*
lemonwood, *Pittosporum eugenioides*, tarata
māhoe (narrow-leaved), *Melicytus lanceolatus*
mānuka, NZ teatree, *Leptospermum scoparium*
marbleleaf, *Carpodetus serratus*, putaputawētā
matagouri, wild Irishman, *Discaria toumatou*
mataī, black pine, *Prumnopitys taxifolia*
Mount Cook buttercup/Mount Cook lily, *Ranunculus lyallii*
ngaio, *Myoporum laetum*
pepperwood/pepperleaf, *Pseudowintera colorata*, horopito
pīngao/pīkao, *Ficinia spiralis*
poataniwha, *Melicope simplex*
rangiora, *Brachyglottis repanda*
rātā (southern), *Metrosideros umbellata*
ribbonwood/lacebark, *Hoheria populnea*, houhere
snowberry/chuckiechuck, *Gaultheria depressa*, karopuka
speargrass/Spaniard, *Aciphylla squarrosa*, kurikuri
supplejack, *Ripogonum scandens*, kareao
tītoki, *Alectryon excelsus*
toetoe/tohetohe/toitoi, *Austroderia richardii*
tōtara, *Podocarpus totara*
tree fuchsia/corninni (berry), *Fuchsia excorticata*, kōtukutuku/kōnini (berry)
tree nettle, *Urtica ferox*, ongaonga

treefern
    black, *Cyathea medullaris*, mamaku
    gully, *Cyathea cunninghamii*, ponga/pūnui
    rough, *Dicksonia squarrosa*, wheki̅
    silver, *Cyathea dealbata*, ponga
    soft/Smith's treefern, *Cyathea smithii*, kātote
tutu, toot, *Coriaria arboria*
violet (NZ), *Viola lyallii*, hāka
whau, NZ mulberry, *Entelea arborescens*
wineberry, *Aristotelia serrata*, makomako

Notes

Preface

1. Alfred, Lord Tennyson, *In Memoriam* (London: Edward Moxon, 1850): 105.1; Exodus 2:22.
2. Helena Drysdale, *Strangerland: A family at war* (London: Picador, 2008), 157.
3. T.H. Potts, 'Old Times', *Canterbury Times*, 4 November 1887.
4. T.H. Potts, 'Diary, 6 April 1855–1 April 1858, and 1 January 1865–2 December 1865', typescript, privately held (Bryony Macmillan), Christchurch. Selections in David Macmillan, 'Memoir: Thomas Henry Potts (1824–88)', *History and Bibliography* (Christchurch) vol. 2 (1948): 160–72, and L.G.D. Acland, *The Early Canterbury Runs* (Christchurch: Whitcombe and Tombs, 1946), 294–97.
5. Henry Phillips, 'Rockwood Journal, 1855–1857', typescript, and Tom Phillips, 'The Point Journal, 1866–1871', typescript, in Rockwood Station, Canterbury, Records 1855–1871, University of Canterbury Library MS9; 'Journal of George Septimus Phillips, Rockwood, 1863–1869', privately held (Reiny Flatt), Napier.
6. Potts diary 11 April 1855.
7. Potts diary 25 December and 3 July 1857.
8. Rhonda L. Hampton, 'Ohinetahi: The place of one daughter' (Ms, n.d.), item no. 138199, Canterbury Museum.
9. See http://rsnz.natlib.govt.nz/
10. T.H. Potts, *Out in the Open: A budget of scraps of natural history, gathered in New Zealand* (Christchurch: Lyttelton Times, 1882; reprinted Christchurch: Capper Press, 1976).
11. For instance Janet Holm, *Nothing but Grass and Wind: The Rutherfords of Canterbury* (Christchurch: Hazard Press, 1992); Geoffrey W. Rice, *Heaton Rhodes of Otahuna: The illustrated biography*, 2nd edn (Christchurch: University of Canterbury Press, 2008); Bruce Ansley with Peter Bush, *A Fabled Land: The story of Canterbury's famous Mesopotamia Station* (Auckland: Random House, 2012); Jennifer Roberts, *Fitz: The colonial adventures of James Edward FitzGerald* (Dunedin: Otago University Press, 2014); Joanna Orwin, *Riccarton and the Deans Family: History and heritage* (Auckland: David Bateman Ltd., 2015); Jenny Abrahamson, *John and Charles Enys: Castle Hill runholders, 1864–1891* (Christchurch: Wily Publications Ltd., 2017).
12. Stevan Eldred-Grigg, *A Southern Gentry: New Zealanders who inherited the earth* (Wellington: A.H. and A.W. Reed, 1980), 85, 92 and 96; Jim McAloon, *No Idle Rich: The wealthy in Canterbury and Otago, 1840–1914* (Dunedin: Otago University Press, 2002). However, he appears in Jim McAloon, 'The radical elite', in John Cookson and Graeme Dunstall, eds, *Southern Capital: Christchurch: Towards a city biography 1850–2000* (Christchurch: Canterbury University Press, 2000), 201.
13. *University of Canterbury Chronicle*, 4 March 1988, vol. 23, no. 3.
14. Potts, *Out in the Open* (reprint of 1976), front flyleaf.

15. See Paul Star, 'Native forest and the rise of preservation in New Zealand, 1903–1913', *Environment and History*, vol. 8 (2002): 275–94; Paul Star, 'Native bird protection, national identity, and the rise of preservation in New Zealand (to 1914)', *New Zealand Journal of History*, vol. 36 (2002): 123–36.
16. Preface to F.W. Hutton and James Drummond, *The Animals of New Zealand* (Christchurch: Whitcombe and Tombs, 1904).
17. A.H. McLintock, ed., *An Encyclopaedia of New Zealand, Volume 2* (Wellington: R.E. Owen, 1966), 847.
18. Robert A. Falla, quoted in *Mr Explorer Douglas: John Pascoe's New Zealand classic revised by Graham Langton* (Christchurch: Canterbury University Press, 2000), 263.
19. Acland, *The Early Canterbury Runs*, 201.
20. Philip Temple, ed., *Lake, Mountain, Tree: An anthology of writing on New Zealand nature and landscape* (Auckland: Godwit Press, 1998); Elisabeth Easther, ed., *Bird Words: New Zealand writers on birds* (Auckland: Random House, 2017).
21. Jonathan West, *The Face of Nature: An environmental history of the Otago Peninsula* (Dunedin: Otago University Press, 2017); Eric Pawson and Tom Brooking, eds, *Making A New Land: Environmental histories of New Zealand: New Edition* (Dunedin: Otago University Press, 2013).
22. A.H. Clark, *The Invasion of New Zealand by People, Plants and Animals: The South Island* (New Brunswick: Rutgers University Press, 1949); Kenneth B. Cumberland, *Landmarks: How New Zealanders remade their landscape* (Surry Hills, NSW: Reader's Digest, 1981).
23. Eric Pawson and Tom Brooking, eds, *Environmental Histories of New Zealand* (Melbourne: Oxford University Press, 2002), later revised and expanded as Pawson and Brooking, eds, *Making a New Land*. See also the articles in *Environment and History*, vol. 9, no. 4 (2003).
24. Robert Peden, *Making Sheep Country: Mt Peel Station and the transformation of the tussock lands* (Auckland: Auckland University Press, 2011); Peter Holland, *Home in the Howling Wilderness: Settlers and the environment in southern New Zealand* (Auckland: Auckland University Press, 2013); West, *The Face of Nature*.

Part One: Thomas Potts and the New Zealand Environment

When referring to articles that were republished by Potts in Out in the Open, *the page numbers given relate to the 1882 collection or its reprint. The original date of publication appears in brackets.*

The Early Years, to 1853

1. Samuel Butler, *A First Year in Canterbury Settlement* (London: Longman Green, 1863), 28.
2. L.G.D. Acland, *The Early Canterbury Runs* (Christchurch: Whitcombe and Tombs, 1946), 297.
3. B.J. Gill et al., *Checklist of the Birds of New Zealand*, 4th edn (Wellington: Te Papa Press and Ornithological Society of New Zealand, 2010), 22–23.

4. H.F. von Haast, *Life and Times of Sir Julius von Haast, Explorer, Geologist, Museum Builder* (Wellington: The author, 1948), 551.
5. See Jock Phillips, 'Kiwi and people: Early history': https://teara.govt.nz/en/kiwi/page-4
6. David Macmillan, 'Memoir: Thomas Henry Potts (1824–88)', *History and Bibliography* (Christchurch) vol. 2 (1948), 161.
7. H.L. Blackmore, *Gunmakers of London, 1350–1850* (York, PA: George Shumway, 1986), 59.
8. *Sir Joseph Banks Papers, State Library of New South Wales:* www.sl.nsw.gov.au/banks *Series 81.03*
9. Arthur Thistlewood, *The Trials at Large of Arthur Thistlewood, … for High Treason* (London: W. Lewis, 1817), 124.
10. http://foundersandsurvivors.org/pubsearch/convict/chain/c31a31190396
11. See Potts diary 23 November 1855, 23 November 1857.
12. Macmillan, 'Memoir: Thomas Henry Potts', 160.
13. T.H. Potts, *Out in the Open: A budget of scraps of natural history, gathered in New Zealand* (Christchurch: Lyttelton Times, 1882), 80–81, 182, 300; Potts diary 20 November 1855.
14. Craig L. Barry, *The Civil War Musket: A handbook for historical accuracy – lock, stock and barrel* (Warren, MI: Watchdog Quarterly, 2006).
15. See gracesguide.co.uk/History_and_Directory_of_Birmingham,_1849:_Guns
16. See *The Mechanics' Magazine*, vol. 58 (1853): 213, 292.
17. en.wikipedia.org/wiki/Pattern_1853_Enfield
18. Comment on North South Skirmish Association website: www.n-ssa.org forum
19. en.wikipedia.org/wiki/Royal_Small_Arms_Factory
20. Macmillan, 'Memoir: Thomas Henry Potts', 161.
21. Listed in *Catalogue of the well known and very valuable library of T.H. Potts, esq., … to be sold by auction* (Christchurch: Lyttelton Times, 1888), 6.
22. John B. Gent, ed., *Croydon: The story of a hundred years* (Croydon Natural History and Science Society, 1970), 11.
23. Mike Brown, 'On the trail of the Phillips', *Brewery History*, vol. 111 (2003): 37–63; vol. 112 (2004): 16–30.
24. www leamingtonhistory.co.uk/15-warwick-new-road/
25. See photo at https://britishlistedbuildings.co.uk/101358822-kingswood-lodge
26. 'Francis Grose in Croydon', *Local History Gleanings*, no. 3, TS X570 (9), held at Croydon Local Studies Library, Norbury.
27. D. Clenet et al., *Nature Conservation in Croydon* (London Ecology Unit, 1988), 13–14, 26–28.
28. Basil H. Tripp, *The Story of Sanderstead* (Sanderstead Preservation Society, 1972), 19.
29. Macmillan, 'Memoir: Thomas Henry Potts', 171. See also the description of a Wiltshire hunt in 'Rambler' (T.H. Potts), 'Christmas here and there', *Canterbury Times*, 30 December 1887.
30. Rambler (T.H. Potts), 'Recollections' (1886), reprinted in *New Zealand Country Journal*, vol. 15 (1891): 380.
31. T.H. Potts, 'Notes on an egg of *Alca impennis*, Linn., in the collection of the writer', *Transactions of the New Zealand Institute*, vol. 3 (1870): 110.

32. John E. Thayer, 'Great auk eggs in the Thayer Museum', *The Auk*, vol. 29, no. 2 (April 1912): 208–09.
33. A.F. Hunter, *The Asiatics: Brahmas, Cochins and Langshans* (Quincy, IL: Reliable Poultry Journal Publishing Co., n.d.).
34. William Wingfield and G.W. Johnson, *The Poultry Book: Comprising the characteristics, management, breeding, and medical treatment of poultry* (London: W.S. Orr and Co., 1853).
35. *Lyttelton Times*, 10 September 1853.
36. Macmillan, 'Memoir: Thomas Henry Potts', 161.
37. Rambler (T.H. Potts), 'Recollections' (1886), reprinted in *New Zealand Country Journal*, vol. 15 (1891): 479.
38. See 'G.R. Macdonald, Dictionary of Canterbury Biographies (1952–64)', 62, Canterbury Museum.
39. *Lyttelton Times*, 22 October 1853.
40. For Wakefield and his family, see Philip Temple, *A Sort of Conscience: The Wakefields* (Auckland: Auckland University Press, 2002).
41. James Bertram, ed., *The New Zealand Letters of Thomas Arnold the Younger, 1847–1851* (Auckland: Auckland University Press, 1966).
42. T.H. Potts, 'Old Times', *Canterbury Times*, 28 October 1887.
43. Minutes Book, Society of Canterbury Colonists, 1850–52, 2 May 1850. Tūranga Christchurch City Libraries, Z Arch 16.
44. Geoff Norman, *Birdstories: A history of the birds of New Zealand* (Nelson: Potton and Burton, 2018), 35.
45. J.H.R. Andrews, *The Southern Ark: Zoological discovery in New Zealand 1769–1900* (Auckland: Century Hutchinson, 1986), 75, 141, 152.
46. C.R. Fay, *Palace of Industry, 1851* (Cambridge: Cambridge University Press, 1951 and 2011), 8. See also Tatiana Holway, *The Flower of Empire: An Amazonian water lily, the quest to make it bloom, and the world it created* (Oxford: Oxford University Press, 2013).
47. Entry 207 in Class VIII: Thomas Henry Potts: www.gracesguide.co.uk/1851_Great_Exhibition:_Official_Catalogue
48. Obituary of T.H. Potts, *Lyttelton Times*, 28 July 1888.
49. See Luke Keogh, 'The Wardian Case: Environmental histories of a box for moving plants', *Environment and History*, vol. 25 (2019): 219-44; James Beattie, 'The empire of the rhododendron: Reorienting New Zealand garden history', in Eric Pawson and Tom Brooking, eds, *Making a New Land: Environmental histories of New Zealand* (Dunedin: Otago University Press, 2013), 241–57.
50. See Peter Laslett, *The World We Have Lost: Further explored* (London: Routledge, 2015), especially Chapter 3, 'The village community: The scale of life in cottage, farmstead, manorhouse and church'.
51. T.H. Potts, 'Old Times', *Canterbury Times*, 4 November 1887.
52. Henry F. Wigram, *The Story of Christchurch, New Zealand* (Christchurch: Lyttelton Times, 1916), 100–01; and see Beattie, 'The empire of the rhododendron': 247.
53. T.H. Potts, 'Old Times', *Canterbury Times*, 18 November 1887.

Changes at Rockwood, 1854–58

1. Rambler (T.H. Potts), 'Recollections' (1886), reprinted in *New Zealand Country Journal*, vol. 15 (1891): 195.
2. Thomas Arnold, 'Reminiscences of New Zealand', *Fraser's Magazine* (August 1861), quoted and discussed in Geoff Park, *Ngā Uruora, The Groves of Life: Ecology and history in a New Zealand landscape* (Wellington: Victoria University Press, 1993), 323; and George Seddon, *Landprints: Reflections on place and landscape* (Cambridge: Cambridge University Press, 1997), 181.
3. Thomas McDonnell in 1844, quoted by James Beattie, 'Thomas McDonnell's opium: Circulating, plants, patronage, and power in Britain, China and New Zealand, 1830s–1850s', in Yota Batsaki and Anatole Tchikine, eds, *The Botany of Empire in the Long Eighteenth Century* (Washington, DC: Dumbarton Oaks Research Library, 2017), 177.
4. W.D. McIntyre, ed., *The Journal of Henry Sewell: Volume 1: February 1853 to May 1854* (Christchurch: Whitcoulls Publishers, 1980), 427. See Eric Pawson, 'Confronting Nature', in John Cookson and Graeme Dunstall, eds, *Southern Capital: Christchurch: Towards a city biography 1850–2000* (Christchurch: Canterbury University Press, 2000), 60–84.
5. See Atholl Anderson, 'A fragile plenty: Pre-European Maori and the New Zealand environment', in Eric Pawson and Tom Brooking, *Making a New Land: Environmental histories of New Zealand* (Dunedin: Otago University Press, 2013), 35–51; and Graeme Wynn, 'Destruction under the guise of improvement? The forest, 1840–1920', in Pawson and Brooking, *Making a New Land*, 127.
6. Alfred W. Crosby, *Ecological Imperialism: The biological expansion of Europe, 900–1900* (Cambridge: Cambridge University Press, 1986).
7. William Pember Reeves, 'The Passing of the Forest' and Matthew Arnold, 'Thyrsis', quoted in Eric Godley, *A Botanist's Notebook* (Christchurch: Manuka Press, 2006), 213.
8. *Twenty-third Report of the Court of Directors of the New Zealand Company* (London: 1847), 2.
9. Henry F. Wigram, *The Story of Christchurch, New Zealand* (Christchurch: Lyttelton Times, 1916), vii–viii.
10. L.G.D. Acland, *The Early Canterbury Runs* (Christchurch: Whitcombe and Tombs, 1946), 101.
11. Henry Phillips in 'Macdonald Dictionary of Canterbury Biographies': 362.
12. T.H. Potts, 'With the gun now – and then' (1882), in T.H. Potts, *Out in the Open: A budget of scraps of natural history, gathered in New Zealand* (Christchurch: Lyttelton Times, 1882), 284. Cf. the evocation of Rockwood in Lady M.A. Barker, *Station Life in New Zealand* (London: Macmillan, 1870), 91.
13. Rambler (T.H. Potts), 'Recollections' (1886), reprinted in *New Zealand Country Journal*, vol. 15 (1891): 105–06.
14. Ibid., 288.
15. T.H. Potts. 'Out in the open [On rātā]', *New Zealand Country Journal*, vol. 9, no. 1 (1885): 4.

16. Rambler (T.H. Potts), 'Recollections' (1886), reprinted in *New Zealand Country Journal*, vol. 15 (1891): 102.
17. See P.G. Holland and R.P. Hargreaves, 'The trivial round, the common task: Work and leisure on a Canterbury hill-country run in the 1860s and 1870s', *New Zealand Geographer*, vol. 47, no. 1 (1991): 19–25; Peter Holland, *Home in the Howling Wilderness: Settlers and the environment in southern New Zealand* (Auckland: Auckland University Press, 2013).
18. T.H. Potts, 'Diary, 4 April 1855–March 1858, and 1865', typescript, privately held (Bryony Macmillan), Christchurch.
19. Potts diary 24 April 1855.
20. Potts diary 28 April 1885.
21. Potts diary 25 December 1855.
22. Potts diary 27 May and 31 May 1855.
23. Potts diary 11 September 1857.
24. Potts diary 1 June 1855.
25. Potts diary 14 June 1855.
26. See Jennifer Queree, ed., *Set Sail for Canterbury: A record of the preparation of Henry Slater Richards of Bridgnorth, England, for his sons' emigration to the Canterbury Settlement, New Zealand, in 1850* (Christchurch: Canterbury Museum, 2002).
27. Potts diary 8 September 1857.
28. Potts diary 5 November and 6 November 1855.
29. See T.H. Potts, 'Changes in the habits of animals and plants', *Nature* (1 February 1872): 262.
30. Potts diary 10 November 1855.
31. Potts diary 12 November 1855.
32. Potts diary 2 October 1857.
33. Potts diary 13 September 1856.
34. Potts diary 2 March 1857 and 24 August 1856.
35. Potts diary 10 September 1856.
36. Potts diary 18 September and 19 September 1856.
37. H.F. von Haast, *Life and Times of Sir Julius von Haast, Explorer, Geologist, Museum Builder* (Wellington: The author, 1948), 166–67.
38. Potts diary 28 September 1855.
39. Potts diary 31 December 1855.
40. Potts diary 3 April and 17 February 1856.
41. Potts diary 29 October 1856.
42. Potts diary 10 April, 5–6 July, 1 August, 6 August, 28 August, 7 September 1855; 7 August and 13 August 1856.
43. Potts diary 10 September 1855 and 25 February 1856.
44. Potts diary 26 January, 27 January and 20 February 1856.
45. Potts diary 13 April 1855 and 19 May 1856.
46. Potts diary 3 January and 17 April 1856.
47. Potts diary 16 April 1855.

48. Barker, *Station Life in New Zealand*, 195, and as in Robert Peden, '"The exceeding joy of burning": Pastoralists and the lucifer match: Burning the rangelands of the South Island of New Zealand in the nineteenth century', *Agricultural History*, vol. 80, no. 1 (Winter 2006): 17–34. See also Robert Peden, *Making Sheep Country: Mt Peel Station and the transformation of the tussock lands* (Auckland: Auckland University Press, 2011).
49. See Tom Brooking and Eric Pawson, eds, *Seeds of Empire: The environmental transformation of New Zealand* (London and New York: I.B. Taurus, 2011).
50. Potts diary 11 September 1857.
51. Potts diary 25 July 1856.
52. Potts diary 2 January 1856.
53. Potts diary 30 June 1855, 22 April and 17 August 1856, 27 June 1857 and 12 March 1858.
54. Potts diary 6 November 1855.
55. Potts diary 27 March 1855 and 16 March 1857.
56. Potts diary 14 March and 16 March 1858.
57. Potts diary 20 April and 22 April 1856.
58. Potts diary 17 September 1855.
59. Potts diary 28 July 1856.
60. T.H. Potts, 'Oology of New Zealand', *New Zealand Journal of Science*, vol. 2 (1884–85): 222–26, 274–88, 373–78, 475–84, 505–11, 556–59.
61. T.H. Potts, 'Nest book', privately held (Bryony Macmillan), Christchurch.
62. Potts diary 12 October 1855.
63. Potts diary 15 October 1855.
64. Potts diary 16 June 1856.
65. For fuller detail see Acland, *Early Canterbury Runs*, 14.
66. Potts diary 16–27 April 1856.
67. Acland, *Early Canterbury Runs*, 295–97. See also T.N. Beckett, *The Mountains of Erewhon* (Wellington: A.H. and A.W. Reed, 1978), 140–42.
68. Potts diary 14 April 1857.
69. Matthew Morris diary 7 April 1857, in Mary Stapylton-Smith, ed., *Wet to the Skin (Again): The 1857–66 journal of Dr Matthew Morris, early Canterbury shepherd, drover and doctor* (Diamond Harbour: Friends of Diamond Harbour Library, 2018), 11–12.
70. Potts diary 28 April 1857.
71. Potts diary 13 May 1858.
72. Beckett, *The Mountains of Erewhon*, 143.
73. Potts diary 18 June 1857.
74. Potts diary 24 January 1858.
75. Potts diary 8 February and 23 February 1858.
76. Sarah Courage, *Lights and Shadows of Colonial Life: Twenty-six years in Canterbury, New Zealand*, quoted in Stevan Eldred-Grigg, *A Southern Gentry* (Wellington: A.H. and A.W. Reed, 1980), 79.

Governors Bay, 1858 to about 1870

1. Table 1, no. 1 in 'Statistics of New Zealand for 1860': www3.stats.govt.nz/
2. Rambler (T.H. Potts), 'Old Times [A forest ramble]', *Canterbury Times*, 2 December 1887: 28; 9 December 1887: 28.
3. *Lyttelton Times*, 27 November 1858.
4. See David Welsh, *Port to Plains: Over and under the Port Hills. The story of the Lyttelton railway tunnel* (Invercargill: Craigs Design and Print, 2017).
5. *Lyttelton Times*, 18 May 1861.
6. T.H. Potts, 7 October 1868, in *New Zealand Parliamentary Debates*, 14 (1868), 188.
7. *Lyttelton Times*, 29 October 1862.
8. *Lyttelton Times*, 23 September 1863.
9. *Lyttelton Times*, 26 September 1863.
10. W.T.L. Travers, 7 October 1868, in *New Zealand Parliamentary Debates*, 14 (1868), 191.
11. T.H. Potts, 7 October 1868, in *New Zealand Parliamentary Debates*, 14 (1868), 189.
12. Potts diary 27 January 1865.
13. Potts diary 27 January and 10 February 1865.
14. Bryony Macmillan (great-granddaughter of Potts) to Paul Star, 14 April 2018.
15. von Haast, *Life and Times of Sir Julius von Haast*, 142.
16. Quoted in Jenifer Roberts, *Fitz: The colonial adventures of James Edward FitzGerald* (Dunedin: Otago University Press, 2014), 279.
17. Potts diary 12 January 1865.
18. See 'First Canterbury representative rugby team': https://nzhistory.govt.nz/media/photo/first-canterbury-rugby-team; Potts diary 24 June 1865.
19. Potts diary 17 June and 14 May 1865.
20. Potts diary 28 April, 6 June and 8 July 1865.
21. Potts diary 20 March and 29 April 1865.
22. Rambler (T.H. Potts), 'Recollections' (1886), reprinted in *New Zealand Country Journal*, vol. 16 (1892): 110.
23. Lyn Neil and Judith Stratford, eds, *West of Windwhistle: Stories of the Lake Coleridge area* (Windwhistle: Lake Coleridge Tourism Group, 2005), 159–64.
24. Journal of G.S. Phillips 11–20 July and 15–23 December 1864.
25. The Point diary 20–28 October 1867.
26. Journal of G.S. Phillips 26–28 January, 19–25 May and 2 December 1864; The Point diary 17 November 1866.
27. L.G.D. Acland, *The Early Canterbury Runs* (Christchurch: Whitcombe and Tombs, 1946), 297.
28. T.H. Potts, 'On the birds of New Zealand, Part IV, read before the Philosophical Institute of Canterbury 4 December 1873', *Transactions of the New Zealand Institute*, vol. 6 (1873): 141.
29. Potts diary 16 March 1865.
30. Potts diary 21 January, 16 March, 4 April and 22 July 1865.
31. Peter Jackson, *Quail Island* (Wellington: Department of Conservation, 1990), 29, 36; Robyn Burgess, 'Report for a Historic Area: Otamahua/Quail Island Historic Area,

Lyttelton Harbour/Whakaraupo' (Christchurch: Heritage New Zealand, Pouhere Taonga, 2018).

32. Potts diary 9 February 1865.
33. Potts diary 3 June 1865.
34. Potts diary 5 August and 16 November 1865.
35. Potts diary 29 January, 8 February, 13 May, 12 August, 18 August and 26 August 1865.
36. Mrs F.R. Inwood, 'Governor's Bay: Reminiscences of past and present days' (Typescript, 1935), 12, in Governors Bay Public Library Records, 1873–1962. Tūranga Christchurch City Libraries, Arch GBL.
37. *Lyttelton Times*, 10 December 1863.
38. *Lyttelton Times*, 27 December 1865.
39. Potts diary 11 March 1865.
40. Potts diary 10 March, 16 March and 17 April 1865.
41. Potts diary 1 May and 15 May 1865.
42. Potts diary 7 August and 8 August 1865.
43. Potts diary, 25 January 1865, 3 April and 29 April 1865.
44. Potts diary 25 October 1865. For the Deans, see Joanna Orwin, *Riccarton and the Deans Family: History and heritage* (Auckland: David Bateman, 2015).
45. Potts diary 23 April and 1 January 1865.
46. Potts diary 9, 10 and 29 January, 1 June, 10 July, 11 October, 21 October and 27 November 1865.
47. Potts diary 10 and 21 January, 11 July, 13 November, 25 November and 27 November 1865.
48. Potts diary 24 June and 29 June 1865.
49. Potts diary 10 July 1865.
50. Potts diary 13–14 April 1856. See Ged Martin and Jim McAloon, *The Iron Priest: William Wellington Willock and the vision of Anglican Canterbury* (2014), at Project Canterbury: http://anglicanhistory.org
51. T.H. Potts, 'Old Times', *Canterbury Times*, 25 November 1887: 25.
52. *Lyttelton Times*, 12 January 1859.
53. *Lyttelton Times*, 6 August 1859.
54. *Lyttelton Times*, 1 February 1860. David Macmillan, 'Memoir: Thomas Henry Potts (1824–88)', History and Bibliography (Christchurch) vol. 2 (1948), 169.
55. Potts diary 1 January, 2 April and 23 April 1865. See also 28 May 1865.
56. Potts diary 6 August 1865.
57. Potts diary 14 August, 23 August and 10 October 1865.
58. *Lyttelton Times*, 30 December 1865.
59. *Lyttelton Times*, 4 February 1864.
60. Potts diary 2 August, 11 August and 12 October 1865. See also 3 January, 25 January and 28 July 1865.
61. *Lyttelton Times*, 31 July 1866.
62. Potts diary 14 February, 15 February and 29 March 1865.
63. Potts diary 17 February, 1 March and 16 March 1865.

A Brief Role in Politics, 1865–70

1. Potts diary 16 March and 17 March 1865.
2. Potts diary 1 June 1865.
3. (T.H. Potts),'Recollections: Old election days (by Rambler)', *Canterbury Times*, 26 August 1887: 9–10.
4. P.R. May, *The West Coast Gold Rushes*, 2nd edn (Christchurch: Pegasus, 1967), 401–03.
5. *Lyttelton Times*, 23 July 1866.
6. Potts,' Old election days': 9–10.
7. W.J. Gardner, 'John Hall', in W.H. Oliver, ed., *The Dictionary of New Zealand Biography, Volume One, 1769–1869* (Wellington: Bridget Williams Books and Department of Internal Affairs, 1990), 172–74.
8. Potts diary 1 March, 7 March 1865 and 4 April 1865.
9. *Lyttelton Times*, 6 and 25 June 1866.
10. *New Zealand Parliamentary Debates*, 27 July 1870, 109.
11. Potts obituary, *Lyttelton Times*, 28 July 1888.
12. *New Zealand Parliamentary Debates*, 14 August 1869, 574.
13. T.H. Potts, 'Out in the open [On Māori]', *New Zealand Country Journal*, vol. 7, no. 3 (1883): 208.
14. G.R. Hart, 'The Parliament of 1870: Some of its members sketched from the press gallery', *New Zealand Illustrated Magazine*, vol. 2 (1901): 438.
15. 'Rambler' (T.H. Potts),'Jottings from an old note book: To the Hot Lakes', *Canterbury Times*, 27 January 1888: 28; *New Zealand Parliamentary Debates*, 18 June 1869, 188.
16. *New Zealand Parliamentary Debates*, 19 August 1869, 597.
17. *New Zealand Parliamentary Debates*, 13 October 1868, 287; 15 October 1868, 348.
18. *New Zealand Parliamentary Debates*, 8 October 1868, 228.
19. *New Zealand Parliamentary Debates*, 24 September 1868, 551–52; 22 July 1869, 59; 8 July 1870, 292.
20. *New Zealand Parliamentary Debates*, 30 September 1868, 60–61; 16 July 1869, 544.
21. *New Zealand Parliamentary Debates*, 7 July 1870, 260.
22. *New Zealand Parliamentary Debates*, 17 September 1868, 405; 23 September 1868, 522–23; 30 September 1868, 79; 15 October 1868, 342.
23. *Canterbury Provincial Council Votes and Proceedings*, vol. 2: 67.
24. *New Zealand Parliamentary Debates*, vol. 8 (28 July 1870), 147.
25. E.N. Reid and A. Eccles, *Donald Reid: Pioneer, statesman, merchant* (Dunedin: A.H. and A.W. Reed, 1939), 158.

Natural Science and Scientists, 1860–74

1. H.F. von Haast, *Life and Times of Sir Julius von Haast, Explorer, Geologist, Museum Builder* (Wellington: The author, 1948), 824–29; and Julius von Haast, *The Geology of the Provinces of Canterbury and Westland* (Christchurch: Lyttelton Times, 1879).
2. Philosophical Institute of Canterbury Minutes Book, 1864–1884, in Royal Society (Canterbury Branch) Papers, University of Canterbury.

3. von Haast, *Life and Times of Sir Julius von Haast*, 543.
4. Ibid., 771, 517.
5. Julius Haast, 'Report on the arrangement of the collections of the Canterbury Museum', Canterbury Provincial Council Votes and Proceedings (1870), Session 34. Printed Catalogue of Museum Donations 1872–87, and photocopy of handwritten report by Haast for 1871–72, Museum Records, Canterbury Museum. Julius Haast, 'On the occurrence of a new species of *Euphysetes* (*E. pottsii*), a remarkably small catodont whale, on the coast of New Zealand', *Transactions of the New Zealand Institute*, vol. 6 (1873): 97–102. See also Kenneth S. Norris, ed., *Whales, Dolphins and Porpoises* (Berkeley: University of California Press, 1966), 64–65.
6. See T.H. Potts in *New Zealand Parliamentary Debates*, 8 October 1868, 224; von Haast, *Life and Times of Sir Julius von Haast*, 605.
7. For Enys, see Paul Star, 'John Enys, Cornish patron of New Zealand science', *New Series*, vol. 2, no. 2 (1996): 30–39, and Jenny Abrahamson, *John and Charles Enys, Castle Hill Runholders, 1864–1891* (Christchurch: Wily Publications, 2017).
8. von Haast, *Life and Times of Sir Julius von Haast*, 614.
9. W.J. Gardner, E.T. Beardsley and T.E. Carter, *A History of the University of Canterbury, 1873–1973* (Christchurch: University of Canterbury, 1973), 36.
10. See von Haast, *Life and Times of Sir Julius von Haast*, 557–58.
11. For Hector, see Simon Nathan and Mary Varnham, eds, *The Amazing World of James Hector* (Wellington: Awa Press, 2008); and Simon Nathan, *James Hector: Explorer, scientist, leader* (Wellington: Geoscience Society of New Zealand, 2015).
12. Bruno Latour, *Science in Action: How to follow scientists and engineers through society* (Cambridge, MA: Harvard University Press, 1987); David Philip Miller, 'Joseph Banks, empire, and "centers of calculation" in late Hanoverian London', in David Philip Miller and Peter Hanns Reill, eds, *Visions of Empire: Voyages, botany and representations of nature* (Cambridge: Cambridge University Press, 1996 and 2010), 23–25. See also Nuala C. Johnson, *Nature Displaced, Nature Displayed: Order and beauty in botanical gardens* (London and New York: I.B. Taurus, 2011), 129 ff.
13. Jim Endersby, 'A garden enclosed: Botanical barter in Sydney, 1818–39', *British Journal for the History of Science*, vol. 33, no. 3 (2000): 326.
14. George Bentham, *Flora Australiensis* (London: L. Reeve and Co., 1863–78).
15. J.W. Gruber, 'The moa and the professionalising of New Zealand science', *Turnbull Library Record* (Wellington), vol. 20 (1987): 61–100.
16. Ruth Barton, 'Haast and the moa: Reversing the tyranny of distance', *Pacific Science*, vol. 54, no. 3 (2000): 253, 257.
17. Potts, 'Oology of New Zealand', 223.
18. William Colenso to J.D. Hooker, 27 December 1884, quoted in Jim Endersby, '"From having no herbarium": Local knowledge versus metropolitan expertise: Joseph Hooker's Australasian correspondence with William Colenso and Ronald Gunn', *Pacific Science*, vol. 55, no. 4 (2001): 352. See also Jim Endersby, *Imperial Nature: Joseph Hooker and the practices of Victorian science* (Chicago and London: University of Chicago Press, 2008), 200–08.

19. C.A. Fleming, *Science, Settlers and Scholars* (Wellington: Royal Society of New Zealand, 1987), 26.
20. Philosophical Institute of Canterbury Minutes Book, 1864–1884, in Royal Society (Canterbury Branch) Papers, University of Canterbury, 125.
21. T.H. Potts, 'Notes from New Zealand', *Nature*, vol. 19 (7 November 1878): 21–22. See Atholl Anderson, *Prodigious Birds: Moas and moa-hunting in prehistoric New Zealand* (Melbourne: Cambridge University Press, 1989), 99.
22. Potts to Haast, 29 April 1878, Haast Papers, Alexander Turnbull Library, Wellington.
23. For Thomson, see Ross Galbreath, *Scholars and Gentlemen Both: G.M. and Allan Thomson in New Zealand science and education* (Wellington: Royal Society of New Zealand, 2002).
24. Potts, 'Oology of New Zealand'.
25. T.H. Potts, 'On the birds of New Zealand, Part II, read before the Wellington Philosophical Society, June 25, September 17, and October 22, and before the Philosophical Institute of Canterbury, September 7, 1870', *Transactions of the New Zealand Institute*, vol. 3 (1870): 59.
26. Walter L. Buller, *A History of the Birds of New Zealand* (London: the author, 1873) , iii.
27. Ross Galbreath, *Walter Buller: The reluctant conservationist* (Wellington: GP Books, 1989).
28. Geoff Norman, *Birdstories: A history of the birds of New Zealand* (Nelson: Potton and Burton, 2018), 219.
29. T.H. Potts, 'On the birds of New Zealand, Part III, read before the Wellington Philosophic Society, 23 October 1872, and before the Philosophical Institute of Canterbury, 4 September and 12 December 1872', *Transactions of the New Zealand Institute*, vol. 5 (1872): 193.
30. See 'We are gentlefolks now', in Endersby, *Imperial Nature*, 251–54; Barton, 'Haast and the moa': 260–61.
31. T.H. Potts, 'On the birds of New Zealand, read before the Wellington Philosophical Society, 17 July 1869', *Transactions of the New Zealand Institute*, vol. 2 (1869): 40–41.
32. T.H. Potts to W.B. Mantell, 22 August 1872, MS Papers 83, Alexander Turnbull Library, Wellington.
33. *Lyttelton Times*, 23 December 1874.
34. Galbreath, *Walter Buller*, 160, 122.
35. *Lyttelton Times*, 3 August 1871; T.H. Potts, 'Notes on a new species of *Apteryx* (*A. haastii*, Potts)', *Transactions of the New Zealand Institute*, vol. 4 (1871): 204–05. See also T.H. Potts, 'Recent occurrence of *Apteryx haastii* of Potts', *Zoologist* (September 1874): 4158.
36. Potts, 'On the birds of New Zealand, Part III': 195.
37. J.A. McLennan in E. Fuller, ed., *Kiwis: A monograph of the family Apterygidae* (Auckland: SeTo Publishing, 1990), 74.
38. A.J.D. Tennyson, R.L. Palma, H.A. Robertson, T.H. Worthy and B.J. Gill, 'A new species of kiwi (*Aves, Apterygiformes*) from Okarito, New Zealand', *Records of the Auckland Museum*, vol. 40 (2003): 55–64.
39. Potts, 'On the birds of New Zealand, Part IV': 139.

The Forest and the Trees, 1868–74

1. For fuller discussion, see Paul Star, 'Thomas Potts and the forest question: Conservation and development in New Zealand in the 1860s', *International Review of Environmental History*, vol. 1 (2015): 173–206.
2. See Nuno Luis Madureira, 'The anxiety of abundance: William Stanley Jevons and coal scarcity in the nineteenth century', *Environment and* History, vol. 18 (2012): 395–421. See also 'The duration of our supply of coal', *Press*, 18 April 1866.
3. *New Zealand Parliamentary Debates*, 7 October 1868, 188.
4. David Lowenthal, *George Perkins Marsh: Prophet of conservation* (Seattle and London: University of Washington Press, 2000), 273.
5. Lowenthal, *George Perkins Marsh*, 305, 302.
6. *Nelson Examiner*, 6 September 1864; *New Zealand Herald*, 7 November 1864; George P. Marsh, *Man and Nature, or, Physical Geography as Modified by Human Action* (New York: Charles Scribner, 1864), iii.
7. *Otago Daily Times*, 6 April 1866.
8. Charles O'Neill, 7 October 1868, in *New Zealand Parliamentary Debates*, 14 (1868), 191–92; Marsh, *Man and Nature*, 279, 370, 512.
9. T.H. Potts, 7 October 1868, in *New Zealand Parliamentary Debates*, 14 (1868), 188.
10. *Lyttelton Times*, 26 January 1869, 23 February 1869.
11. See *Otago Provincial Council Votes and Proceedings*, Dunedin, 1867, Session XXIII, 11. For Lindsay, see James Beattie, 'Natural history, conservation and health: Scottish-trained doctors in New Zealand, 1790–1920s', *Immigrants and Minorities*, vol. 29, no. 3 (2011): 281–307.
12. Michael Roche, *History of New Zealand Forestry* (Wellington: GP Books, 1970), 67–68. See also *Otago Daily Times*, 31 March 1868 and 1 April 1868.
13. See Potts to William Rolleston, 12 December 1868, in CAAR CH287 19936 Box CP 180, National Archives Christchurch.
14. See *Appendices to the Journal of the House of Representatives* (1869) D22: 3.
15. Minutes Book, Society of Canterbury Colonists, 1850–52: 7 January 1851. Christchurch City Libraries, Z Arch 16). See also Roche, *History of New Zealand Forestry*, 74–83.
16. *Appendices to the Journal of the House of Representatives* (1869) D22: 4–16.
17. Roche, *History of New Zealand Forestry*, 91, 94.
18. *Appendices to the Journal of the House of Representatives* (1869) D22.
19. T.H. Potts in *New Zealand Parliamentary Debates*, 15 July 1870, 472.
20. On O'Neill generally, see Stephen Utick, *Captain Charles, Engineer of Charity: The remarkable life of Charles Gordon O'Neill* (Sydney: Allen and Unwin, 2008).
21. On Vogel's role, see Raewyn Dalziell, *Julius Vogel, Business Politician* (Auckland: Auckland University Press, 1986), 171.
22. For details, see Michael Roche, *Forest Policy in New Zealand: An historical geography, 1840–1919* (Palmerston North: Dunmore Press, 1987), 73–80, and Roche, *History of New Zealand Forestry*, 83–88.
23. *Appendices to the Journal of the House of Representatives* (1869) D22.

24. *Lyttelton Times*, 26 April 1856.
25. The Ordinances of the Canterbury Provincial Council Session 10, October to December 1858.
26. See Jean Garner, *By His Own Merits: Sir John Hall – pioneer, pastoralist and premier* (Hororata: Dryden Press, 1995), 67–68 and 128–29.
27. T.H. Potts and William Gray, 'On the cultivation of some species of native trees and shrubs', *Transactions of the New Zealand Institute*, vol. 3 (1870): 181–202.
28. Potts and Gray, 'On the cultivation of some species of native trees and shrubs': 181.
29. R.W. Shepherd, 'Early importations of *Pinus radiata* to New Zealand and distribution in Canterbury to 1885: Implications for the genetic make-up of *Pinus radiata* stocks', *Horticulture in New Zealand*, vol. 1, no. 1 (1990): 33–38.
30. Winsome Shepherd and Walter Cook, *The Botanic Garden, Wellington: A New Zealand history, 1840–1987* (Wellington: Millwood Press, 1988), 95–96.
31. See M.J. Barnett, ed., *A Garden Century: The Christchurch Botanic Gardens, 1863–1963* (Christchurch: Christchurch City Council, 1963), 19–24.
32. See T.H. Potts, 'Through a young plantation', *New Zealand Country Journal*, vol. 2 (1878): 390–97, and vol. 3 (1879): 34–38; T.H. Potts, 'Measurements of some coniferous trees planted in 1866 in Ohinitahi, Canterbury', *New Zealand Country Journal*, vol. 9 (1885): 477.
33. *Lyttelton Times*, 15 October 1864.
34. Potts to Hector, 30 May 1872, Inward Letters, Colonial Museum, Box 53 Folder iii, Museum of New Zealand Te Papa Tongarewa, Wellington; Potts and Gray, 'On the cultivation of some species of native trees and shrubs', 182–83. T.H. Potts to James Hector, 30 May 1872, Hector correspondence, Museum of New Zealand Te Papa Tongarewa, Wellington.
35. 'Report of the Joint Committee on Colonial Industries', *Appendices to the Journal of the House of Representatives*, 1870, Session I, F-01.
36. Shepherd and Cook, *The Botanic Garden, Wellington*, 95–98.
37. Donal P. McCracken, *Gardens of Empire: Botanical institutions of the Victorian British Empire* (London and Washington: Leicester University Press, 1997), 39; Shepherd and Cook, *The Botanic Garden, Wellington*, 130, 25.
38. T.H. Potts, 'Public plantations', *Lyttelton Times*, 23 February 1869.
39. *Lyttelton Times*, 2 March 1869.
40. Review of *Transactions of the New Zealand Institute*, vol. 1, in *Otago Daily Times*, 13 July 1869.
41. See Roche, *Forest Policy in New Zealand*, 60.
42. *Lyttelton Times*, 3 December 1868.
43. T.H. Potts, 7 October 1868, in *New Zealand Parliamentary Debates*, vol. 14 (1868), 188.
44. 'Report of the Joint Committee on Colonial Industries', *Appendix to the Journal of the House of Representatives* (1870) Session I, F-1.
45. M.J.J. Donlan, *Phormium Tenax, or Neptune New Rigg'd: Statement of facts relative to experiments made upon* Phormium tenax *or New Zealand flax* (London: W. Glindon, 1833).

46. J.S. Williams in Canterbury Provincial Council, 2 December 1868, as reported in *Lyttelton Times*, 3 December 1868.
47. T.H. Potts, 'Flax culture', Letter to the editor, *Lyttelton Times*, 8 February 1869.
48. *Lyttelton Times*, 18 February 1869.

Introduction to Acclimatisation, to 1874

1. For fuller discussion, see Paul Star, 'Regarding New Zealand's environment: The anxieties of Thomas Potts, c. 1868–1888', *International Review of Environmental History*, vol. 3, no. 1 (2017): 101–38.
2. T.H. Potts, 'On the birds of New Zealand, Part I, read before the Wellington Philosophical Society, July 17, 1869', *Transactions of the New Zealand Institute*, vol. 2 (1869): 43.
3. T.H. Potts, 'Fern leaves' (1877–78), in T.H. Potts, *Out in the Open: A budget of scraps of natural history, gathered in New Zealand* (Christchurch: Lyttelton Times, 1882), 99; *Press*, 1 January 1872; 15 June 1872; 3 September 1872; 16 April 1874.
4. *Otago Daily Times*, 22 May 1866.
5. W.T.L. Travers, 'Acclimatisation in Canterbury', *New Zealand Country Journal*, vol. 8 (1884): 410; vol. 10 (1886): 136. For more on Travers, see James Beattie and John Stenhouse, 'Empire, environment and religion: God and the natural world in nineteenth-century New Zealand', *Environment and History*, vol. 13 (2007): 432–34.
6. Potts, *Out in the Open*, 235.
7. *Lyttelton Times*, 26 April 1864 and 27 August 1864.
8. *Lyttelton Times*, 26 January 1866.
9. *Press*, 28 March 1868 and 29 February 1868.
10. Potts, 'On the birds of New Zealand' (Part I): 49–50.
11. *Press*, 23 February 1867 and 1 March 1873; *Christchurch Star*, 8 March 1873; Records of the North Canterbury Acclimatisation Society, August 1873, 1, 27. Tūranga Christchurch City Libraries, Z Arch 5.
12. *Lyttelton Times*, 4 and 9 May 1874.

A Fascination for Birds, to 1872

1. H. Guthrie-Smith, 'Bird-life on a run', *Transactions of the New Zealand Institute*, vol. 28 (1895): 367–75.
2. W.H. Guthrie-Smith, *Tutira: The story of a New Zealand sheep station* (Dunedin: Reed, 1921); Michael King, quoted by Philip Steer: https://thespinoff.co.nz/books/19-04-2017/bottom-of-the-lake-how-the-setting-for-a-classic-book-of-new-zealand-literature-became-a-toxic-swamp/. See also Graeme Wynn, 'Remapping Tutira: Contours in the environmental history of New Zealand', *Journal of Historical Geography*, vol. 23, no. 4 (1997): 418–46.
3. 'Sketches in the House', *Press*, 12 July 1870.
4. Newton to Hector, 4 November 1869, Inward Letters, James Hector archive, Museum of New Zealand Te Papa Tongarewa, Wellington.

5. See John F. Reiger, *American Sportsmen and the Origins of Conservation* (Norman, OK: University of Oklahoma Press, 1986); Kate Hunter, *Hunting: A New Zealand history* (Auckland: Random House, 2009).
6. See for instance W.D. Murison, *New Zealand Parliamentary Debates*, vol. 1 (15 August 1867), 471 and (2 October 1867), 1230.
7. For precise detail see Colin M. Miskelly, 'Legal protection of New Zealand's indigenous terrestrial fauna: An historical review', *Tuhinga*, vol. 25 (2014): 25–101.
8. In Raymond Dasmann, *A Different Kind of Country* (London: Collier-Macmillan, 1968).
9. 'An Act to provide for the Protection of certain Animals and the Encouragement of Acclimatization Societies in New Zealand' (10 October 1867), Clause 13. See Miskelly, 'Legal protection of New Zealand's indigenous terrestrial fauna': 25–101.
10. T.H. Potts, 'On the birds of New Zealand, Part I, read before the Wellington Philosophical Society, July 17, 1869', *Transactions of the New Zealand Institute*, vol. 2 (1869): 48–49.
11. T.H. Potts, 'Notes on a new species of rail, *Rallus pictus*, Painted Rail', *Transactions of the New Zealand Institute*, vol. 4 (1871): 202–03; T.H. Potts, 'Notes on a new species of gull, *Larus (Bruchigavis) bulleri*, Potts', *Transactions of the New Zealand Institute*, vol. 4 (1871): 203–04; Potts, 'Notes on a new species of *Apteryx*'.
12. T.H. Potts, 'On the birds of New Zealand, Part III, read before the Wellington Philosophic Society, 23 October 1872, and before the Philosophical Institute of Canterbury, 4 September and 12 December 1872', *Transactions of the New Zealand Institute*, vol. 5 (1872): 179.
13. T.H. Potts, 'Notes on the "Piopio", *Keropia crassirostris*, Gml. (1872)', *Linnean Society Journal*, vol. 9 (zoology) (1873): 505–09; T.H. Potts, *Out in the Open: A budget of scraps of natural history, gathered in New Zealand* (Christchurch: Lyttelton Times, 1882), 84–85. See also A. Tennyson and P. Martinson, *Extinct Birds of New Zealand* (Wellington: Te Papa Press, 2006), and Geoff Norman, *Birdstories: A history of the birds of New Zealand* (Nelson: Potton and Burton, 2018), 289–90.
14. Potts, 'On the birds of New Zealand, Part III': 182.
15. Ibid., 179–80, 181.
16. H.F. von Haast, *Life and Times of Sir Julius von Haast, Explorer, Geologist, Museum Builder* (Wellington: The author, 1948), 533.
17. Potts, 'On the birds of New Zealand, Part III': 194, 190–91, 195; T.H. Potts, 'Observations on the natural history of the Night Parrot of New Zealand (Kakapo of the Maories)', *Zoologist*, vol. 8 (1873): 3621–24.
18. Potts, *Out in the Open*, 5; Potts, 'On the birds of New Zealand, Part III': 197.
19. T.H. Potts, 'Help us save our birds', Letter to the editor, *Nature* (2 May 1872): 5–6.
20. T.H. Potts, 'Help us save our birds': 5–6.
21. T.H. Potts, 'On recent changes in the fauna of New Zealand, from a paper read before the Philosophical Institute of Canterbury, December 12, 1872', in Potts, *Out in the Open*, 221–36.
22. See Peter J. Bowler, *The Fontana History of the Environmental Sciences* (London: Harper Collins, 1992), 370–78.
23. Potts, 'On the birds of New Zealand' (Part I): 43.

24. Potts, 'Help us save our birds': 6.
25. See Paul Star, 'Island reserves and mainland islands, including a review of *Ecosanctuaries*', *Environment and Nature in New Zealand*, vol. 9, no. 2 (2014): 61–71.
26. See Hill, *Richard Henry of Resolution Island*, 116 ff.
27. T.H. Potts, 'Kia, kea, or sheep-killer' (1880), in Potts, *Out in the Open*, 184.
28. T.H. Potts, 'White heron' (1878), in Potts, *Out in the Open*, 1; T.H. Potts, 'On the birds of New Zealand, Part II, read before the Wellington Philosophical Society, June 25, September 17, and October 22, and before the Philosophical Institute of Canterbury, September 7, 1870', *Transactions of the New Zealand Institute*, vol. 3 (1870): 59.
29. Evident in T.H. Potts, 'With Tawhaio and the Kingites' (1878), in Potts, *Out in the Open*, 9–29.
30. T.H. Potts, 'Out in the Open' (1883): 207–08.
31. J.D. Enys, 'An account of the Maori manner of preserving the skin of the huia, *Heteralocha auctirostris*, Buller', *Transactions of the New Zealand Institute*, vol. 8 (1875): 204–05.
32. For traditional ecological knowledge, see www.fws.gov/nativeamerican/pdf/tek-fact-sheet.pdf
33. See Jeremy Gaskell, *Who Killed the Great Auk?* (Oxford: Oxford University Press, 2000).
34. Potts, 'Notes on an egg of *Alca impennis*': 109–10. The italics are his.
35. Thomas Kirk, 'The displacement of species in New Zealand', *Transactions of the New Zealand Institute*, vol. 28 (1895): 26.
36. Potts, 'Help us save our birds', 6; Newton to Hector, 28 August 1877, Museum of New Zealand Te Papa Tongarewa, Wellington.
37. See 'The colony in 1874', plate 53 in Malcolm McKinnon, ed., *New Zealand Historical Atlas* (Auckland: David Bateman, 1997).
38. John Enys to his mother, 18 January 1873, Enys papers, 157/55, Canterbury Museum, Christchurch.
39. Potts to Hector, 21 and 30 May 1872, 4 June 1872, 12 October 1872, Inward Letters, James Hector archive, Museum of New Zealand Te Papa Tongarewa, Wellington.
40. Robert A. Stafford, *Scientist of Empire: Sir Roderick Murchison, scientific exploration and Victorian imperialism* (Cambridge: Cambridge University Press, 1989), 190.
41. James Hector, 'Geological expedition to the West Coast of Otago', *Otago Provincial Government Gazette*, vol. 6 (5 November 1863): 458, 460, 461, 463.
42. T.H. Potts, 'On the birds of New Zealand, Part IV, read before the Philosophical Institute of Canterbury 4 December 1873', *Transactions of the New Zealand Institute*, vol. 6 (1873): 151, 152.
43. Potts, 'Fern leaves', in Potts, *Out in the Open*, 66.
44. T.H. Potts, 'Sea-fowl' (1881), in Potts, *Out in the Open*, 218.
45. In 1873: Potts, 'On the birds of New Zealand, Part IV': 145–47; T.H. Potts, 'Notes on rare or little known birds' (1880), in Potts, *Out in the Open*, 195–96.
46. But see Jamie Morton, '"Extinct" South Island kokako could still be alive', *New Zealand Herald*, 27 November 2013.
47. Potts, *Out in the Open*, 196.

48. Email, Colin Miskelly of Te Papa to Paul Star, 4 April 2011.
49. Potts, 'On the birds of New Zealand' (Part I): 43.
50. Ibid., 67.
51. Potts, 'On the birds of New Zealand, Part III': 197.
52. Potts to Hector, 11 July 1872, Inward Letters, Colonial Museum, Box 53 Folder iii, Museum of New Zealand Te Papa Tongarewa, Wellington. See also Potts to Mantell, 22 August 1872, Mantell Papers, Turnbull Library, Wellington.
53. Potts to Mantell, 22 August 1872, Mantell Papers, Turnbull Library, Wellington.
54. P.D. Lowe in A. Warren and F.B. Goldsmith, eds, *Conservation in Perspective* (New York: Wiley, 1983), 330–31.
55. Potts, 'Help us save our birds': 5.
56. *New Zealand Parliamentary Debates*, vol. 12 (30 July 1872), 145–46.
57. Ibid., 145.
58. *New Zealand Parliamentary Debates*, vol. 13, 204.
59. von Haast, *Life and Times of Sir Julius von Haast*, 557.
60. Ibid.

Musings in Maoriland, 1876–78

1. Brian Easton, 'The Long Depression of the 1880s', *Policy Quarterly*, vol. 3, no. 1 (February 2009): 4.
2. W.J. Gardner in W.H. Oliver and B.R. Williams, eds, *The Oxford History of New Zealand*, 1st edn (Wellington: Oxford University Press, 1981), 75.
3. H.F. von Haast, *Life and Times of Sir Julius von Haast, Explorer, Geologist, Museum Builder* (Wellington: The author, 1948), 543.
4. T.N. Beckett, *The Mountains of Erewhon* (Wellington: A.H. and A.W. Reed, 1978), 133.
5. L.G.D. Acland, *The Early Canterbury Runs* (Christchurch: Whitcombe and Tombs, 1946), 299.
6. Beckett, *The Mountains of Erewhon*, 140; W.H. Scotter, *Ashburton: A history, with records of town and county* (Ashburton: Ashburton Borough and County Councils, 1972), 80, 352.
7. Chudleigh diary 12–19 April 1876.
8. T.H. Potts, 'Jottings from an old notebook: To the Hot Lakes' (by Rambler), *Canterbury Times*, 13 January 1888: 28–29.
9. See Jane Robertson, *Head of the Harbour: A history of Governor's Bay, Ohinetahi, Allandale and Teddington* (Christchurch: Philip King Publisher, 2016).
10. Mabel Potts, diary 12 May 1876, from Diary of Mabel Potts, April to June 1876, in Box 5 of Chudleigh papers, Canterbury Museum.
11. T.H. Potts, 'Fern leaves' (1882) in T.H. Potts, *Out in the Open: A budget of scraps of natural history, gathered in New Zealand* (Christchurch: Lyttelton Times, 1882), 69, 74, 85, 86, 89, 90, 95, 98, 101, 102, 103, 105, 110.
12. See Gordon Ell, 'To the Wild Islands', in *Forest and Bird*, vol. 16, no. 4 (November 1985): 11.
13. Potts' blue notebook, 1878, privately held (Bryony Macmillan), Christchurch.

14. See also John O'Leary, '"Zambesi seeds from Mr Moffat": Sir George Grey as imperial botanist', *International Review of Environmental History*, vol. 5, no. 1 (2019): 129–40.
15. 'Petre' (A. Ringland), *In Southern Seas: A trip to the Antipodes* (Edinburgh: R. Grant, 1888), 96; cf. New Zealand as Maoriland in Potts, 'Out in the Open [On Māori]' (1883): 207, and Thomas Bracken, *Musings in Maoriland* (Wellington: Arthur T. Keirle, 1890).
16. Potts, 'With Tawhaio and the Kingites' (1882), in Potts, *Out in the Open*, 9.
17. Ibid., 18.
18. Ibid., 27–28.
19. Potts, 'Jottings from an old notebook', *Canterbury Times*, 20 January 1888: 28–29, and 27 January 1888: 28–29.
20. Potts, 'With Tawhaio and the Kingites' (1882), in Potts, *Out in the Open*, 9.
21. See also James W. Stack, 'An account of the Maori House, attached to the Christchurch Museum', *Transactions of the New Zealand Institute*, vol. 8 (1875): 172–76.
22. Potts to Rolleston, 25 June 1874, in Canterbury Museum Records 4/1 Box 2: Photocopies of correspondence received by Canterbury Provincial Council relating to the Museum.
23. See Andrea Donovan, *William Morris and the Society for the Protection of Ancient Buildings* (London: Routledge, 2007).
24. Potts, 'Jottings from an old notebook', *Canterbury Times*, 10 February 1888: 28.
25. Potts to Grey, 8 July 1876, Sir George Grey Autograph Letter Collection, Auckland Public Library; T.H. Potts, 'Meeting with a Moriori' (1879) in Potts, *Out in the Open*, 160–63.
26. Michael King, *Hidden Places: A memoir in journalism* (Auckland: Sceptre, 1992), 200.
27. Potts, 'Out in the Open [On Māori]' (1883): 207.
28. T.H. Potts, 'Our Maori neighbours', *New Zealand Country Journal*, vol. 9, no. 4 (1885): 260.
29. J.W. Stack, Autobiography, Public Library, Dunedin, 425–26.
30. Mark P. Stoddart, Reminiscences, Canterbury Museum, Christchurch.

In God's Own Country, around 1880

1. James Beattie and John Stenhouse, 'Empire, environment and religion: God and the natural world in nineteenth-century New Zealand', *Environment and History*, vol. 13 (2007): 414, 437; Alfred W. Crosby, *Ecological Imperialism: The biological expansion of Europe, 900–1900* (Cambridge: Cambridge University Press).
2. Beattie and Stenhouse, 'Empire, environment and religion': 424.
3. Listed in *Catalogue of the well known and very valuable library of T.H. Potts, esq., … to be sold by auction* (Christchurch: Lyttelton Times, 1888), 5.
4. John Stenhouse, 'Darwin's captain: F.W. Hutton and the nineteenth century Darwinian debate', *Journal of the History of Biology*, vol. 23, no. 3 (1990): 413.
5. Stenhouse, 'Darwin's captain': 431.
6. See Carolyn King, *Immigrant Killers: Introduced predators and the conservation of birds in New Zealand* (Auckland: Oxford University Press, 1984), 10.

7. T.H. Potts, 'On the retention and colouring of eggs and the protective mimicry of sounds', *Nature* (3 October 1872): 457. See also T.H. Potts, 'Habits of animals transmitted to offspring'; T.H. Potts, *Nature*, vol. 14 (19 October 1874): 544–45; 'Animal intelligence', *Nature* (17 July 1884): 265–67.
8. T.H. Potts, 'On the birds of New Zealand, Part I, read before the Wellington Philosophical Society, July 17, 1869', *Transactions of the New Zealand Institute*, vol. 2 (1869): 61–62.
9. Ibid., 63; T.H. Potts, 'On a case of cross-breeding between two species of fly-catchers of the genus *Rhipidura*', *Zoological Society Proceedings* (1884): 530; 'On *Rhipidurae* of New Zealand (1884)', *New Zealand Journal of Science*, vol. 2 (1884–85): 170–71; Potts, 'Oology of New Zealand': 375.
10. Leonard Cockayne, 'Sketch of the plant geography of the Waimakariri River Basin, considered chiefly from an oecological point of view', *Transactions of the New Zealand Institute*, vol. 32 (1899): 95–131; A.J. Healy in G.A. Knox, ed., *The Natural History of Canterbury* (Wellington: A.H. and A.W. Reed, 1969), 279.
11. Potts, 'On recent changes' (1873), in T.H. Potts, *Out in the Open: A budget of scraps of natural history, gathered in New Zealand* (Christchurch: Lyttelton Times, 1882), 221–23.
12. S.C. Farr to T.H. Potts, 3 March 1873, in Letter Book 1, 193, North Canterbury Acclimatisation Society Records.
13. S.C. Farr to T.H. Potts, 11 August 1873, in Letter Book 1, 217, North Canterbury Acclimatisation Society Records.
14. Potts, *Out in the Open*, 221.
15. S.C. Farr to T.H. Potts, 19 July 1883, in Letter Book 3, 680, North Canterbury Acclimatisation Society Records.
16. T.H. Potts, 'The blackbird' (1882), in Potts, *Out in the Open*, 295.
17. T.H. Potts, 'A countryman in town', *New Zealand Country Journal*, vol. 11, no. 6 (1887): 461.
18. *Press*, 17 September 1874; 'Correspondence relative to determining right to cut timber on road and tramway reserves at Little River', 287/CAAR/SSP/CP663b/2, National Archives Christchurch.
19. As in Graeme Wynn, 'Conservation and society in late nineteenth-century New Zealand', *New Zealand Journal of History*, vol. 11, no. 2 (1977): 124–36; Graeme Wynn, 'Pioneers, politicians and the conservation of forests in early New Zealand', *Journal of Historical Geography*, vol. 5, no. 2 (1979): 171–88; Michael Roche, *Forest Policy in New Zealand: An historical geography, 1840–1919* (Palmerston North: Dunmore Press, 1987), 83 ff; Michael Roche, *History of New Zealand Forestry* (Wellington: GP Books, 1970), 76–93; James Beattie and Paul Star, 'Global networks and local environments: Forest conservation in New Zealand, 1850s–1920s', *British Scholar*, vol. 3 (September 2010): 191–218.
20. See Paul Star, 'Henry Matthews' contribution to tree culture in New Zealand from 1896 to 1909', in Brett J. Stubbs, Jane Lennon, Alison Specht and John Taylor, eds, *Australia's Ever-Changing Forests VI: Proceedings of the Eighth National Conference*

on Australian Forest History (Canberra: Australian Forest History Society, 2012), 201–24.
21. H.D. Thoreau, 'Chesuncook', in *The Atlantic*, vol. 2 (August 1858): 317. See also Thoreau, *The Maine Woods* (Penguin Random House, 1988).
22. George P. Marsh, *Man and Nature, or, Physical Geography as Modified by Human Action* (New York: Charles Scribner, 1864), 235.
23. See Roderick Nash, *Wilderness and the American Mind* (New Haven: Yale University Press, 1967), 108, and later edns.
24. *Appendices to the Journal of the House of Representatives* (1874): H26, 4.
25. T.H. Potts, 'On recreation grounds: The village green or common', *New Zealand Country Journal* (1887): 277–87.
26. H.W. Orsman, ed., *The Dictionary of New Zealand English* (Auckland: Oxford University Press, 1997), 219.
27. 'Canterbury Public Domains Act', 36 Victoriae 1872, no. 19: 59; M.J. Barnett, ed., *A Garden Century: The Christchurch Botanic Gardens, 1863–1963* (Christchurch: Christchurch City Council, 1963), 23.
28. 'An Act to provide for the Management of a Public Domain for the Borough of Lyttelton', 41 Victoriae 1877, no. 3: v.
29. *Christchurch Star*, 26 May 1880. See also correspondence on 'Orphanage Road', 287/CAAR/1 CPS 461/1877/Box CP 295, National Archives, Christchurch.
30. Email, Jane Robertson to Paul Star, 25 July 2019.
31. T.H. Potts, 'National domains' (1878), in Potts, *Out in the Open*, 30.
32. Ian Rockel, *Taking the Waters: Early spas in New Zealand* (Wellington: Government Printing Office, 1986), 6.
33. See Franklin Ginn, 'Extension, subversion, containment: Eco-nationalism and (post) colonial nature in Aotearoa New Zealand', *Transactions of the Institute of British Geographers*, new series, no. 33 (2008): 338.
34. Potts, *Out in the Open*, 33, 32.
35. Ibid., 35.
36. Tom Brooking, *Richard Seddon, King of God's Own: The life and times of New Zealand's longest-serving prime minister* (Auckland: Penguin Books, 2014).
37. See *Timaru Herald*, 23 March 1888; republished in Thomas Bracken, *Lays and Lyrics: God's Own Country and other poems* (1893).

Later Writings, Last Years, 1880–88

1. *Press*, 1 May 1886.
2. As in Potts, 'With the gun, now – and then' (1882), in T.H. Potts, *Out in the Open: A budget of scraps of natural history, gathered in New Zealand* (Christchurch: Lyttelton Times, 1882), 149–58; and many later articles.
3. T.H. Potts,'Out in the open [On robins]', *New Zealand Country Journal*, vol. 7, no. 2 (1883): 87–88. Cf. Tim Flannery, *The Future Eaters: An ecological history of the Australasian lands and people* (Chatswood, NSW: Reed Books, 1994).

4. A. Crosland, 'Port Hills bird life: Inventory, analysis and restoration', Report for the Parks Unit, Christchurch City Council, Christchurch, 1996. Referred to by Pawson in John Cookson and Graeme Dunstall, eds, *Southern Capital: Christchurch: Towards a city biography 1850–2000* (Christchurch: Canterbury University Press, 2000), 72.
5. *New Zealand Country Journal*, vol. 1, no. 1 (1877): 1.
6. Vaughan Wood and Eric Pawson, 'Information exchange and the making of the colonial farm: Agricultural periodicals in late nineteenth-century New Zealand', *Agricultural History*, vol. 62, no. 3 (2008): 345–46.
7. T.H. Potts, 'Fern leaves' (1877–79) and 'Classified list of New Zealand ferns' (1881–82), in Potts, *Out in the Open*, 51–112 and 237–80. See also T.H. Potts, 'Notes on a *Lomaria* collected in the Malvern District', *Transactions of the New Zealand Institute*, vol. 9 (1876): 491; T.H. Potts, 'Habits of the Filices observed about the Malvern Hills, near the gorge of the Rakaia River, Canterbury, New Zealand (1876)', *Linnean Society Journal*, vol. 15 (botany) (1877): 423–26; T.H. Potts, 'Notes on ferns, read before the Philosophical Institute of Canterbury 6 December 1877', *Transactions of the New Zealand Institute*, vol. 10 (1877): 358–62.
8. G.M. Thomson, *The Ferns and Fern Allies of New Zealand* (Dunedin: George Robertson, 1882), viii.
9. J.F. Armstrong, 'On some new species of New Zealand plants', *Transactions of the New Zealand Institute*, vol. 4 (1871): 290–91.
10. M.J. Barnett, ed., *A Garden Century: The Christchurch Botanic Gardens, 1863–1963* (Christchurch: Christchurch City Council, 1963), 24.
11. See Molly Duggins, '"The world's fernery": New Zealand, fern albums, and nineteenth-century fern fever', in Katie Pickles and Catherine Coleborne, eds, *New Zealand's Empire* (Manchester: Manchester University Press, 2015), 102–24; Dimitra Nikolaidou, 'How the Victorian fern-hunting craze led to adventure, romance, and crime': www.atlasobscura.com
12. Potts, 'Old Times [A forest ramble]', *Canterbury Times*, 9 December 1887: 28.
13. T.H. Potts, 'The pulse of spring', *New Zealand Country Journal*, vol. 9, no. 6 (1885): 76.
14. See Alan Bewell, *Natures in Translation: Romanticism and colonial natural history* (Baltimore: Johns Hopkins University Press, 2016), 9 ff.
15. Duggins, 'The world's fernery', 102.
16. Ibid.
17. Phoebe Jaffrey, *Darjeeling's Ferns* (Darjeeling: Privately published, 1878–85), listed in *Catalogue of the well known and very valuable library of T.H. Potts, esq., ... to be sold by auction* (Christchurch: Lyttelton Times, 1888), 11.
18. Potts, 'Classified list of New Zealand ferns' (1882), in Potts, *Out in the Open*, 237, 240.
19. T.H. Potts, 'Farmers' friends' (1879), 'White heron' (1882), and 'Something about hawks' (1878), in Potts, *Out in the Open*, 128, 7–8, and 45.
20. T.H. Potts, 'The White-eye, or Blight Bird', *New Zealand Country Journal*, vol. 6, no. 5 (1882): 301–08.
21. T.H. Potts to Sir George Grey, 6 October 1880, Auckland Public Library archives.
22. As in 'In memoriam T.H. Potts', *New Zealand Country Journal*, vol. 12 (1888): 368; J.C. Anderson, *Bird-Song and New Zealand Song Birds* (Auckland: Whitcombe and Tombs,

1926); Ross Galbreath, *Walter Buller: The reluctant conservationist* (Wellington: GP Books, 1989), 122.
23. T.H. Potts, 'The kea (*Nestor notabilis*) – progress of development', *Nature* (14 October 1871): 489.
24. T.H. Potts. 'Changes in the habits of animals and plants', Letter to the editor, *Nature* (1 February 1872): 262.
25. Potts, 'Kia, kea, or sheep-killer' (1880), in Potts, *Out in the Open*, 185.
26. Ibid., 184.
27. Both paintings are reproduced in Geoff Norman, *Birdstories: A history of the birds of New Zealand* (Nelson: Potton and Burton, 2018), 213.
28. T.H. Potts, 'The kea, or sheep-killer, *Nestor notabilis*, Gould', *New Zealand Country Journal*, vol. 7, no. 4 (1883): 270–74.
29. *Press*, 4 October 1886.
30. T.H. Potts, 'Lost game', *New Zealand Country Journal*, vol. 10, no. 6 (1886): 436.
31. T.H. Potts, 'On the birds of New Zealand, Part II, read before the Wellington Philosophical Society, June 25, September 17, and October 22, and before the Philosophical Institute of Canterbury, September 7, 1870': 65.
32. T.H. Potts, 'Out in the open [On humblebees]', *New Zealand Country Journal*, vol. 9, no. 3 (1886): 174.
33. See Michael Roche, *Forest Policy in New Zealand: An historical geography, 1840–1919* (Palmerston North: Dunmore Press, 1987), 88–93.
34. T.H. Potts, 'Out in the open [On strawberries]', *New Zealand Country Journal*, vol. 9, no. 2 (1886): 87.
35. Ibid., 91.
36. T.H. Potts, 'Eels and eel-fishing' (1880), in Potts, *Out in the Open*, 164.
37. Potts, 'Out in the open [On robins]': 84.
38. Potts, 'Out in the open [On rātā]': 3–5. See also Vaughan Wood, *Akaroa Cocksfoot: King of grasses* (Christchurch: Canterbury University Press, 2014), 19–35.
39. Potts, 'The pulse of spring' (1885): 465 ff.
40. Potts, 'On the birds of New Zealand Part II': 81–82.
41. See Donald Worster, *Nature's Economy: A history of ecological ideas* (Cambridge: Cambridge University Press, 1985).
42. T.H. Potts, 'Parrots' (1880), in Potts, *Out in the Open,* 176–83.
43. Potts, 'Notes on rare or little known birds' (1880), in Potts, *Out in the Open*, 194, repeating what he wrote in T.H. Potts, 'On the birds of New Zealand, Part IV, read before the Philosophical Institute of Canterbury 4 December 1873', *Transactions of the New Zealand Institute*, vol. 6 (1873): 146.
44. Potts, 'On recent changes', in Potts, *Out in the Open*, 221, 223.
45. T.H. Potts, 'A countryman in town: Continued', *New Zealand Country Journal*, vol. 12, no. 1 (1888): 15.
46. T.H. Potts, 'Variegated aloe', *New Zealand Country Journal*, vol. 8, no. 4 (1884): 337.
47. See Paul Star, 'Plants, birds and displacement theory in New Zealand, 1840–1900', *British Review of New Zealand Studies*, no. 10 (1997): 5–21.

48. *Press*, 28 March 1882. For subsequent trials, see 'Indigenous grasses' in the *Press*, 27 September 1887.
49. Potts, 'Out in the open [On humblebees]': 178.
50. S.C. Farr, 'The introduction of the humble bee into New Zealand', *New Zealand Country Journal*, vol. 13 (1889): 284–87, 489–93.
51. T.H. Potts, 'Notes on a native species of *Mantis*', *Transactions of the New Zealand Institute*, vol. 16 (1883): 114–18. For context, see G.W. Ramsay, 'Mantodea (Insecta), *Fauna of New Zealand*, no. 19 (Wellington: DSIR Publishing, 1990): 9–10.
52. Michael King, *Moriori: A people rediscovered* (Auckland: Viking, 1989), 104.
53. Chudleigh diary, 20 April 1881.
54. Fiona Holmes, *Chatham Islands: Rekohu, 1791–1984* (Christchurch: Raven Press, 1985), 61.
55. H.F. von Haast, *Life and Times of Sir Julius von Haast, Explorer, Geologist, Museum Builder* (Wellington: The author, 1948), 543.
56. Inwood, 'Governor's Bay', 14.
57. T.H. Potts to Clara Dobson, 10 January 1884, filed with Chudleigh diary.
58. Potts, 'On recreation grounds', 280.
59. T.N. Beckett, *The Mountains of Erewhon* (Wellington: A.H. and A.W. Reed, 1978), 143; W.H. Scotter, *Ashburton: A history, with records of town and county* (Ashburton: Ashburton Borough and County Councils, 1972), 80.
60. David Macmillan, 'Memoir: Thomas Henry Potts (1824–88)', *History and Bibliography* (Christchurch) vol. 2 (1948), 168; Frances Cresswell, *Old Homes of Lyttelton Harbour*, 2nd edn (Christchurch: Pegasus Press, 1966), 18.
61. *Lyttelton Times*, 22 August 1887.
62. T.H. Potts, 'Old Times', *Canterbury Times*, 4 November 1887: 33, and 11 November 1887: 33; 'Rambler' (T.H. Potts), 'Recollections: The eeling camp', *Canterbury Times*, 29 July 1887: 8, 5 August 1887: 29, 12 August 1887: 10, and 19 August 1887: 28; 'Rambler' (T.H. Potts), 'Recollections', *Canterbury Times*, 29 October 1886: 27, 5 November 1886: 10, 12 November 1886: 28, 19 November 1886: 28, 26 November 1886: 28, 3 December 1886: 24, 10 December 1886: 29, 17 December 1886: 29, and 24 December 1886: 9; 'Rambler' (T.H. Potts), 'Recollections: Old election days', *Canterbury Times*, 26 August 1887: 9–10.
63. Potts, 'A countryman in town': 457.
64. Potts, 'Meeting with a Moriori' (1882), in Potts, *Out in the Open*, 160.
65. Anon. (T.H. Potts), 'Rambles in the Chathams', *Canterbury Times*, 9 March 1888: 28, and 4 May 1888: 5.
66. Potts, 'A countryman in town: Continued', 102.
67. T.H. Potts, 'Stock in the Chathams', *New Zealand Country Journal*, vol. 12, no. 5 (1888): 372–73.
68. Potts, 'Rambles in the Chathams': 5.
69. Potts, 'Stock in the Chathams'.
70. Ibid., 370–71.
71. Leonard Cockayne, 'A sketch of the plant geography of the Waimakariri river basin,

considered chiefly from an oecological point of view', *Transactions of the New Zealand Institute*, vol. 32 (1899): 95–136.

72. See Paul Star, 'Ecology: A science of nation? The utilization of plant ecology in New Zealand, 1896–1930', *Historical Records of Australian Science*, no. 17 (2006): 1–11; and A.D. Thomson, *The Life and Correspondence of Leonard Cockayne* (Christchurch: Caxton Press, 1983).
73. Chudleigh diary 2 February 1888.
74. John Enys diary 29 January 1888, Charles and J.D. Enys Papers, vol. 4, 157/55, Canterbury Museum, Christchurch.
75. Chudleigh diary 11 February 1888.
76. 'Auctions', *Christchurch Star*, 13 October 1887.
77. Canterbury Death Duty Registers 1867–1913, Card Index, Canterbury Museum.
78. Chudleigh diary 23 April 1888.
79. Ibid., 22 June 1888.
80. *Lyttelton Times*, 30 July 1888; Warrant of 28 July 1888, Record of Internments at Linwood Cemetery, Tūranga Christchurch City Libraries.
81. Chudleigh diary 8 October 1888.

The Legacy of Thomas Potts

1. *Press*, 4 June 1919.
2. *Book of Common Prayer*, with annotations by T.H. Potts, 1862. Privately held (Bryony Macmillan), Christchurch.
3. *St Cuthbert's Church, Governor's Bay Souvenir, 1860–1935* (Christchurch: Turners Ltd., 1935), 7. Copy in Governors Bay Public Library records.
4. Frances Cresswell, *Old Homes of Lyttelton Harbour*, 2nd edn (Christchurch: Pegasus Press, 1966), 18.
5. George William, Lord Lyttelton, *Two Lectures on a Visit to the Canterbury Colony* (Stourbridge: T. Mark, 1868), 25.
6. Miles Warren, *Ohinetahi: Garden, house and art* (Lyttelton: Sir Miles Warren, 2014), 14.
7. www.summitroadsociety.org.nz/resource-management/ohinetahi-bush-reserve/
8. Conversation with Paul Ensor, Governors Bay, 20 February 2019.
9. See Peter Jackson, *Otamahua/Quail Island: A link with the past*, 2nd edn (Christchurch: Chaucer Press, 2006); and https://en.wikipedia.org/wiki/Quail_Island (New Zealand).
10. Potts diary 9 January and 28 August 1865.
11. Details from mtpotts.co.nz/history
12. T.N. Beckett, *The Mountains of Erewhon* (Wellington: A.H. and A.W. Reed, 1978), 140.
13. https://en.wikipedia.org/wiki/Mount_Potts; Department of Conservation brochure on Hakatere Conservation Park: www.doc.govt.nz/globalassets/documents/parks-and-recreation/places-to-visit/canterbury/raukapuka/hakatere-conservation-park.pdf
14. *Transactions of the New Zealand Institute*, vol. 16 (1883): 574.
15. *New Zealand Parliamentary Debates*, vol. 49 (7 October 1884), 532.

16. Craig Potton, *Tongariro: A sacred gift* (Auckland: Lansdowne Press, 1987).
17. See also T.H. Potts, 'In the Chathams', *New Zealand Country Journal*, vol. 12, no. 3 (1888): 195 on the word 'biddy'.
18. *Christchurch Star*, 9 January 1884.
19. Potts, 'On Recreation Grounds': 282.
20. R.P. Hargreaves in L.B. Heenan and G.W. Kearsley, eds, *Man, Environment and Planning* (Dunedin: Department of Geography, University of Otago, 1981), 87.
21. Paul Bensemann, *Fight for the Forest: The pivotal campaigns that saved New Zealand's national forests* (Nelson: Potton and Burton, 2018). See also David Young, *Our Islands, Our Selves: A history of conservation in New Zealand* (Dunedin: University of Otago Press, 2004), chapter 7; Catherine Knight, *Beyond Manapouri: 50 years of environmental politics in New Zealand* (Christchurch: Canterbury University Press, 2018).
22. For its first appearance, see Lynne Lochhead, 'The battle for Rai Valley (1898)', *Environment and Nature in New Zealand*, vol. 7 (November 2012): www.environmentalhistory-au-nz. org/2012/11/the-battle-for-the-rai-1898/
23. Paul Star and Lynne Lochhead, 'Children of the burnt bush: New Zealanders and the indigenous remnant', in Eric Pawson and Tom Brooking, eds, *Making a New Land: Environmental histories of New Zealand* (Dunedin: Otago University Press, 2013), 141–57; Brooking, *Richard Seddon*, 365–71.
24. See Ross Galbreath, *Scholars and Gentlemen Both* (Wellington: Royal Society of New Zealand, 2002), 84.
25. Email, John Hill to Paul Star, 24 January 2019.
26. But see Hill, *Richard Henry of Resolution Island*, 107–09, and Marty Taylor, 'Resolution for Richard Henry', *New Zealand Geographic*, no. 83 (January–February 2007).
27. See Geoff Norman, *Buller's Birds of New Zealand: The complete works of J.G. Keulemans* (Wellington: Te Papa Press, 2012).
28. Geoff Norman, *Birdstories: A history of the birds of New Zealand* (Nelson: Potton and Burton, 2018), 249.
29. See Miskelly, 'Legal protection of New Zealand's indigenous terrestrial fauna': 69.
30. John Aspinall, *Keas* (Wanaka: The author, 1990).
31. Philip Temple, 'Kea, the feisty parrot', *New Zealand Geographic*, no. 24 (October–December 1994).
32. See Dave Hansford, *Protecting Paradise: 1080 and the fight to save New Zealand's wildlife* (Nelson: Potton and Burton, 2016).
33. But see Paul Star, 'Human agency and exotic birds in New Zealand', *Environment and History*, vol. 20, no. 2 (2014): 275–99; and Pavel Pipek, Tim M. Blackburn and Petr Pysek, 'The ins and outs of acclimatisation: Imports versus translocations of skylarks and starlings in 19th century New Zealand', *Biological Invasions* (2018): doi.org/10.1007/s10530-018-1905-y
34. See M. Heginbotham, 'Norman Potts – Opotiki', *Auckland Botanical Society Journal*, vol. 30, no. 3 (1973): 5–7.
35. For Schourup, see http://canterburyphotography.blogspot.com/2008/08/peter-schourup-christchurch.html

Part Two: Seeking a Stranger-Land

Selections from the diary of Thomas Potts, 1855–58

1. Waikirikiri is the Hororata tributary of the Selwyn River.
2. A. Bayfield, Lyttelton and Christchurch, chemist.
3. Nicolas I of Russia, died 2 March 1855.
4. A novel by Walter Scott, 1825.
5. Psalms 16.6.
6. Emma was also away, staying at Rockwood.
7. See Milton, *Paradise Lost* (1667): 12.646.
8. From 'Elegy written in a country churchyard' (1751) by English poet Thomas Gray.
9. From 'The grave' (1743) by Scottish poet Robert Blair.
10. These lines appear on page 123.
11. Potts wrote up the following account on 28 April, but events are included here in chronological order. The group did not reach the West Coast.
12. Potts is here referring not to the Rakaia proper, but to the large tributary of the Rakaia later named the Wilberforce River..
13. The name celebrated the ultimately successful Siege of Sebastopol (1854–55) by the British during the Crimean War.
14. Potts wrote up the account of this trip on 5 July, but events are included here in chronological order.
15. Louis-Napoleon Bonaparte, born 16 March 1856.
16. A novel by Charles Dickens, 1852–53.
17. Thomas Babington Macaulay's *History of England*, published 1849–55.
18. A site rich in fossils, 8–9 kilometres below the Rakaia Gorge.
19. That is, W.H. Heywood Dansey had bought J.P. Taylor's run in the Waitaki.
20. Potts wrote up the account of this trip on 14 April, but events are included here in chronological order.
21. 'Lake Constance' is a large pond near The Point (the station immediately to the west of Rockwood).
22. George William Lee of Kaiapoi.
23. William Hone, *The Every-day Book: or, A guide to the year: Describing the popular amusements, sports, ceremonies, manners, customs, and events, incident to the three hundred and sixty-five days, in past and present times*, 1826.
24. A statement in *The Art of Cookery* by Hannah Glasse, 1747.
25. Rev Thomas Wintle, in *A Commentary on Daniel*, 1794, referred to Nebuchadnezzar's 'honour and glory' when in his kingdom.
26. Edward Knapman, Christchurch veterinarian.
27. For the purpose of hosing them down.
28. Joseph Brittan and William Sefton Moorhouse (presently his Honor) were the candidates for Canterbury's superintendency in 1857.

Part Three: Still Out in the Open

Eleven essays by Thomas Potts, 1882–88

1. Kōnini is the te reo name for the fruit of kōtukutuku or New Zealand fuchsia.
2. Daniel 12:11.
3. Partial legal protection for tūī was introduced in 1878.
4. Alexander Pope, 1733.
5. Shakespeare, *Othello*, Act 1 Scene 3.
6. From John Milton, *Comus*, 1637.
7. Robert Burns, 'The cotter's Saturday night', 1785.
8. A reference to the London Brighton and South Coast Railway locomotive 'Gladstone', built in 1882.
9. Matthew 3:10.
10. Ecclesiastes 11:1. The mayor was Aaron Ayers, an avid gardener.
11. Lucius originally appears in *The Golden Ass* by Apuleius.
12. A misprinted reference to the equine Houyhnhnms in Jonathan Swift's *Gulliver's Travels*, 1726.
13. How the English poet John Skelton described the bittern and the 'bumping' noise the bird makes.
14. Now *Mohoua mochrocephala*, the mohua.
15. Their family names are now, respectively, *Cicindelinae*, *Phasmatodea* and *Sphecidae*.
16. Thomas Gray, 'Ode on a distant prospect of Eton College', 1747.
17. Shakespeare, *Hamlet*, Act 3 Scene 4.
18. Now *Dodonaea viscosa*.
19. The mathematician of Ancient Greece who founded geometry.
20. Potts here adds a footnote for the reader: 'See *Nature*, Sept., 1884. Potts on Animal Intelligence'.
21. Now generally called silvereye or waxeye.
22. There are 12 lines to one inch.
23. Shakespeare, *Hamlet*, Act 3 Scene 4.
24. Scab is a skin disease affecting sheep, caused by the mite *Psoroptes ovis*.
25. The title of an 1862 article by Charles Dickens.
26. Numbers 11:31.
27. Shakespeare, *All's Well That Ends Well*, Act 1 Scene 1.
28. Now *Metrosideros umbellata*.
29. 'Confidence is a plant of slow growth in an aged bosom': William Pitt the Elder, 1766.
30. That is, from the very beginning; the full phrase, from Horace, is '*ab ovo usque ad mala*': 'from the egg to the apples'.
31. The subject of a cartoon by William Hogarth, 1747.
32. Shakespeare, *As You Like It*, Act 2 Scene 7.
33. From Isaac Watts' poem 'Against Idleness and Mischief', 1715.
34. A word first used by Nathaniel Hawthorne in 1843 – the daffodil.
35. That is, the male fern, now *Dryopteris filis-mas*.

36. Shakespeare, *Romeo and Juliet*, Act 3 Scene 2.
37. The Primrose League was founded in Britain in 1883 to promote the Conservative Party.
38. From Oliver Goldsmith, 'Retaliation: A Poem', 1774.
39. The banded dotterel, *Charadrius bicinctus*.
40. 'A countryman in the Chathams' combines the titles under which the first and second parts of the essay ('Out in the Open: A countryman in town' and 'Out in the Open: In the Chathams') first appeared.
41. Thomas Abbott of Exeter Nursery, Papanui Road, Christchurch.
42. That is, wood ear fungus, now *Airucularia cornea*.
43. Now *Asplenium polyodon*, sickle spleenwort.
44. Now *Brachyglottis huntii*, the Chatham Island Christmas tree.
45. Smith's tree fern, now *Cyathea smithii*.
46. Tarahinau, Chatham Island grass tree, now *Dracophyllum arboreum*.
47. Chatham Island akeake, now *Olearia traversiorum*.
48. Now *Poa billardierei*, referred to later in the paragraph as 'fescue'.

Bibliography

The published writings of Thomas (T.H.) Potts

'Local manufactures', Letter to the editor, *Lyttelton Times*, 26 January 1869

'Flax culture', Letter to the editor, *Lyttelton Times*, 8 February 1869

'Public plantations', Letter to the editor, *Lyttelton Times*, 23 February 1869

'On the birds of New Zealand, read before the Wellington Philosophical Society, July 17, 1869', *Transactions of the New Zealand Institute*, vol. 2 (1869): 40–78. Same as 'Notes on the breeding habits of New Zealand birds' (Part I), Wellington, 1870. Also in *Zoologist*, vol. 6 (1871): 2793–802, 2853–59

'Notes on the little bittern (*Ardetta pusilla*) read before the Philosophical Institute', *The Press*, 12 September 1870 (supplement)

'On the birds of New Zealand, Part II, read before the Wellington Philosophical Society, June 25, September 17, and October 22, and before the Philosophical Institute of Canterbury, September 7, 1870', *Transactions of the New Zealand Institute*, vol. 3 (1870): 59–109. Also in *Zoologist*, vol. 7 (1872): 3052–56, 3089–95

'Notes on an egg of *Alca impennis*, Linn., in the collection of the writer', *Transactions of the New Zealand Institute*, vol. 3 (1870): 109–10

'On the cultivation of some species of native trees and shrubs' (by T.H. Potts and W. Gray), *Transactions of the New Zealand Institute*, vol. 3 (1870): 181–202

'The kea (*Nestor notabilis*) – progress of development', *Nature* (14 October 1871): 489

'Notes on a new species of rail, *Rallus pictus*, painted rail', *Transactions of the New Zealand Institute*, vol. 4 (1871): 202–03

'Notes on a new species of gull, *Larus (Bruchigavis) bulleri*, Potts', *Transactions of the New Zealand Institute*, vol. 4 (1871): 203–04

'Notes on a new species of *Apteryx* (*A. haastii*, Potts)', *Transactions of the New Zealand Institute*, vol. 4 (1871): 204–05

'Notes and descriptions of some birds lately added to the museum, Canterbury, New Zealand: *Apteryx haastii*, *Apteryx australis*, *Rallus pictus*, *Larus bulleri*', *Ibis*, series 3 no. 5 (1872): 35–39

'Discovery of a *Gerygone* (*G. albofrontata*?) in New Zealand', *Ibis*, series 3 no. 7 (1872): 325–26

'Changes in the habits of animals and plants', Letter to the editor, *Nature* (1 February 1872): 262

'Cuckoo's eggs', *Nature* (25 April 1872): 501

'Help us save our birds', Letter to the editor, *Nature* (2 May 1872): 5–6

'Rain after fire', Letter to the editor, *Nature* (13 June 1872): 121

'Verspertilio', Letter to the editor, *Nature* (27 June 1872): 162

'On the retention and colouring of eggs and the protective mimicry of sounds', *Nature* (3 October 1872): 457

'On the birds of New Zealand, Part III, read before the Wellington Philosophical Society 23 October 1872, and before the Philosophical Institute of Canterbury 4 September and 12 December 1872', *Transactions of the New Zealand Institute*, vol. 5 (1872): 171–205

'On recent changes in the fauna of New Zealand, from a paper read before the Philosophical Institute of Canterbury, December 12, 1872', *The Field* (25 October 1873). Also in *Otago Witness*, 14 February 1874. Also in *Lyttelton Times*, 28 April, 30 April and 9 May 1874. Also published separately, Christchurch: Lyttelton Times, 1874. Also in *Zoologist*, vol. 9 (1874): 4135–53. Also in *New Zealand Country Journal*, vol. 5 no. 6 (1881): 385–400. Also in T.H. Potts, *Out in the Open* (Christchurch: Lyttelton Times, 1882), 221–36

'Notes on the "Piopio", *Keropia crassirostris*, Gml. (1872)', *Linnean Society Journal*, vol. 9 (zoology) (1873): 505–09

'Observations on the natural history of the night parrot of New Zealand (kakapo of the Maories)', *Zoologist*, vol. 8 (1873): 3621–24

'Notes on a supposed new species of *Prion* (*P. australis*)', *Ibis*, series 3 no. 9 (January 1873): 85–86

'On the birds of New Zealand, Part IV, read before the Philosophical Institute of Canterbury 4 December 1873', *Transactions of the New Zealand Institute*, vol. 6 (1873): 139–53. Also in *Zoologist*, vol. 10 (1875): 4409–13, 4477–87

Letter to the editor, *Lyttelton Times*, 9 May 1874

'Recent occurrence of *Apteryx haastii* of Potts', *Zoologist* (September 1874): 4158

'Habits of animals transmitted to offspring', *Nature*, vol. 14 (19 October 1874): 544–45

'Notes on a *Lomaria* collected in the Malvern District', *Transactions of the New Zealand Institute*, vol. 9 (1876): 491

'Habits of the Filices observed about the Malvern Hills, near the gorge of the Rakaia River, Canterbury, New Zealand (1876)', *Linnean Society Journal*, vol. 15 (botany) (1877): 423–26

'Fern leaves' (by 'G.'), *New Zealand Country Journal*, vol. 1 no. 4 (1877): 227–31; vol. 2 no. 1 (1878): 21–28; vol. 2 no. 2 (1878): 106–16; vol. 2 no. 3 (1878): 174–80; vol. 2 no. 4 (1878): 245–49; vol. 2 no. 5 (1878): 300–08; vol. 2 no. 6 (1878): 360–69; vol. 3 no. 1 (1879): 15–19. Also in T.H. Potts, *Out in the Open* (Christchurch: Lyttelton Times, 1882), 51–112

'Notes on ferns, read before the Philosophical Institute of Canterbury 6 December 1877', *Transactions of the New Zealand Institute*, vol. 10 (1877): 358–62

'Noxious trees, etc.' (by 'G.'), *New Zealand Country Journal*, vol. 2 no. 2 (1878): 94–95

'On hedge plants' (by 'G.'), *New Zealand Country Journal*, vol. 2 no. 2 (1878): 125–27

'Out in the Open (A budget of scraps of natural history)', *New Zealand Country Journal*, vol. 2 no. 3 (1878): 139–46. Also as 'White heron' in T.H. Potts, *Out in the Open* (Christchurch: Lyttelton Times, 1882), 1–8

'With Tawhaio and the Kingites', *New Zealand Country Journal*, vol. 2 no. 4 (1878): 207–27. Also in T.H. Potts, *Out in the Open* (Christchurch: Lyttelton Times, 1882), 9–29

'National domains', *New Zealand Country Journal*, vol. 2 no. 4 (1878): 227–33. Also in T.H. Potts, *Out in the Open* (Christchurch: Lyttelton Times, 1882), 30–36.

'Something about hawks', *New Zealand Country Journal*, vol. 2 no. 5 (1878): 275–88. Also in T.H. Potts, *Out in the Open* (Christchurch: Lyttelton Times, 1882), 37–50

'Through a young plantation' (anonymous), *New Zealand Country Journal*, vol. 2 no. 6 (1878): 390–97

'Notes from New Zealand', *Nature* (7 November 1878): 21–22 (9 January 1879): 234

'Through a young plantation (continued)' (anonymous), *New Zealand Country Journal*, vol. 3 no. 1 (1879): 34–38

'A chime of the bell-bird', *New Zealand Country Journal*, vol. 3 no. 2 (1879): 81–84. Also in T.H. Potts, *Out in the Open* (Christchurch: Lyttelton Times, 1882), 113–16

'Farmers' friends', *New Zealand Country Journal*, vol. 3 no. 3 (1879): 153–57. Also in T.H. Potts, *Out in the Open* (Christchurch: Lyttelton Times, 1882), 117–28

'Farmers' friends (continued)', *New Zealand Country Journal*, vol. 3 no. 4 (1879): 211–20. Also as 'Still with friends', in T.H. Potts, *Out in the Open* (Christchurch: Lyttelton Times, 1882), 129–32

'Under the mistletoe bough', *New Zealand Country Journal*, vol. 3 no. 5 (1879): 267–74. Also in T.H. Potts, *Out in the Open* (Christchurch: Lyttelton Times, 1882), 133–40

'Meeting with a Moriori', *New Zealand Country Journal*, vol. 3 no. 6 (1879): 333–36. Also in T.H. Potts, *Out in the Open* (Christchurch: Lyttelton Times, 1882), 160–63

'Kingfishers', *New Zealand Country Journal*, vol. 3 no. 6 (1879): 343–52. Also in T.H. Potts, *Out in the Open* (Christchurch: Lyttelton Times, 1882), 141–51

'Flycatchers', *New Zealand Country Journal*, vol. 4 no. 1 (1880): 41–48. Also in T.H. Potts, *Out in the Open* (Christchurch: Lyttelton Times, 1882), 152–59

'Parrots', *New Zealand Country Journal*, vol. 4 no. 2 (1880): 87–94. Also in T.H. Potts, *Out in the Open* (Christchurch: Lyttelton Times, 1882), 176–83

'Eels and eel-fishing', *New Zealand Country Journal*, vol. 4 no. 3 (1880): 159–69. Also in T.H. Potts, *Out in the Open* (Christchurch: Lyttelton Times, 1882), 164–75

'Kia, kea, or sheep-killer', *New Zealand Country Journal*, vol. 4 no. 4 (1880): 209–19. Also as 'On the habits of the kea or mountain parrot of New Zealand', *Zoologist*, vol. 5 (1881): 290–301. Also in T.H. Potts, *Out in the Open* (Christchurch: Lyttelton Times, 1882), 184–93

'Notes on rare or little known birds', *New Zealand Country Journal*, vol. 4 no. 5 (1880): 288–93 and vol. 4 no. 6 (1880): 344–48. Also in T.H. Potts, *Out in the Open* (Christchurch: Lyttelton Times, 1882), 194–203

'Notes on eels and eel-catching', *New Zealand Country Journal*, vol. 4 no. 6 (1880): 379–80

'Sea-fowl', *New Zealand Country Journal*, vol 5 no. 1 (1881): 9–14 and vol. 5 no. 2 (1881): 92–102. Also in T.H. Potts, *Out in the Open* (Christchurch: Lyttelton Times, 1882), 204–20

'Classified list of New Zealand ferns' (anonymous), *New Zealand Country Journal*, vol. 5 no. 4 (1881): 235–39; vol. 5 no. 5 (1881): 305–10; vol. 5 no. 6 (1881): 373–77; vol. 6 no. 1 (1882): 11–14; vol. 6 no. 2 (1882): 78–87; vol. 6 no. 3 (1882): 177–92. Also in T.H. Potts, *Out in the Open* (Christchurch: Lyttelton Times, 1882), 237–80

'Black oystercatcher (*Haematopus unicolor*), Torea-pango', *New Zealand Country Journal*, vol. 6 no. 1 (1882): 6–8. Also in T.H. Potts, *Out in the Open* (Christchurch: Lyttelton Times, 1882), 291–93

'With the gun, now – and then', *New Zealand Country Journal*, vol. 6 no. 3 (1882): 149–58. Also in T.H. Potts, *Out in the Open* (Christchurch: Lyttelton Times, 1882), 281–90

'Introduced birds – the blackbird', *New Zealand Country Journal*, vol. 6 no. 4 (1882): 235–42. Also in T.H. Potts, *Out in the Open* (Christchurch: Lyttelton Times, 1882), 204–301

Out in the Open: A budget of scraps of natural history, gathered in New Zealand (Christchurch: Lyttelton Times, 1882). (Includes an original preface.)

'Aurora australis', Letter to the editor, *Nature* (8 June 1882): 126

'The white-eye, or blight bird, tauhou of the Maoris, *Zosterops lateralis*, Reich', *New Zealand Country Journal*, vol. 6 no. 5 (1882): 301–08

'Plovers', *New Zealand Country Journal*, vol. 7 no. 1 (1883): 3–5

'Out in the Open [On robins]', *New Zealand Country Journal*, vol. 7 no. 2 (1883): 83–92

'Out in the Open [On Māori]', *New Zealand Country Journal*, vol. 7 no. 3 (1883): 207–10

'The kea, or sheep-killer, *Nestor notabilis*, Gould', *New Zealand Country Journal*, vol. 7 no. 4 (1883): 270–74

'Meteor', Letter to the editor. *Nature* (13 September 1883): 462

'Note on an egg of a kea', *Zoologist* (September 1883): 376

'Notes on a native species of *Mantis*', *Transactions of the New Zealand Institute*, vol. 16 (1883): 114–18

'Iridescent lunar halos', Letter to the editor, *Nature* (13 September 1884): 464

'Animal intelligence', *Nature* (17 July 1884): 265–67

'Uber Vererbung und Aenderungder Lebensweise' ('On heredity and changes of habit'), *Wien Ornith Ver Mitth*, vol. 8 (1884): 35–37

'Ornithologische Notizen aus Neu-Seeland' ('Bird notes from New Zealand'), *Wien Ornith Ver Mitth*, vol. 8 (1884):168–70

'On some introduced birds in New Zealand', *Zoologist*, vol. 8 (November 1884): 448–50

'On a case of cross-breeding between two species of fly-catchers of the genus *Rhipidura*', *Zoological Society Proceedings* (1884): 530

'On recreation grounds – the village green or common', *New Zealand Country Journal*, vol. 8 no. 4 (1884): 277–87

'Variegated aloe', *New Zealand Country Journal*, vol. 8 no. 4 (1884): 336–37

'Habits of the huia', *Zoologist*, vol. 8 (September 1884): 386–87

'On an abnormally-coloured specimen of *Petroica albifrons*, Gray, *Myioscopus albifrons*, Gml. (1884)', *New Zealand Journal of Science*, vol. 2 (1884–85): 169–70

'On *Rhipidurae* of New Zealand (1884)', *New Zealand Journal of Science*, vol. 2 (1884–85): 170–71

'*Lomaria pumila*, Raoul (1884)', *New Zealand Journal of Science*, vol. 2 (1884–85): 173–74

'Oology of New Zealand', *New Zealand Journal of Science*, vol. 2 (1884–85): 222–26, 274–88, 373–78, 475–84, 505–11, 556–59

'Out in the Open [On rātā]', *New Zealand Country Journal*, vol. 9 no. 1 (1885): 3–5

'Out in the Open: The pulse of spring', *New Zealand Country Journal*, vol. 9 no. 6 (1885): 465–76

'Measurements of some conifers planted in 1866 at Ohinitahi, Canterbury, New Zealand', *New Zealand Country Journal*, vol. 9 no. 6 (1885): 476–77

'Breeding habits of the Lake Gull', *Zoologist*, vol. 9 (August 1885): 148–50

'Notes on New Zealand birds', *Zoologist*, vol. 9 (November 1885): 421–23

'Out in the Open [On strawberries], *New Zealand Country Journal*, vol. 9 no. 2 (1886): 87–95
'Out in the Open' [On humblebees]', *New Zealand Country Journal*, vol. 9 no. 3 (1886): 173–85
'Our Maori neighbours', *New Zealand Country Journal*, vol. 9 no. 4 (1885): 259–62
'Recollections' (by 'Rambler'), *Canterbury Times*, 29 October 1886: 27; 5 November 1886: 10; 12 November 1886: 28; 19 November 1886: 28; 26 November 1886: 28; 3 December 1886: 24; 10 December 1886: 29; 17 December 1886: 29; 24 December 1886: 9. Also in *New Zealand Country Journal*, vol. 15 no. 2 (1891): 100–07; vol. 15 no. 3 (1891): 194–201; vol. 15 no. 4 (1891): 287–95; vol. 15 no. 5 (1891): 380–88; vol. 15 no. 6 (1891): 474–79; vol. 16 no. 1 (1892): 7–12; vol. 16 no. 2 (1892): 103–10
'Lost game', *New Zealand Country Journal*, vol. 10 no. 6 (1886): 435–39
'Out in the Open: A countryman in town', *New Zealand Country Journal*, vol. 11 no. 6 (1887): 457–61
'Recollections: The eeling camp' (by 'Rambler'), *Canterbury Times*, 29 July 1887: 8; 5 August 1887: 29; 12 August 1887: 10; 19 August 1887: 28. Also in *Lyttelton Times*, 2 August 1887, 11 August 1887, 17 August 1887, 25 August 1887
'Recollections: Old election days' (by 'Rambler'), *Canterbury Times*, 26 August 1887: 9–10. Also in *Lyttelton Times*, 30 August 1887
'Old Times', *Canterbury Times*, 28 October 1887: 28; 4 November 1887: 33; 11 November 1887: 33; 18 November 1887: 25; 25 November 1887: 25; 2 December 1887: 28 ['A forest ramble']; 9 December 1887: 28 ['A forest ramble: continued']
'Christmas here and there (Specially written for the Christmas number by "The Rambler")', *Canterbury Times*, c. 23 December 1887; 30 December 1887
'Jottings from an old notebook: To the Hot Lakes' (by 'Rambler'), *Canterbury Times*, 16 December 1887: 29; 13 January 1888: 28–29; 20 January 1888: 28–29; 27 January 1888: 28–29; 10 February 1888: 28; 17 February 1888: 28. Also as 'Old reminiscences', *Lyttelton Times*, 20 January 1888: 3; 21 January 1888: 6; 30 January 1888: 6; 11 February 1888: 6; 18 February 1888: 6
'Out in the Open: A countryman in town: continued', *New Zealand Country Journal*, vol. 12 no. 1 (1888): 15–20; vol. 12 no. 2 (1888): 98–102
'Rambles in the Chathams' (anonymous), *Canterbury Times*, 9 March 1888: 28; 23 March 1888; 27 April 1888: 5; 4 May 1888: 5. Also as 'The Chatham Islands', *Lyttelton Times*, 10 March 1888: 6; 24 March 1888: 6; 2 May 1888: 2; 8 May 1888: 2
'Out in the Open: [A countryman] In the Chathams', *New Zealand Country Journal*, vol. 12 no. 3 (1888): 193–98
'Out in the Open: Stock in the Chathams', *New Zealand Country Journal*, vol. 12 no. 5 (1888): 370–75

Index

Bold denotes an illustration in the picture section